Civil War Wives

Civil War Wives

The Lives and Times of
ANGELINA GRIMKÉ WELD,
VARINA HOWELL DAVIS,
and JULIA DENT GRANT

Carol Berkin

ALFRED A. KNOPF NEW YORK 2009

THIS IS A BORZOI BOOK
PUBLISHED BY ALFRED A. KNOPF

www.aaknopf.com

Knopf, Borzoi Books, and the colophon are registered
trademarks of Random House, Inc.

Library of Congress Cataloging-in-Publication Data

Berkin, Carol.
Civil War wives : the lives and times of Angelina Grimké Weld, Varina Howell
Davis, and Julia Dent Grant / Carol Berkin.—1st ed.
p.   cm.
Includes bibliographical references and index.
ISBN 978-1-4000-4446-7
1. United States—History—Civil War, 1861–1865—Women.   2. United States—
History—Civil War, 1861–1865—Biography.   3. Grimké, Angelina Emily,
1805–1879.   4. Grimké, Angelina Emily, 1805–1879—Marriage.   5. Davis, Varina,
1826–1906.   6. Davis, Varina, 1826–1906—Marriage.   7. Grant, Julia Dent,
1826–1902.   8. Grant, Julia Dent, 1826–1902—Marriage.   9. Women—United
States—Biography.   10. Wives—United States—Biography.   I. Title.
E628.B47   2009   973.7082—dc22   2009019476

Manufactured in the United States of America
First Edition

To Hannah and Matthew,
The Best of My Past, Present, and Future

Contents

THREE *Julia Dent Grant*

Preface

THE NAMES AND DEEDS of the politicians, statesmen, generals, and reformers of the Civil War era are familiar to most Americans. Lincoln, Douglass, Lee, Grant, Davis, Sherman, Calhoun, Clay, Jackson, Weld, and Garrison . . . they are part of a history written and rewritten by every generation since the war began. Bookshelves teem with biographies and with narratives and analyses of the political crises in which these larger-than-life figures shaped our national destiny. Almost 150 years after the war, thousands of American families visit the battlefields where blue and gray waged their desperate struggles or watch reenactors bring those battles to life once again. Thousands more visit the homes and churches where African Americans found shelter as they escaped to freedom. In countless monuments, in songs and flags, and in museums and shrines, we honor the memory of causes both lost and won.

Over the past few decades, the stories of ordinary men and women have been added to the history of our nation's epic crisis. Social historians have helped us grow familiar with the experiences of common soldiers, wives and mothers, field hands and factory workers, immigrants and native sons and daughters. Although these nineteenth-century women and men did not hold the reins of power, their lives were changed forever by the end of slavery, the promise and failure of Reconstruction, the decline of the Cotton Kingdom and the rise of industrial America, widowhood and mourning, and the challenges to gender and racial roles that followed as modern America took shape. The portraits that have emerged have been, of necessity, collective more often than individual, for few of these Americans left behind the rich records bequeathed to us by presidents, generals, and reformers. Their stories come to us in a rich collective tapestry, woven together from the fragments each left behind.

The women who are the subject of this book stand between the powerful and the anonymous, the famous and the ordinary. Their lives were in many ways privileged, but in others they were anomalous, for through their marriages to leading figures they had access to the seats of power but no power themselves. Their positions in society gave them a unique perspective on the decisions and events that changed their world. Their marriages gave them intimate knowledge of the men who made those decisions and shaped those events. They were white and thus they were free, yet marriage and motherhood created barriers to their autonomy that only spinsterhood or widowhood could overcome. In their privileged yet restricted lives, they have much to tell us about their era if we listen to their voices and recover their stories.

The origins of this book lay in a series of questions: What would the memoirs, letters, and diaries of such women reveal? How did women who had intimate knowledge of statesmen, generals, and reformers judge these men in their public and private roles? How did women who were in the public eye adjust to the rapid social change and the challenges to customary beliefs and behaviors? And how did marriage shape the choices they made over long and complex lives?

I began with an extensive list of potential subjects for this book—and quickly found their numbers dwindling. Some, such as Mary Lincoln, are studies in idiosyncrasy if not madness; others, including Mary Anna Lee, wife of Robert E. Lee, did not leave behind the sources needed to tell their stories. I did not want to reconstruct a lunar landscape, filled with women who could be known only in the reflected light of their husbands' commentary. In the end, there proved to be few women who left behind the records that would allow me and my readers to hear their voices clearly and see their world as they saw it. From among them, three women emerged as my subjects: Angelina Grimké Weld, Varina Howell Davis, and Julia Dent Grant.

Although each of these three women left richly detailed and revealing accounts of her life, there are important differences in these sources. Angelina Grimké Weld left a record of her thoughts in real time, in the diary she kept as a young woman in South Carolina, in the letters she wrote, and in the essays and speeches she produced in the causes of abolition, racial equality, and women's rights. Varina Howell Davis's life can be narrated from both real-time letters and from the memoirs she wrote as an aging widow. Julia Dent Grant's life, however, must be reconstructed primarily from the memories she set down in old age, for she wrote few letters and not many of them have survived. Memory, of course, can be faulty and memoirs can have agendas that make them suspect. Even diaries can present desired personas rather than true identities. Yet Angelina, Varina, and Julia reveal much about themselves as they narrate their own stories, and, because they were in the public eye, contemporaries commented on everything from their personalities to their diets to the way they raised their children. All these sources, along with decades of literature produced by historians of the era, have been marshaled to tell these stories.

As individuals, these women differed greatly in personality, character, temperament, and intellect. The winds of change that blew within their lifetimes carried them down quite different paths. Yet the paths they chose and the paths chosen for them by their husbands illustrate both the limitations and the possibilities for married white women in an age that saw both reform and reaction, rapid change and a rising nostalgia for the past. More often than not, things did not turn out in their lives as they might have hoped or planned. Angelina Grimké embraced both the antislavery movement of the 1830s and the man who most famously represented it, and for a brief moment she became a central figure in the struggle for abolition. But if marriage to Theodore Weld solidified her place in the reform community, it also limited her participation and silenced her public voice. Varina Howell nurtured her intellect as a young woman and believed that the man she married loved her independent mind and spirit. But in her marriage to Jefferson Davis she found herself the frequent object of his disapproval and criticism because she would not behave as an obedient wife. Alone among these three women, Julia Dent seemed content with the restrictions marriage placed upon her. She was fortunate to marry Ulysses S. Grant, a man who, like herself, accepted the social norms and conventions of the day. Julia embraced the status quo, resisted change until it could no longer be ignored or repelled, and only late in life caught a fleeting glimpse of the price of the perpetual dependency that had defined her.

Over the months, as their biographies took shape, I came to know these three women with the intimacy that biographers often acquire and with an affection that biographers do not always sustain. Angelina's bravery won my respect, Varina's brilliance won my admiration, and Julia's contentment won my envy. Each performed remarkable deeds, some of their own initiative, others in response to the exigencies of the moment. Each made striking sacrifices to husband and family and saw this as their duty. For whether they struggled against the limits set on their autonomy and independence because they were women or took comfort and satisfaction in those limits, their lives played out in response to social conventions and ideals they could never fully escape. For this reason, they viewed the events of their lifetime through a very different prism than did their famous husbands, and that is one reason why their story must be told.

Because their stories give a human face to what often seems an overpowering series of grand, impersonal events, I knew they must be told with sympathy and empathy. Angelina, Varina, and Julia were not without their faults. In her twenties, Angelina was tiresomely self-centered and ungenerous in her constant criticism of the family who loved her and tolerated her verbal attacks. As a woman of impressive intelligence and great wit, Varina could be callously judgmental about those with slower tongues and less agile minds. And throughout her life, Julia maintained a myopia about the clash of ideas that prompted the war and moved women and men to demand an end to slavery. Yet the hardships and challenges that the era brought into their lives awakened reserves of strength and ingenuity in each of them that earned my respect. They were, to a great extent, accidental heroes, but heroes nonetheless. Neither generals nor presidents, political leaders nor founders of movements, these women remind us why our generation still reaches out across the centuries to understand theirs.

Angelina Grimké Weld

Angela Grimké Weld.
Courtesy of the Library of Congress.

One

"WE ARE A NATION OF CHANGES"

America at the Crossroads in the 1830s

"IT WAS THE BEST OF TIMES. It was the worst of times." When Charles Dickens penned these now familiar words of contradiction, he was not speaking of the United States in 1830. Yet the contradiction surely applied, for during this turbulent decade Americans agreed that their country was changing rapidly. But whether the changes they witnessed were for the good or bad, they sharply disagreed.

No one could deny that the nation was growing, both physically and in population. Eight new states had come into the Union since the century began and two more would join before the decade ended. The nation's population had soared, growing from under four million in 1790 to almost thirteen million by 1830. Although the great wave of German and Irish immigration lay ahead in the 1840s, roughly a hundred thousand new Americans would arrive in the United States before the decade was over. Yet if the nation was growing larger, there was a sense that it was also becoming more intimate, for a revolution in transportation and communication was in full swing. Toll roads crisscrossed the country, creating a transportation network unimagined in the eighteenth century. The heavily traveled National Road had snaked its way through the Appalachian Mountains since the 1820s, and by 1830 it reached as far as the Ohio River. Construction on a state-of-the-art highway soon followed, and by 1838 it carried people and produce as far as Illinois. A system of canals, including the famous Erie Canal, now linked the western countryside to the cities of the Northeast. Americans were already growing accustomed to the marvels of new technology, for since the late eighteenth century, steamboats with fanciful names such as *Car of Neptune*, *Firefly*, and *Vesuvius* could be seen on the Hudson, Delaware, and Savannah rivers. But an even faster, if noisier, form of transportation was beginning to appear on the landscape: the railroad. Americans who had seen Peter Cooper's "Tom Thumb" steam loco-

Theodore Weld.
Courtesy of the Ohio Historical Society.

motive make its first run in 1830 knew they had been given a glimpse of the future.

Cheaper printing technology and improved mail service were creating a more intimate America as well. Letters posted in Buffalo, New York, sped south in the holds of canal boats, reaching New York City in a remarkable six days. The same letter could reach New Orleans in only two weeks. Affordable books, pamphlets, and newspapers now reached homes that had once boasted of nothing but a family Bible. The statistics were dazzling: in 1790, 92 newspapers were published in the United States, with a circulation of four million; by 1835, there were 1,258 newspapers reaching ninety million readers. By 1836, instant communication seemed possible, as Samuel F. B. Morse perfected his electric telegraph.

Changes in the American economy were no less dramatic. In the North, production had begun to move out of the household and into shops and factories, while in the South, King Cotton claimed its throne. The signs of prosperity were everywhere: not only in urban mansions and Southern plantation homes but also in the luxuries that graced the tables of the nation's middle class. Signs of expanding democracy were just as obvious, at least for the white male population. The older notion that only men of property should enjoy full citizenship had given way to the demand for wider participation in choosing those who made the laws and set the policies for the nation. The "era of the common man" was in full swing by the 1830s, and as the number of voters swelled, a new breed of professional politicians emerged to woo their support and to offer policies that served their interests.

Along with these changes came a new national ethos. The brash nationalism that had followed the War of 1812 produced a cultural revolution. Young American artists turned their backs on Old World subjects, preferring to capture on their canvases the natural beauty of their country's mountains and rivers. The romance with the American landscape, embodied in the Hudson River school of artists, had its literary counterpart in the works of writers such as James Fenimore Cooper, who created characters and plots drawn from local myths and local history. Americans even had their own dictionary, thanks to Noah Webster—another sign, if one was needed, of independence from their English past.

At the same time that American artists were discovering the aesthetic soul of the nation, American religious leaders were discovering the democratization of the human soul. A religious revival swept the nation in the early nineteenth century, carrying the message that everyone was capable of attaining salvation, that heaven's doors opened to the penitent sinner, and that there was room for all in paradise. This Second Great Awakening, as historians came to call it, declared that men and women could shape their own destiny if they embraced Christ. And if salvation was within the reach of everyone, surely life on earth could also be improved. Missionary societies took up the task of converting those they called heathens at home and abroad. Utopian communities sprang up, each an experiment in new social arrangements that might guide the way to a perfect society. Reformers organized campaigns against alcoholism; sexual immorality; and the abuse of the insane, the handicapped, and the criminal. By the 1830s, Americans could speak of a "benevolent empire" of devoted men and women, eager to eradicate all social ills and imperfections.

And yet there was a darker side to all this change. The expansion of the South's Cotton Kingdom also meant the expansion of slavery. If many of the framers of the Constitution had quietly hoped African American slavery would vanish from their republic, the soaring profits enjoyed by Southern planters destroyed that dream. The westward movement of the white population, made possible by improved transportation and fueled by the insatiable thirst for land, was already setting slave master against small farmer in the territories. The West was becoming, in the minds of both political leaders and ordinary citizens, a competitive battleground between the systems of slave and free labor. The decade had begun with an attempt to control the tensions, but few were convinced that the political bandage known as the Missouri Compromise would stop the spread of sectional tensions.

Americans also discovered there was a price to pay for rapid economic growth and expansion when the boom economy of the early 1830s morphed into the bust economy of its later years. In 1837, panic and widespread depression wiped out rich men's fortunes and destroyed poor men's dreams. Banks that had swung their doors wide closed them tightly soon afterward, leaving farmers and small merchants to mourn the loss of their life savings. Debtors' prisons overflowed and businessmen learned that social mobility was a ladder that could carry them down as well as up.

A new anxiety about rapid change rippled beneath the surface of this age of optimism and belief in progress. By the mid-thirties, a disturbing question began to be raised: where was America headed? Many feared that the land of Jefferson's Protestant yeoman farmer was becoming the land of speculators, bankers, African American slaves, and Catholic immigrants. A belief in conspiracies began to take hold, prompting the rise of the Know-Nothing Party, which accused American Freemasons of dangerous secret rituals, undue influence in business and politics, and even murder. Northern reformers spoke ominously, and often, of the "slaveocracy," a conspiratorial coalition of Southern planters and their Northern business allies. Even the consumer revolution that brought luxuries such as ice cream to day laborers and fashionable gowns to the wives of clerks proved troubling. The eager embrace of goods seemed to spell a victory for Mammon over God.

Other Americans wondered what traditional values were being lost in the race to modernity. They viewed the lure of the city with alarm, for urban opportunities drew young men and young women away from the watchful eyes of parents and ministers. The city's anonymity—and its decadence—were destroying the morality of their sons and daughters. Certainly those who read the headlines in 1836, detailing the brutal and mysterious death of a young New York prostitute, had reason to fear that vice, violence, and moral corruption were dangers lurking on every city street.

Still others asked who controlled politics in this new age of interest groups and professional officeholders. The expansion of suffrage to all adult white males in most states had unexpected political consequences. Political parties were developing efficient vote-garnering machinery, their candidates willing to make promises to the common man they could not (and never intended to) keep while selling their votes to powerful interests such as the planters, manufacturers, and merchants whose bidding they were more than eager to do.

Everywhere some Americans looked they saw greed, exploitation, sin, and excess—and, just as their more optimistic neighbors were doing, they mounted a determined crusade to improve the world around them. But their reform was harder-edged: if the promise of perfectability resonated with them as it did with their counterparts, the stakes for these reformers were higher. Unless Americans fought the temptations of their changing world, God's wrath would be felt and the nation would be punished. The focus of the energies of a small but determined group soon became the abolition of slavery, for it would carry with it the end to the political and economic power of Southern slave masters and their Northern commercial allies. Abolition would guarantee the fulfillment of the promise of the Revolution: life, liberty, and the pursuit of happiness for all.

Over the next two decades, these abolitionists waged a dogged battle against what they considered the unholy alliances of cotton magnates and Northern merchants, Southern and Northern politicians, slave owners and those in the free states who closed their eyes to the evils of the "peculiar institution." Although they were always a small minority, their crusade moved the nation closer to both civil war and emancipation. One of the most remarkable of these crusaders was Angelina Grimké, who began life as a pampered and self-absorbed child of privilege and ended it as a woman dedicated not only to abolition but also to racial equality.

Two

"I THINK MUCH SUFFERING AWAITS ME"

Angelina Grimké's Journey to Reform

ON FEBRUARY 20, 1805, Angelina Emily Grimké became the fourteenth and last child born to Mary Smith Grimké and John Faucheraud Grimké, and the eleventh to survive her infancy. Blue-eyed and curly-headed, "baby Nina" did not yet realize what a privileged world she had entered. Her father was a South Carolina planter, slaveholder, lawyer, politician, and judge who owned two profitable plantations as well as the large and gracious town house in Charleston where Angelina would spend most of her childhood. Judge Grimké, a man of great learning and even greater confidence in the correctness of his own views and values, had studied law in England, served as a captain in the Revolutionary War, and returned home to take his place in state government. His wife's lineage was as aristocratic as was possible in a republic: she was a direct descendant of the first landgrave of colonial Carolina, a quasi-noble rank that reflected the proprietors' dream of reviving feudalism in the New World. Men in her family had served as governors and speakers of the colonial legislature. Smiths had earned a reputation for civic responsibility with a dash of derring-do, for one among them had delivered Charleston from the clutches of pirates. Mary Smith's own father, a banker, was one of the richest men in a state not lacking in wealthy citizens. The Grimkés' position as leaders of glittering Charleston society seemed to rest comfortably upon their shoulders—and heavily upon the shoulders of the many slaves who secured the family's place in the land where cotton was king.

Like most of South Carolina's planter elite, the Grimkés often divided their time between their country plantation and their Charleston residence, preferring the less disease-prone and less humid city in the summer. Wherever they resided, they enjoyed the comforts that only those with housekeepers, parlor maids, nursemaids, valets, butlers, footmen, cooks, coachmen, stable boys, and other servants at their beck and call were likely to know. Despite the panoply of servants, Mary Smith Grimké had little leisure time. Managing two complex households, directing the activities of the African American slaves who served the family's needs, and carrying out the charity work and church-related activities that were expected of the fortunate members of Southern society filled her days. She lived, as one historian has put it, a life of duty, fulfilling her society's gender ideals of piety and self-sacrifice—as well as admirable fertility. But if her last child was to be doted upon, it was not likely to be by her mother. For Mary Smith Grimké, the novelty of motherhood had long ago worn off.[1]

Fortunately, Angelina had someone ready to lavish attention upon her: one of her older sisters, Sarah. Sarah, twelve years old when baby Nina was born, was a plain-looking, awkward young woman despite all the appropriate preparation in French, singing, piano, and manners her family ensured she received. Sarah had brains rather than beauty, no advantage in antebellum Southern society. Her ardent desire to become a lawyer was greeted with amusement by the Grimké men, and thus while brothers Thomas and Fred went on to be lawyers and John became a doctor, Sarah was primed for marriage, motherhood, and household management. Instead of reading law books, she was set to work at womanly tasks such as making clothes for the family's slaves. Her ambitions thwarted, Sarah looked for a challenge that was acceptable within the rigid separation of spheres that consigned her to domestic duties. When Angelina was born, she begged to be the baby's godmother. For the rest of Sarah's life, Angelina would be the focus of her most intense and often overpowering affection. And for much of *her* life, Angelina would call Sarah "Mother."[2]

As the two girls grew up, their futures seemed to move in quite different directions. Sarah did not fare well in the marriage market, for Charleston suitors were not drawn to a woman of great intelligence and articulated opinions. She earned a reputation as an eccentric rather than a belle. Her restless mind sought an outlet in one of the few acceptable pursuits for unmarried women: the quest for salvation. Piety was one of the cornerstones of that nineteenth-century feminine ideal known to historians as the "cult of true womanhood." Quietly but deliberately, Sarah Grimké turned her thoughts inward and searched her soul. Although she may not have intended to set in motion a rebellion against family or community, Sarah's quest led her to defy both their social values and their gender expectations. In 1817, at the age of twenty-four, she troubled her parents by renouncing her Episcopal roots and converting to the déclassé faith of Presbyterianism. Guided by a local minister, she began to attend prayer meetings rather than dances or parties and to read religious treatises rather than romantic novels. Sarah struggled with the demands of this more Spartan life, suffering frequent lapses in her devotion, reverting to familiar pastimes only to return, humbly, to the evangelical fold. By 1821, two years after her father's death, her search for spiritual fulfillment had led her to the furthest margins of religious respectability. In that year she moved to Philadelphia and joined the Society of Friends. Something of her old intellectual ambition reemerged as she embraced this Quaker faith, for in this sect, a woman of devotion and intelligence could be a preacher rather than a silent worshiper, a leader rather than a submissive congregant.

Angelina, on the other hand, was perfectly suited to the expectations placed upon wealthy young Charleston women. She was attractive, tall, graceful, and delicately made, and she was accomplished in those arts that the daughters of South Carolina's elite learned from boarding-school mistresses or tutors. She seemed destined for success in the intricate courtship dance that friends and peers looked forward to with relish. And yet Angelina rejected the future spreading so smoothly before her. In 1821, the same year that Sarah left for Philadelphia, Angelina announced a second, even more surprising apostasy by refusing to be confirmed in the Episcopal Church. Mary Smith Grimké was relieved, no doubt, that her husband had not lived to see such acts of rebellion by his daughters. No son of John Grimké ever resisted his father's wishes, rejected his mother's church, or renounced the luxuries and privileges of their class. Yet, different as they were in temperament, experience, and motivation, the sisters had begun a journey down the same deviant, and defiant, path.

Surely Sarah's decisions influenced Angelina. The younger Grimké had followed her sister's spiritual journey closely as Sarah confided her loneliness, self-doubts, ecstasies, and revelations of intense religious experiences. An intimacy that had few boundaries had developed between the sisters, born of their emotional neediness. But there was more to Angelina's rebellion than a desire, or need, to walk in her sister's footsteps. She was propelled by a powerful ambition to live out her life on a grander scale than Charleston provided a genteel woman. Later in life, she would confess that this ambition had never died. An equally powerful belief that she had a special destiny gave her the courage to turn her back on all that was expected of her and all that was promised to her. The roots of this belief in her special destiny surely lay in Sarah's doting attention, but much had to do with the impatience that Angelina, like her father, felt toward those who did not see the world as she saw it. If Sarah regretted being considered an eccentric, Angelina chose to become one.

The path Angelina chose would prove to be difficult, even for a tough-minded and determined young Southern woman. Rebellion was not an accepted rite of passage for sons and daughters of the planter class, and there was no welcoming and reaffirming youth culture that parents shook their heads at but tolerated just the same. If utopian communities would soon spring up in America, testing new male and female relationships and new theologies, they would not take root in South Carolina. Every step that Angelina took outside the protective circle of family values and family traditions was precipitous; every challenge to accepted social norms carried her onto unfamiliar ground. Like Sarah, she sought an authority higher than parents, a code of behavior even more legitimate than Charleston manners and mores, and like Sarah she found both in Christ and His teachings.

By 1826, the twenty-one-year-old Angelina had followed her sister's path to a local Presbyterian church. With Sarah far away, she was lucky to find a minister who served as mentor and guide in the first months of her religious explorations. The friendship that developed between the young and dynamic but married Reverend William McDowell and the headstrong but eager acolyte became precariously intimate. Yet Angelina's temperament and character proved to be bolder, and her vision broader, than her mentor's. Her religious rebellion had done more than move her away from the comfortable Episcopalian worldview. It had given her a new perspective from which to view not only her family's tenets of faith but their social values as well. She came to see slavery and the privileges it ensured the planter class in a new and horrifying way. Older, once disconnected memories of cries from the workhouse where slaves were taken to be punished, recollections of a young African American boy scarred and crippled by his beatings, the daily mistreatment of family servants—these gained a coherence in Angelina's mind as she stepped back, and away, from a world that had once seemed natural and even inevitable. Reverend McDowell, she would discover, was content to pray silently for the repentance of South Carolina's slaveholding class. But Angelina Grimké felt compelled to testify against their sins. For her, faith and religious commitment demanded action; they were an enabling force rather than ends in themselves.

McDowell had no answers for the questions that now plagued Angelina Grimké. Her questions seemed both naive and grandiose, but they were much like the questions that were beginning to spur small bands of reformers in New England, New York, Pennsylvania, and Ohio to oppose slavery. The religious revival of the early nineteenth century had created the vocabulary of social reform, and antislavery and temperance advocates as much as missionaries believed that the tasks they shouldered could be achieved only if they passed the test of faith and carried the banner of Christ. For Angelina, the burning question was what God was steeling her to do and whether she had the strength of character and the faith to do it. What must she sacrifice and what must she embrace in order to carry what she called the "yoke of Jesus Christ" on earth? She did not yet have the answers, but she knew that her burden would include more than a personal rejection of slavery. It required a public renunciation of slavery as an institution. The task was daunting: to be openly antislavery was, as she knew, to be very much alone in the Charleston of the 1820s.

In 1828, Angelina began to keep a journal that was both an intellectual and emotional record of her effort to delineate her faith and discover her purpose. The journal was a pilgrim's progress, with an agonizing and harsh self-examination, a meticulous accounting of what she saw as her character flaws and her moral weaknesses, and a litany of self-doubt and fears of inadequacy to serve God's purpose on earth. In its relentless self-evaluation, Angelina's journal is similar to the records of spiritual awakenings kept by Puritan Calvinists of an earlier century. But in its quest for the revelation of a social purpose, its desire for divine guidance on how to refashion the world and not simply one's own soul, Angelina Grimké's journal embodied the early-nineteenth-century age of reform.[3]

Angelina's journal begins on January 10, 1828, with this simple yet significant declaration: "Today I have torn up my novels." The act was symbolic, for novel reading was a mark of the leisure enjoyed by elite women at the expense of servants and slaves. Other sacrifices followed: her cashmere mantle, her fashionable hats adorned with lace and ribbons. She vowed to dress in coarse fabric and clothes of plain design just as Sarah now wore. Her friends scoffed at her, insisting that such acts of self-denial were not holy but unseemly. "My friends," she wrote, "tell me that I render myself ridiculous and expose the Crown of Jesus to reproach on account of my plain dressing, they tell me that it is wrong to make myself so conspicuous." But peer pressure no longer held any power over the determined Angelina. "The more I ponder on this subject," she wrote, "the more I feel that I am called with a high and holy calling."[4]

Angelina was not blind to what she was giving up. Like Sarah, she confessed to her journal how painful it was to renounce the many advantages of her birth. "It is my grief & shame," she admitted, "that I find it so hard to yield willingly." But the struggle to reform herself took on an urgency, for she believed, as thousands of other evangelicals believed in these ante-

bellum decades, that Judgment Day was imminent and Christ was preparing to take possession of the earth. Sides must be chosen for the coming
battle between "the Soldiers of the Cross" and "Gog and Magog"—and
Angelina Emily Grimké wanted fervently to be in God's army. At each step
along the way to salvation, however, the chasm between her and the society
of her birth would grow. She was intensely aware of her alienation from
friends, family, and even the Reverend McDowell. By April, she no longer
believed that the Presbyterian Church or its minister could help her find
her way. "Now its Pastor can do no more for me," she confided to her journal, "for he knows nothing about the exercises of my mind & he can teach
me no more." By May 1828, she and McDowell had reached a spiritual and
intellectual impasse and a wave of loneliness swept over her. Small wonder
that she feared she would soon be "a stranger in the midst of those with
whom I once took sweet counsel . . . forsaken of all & condemned."[5]

That July, Angelina sought relief from both her loneliness and her continuing self-doubts by taking a trip to Philadelphia to visit Sarah. By now,
she had begun a tentative association with the small Quaker meeting in
Charleston, but her sympathies with the sect deepened during her stay
with her sister. And in Philadelphia, she had her first exposure to a culture
in which neither she nor her sister was eccentric. By the time she returned
to Charleston, she considered herself a Friend. The language of her journal
confirmed this second religious conversion, as "you" became "thee" and the
dates of her entries shifted from "Monday" or "Tuesday" to "second day" or
"third day." Her new faith proved even more demanding than her first, for
the Quakers required their followers to "be still before the Lord" and to
wait for His will to be revealed. For Angelina, being still was the biggest
challenge she had faced.

The rest of the Grimké family wished fervently, however, that Angelina
would be still—and be quiet. Sarah had said farewell to family and friends
quietly and put hundreds of miles between herself and the society she
rejected. But Angelina remained in the Grimké home, unable to make a
final separation despite constant talk of moving to Philadelphia. Her journal for these months reflects the fragile yet aggressive state of mind of the
newly converted. She burned with an unrelenting evangelical energy that
she released upon her mother, her brothers, and her sisters. She turned the
Grimké household into her own captive congregation and, like many of
the most spirited revivalist ministers, bombarded its members with an
account of their sins, their personal failings, and their need to repent. She
practiced her by now sharply honed talent for criticism on Mary Smith

Grimké, on her brothers Henry and Charles—in fact, upon any family member who crossed her threshold. She pointed out their excessive love of luxury, their preference for sociability rather than quiet contemplation, and their inexcusable willingness to reap the rewards of slavery. She had a desperate, often touching desire to rescue them from themselves, to convert them to the truths that were daily revealed to her. But she had an equally desperate desire to place the blame for all of her own earlier sins and moral failings on their influence and example. And blame them she did.[6]

Angelina did not have to look far for the greatest culprit in the spiritual and emotional ruin of the Grimké household. Her mother, Mary Smith Grimké, was responsible for Charles's decadence, for Henry's temper, and for her own improper upbringing as a child. The litany of her mother's sins was long: she had failed to nurture Angelina, failed to set an example of moral strength for the family, failed to shape the consciences of her children. Rather than teach her family the values of simplicity and sobriety, Mrs. Grimké had wasted money on new draperies, wasted food on a table groaning with excess, wasted attention on a circle of shallow acquaintances. She had devoted herself to a church that taught false doctrine. Most damning of all, she refused to see slavery as a sin.

Angelina was certain that her motives were pure, and she was puzzled when her efforts to save a family "without natural affection, hateful & hating one another" were greeted with annoyance and anger rather than gratitude. She recorded her exchanges with her mother with genuine frustration, for she saw no improvement in Mary Smith Grimké's behavior and no willingness to mend her ways. Still, Angelina persisted. "I feel the necessity," she wrote, "of dear Mother's seeing the bitter fruit of her system of education." The moral and emotional wreckage Angelina believed she saw in her family was due, she concluded, to her mother's willingness to "let every one do as they pleased." She never stopped to consider that her own individualism owed much to her mother's tolerance.[7]

Despite Mrs. Grimké's many flaws, Angelina longed to establish a greater intimacy with her mother. She longed to awaken what she saw as her mother's stillborn maternal instinct, and she orchestrated opportunities for Mary to profess and demonstrate her love. One evening she sat beside her mother and laid her head on her lap. Neither the patient Mrs. Grimké nor her desperate daughter said a word. "My tears began to flow," Angelina wrote that April night, "& she felt much also—putting her hand on my face she assured me that she loved me very much but that it was not her way to show her love by outward caresses." After this, the evening sessions became a ritual: the two women, old and young, sitting in darkness, saying little or nothing as the hours passed. Yet no matter how many assurances she received, Angelina did not trust her mother's affection. Mary's true nature, she believed, was cold and indifferent, and her occasional kisses were motivated by duty—or pity—rather than love. "I don't think she ever has experienced that deep & tender affection for me which is right to exist in a parents bosom." The judgment would come home to haunt Angelina many years later, when her own children turned to another, more openly affectionate Grimké sister for nurturance.[8]

Angelina's criticism of her brothers was equally blunt. She pointed out Charles's idleness and irresponsibility, for he followed no occupation and lived off the generosity of his mother. Although she offered her comments "candidly & affectionately," Charles Grimké was not grateful for her insights. Despite his obvious annoyance with her suggestions that he give up all small luxuries such as butter and live "in the plainest fashion since he paid no rent," Angelina persisted. She told him that she did not feel condemned for anything she had said, for "my opinions were based on principle." In later years, Angelina's willingness to stand her ground when she believed she was morally right would win her the admiration of reformers; in the Grimké household, it gained her nothing but a door slammed in her face.[9]

Angelina's early efforts to reform others clearly lacked subtlety and empathy. They took the form of frontal assaults rather than sympathetic efforts to persuade—and they failed. In time, she would learn to teach rather than preach, to urge rather than demand, and to speak to others with firmness of belief rather than with pride. But in her last months at home, she seemed more determined to drive a wedge between herself and her family than to strengthen bonds of affection. Discouraged by her failures, she turned her thoughts to an escape from both her family and Charleston.

The tense situation at home was not Angelina's only motive for flight. She had grown more sensitive to the cruelties of slavery, and at every turn she saw its impact on the enslaved men and women whom she still thought of as "poor creatures," "miserable creatures," rather than as full members of humanity. Her deepest sympathy was not yet for the enslaved but rather for herself, an outcast in her native land because of slavery. She had come home from Philadelphia "to suffer—& be nothing among those who once caressed & loved me much." Now she longed to return to the Quaker community in Philadelphia. By the summer of 1829, she was often deeply depressed and weary, with "no bosom for me to lean upon, no heart to sympathize with me." A woman of weaker will might have given up the struggle and returned to the Charleston fold, but Angelina never considered this option. Instead she turned repeatedly to the subject of slavery with both friends and family, challenging the sanctity of the parlor and its polite conversation with her insistence that her slave-owning guests were not living by the gospel of love.[10]

On June 5, 1829, Angelina observed the anniversary of her sailing to Philadelphia a year before. She was ready, at last, to return to Pennsylvania, for "every cord [had been] broken which bound me to Carolina at that time." It was true. Only a week later, in another of her almost daily confrontations with her daughter, Mary Smith Grimké's patience had come to an end. Not everyone, she told Angelina, thinks as a Quaker thinks about slavery. Reluctantly, Angelina concluded that she had failed to rescue her mother from sin. "The root of corruption," she told her journal, was still in her mother's heart. Her siblings were equally hopeless. Sister Eliza continued to revel in fashion and folly. Charles remained shiftless and idle. Henry held late-night parties, serving alcohol to his guests. The minds of her friends were "closed against her opinions" as well. The Presbyterian elders had declared her unwelcome in their church. Even the local Quakers, small in number and weak in influence, had greeted her criticisms of their squabbles coldly.[11]

That August, Angelina turned her attention to her own soul and once again took stock of her progress toward true salvation. She found herself sorely wanting. With a new and hard-won maturity, she recognized that her greatest failing had been, and remained, a pride in her own righteousness. "All that righteousness of which we are proud," she declared in her journal, "is literally filthy rags." She suddenly saw her persistent criticism of her family in a new light: "though it was deserved it was still sinful of me." The revelation was a turning point. She would never again act the avenging angel; the truth would be a burden to bear rather than a sword to wield against others.[12]

In October, a very different Angelina Emily Grimké sailed for Philadelphia once again. Despite all their unresolved differences, mother and daughter found it difficult to say their goodbyes. Mary Smith Grimké confessed that this separation was the hardest she had ever experienced with a child. Angelina recorded her mother's parting words: "It is vain for me to reason about my feelings she said, why I am so afflicted I know not, I have parted with other of my children but never felt as I now do, some-times I think I should never see you again, but it is in vain to reason." Mary's premonition proved correct; although she and Angelina would keep their connection alive through letters, mother and daughter would never meet again.[13]

Three

"MAKE ME INSTRUMENTAL IN THE GREAT WORK OF EMANCIPATION"

Angelina Grimké's Letter to The Liberator

THE PHILADELPHIA AWAITING Angelina Grimké in 1829 was the largest city in the United States, a thriving seaport whose waterfront hosted numerous boatyards and docks and whose city streets were lined with the elegant homes of merchants, shippers, and financiers and the crowded boardinghouses of the poor and African American laborers and servants. It boasted private and public schools, colleges, newspaper offices, print shops, libraries, theaters, and specialty shops that sold luxury items from around the world. The city offered cultural and social opportunities for everyone: rich men could attend lectures at the American Philosophical Society, poor men could argue politics at the city's many taverns, and the middle classes could entertain themselves at amusement parks and public gardens. Although it was no longer the nation's capital, Philadelphia was a magnet for reformers, revivalists, and political reactionaries, all of whom found a ready audience among those whose religions ran the gamut from Quaker to German Pietist to Methodist and Presbyterian and whose politics ranged from Anti-Masonic to Working Men's parties as well as Democratic and Whig. In short, Philadelphia was a city of infinite possibilities, alive with political, social, and cultural activity that invited a newcomer's participation.

None of these possibilities had drawn the twenty-four-year-old Angelina Grimké to the City of Brotherly Love. She had no interest in amusements or entertainment, no desire to patronize the shops offering the latest fashions or delicacies, and, with her more than adequate inheritance from her father, no need to find employment of any kind. And, despite the role her opposition to slavery played in her flight from South Carolina, Angelina showed no interest in national policies or in the movements arising to reform them. Indeed, she was almost oblivious to the major events of the day. She had come to Philadelphia for a single, all-consuming reason: to find a haven, a community in which she could feel she truly belonged. She had come to find a home among the Quakers.

At first, Philadelphia seemed indeed to be her promised land. After years of unhappiness among Charleston belles, she reveled in the company of women such as her sister Sarah, Catherine Morris, and Jane Bettle, all of whom wore the same plain dresses and unadorned bonnets and spoke the same distinctive language that had once set her painfully apart from female society. Once she settled in at Catherine Morris's home, Angelina entered easily into the flow of charity work and Bible study that filled the days of orthodox Quaker women, and she worked diligently to ready herself for formal admission to the Society of Friends. But to preserve her idealized image of the community that seemed to welcome her, she also closed her eyes to the signs that Quakerism was in turmoil, racked by dissension and disagreement over participation in social reform. Already the local Hicksite faction had broken ranks with the orthodox Quakers, preferring to play an active role in political and social reform while the more conservative Arch Street Meeting Angelina attended maintained its insular stance. She closed her eyes as well to the sometimes brutal discouragement meted out by Quaker elders that had crushed her sister Sarah's hopes of preaching. Most of all, she did not acknowledge the ironic similarities between the society she had left and the society she was so eager to join. The Quaker world, like the planter world, had a rigid code of behavior, firm demands for conformity, and its own methods of punishing those who challenged their rules. For almost five years, Angelina would continue her struggle to belong, but she would find the cost too high and, in the end, the rewards too few. Her experiences would make her realize, as Sarah also slowly realized, that there was no room for a woman of independent mind and restless spirit among orthodox Quakers.[1]

In 1830, Angelina gained formal admission to the Society of Friends. Soon afterward, Jane Bettle's son Edward began to court her. Edward, a widower with a young son of his own, was by Quaker standards a desirable suitor. Although he was physically frail and somewhat stolid, he was sober and honest and his father was the wealthy and prestigious Samuel Bettle. Angelina had rejected the idea of marriage to a slave-owning man of the South, not simply because slavery was a sin but also because she had seen the living evidence of infidelity in the mulatto children of Charleston. She had concluded that in planter society the sanctity of marriage was a farce. But she had not rejected the idea of marriage itself. Her sister Sarah had committed herself to spinsterhood when she turned down her only Quaker suitor, the widowed Israel Morris. But Angelina had no reason to believe she would follow her sister down that path.[2]

Unfortunately, courtship patterns among Pennsylvania's orthodox Quakers were not the same as those Angelina had witnessed in South Carolina's planter society. If flirtation and cupidity were an accepted part of the process in Charleston, in Quaker Philadelphia the path to marriage was straight and narrow. Bettle knew the rules and followed them: a man called on an eligible woman; his intentions were noted in the meeting minutes; the parents' approval was sought and received; the Society consented; the couple married. Angelina was unaware of this rigid script, and in the midst of Edward Bettle's courtship, the object of his desire decided to take a trip out of town.[3]

The decision seemed perfectly reasonable to Angelina. For several months since her admission to the Society, she had been contemplating her future. Despite her relief at being among like-minded people, and despite Edward's attentions, she had grown restless. The endless rounds of charity work that had filled her days since the move to Philadelphia were no longer satisfying, and she sought something more challenging and more productive. But what? The answer seemed to come when Catharine Beecher visited Philadelphia. Beecher, the daughter of the famous Presbyterian minister Lyman Beecher, had established a female academy in Hartford where she trained women teachers. A few years later, Beecher and Grimké would engage in an acrimonious public debate over how to end slavery, but in 1831 Angelina was deeply impressed by this intelligent and charming woman. She decided to see Beecher's school firsthand. Thus, in July, she headed north with companions, oblivious to the many infractions she was committing. Her departure not only embarrassed and insulted her suitor but also offended the Quaker community. For Angelina had broken yet another rule: she had left Philadelphia without first asking permission to go.

The monthlong trip opened up a new and very different world for Angelina Grimké from the world she had found among Philadelphia's orthodox Quakers. Her journal offers a portrait of an enthusiastic traveler, reveling in the natural beauty of the region as she climbed Mt. Holyoke, marveling at the early signs of industrialization at a wool factory, and admiring the institutions that bore the stamp of Northern reformers—prisons, the Hartford Deaf and Dumb Asylum, and, above all, Beecher's Hartford Female Seminary. She was stimulated by conversation with the witty Catharine Beecher, her talented and empathetic sister Harriet, and the celebrated author Lydia Howard Sigourney. Wherever she went, in Massachusetts and later in New York, she was surrounded by vibrant and interesting people, women and men engaged with the political and intellectual currents of the day. The contrast to the Quaker community in which she had lived for three years was striking; there, events such as President Jackson's cabinet scandal over the morals of Peggy Eaton, the Webster-Hayne debate, and even the Nullification Controversy had passed unnoted, but here, the issues of the day were topics of parlor conversation. By the time she headed home, Angelina had resolved to enroll in Beecher's academy and to return to the stimulating environment of New England.

None of these plans would materialize. On her return to Philadelphia, she faced a barrage of criticism. Friends were eager to explain the many ways her trip had offended: she had abandoned her charitable duties for frivolous pleasure; she had left Philadelphia without receiving permission; she had dared to choose a career without seeking advice; and she now proposed to return to the dangerous company of Hartford's Presbyterians. Worst of all in the eyes of Edward Bettle's parents, Samuel and Jane, she had interrupted a proper courtship. Angelina had no one to blame but herself when Edward no longer came to call.

Angelina's resolve crumbled in the face of community criticism and a lover's apparent rejection. She tried frantically to repair the damage she had done, renouncing all plans to attend Beecher's school or to train as a teacher. As penance, she agreed to work as the assistant in Catherine Morris's infant school, although she proved ill-suited to the job and thoroughly disliked it. Each evening, she waited for Edward to reappear. Through much of August, Angelina hoped in vain. The longer Edward stayed away, the more cherished he became in her mind and heart. Little else seemed to matter. In South Carolina, a slave named Nat Turner rose up in rebellion against his masters, but the young woman who had feared violence would come to her homeland if justice was not done knew nothing of it. "Hope & fear anxiety & doubt are my daily, hearty portion," she confessed to her journal; "how humbling to any woman to feel that her affections are fixed on one who no longer pays her any attention." She now blamed herself for his desertion, and she blamed New England Presbyterians for setting her on the foolish path that had destroyed his affections.[4]

By September, Angelina's self-confidence was so shaken that she added a long list of personal inadequacies to the reasons for Edward's rejection. It was not simply that she had defied the rules; she was unsuited to be a wife and mother. "My incapacity to fill the responsible stations of wife, mother

& mistress," she wrote, was the true reason he had given up the courtship. "Surely he knows as well as I do," she continued, "how poor a creature I am & cannot still think of placing his own & his childs happiness in such unworthy hands." What she did not do, despite pages and pages of her journal devoted to the relationship, was consider that she was suffering from a bruised ego more than a broken heart.[5]

At last, after months of Angelina's waiting, hoping, and doubting, the young widower reappeared. As an encouragement to their courtship, Angelina moved away from the close supervision of Catherine Morris and into the home of Anna Frost, a widowed Grimké sister who now lived in Philadelphia. Yet, now that Edward had returned and her self-confidence was restored, doubts crept in. There was no intense meeting of the minds between them, no deep empathy. "I do not understand how we ever are to understand each other fully," she confessed to her journal, for "there is never that unreserved spiritual intercourse which I so much desire." Her thoughts turned to the communion of minds she had once shared with William McDowell. Rereading the letters she had exchanged with the young minister only heightened her sense that something vital was missing in Edward Bettle.[6]

Was she simply fickle? she wondered. This had been the judgment of her critics when she returned from New England. Angelina hoped desperately they were wrong. The truth was she did not know her own mind and feared what she might find if she honestly explored her feelings. In fact, she had many good reasons to question the wisdom of a commitment to Edward: his health was poor and the prospect lay ahead that she would spend her life caring for an invalid; he had a child whose affection and respect were uncertain; and he had parents who were now less than welcoming. But such considerations made her feel cold-blooded. The truth was that, at twenty-six, Angelina Grimké was a romantic like so many young women of her era and social class, drawn to the idea of self-sacrifice in the name of love, although her inner language was the language of spirituality: "Oh how my soul shrinks from such selfish calculation on the holy & solemn subject of marriage." She reassured herself that she was willing to make any sacrifice: "Lord, give him unto me, even if I should have to be his nurse all his life."

In the end, fate and cholera freed Angelina from this agonizing decision. In September 1831 the disease swept through Philadelphia, taking the lives of almost a thousand residents. Edward Bettle was one of its victims. Whatever doubts Angelina had entertained while he was alive, she was devastated by his death. "Death has snatched from me one whom I had fondly hoped would [be] my friend & counselor, my help mate in best things." She feared that his death was a judgment upon her, a sign that God intended her to have no other in her life but Him "as my head & husband."[7]

Edward's parents did little to dispel her grief or ease her sense of guilt. They would not allow her to join the intimate circle of grieving family. Months later, in May 1833, Angelina still silently mourned Edward's loss, confiding to her journal, "The sorrows of my heart are like hidden waters in a deep well, unseen, unknown even to my dearest friends. God only knows the grief of my soul even now when I remember the wormwood & the gall." And yet she now acknowledged her ambivalence toward the marriage. "I not only feel the loss of my friends society . . . but I also feel renewed by the loss of him . . . such was the continual conflict of my spirit during that time . . . and I have often tho't on the whole I am happier since he was taken than I was before." These were not the comments of a callous heart but the recognition of a nineteenth-century woman that marriage and motherhood would surely close off the pursuit of a special destiny.[8]

By the end of 1832, much had changed in Angelina's life. She felt cut adrift from the Quaker community and now thought of Philadelphia as "this strange land," no longer confident that in coming here she had really been coming home. She was twenty-seven years old and resigned to sharing spinsterhood with Sarah, who was almost forty. Although both sisters had inherited ample means to live a genteel spinsterhood, Angelina viewed her future with despair. The years stretched before her as a woman unencumbered by the demands of domesticity or by the need to earn a livelihood. With a sense of urgency, she began to ask herself what useful work she could do. She had once insisted to William McDowell that one must do as well as pray, and now the Quaker injunction to be still and wait seemed a deeply flawed approach. "I am tired beyond what I am able to bear with patience and resignation," she wrote, and acknowledged that she, unlike her Quaker friends, had a "rebellious soul."[9]

Angelina's rebellious soul had carried her on a long and as yet not fully satisfactory religious quest. It had given her the strength to defy social custom in Charleston and to take the measure of Quaker insularity in Philadelphia. And, after her trip to New England, it had prompted her to undertake a rigorous course of self-education. She had devoured books on geometry, arithmetic, chemistry, anatomy, and history. Now her rebellious soul carried her into the heart of a rising movement, abolitionism—and here, at last, she would find her home. In 1833, she began to devour newspapers and pamphlets that brought the arguments over slavery, national politics, and reform into view. Philadelphia's promise now seemed to lie in the Female Anti-Slavery Society rather than in the insular Society of Friends, and Angelina began to attend these abolitionist meetings. In these first, tentative steps toward activism, she was leaving Sarah behind; for the first time, Angelina was paving the way for "Mother" to follow if she dared.

It was an auspicious moment to turn to the antislavery movement. For over a decade, the American Colonization Society had dominated the discussion of slavery, calling for the voluntary emigration of free blacks to Africa and the voluntary emancipation of slaves who would be sent there as well. But a movement for emancipation without any forced relocation had grown strong in England, and on August 23, 1833, the English Parliament passed a Slavery Abolition Act that outlawed slavery in the British colonies. By the following August, every slave in the British Empire had been emancipated. The call for this type of emancipation spread to America, where the son of an alcoholic sailor and a Baptist evangelical mother named William Lloyd Garrison issued a clarion call for "immediate emancipation gradually accomplished." On January 1, 1831, Garrison's antislavery newspaper, *The Liberator,* had ushered in a new phase of antislavery agitation by issuing a direct attack upon the American Colonization Society and its unrealistic, and thus far unsuccessful, solution to racial issues. Garrison set the tone of each issue to come—brash, radical, provocative—with his declaration, "I will not equivocate—I will not excuse—I will not retreat a single inch." His insistent call for public action on the slavery issue was a daring advocacy of a cause most Americans considered dangerously radical and politically disruptive. Since 1820, national politics had dealt gingerly with the growing sectional tensions between the slave-based economy of the South and the free-labor world of the Northern and Ohio Valley states. The moral outrage of those such as Garrison, John Greenleaf Whittier, and the brilliant orator Theodore Weld might make the politics of compromise, practiced so carefully by the Congress, more difficult. But *The Liberator*'s demand for immediate emancipation resonated in the hearts of that small and still marginalized group of Americans who worried that their nation had lost its soul, that a materialist society worshiped Mammon rather than God, and that Northerners were complicit in the sin of slavery. Few of the women and men who flocked to the cause of abolition were politically influential or wealthy; they were ordinary middle-class Americans, eager to have their voices heard by those with the power to effect change.[10]

The abolitionist movement grew quickly, although it was opposed by the majority of Americans in the free states and despised by white Americans in the South. In December 1833, the American Anti-Slavery Society held its first convention in Philadelphia, bringing together three strands of the growing movement: Garrison's Massachusetts Anti-Slavery Society; the New York Anti-Slavery Society, backed by the state's wealthy Tappan brothers; and the Western Movement, formed by abolitionists in Ohio. The following year, an eighteen-month debate between supporters of colonization and supporters of emancipation raged at Lane Seminary in Ohio. When it was over, the argument for colonization had lost legitimacy and abolition had come into its own.

As the movement grew, hostility toward it also grew. Angelina followed with alarm the waves of violence that broke out across the country: riots against antislavery advocates in New York and in her own Philadelphia; the stoning of the abolitionist poet John Greenleaf Whittier and the Reverend Samuel May in Concord, Massachusetts; the beatings taken by antislavery organizers in Ohio; and in New England, the imprisonment of a young Quaker schoolteacher named Prudence Crandall, who had dared to open a school for black girls in Canterbury, Connecticut. In her hometown of Charleston, angry mobs greeted the arrival of abolitionist pamphlets by storming the post office and burning the offending literature.[11]

Angelina's self-education in abolition continued throughout 1834. Then, on February 12, 1835, she went to hear the British abolitionist George Thompson speak at a local Presbyterian church. Thompson had been the driving force behind Britain's abolition of slavery, and his call in 1833 for "the abolition of slavery throughout the world" had inspired William Lloyd Garrison's commitment to immediatism. In 1834, Thompson came to America to lecture and to assist abolitionists in forming antislavery societies across the free states. Mainstream politicians, including Andrew Jackson, denounced him as a rabble-rouser, and his lectures were often disrupted by violent crowds. But for Angelina, Thompson's impassioned call for women to join the great moral crusade of abolition was electric. She had found her community in 1834; now she had found her special destiny as well.[12]

In the wake of the violent attacks on abolitionists, William Lloyd Garrison issued an appeal to the citizens of Boston, asking them to repudiate mob violence and to give his friend George Thompson a fair hearing when he arrived there to lecture. Angelina was deeply touched by Garrison's appeal, and on August 30, 1835, she wrote to him, praising him for his commitment to nonviolence and urging him to stand fast against all physical and emotional opposition to his cause. Her own passionate commitment to the crusade against slavery gave her eloquence: "The ground upon which you stand is holy ground," she wrote, "never—never surrender it. If you Surrender it, the hope of the slave is extinguished." She urged Garrison to accept with serenity the violence that awaited him. "If persecution is the means which God has ordained for the accomplishment of this great end, EMANCIPATION," she wrote, "I feel as if I could say, LET IT COME; for it is my deep, solemn, deliberate conviction, that *this* is a *cause worth dying for.* I say so, from what I have seen and heard, and known in a land of slavery, where rests the darkness of Egypt, and where is found the sin of Sodom."[13]

Angelina had meant her words of encouragement for Garrison alone. But the editor of *The Liberator* recognized the power and moral clarity of her comments. On September 19, 1835, Garrison printed Angelina's letter with an introduction that left no doubt how important he considered this new convert to his cause to be. Here was a woman who, like all proper women, "ordinarily shuns public observation," but who was willing to risk criticism to advance a righteous cause. He, in turn, had breached the etiquette of the day in order that "female abolitionists may derive support and comfort from its perusal." But Garrison knew that Angelina's letter was more than a spur to women activists. Its power lay in the author's personal history as much as in its words, for Angelina Grimké of Charleston, South Carolina, had experienced the benefits of slavery firsthand—and had renounced them.[14]

Other abolitionist papers quickly picked up Angelina's letter and reprinted it. Before the year was out, Angelina Grimké was no longer simply a member of the growing army of abolition; she was a public figure in the antislavery movement. She had found her cause—and it had found her.

Four

"THIS IS ALL LIKE A DREAM NOW;
BUT I CAN'T UNDREAM IT"

Angelina Becomes an Abolitionist

THE PUBLICATION OF ANGELINA'S LETTER roused the ire of Philadelphia's orthodox Quaker community. They immediately pressured her to make a public retraction. Angelina was saddened by their criticism, but she was not surprised by it. Nor did it influence her, for if she still could not make a final, formal break with these Quakers, she had already made an intellectual and emotional one. But Angelina was deeply troubled when her sister Sarah voiced her disapproval. Sarah believed Angelina had allowed herself to become the dupe of a demagogue, a man whose organization was too radical to be endorsed privately, let alone publicly. She feared that her sister's name in print gave the appearance of female impropriety, even if Angelina had not sought public notice. On September 25, only a few days after the letter appeared in *The Liberator,* Sarah wrote a stinging condemnation of Angelina in her diary: "The suffering which my precious sister has brought upon herself, by her connection with the anti-slavery society, which has been a sorrow of heart to me, is another proof how dangerous it is to slight the clear convictions of Truth."[1]

But Angelina's "clear convictions" were no longer the same as Sarah's. Two days later, Angelina wrote to her sister in tones both defensive and accusatory. Had Sarah forgotten how agonizing her decision to oppose slavery had been? "Thou knowest," she chided her older sister, "I am an exile from the home of my birth because of slavery."

Yet in her own diary Angelina recorded her confusion over the response to her letter. "It is now more than 4 weeks since I tho't it felt right to write WLG a letter of sympathy & encouragement," Angelina wrote that autumn. She was prepared to face the hostile reactions the letter might provoke, for God had made her "instrumental in the great work of Emancipation" and given her the strength to "bear any suffering." But she found herself totally unprepared to deal with the approval it garnered. As praise from abolitionists began to reach her, she was as embarrassed by this public acclaim as she was resolute against the criticism heaped upon her. "O! the extreme pain of extravagant prais[e] to be held up as a saint in a public Newspaper before thousands of people when I felt I was the chief of sinners."[2]

More than anything else, Angelina was chagrined that the often tactless Garrison had identified her as the sister of the reformer Thomas Grimké in his introduction to the letter. Thomas had been Angelina's favorite brother, and a rebel in his own fashion. During the tariff dispute of 1832, he had opposed South Carolina's states' rights advocates when they invoked the right to nullify a federal law. Soon afterward, he had abandoned both his legal practice and his political career to travel the country, advocating world peace, temperance, and improved women's education. He had visited Sarah and Angelina in the troubled summer of 1834, on his way to Ohio to lecture. That October he died suddenly, the victim, like Edward Bettle, of a deadly cholera. To have the family name "associated with that of the despised Garrison," Angelina confessed, "seemd like bringing disgrace upon my family not myself alone. I felt as tho' the name had been tarnishd in the eye of thousands who had before lovd & revered it."[3]

Angelina may have regretted her impulsive actions, but it was too late to undo their effect. By autumn, abolitionists across the country had read her letter, which had been reprinted in their local antislavery newspapers. Unaware of her embarrassment or her discomfort, Northern abolitionists rapidly turned her into a symbol of their movement. They both admired and envied her, for she had sacrificed home and family for the cause—a sacrifice greater than any they had been called upon to make. But before the year ended, the price of carrying the antislavery banner was brought home to many of these admirers. The fall of 1835 was a season of violence, and many of those who spoke out against slavery fell victim to the hatred and fears of their neighbors. In western New York, mobs attacked abolitionists, including the eccentric retired British army officer Charles Stuart. In Connecticut, Amos Phelps, a Congregational clergyman and officer in the American Anti-Slavery Society, was almost killed by a brick hurled at him as he spoke. And despite Garrison's plea for tolerance, George Thompson's life had been threatened by armed men and he had barely escaped Boston with his life. Organizers such as Henry B. Stanton, James A. Thome, and Theodore Weld, whom abolitionists would come to call the "most mobbed man in America," along with dozens of other antislavery men, were pelted with rotten eggs and bricks, tarred and feathered, or ridden out of town on a rail. Yet the movement continued to grow. Although abolition would never win the loyalties of more than a fraction of the population, dedicated cadres of antislavery activists sprang up wherever men like Weld or Stanton visited.[4]

Angelina admired these activists from afar. She remained uncertain what her course of action should be, uncertain what positive use to make of her new celebrity. She realized that she had formed a broader view of the movement's goals than many abolitionists. Her experiences, both in Charleston and in Philadelphia, had convinced her that emancipation and the dismantling of the institution of slavery were not enough. The movement must also work to eradicate racism and end the discrimination against free blacks that restricted the daily lives of African Americans. She had seen the horrors of slavery firsthand in South Carolina, but she could not hold Southerners alone guilty of the sins of slavery and racism: all Americans who enjoyed the fruits of slave labor and all those who denied equality to those of a different race were complicit in those sins. To Angelina, nothing signified the shame of racial prejudice as much as the existence of a "colored bench" in the Philadelphia meetinghouse where she had worshiped. When she felt ready to speak out on the subject of slavery and race, she articulated a philosophy far more radical than many abolitionists were ready to embrace.

Although their relationship was still strained, in February 1836 Sarah and Angelina decided to travel together to Providence, Rhode Island. The trip proved therapeutic for Sarah, giving her respite from her inner conflict over remaining within the Philadelphia Quaker fold. Leaving Pennsylvania, she wrote, opened a "door of escape for me out of that city of bonds and conflicts." Angelina breathed easier now, too. She reveled once again in the intellectual exchanges and the debates over important issues that she had experienced on her last trip to New England. Wherever she went, abolitionists were impressed by her impassioned condemnation of slavery and by her ability now to speak of the slave as a human being rather than an object of scorn or pity.[5]

On their return to Philadelphia, the sisters took another step toward separation from the Quaker community by moving out of Catherine Morris's home. Still, neither Angelina nor Sarah seemed able to make the final break with the group that had given them refuge when they left Charleston. For Angelina, the problem was not so much severing ties with her Quaker past but discovering where the new ties she had formed might lead her. That summer, she sought some respite from her uncertainties by visiting friends in Shrewsbury, New Jersey, but she was far too restless to give herself up to the delights of the country. Once again she felt an intense need to do productive, useful work—work that would help her define who she was or who she wanted to become. She was, after all, an anomalous figure in the America of the 1830s: a spinster with an independent income, a genteel woman with a public reputation, a daughter of a slave owner and an advocate of abolition, a Quaker who questioned the morality of her congregation, a gifted writer and thinker without formal education—and, perhaps above all, a neophyte in a new and radical community.

In Shrewsbury, Angelina resolved to write a history of the United States based on "peace principles." No doubt this project was designed as a tribute to her brother Thomas and perhaps as an effort to atone for the damage her letter to Garrison had done to his memory. But the peace history quickly came to nothing. Other ambitious writing projects followed—and were just as quickly abandoned. With every failure, she grew more desperate, until her hosts could hear her crying in her room at night. The thought of returning to Philadelphia filled her with dread, but she had no idea what she could or should do or where she should go. An invitation from abolitionists in New York had come to her at Shrewsbury, asking her to speak to women's sewing circles and in private parlors about her firsthand experiences of slavery. But Angelina recoiled from the thought of becoming an even more public figure. She had never spoken in front of a group before, never even risen in meeting to speak her thoughts. "The bare idea that such a thing may be required of me is truly alarming," she wrote, "and that my mind should be resigned to it increases the fear that I may have to do it. . . . One thing, however, I do see clearly, that I am not to do it *now*."[6]

Despair as deep as she had once felt in Charleston now enveloped Angelina. "My spirit is oppressed and heavy laden, & wrout up in passion," she wrote in her journal. "What am I to do?" The answer came to her at last. She would write an appeal to the women of the South, asking them to join the crusade to end slavery. Writing to Sarah, Angelina called her decision "a pretty bold step," but one she must take even though "my friends will highly disapprove." In truth, it was a remarkable project, contradictory in its purpose and outcome: in the writing, she reached out to her past; in the message she carried, she severed all ties with her native land.[7]

Angelina Grimké's *Appeal to the Christian Women of the South* was printed in September 1836.[8] Its tone was strikingly intimate, for Angelina knew her audience well. She knew the social ideology that shaped the identity of planters' wives and daughters and prescribed the acceptable outlets for their intellect and emotions. She knew the moral authority that ideology granted women and the political and economic independence it denied them. She spoke to them as "true women," as the moral center of their family. Some were relatives and friends; others, though they were strangers, were, she wrote, "sisters in Christ."

The *Appeal* moved effortlessly from an emotional greeting to an analysis of the arguments for and against slavery and finally to a call for action. It was part exegesis, an impressive display of Angelina's biblical knowledge, and part exhortation, an impassioned call for women to use their moral powers effectively. But, like her later speeches and essays, it reflected Angelina's conviction that an appeal to emotions was not enough; evidence must be mustered and a rational argument must be made even if the issues were moral ones.

In the *Appeal,* Grimke first addressed the women of Charleston, still joined to her in "Christian sympathy and Gospel fellowship" although she had broken "those outward bonds of union" with them by leaving the South. She asked them, "for the sake of former confidence, and former friendship," to read her appeal. "It is because you have known me, that I write thus to you." But she quickly broadened the circle of intimacy she had drawn, addressing all Christian women of the South whose salvation she prayed for daily though she did not know their names. She assured them all, friends and strangers alike, that she did not write "in the heat of passion or prejudice, but in that solemn calmness which is the result of conviction and duty." The "unwelcome truths" she offered them might wound, but those wounds were inflicted "in tenderness and love." In much the same way, a young and troubled Angelina had once laid out what she believed were the many sins and faults of her own mother.

The unwelcome truths she offered were embedded in the strong and thorough arguments that neither natural law nor the Bible justified slavery as it was practiced in the South. The principles of a republic denied it; Mosaic law and Christian precept condemned it. Her argument was blunt: our republic was founded upon a conviction that all men were equal. "The laws of Moses *protected servants* in their *rights as men and women,* guarded them from oppression and defended them from wrong"; Christ taught that no man should do to another what he would not have done to him. But "the Code Noir of the South *robs the slave of all his rights as a man,*" and thus it could find no legitimacy in the secular or religious foundations of the country.

The *Appeal* insisted that the burden of the sin of slavery fell on all white Southerners. It was not simply the slave trader—"whose daily work is to break human hearts, by tearing wives from their husbands, and children from their parents"—who bore the guilt; the Christian who bought the slave was as guilty as the despised slave trader from whom he made his purchase. As Christians, Southern slave owners had been shown the path to righteousness, but as slaveholders, they had strayed from it.

No matter how sound or how compelling her arguments, Angelina knew the question in the minds of all her intended female readers, and she gave it voice: "Why appeal to *women* on this subject? We do not make the laws which perpetuate slavery. *No* legislative power is vested in *us;* we can do nothing to overthrow the system, even if we wished to do so." Angelina's answer was simple: women could not and must not hide behind claims of helplessness, for they "*are the wives and mothers, the sisters and daughters of those who do.*" Their power lay in these intimate relationships and in the moral influence women held over men. It was an argument firmly grounded in the nineteenth-century ideology that made women the moral guardians of their civilization, the exemplars of virtue for husbands, brothers, and sons. For these "moral mothers" of the South, Angelina laid out a set of four simple steps that formed a progression from intellectual understanding to spiritual commitment to social action. Read on the subject, she urged; then pray over the subject; speak on the subject; and, finally, act on the subject. She was asking them to do no less than the female martyrs of Christianity and no more than those antislavery women of Boston who stood their moral ground when they were mobbed by "gentlemen of property and standing."

Angelina ended her appeal with a defense of the abolitionist movement and its tactics—and, in the process, she seemed to clarify her own commitment to that movement. Antislavery activists were not, she wrote, "insurrectionary and mischievious, fanatical and dangerous." She could never associate herself, as "a Southerner . . . a daughter and a sister" of a Southern family, with any who sought to overthrow slavery "by falsehood, bloodshed, and murder." Powerful northerners caught in King Cotton's web of profit might attack abolitionists in the halls of government; ordinary Northerners, fearful of amalgamation and prejudiced against the African race, might attack them on the streets. But what abolitionists said about the horrors of slavery was true. And what abolitionists called for was just.

Having made her case, Angelina declared: "Sisters in Christ, I have done. As a Southerner, I have felt it was my duty to address you . . . I have done— I have sowed the seeds of truth, but I well know, that even if an Apollos were to follow in my steps to water them, *God only* can give the increase. To

Him then . . . I commend this Appeal in fervent prayer. . . . Farewell—
Count me not your 'enemy because I have told you the truth,' but believe
me in unfeigned affection, Your sympathizing Friend." To this most public
declaration of her commitment to abolition, Angelina E. Grimké proudly
signed her name. Whatever shame she had once harbored about soiling her
family reputation had clearly vanished; she was now ready to carry the
banner of abolition directly to her place of birth.

If Angelina had expected to turn the hearts and minds of Southern
women toward abolition, she was naive. Few if any ever saw her *Appeal,* for
it, like most abolitionist literature, was confiscated, banned, or destroyed
before it could be distributed in the Southern states. In her own hometown
of Charleston, the pamphlets would be seized and the mayor would warn
her mother that Angelina risked arrest and imprisonment if she set foot in
the city. But the *Appeal was* read in New York, Ohio, and New England, and
it made a deep and positive impression on abolitionist leaders including
Theodore Weld and Elizur Wright. Elizur Wright renewed his efforts to
bring Angelina to New York—and this time she was ready. For this time,
Sarah had agreed to come with her.

Sarah's conversion to abolition had been nurtured by bitter disappointment. In early August, as Angelina was laboring over her *Appeal,* Sarah had
faced a personal crisis of her own. She had joined the Society of Friends a
decade earlier, hoping to find a community in which her intellect was
respected and her voice could be heard. She did not claim to be as charismatic as Angelina was proving to be; she claimed only to be sincere and to
speak truthfully. But if the Friends had welcomed her into meeting, they
did not support her calling to be a leader of their flock. She had endured
their discouragement for many years, but on August 3, she encountered
their cruelty. When she rose in meeting to express herself, she was interrupted and told brusquely to stop talking and sit down. "This incident," she
later wrote in her diary, "has proved the means of releasing me from those
bonds which almost destroyed my mind." Angelina had abandoned the
Quakers when she no longer felt comfortable in their community. Sarah
had to be rejected.[9]

The sisters' visit to New York was a success. Female abolitionists pressed
them to work as agents for a national antislavery association that activists
in Philadelphia, Boston, and New York were hoping to organize. Elizur
Wright, meanwhile, pressed Angelina to work for the men's New York Anti-
Slavery Committee. Angelina returned to Philadelphia, determined to pursue one or the other of these options. But Sarah once again hesitated. Only

a letter from their mother made her agree. Mary Smith Grimké pleaded with Sarah not to let her sister go to a strange city and embark on dangerous work alone, and Sarah could not refuse to play the role of mother and protector that she had so often played for Angelina in the past.[10]

Thus, in October 1836, the Grimké sisters arrived in New York once again. Their careers as public speakers for a highly unpopular cause were about to begin. No matter what lay in store, they could not turn back: they had left behind the Quaker community in Philadelphia, and the planter community of Charleston had forbidden them to ever return. Abolitionism must be their home.

Five

"I LAID MY DIFFICULTY AT THE FEET OF JESUS"

The Burden of Being a Woman

EIGHTEEN THIRTY-SIX WAS AN AUSPICIOUS YEAR to begin a career as an abolitionist speaker. Since the Lane Seminary debates, the ranks of the abolitionist movement had swelled, and the surprising unity of Garrisonians, Western abolitionists, and the more conservative New York antislavery organization forged in 1833 helped the membership grow from three hundred societies in 1835 to almost a thousand in 1836. Although the male organizations were better funded, female antislavery organizations were thriving, too. Hicksite Quakers such as Lucretia Mott had already begun to play a role in the movement by the time Angelina moved to Philadelphia, and it was their Philadelphia Female Anti-Slavery Society that she would officially join in 1835. By 1832, Maria Weston Chapman and her sisters, along with eight other Massachusetts women, had organized the Boston Female Anti-Slavery Society, and smaller societies sprang up across New England. Plans to create a national female antislavery society were already being discussed when the Grimké sisters arrived in New York. Irreconcilable disagreements over strategy and policies that would shatter the unity of the movement lay ahead; the Panic of 1837 and the depression that followed, which would dry up funds flowing to the movement, lay ahead; organized and effective clerical resistance to antislavery activism lay ahead—but in the fall of 1836, as Angelina and Sarah took their first tentative steps into the world of abolitionist speakers, optimism reigned.[1]

That optimism was evident in the American Anti-Slavery Association's ambitious plan to train seventy "apostles" to help carry out the work of organizing. And Congress had inadvertently given the movement both an issue and a tactic that would win converts to the cause. Pressed by Southern leaders such as South Carolina's John C. Calhoun, in 1836 the Senate began to systematically reject all petitions calling for the abolition of slavery. Abolitionists insisted that this "gag rule" was unconstitutional, an infringement of the Bill of Rights. A defense of the right to petition appealed to many Americans and gave much-needed respectability to the antislavery cause. Even northern Whig Party politicians, eager to see the Democrats embarrassed, endorsed the abolitionists' call to protest the gag rule. Beginning in 1836, the antislavery movement launched an impressive petition-signing campaign, garnering hundreds of thousands of signatures in communities across the Northeast and the Midwest. Many of these petitions included demands that slavery be ended in the District of Columbia and banned in the territory of Florida. Often those who supported an end to the gag rule wound up supporting abolition as well.

Angelina was the only woman recruited for the new apostle program. Hers was a unique invitation, and a bold one, for a strict segregation of women and men had always been the rule in the movement, not only in organizational membership but also in the understanding that women never spoke in front of mixed—or, as nineteenth-century Americans put it, "promiscuous"—audiences. The organizers of the training program clearly saw the value of a Southern woman who could speak of the horrors of slavery from firsthand knowledge, but the conservative New York abolitionists remained wary that they were opening the door to scandal. The recent damage done by the Scottish radical Fanny Wright was fresh in their minds when Angelina arrived.

Angelina had no doubt heard of the infamous Fanny. Wright had begun her career in America as a celebrated travel writer, praising America's democratic principles in her 1821 *Views of Society and Manners in America.* But in 1825, she stunned many of her admirers by establishing Nashoba, a community of freed African Americans in Tennessee based on principles of free love and the sexual mixing of the races. Wright's social philosophy grew steadily more radical; by 1829, she had settled in New York City, where she published a second book, *Course of Popular Lectures,* and wrote editorials advocating socialism, abolition, woman suffrage, birth control, and the liberalization of marriage laws. By 1833, this outspoken—and, by nineteenth-century standards, crude and unfeminine—woman was traveling the Northeast, giving antislavery and feminist lectures to promiscuous audiences of males and females. Although admiring Fanny Wright societies were formed, the press mercilessly attacked her demeanor and the clergy condemned her social views. Abolitionists such as Arthur and Lewis Tappan, radical in their views on slavery but highly traditional in their views on marriage and women's proper sphere, wanted to avoid the taint of Fanny Wrightism at any cost. The Tappans must have breathed easier when Angelina arrived with her sister as chaperone. In their "tight crimped caps, seven by nine bonnets [and] that impenetrable drab that defieth utterly all amalgamation of colors," the soft-spoken and genteel spinsters from Charleston seemed models of propriety.[2]

The apostles' training sessions began in November under the direction of the man abolitionists called "the lion of the tribe," Theodore Dwight Weld. Weld was already a legend among reformers: tall and thin, with sharp features set off by uncombed hair and untrimmed beard, Weld was as charismatic as he was eccentric. In repose, he seemed lost in "deep, wild gloom," but once he rose to speak on abolition, his countenance was transformed. His voice was rich and full, and he spoke with a sincerity and conviction that captured the attention of even the most hostile audience. He had begun his reform career in the late 1820s, traveling around the country lecturing on the virtues of manual labor, on temperance, and on moral reform. Along with other followers of the evangelical minister Charles Finney, Weld studied at Lane Seminary in Cincinnati. It was Weld who organized the famous Lane Debates over slavery, and when he was dismissed from the seminary most of the student body left with him. Weld was widely acknowledged to be the most effective abolitionist lecturer the movement had ever produced, but by November 1836, his many speeches before large crowds had ruined his voice. Unable to be heard by his audiences, he had given up public speaking. He now worked in the offices of the American Anti-Slavery Association in New York City, writing pamphlet literature. When the training sessions were designed, the association insisted that Weld was the only man to lead them. The other instructors were equally stellar: New York lawyer and journalist Henry Stanton, the Quaker poet John Greenleaf Whittier, Charles Stuart, and the editor of *The Liberator* himself, William Lloyd Garrison.[3]

The session schedule was grueling, running from early morning until nine at night, with only short breaks during the day. The Grimkés—for Sarah too had been invited to attend with her apostle sister—barely had time to eat. But neither of the women minded, for they found the experience thrilling. Sarah reveled in the fact that she was, at last, among men who treated her as an intellectual equal; Angelina reveled in the education she was receiving from experienced crusaders for the emancipation of the slave. She was delighted to discover that Garrison was a soft-spoken, gentle, even sweet man, far different from the persona he presented on the pages of his newspaper. But the man who captured Angelina's attention most was Theodore Weld, who now stood before his students, straining his damaged voice to the utmost by lecturing eight or nine hours a day.

On November 11, 1836, Angelina described the training sessions to the sisters' closest friend in Philadelphia, Jane Smith. The meetings, she wrote, "are increasingly interesting, & to-day we enjoyd a moral & intellectual feast in a most notable speech from T D Weld of more than two hours on the question of what is slavery." Angelina could barely contain her admiration for Weld. "I never heard so grand & beautiful an exposition of the dignity & nobility of man in my life. . . . He then spoke on the *duty* of immediate emancipation, regardless of all consequences, even to the slave." She was flattered when Weld "greeted me with the appellation of my dear sister," she told Smith, and then added more praise for Weld's devotion to the slave. But Angelina also took the time to describe Weld's physical appearance. "Well, at first sight, there was nothing remarkable to me," she began, "& I wonderd whether he realy was as great as I had heard. But as soon as his countenance became animated by speaking, I found it was one which portrayd the noblest quality of the heart & head, beaming with benevolence, intelligence & frankness."[4]

After weeks as Weld's students, it was time at last for Angelina and Sarah to talk rather than to listen. That December, they began a series of parlor talks. Sarah, a bit stilted and monotone, just as she had been in meeting, focused on moral and theological issues. Not surprisingly, given her humiliating experiences with the Arch Street Meeting, she was especially critical of the hypocrisy and self-interest of the clergy and the churches. Angelina, who admitted to Jane Smith that "the day I have to speak is always a day of suffering," nevertheless showed a natural talent for lecturing. Her anxiety beforehand was great, yet once she began to speak, she lost all self-consciousness and hesitancy. Her talks—she modestly insisted that they were not lectures in the masculine mode—dealt largely with the politics of slavery and the organizational tactics and strategies that best advanced the cause of abolition. But it was her insistence that Northerners must overcome their race prejudice as well as work for emancipation that made her lectures unique. In no time, the sisters' audiences outgrew the capacities of even the roomiest of parlors. They were offered space in a Baptist church, a venue the most cautious abolitionists feared was a bit too public for a female gathering. Nevertheless, Theodore Weld encouraged them to accept.[5]

Emboldened by Weld's approval—"his visit was really a strength to us," Angelina wrote—the sisters agreed to accept the offer from the church. Three hundred women flocked to hear them. When they had finished speaking, their audience was unanimous in insisting that they lecture at the church regularly. Afterward, Angelina and Sarah recounted the day's events to Weld, who was waiting with others at the Tappan house for their report. When Angelina told them that a man had tried to get into the meeting and had to be escorted out, Weld alone was outraged rather than disturbed. He considered it ridiculous, he said, that a man could not hear a woman speak. Angelina's admiration for him, already high, increased.[6]

Throughout January and February 1837, the sisters continued to lecture in the church. They were so busy that Angelina's thirty-second birthday passed without note. The crowds for their lectures had increased in size until the side room in the church was no longer adequate, and with some trepidation, Angelina and Sarah agreed to move their talks to the main sanctuary. Despite their success, Angelina's pre-lecture jitters continued, but as she warmed to her subject, she became confident and animated. When critics suggested that her gestures were too frequent to be considered ladylike, she replied that the subject of slavery simply carried her away.[7]

By spring the sisters were lecturing in New Jersey as well as New York City—and invitations poured in for them to speak in upstate New York. Angelina admitted to Jane Smith, "I love the work." But she also confessed that the success of the past few months overwhelmed her. "How little! How *very little* I supposed when I used so often to say 'I wish I was a *man* that I might go out and lecture'—that *I* ever would do such a thing—the idea never crossed my mind that *as a woman* such work could possibly be assigned to me."[8]

More amazements would follow. That spring, the sisters spoke to three hundred African American women—and men—who gathered to hear them in Poughkeepsie, New York. Angelina recognized this as a milestone event: "For the first time in my life," she wrote, "I spoke to a promiscuous assembly . . . and found the men were no more to me than the women." Perhaps because the audience was black, no shock waves flowed through the abolitionist organization. But as the news spread that two Southern sisters, daughters of slaveholders, were lecturing not only on the sins of slavery and the sexual exploitation it allowed but also on the physical horrors of that institution, which they had witnessed firsthand, it was only a matter of time before their lectures would become a magnet for curious or hostile men. The issue of women's role in the public sphere would inevitably be thrust upon them. When it was, they met it head-on.[9]

That February a Connecticut man had published a sarcastic reprimand of the Grimkés in the New Haven *Religious Intelligencer.* Northerners were well aware of the wickedness of slavery, he wrote, and "you may therefore spare the trouble of further efforts to 'undeceive us.' " He challenged the

Grimkés to provide a concrete, practical program for emancipation. It was a challenge that did not go unanswered. On March 1, 1837, the sisters replied, listing the ways in which Northerners were complicit in sustaining slavery and then proposing how they might act to undermine the "peculiar institution." Their suggestions included the current abolitionist focus on petitions to end slavery in the nation's capital and in the Florida territory. But Sarah's hand could be seen in the criticism of the clergy and the insistence that Northern ministers withhold communion from slaveholders and refuse their pulpits to slaveholding clergy. Angelina's influence could be seen in the strong call to boycott all goods made by slave labor and in the appeal to Northerners to abandon their racial prejudice.[10]

Neither Angelina nor Sarah was optimistic that Northern men would rally to their suggestions. After a winter spent in New York and New Jersey, the sisters had come to appreciate how powerful the Northern forces operating against abolition were. New York, Sarah wrote to her friend Sarah Douglass in Philadelphia, "is a hard place to labor in; ten thousand cords of interest, are linked with the Southern slave holder." Newark was little better. "Southern interest is powerful, shoes and carriages, etc. made in Newark are bartered for the gold of the South, which is gotten by the unrequited toil of the slave." And, despite a winter of lecturing success, the sisters had also come to appreciate how little expertise they had in discussing the institution of slavery. Personal experience was simply not enough, and Angelina told Sarah Douglass that "we feel as yet unprepared to go fully into our delightful work, because the subject of Slavery is one of such length and breadth, height and depth." To correct the gaps in their knowledge, they began a regimen of reading and studying that would continue for years to come. From 1837 onward, Sarah peppered her letters to Theodore Weld with questions about such issues as the Kentucky laws regarding slavery or past debates over slavery in Southern legislatures.[11]

In March, however, most of the sisters' thoughts were taken up by the first national female antislavery convention, to be held in New York that April. Angelina, who had been disturbed by the absence of black women at the local New York City antislavery meetings, actively recruited African American delegates. Male abolitionists, including Theodore Weld, offered a great deal of unsolicited advice to the organizers, but it became clear when the convention sessions began that the delegates were more than competent to run the meetings. The Boston women, in particular, impressed Angelina with their organizational skills. Later that year, she would convey the women's amusement and annoyance at Weld's meddling, writing with humor to him that she had a message from one of the convention secretaries: "Tell Mr Weld said she, that when the women got together, they found they had *minds* of their own, and could transact their business *without* his directions."[12]

Angelina and Sarah were among the seventy-one official delegates. They registered not as Pennsylvanians but as delegates from the heart of slavery, South Carolina. Leaders from the Northern states joined them, including Lucretia Mott of Philadelphia and Maria Weston Chapman and Lydia Maria Child of Massachusetts. Perhaps a hundred more women came to the sessions. When Angelina rose to address the gathering, she drove home her unique call for racial harmony. Sisterhood, she said, must know no color boundaries. But she also drew a telling analogy between women and the enslaved, one that suggested that gender issues as much as race were much on her mind. "Women ought to feel a peculiar sympathy in the colored man's wrong," she said, "for, like him, she has been accused of mental inferiority, and denied the privileges of a liberal education."[13]

The convention published two works by their South Carolina delegates: Angelina's *Appeal to the Women of the Nominally Free States* and Sarah's *Address to Free Colored Americans.* Just as she had done in the reply to her New Haven critic, Angelina focused her *Appeal* first on the problem of slavery and then on a program for solving it. What could Northern women do? Angelina asked, and her answer was, in its broadest strokes, much the same as that she had offered to Northern men: organize antislavery societies, read and educate themselves on the subject of slavery, petition both religious and civil authorities, and boycott slave-grown products. But more basic, more essential than all of these other steps, must be a commitment to end racial prejudice. Sympathize with "our oppressed colored sisters," she urged; "extend to them the right hand of fellowship on the broad principles of humanity and Christianity, treat them as *equals,* visit them as *equals,* invite them to co-operate with you in Anti-Slavery and Temperance and Moral Reform Societies—in Maternal Associations and Prayer Meetings and Reading Companies." Only when racism "has been cast out of your own hearts" could Northern women appeal to the morality of Southern women as they must. Angelina also called on black women to become more active in the movement despite the residual racism they would encounter. "Bear with us a little in our *folly,*" she pleaded, and show charity toward white women, who "crave your sympathy and prayers."[14]

In her ardent appeal for racial equality, Angelina was far more radical than many of her male and female abolitionist peers. The fear of being labeled "amalgamationists" made men such as Arthur Tappan oppose any private socializing with African Americans. Even Theodore Weld, who Angelina believed treated blacks with respect and was at ease among them, mingled with them socially only at black events, never white ones. To Angelina and to Sarah, abolition was a step toward a greater goal: human equality. The barriers that stood in the way—race and gender bias—were as important to address as slavery. Men such as the Tappans, Whittier, and Stuart would never agree.[15]

Angelina was deeply impressed by the women of New England who so dominated the convention. The New England delegates were equally impressed with Angelina. After the convention, she was invited to come north and lecture throughout Massachusetts and Connecticut. Theodore Weld encouraged her to go, and urged Sarah to accompany her. A single woman, he wrote with sincere but patronizing nineteenth-century gallantry, needed a protector, and if no husband or brother was available, a sister would have to do. That May, both Grimkés headed for Boston. They were optimistic and excited, for Massachusetts was the home of William Lloyd Garrison, the outspoken champion of women's rights, nonviolence, temperance, and an immediate commitment to abolition as well as to some eighty thousand members of the American Anti-Slavery Society. What they did not fully consider, however, was that it was also the home of staunch opponents of Garrison and his causes.[16]

Maria Chapman paved the way for the Grimkés' tour that summer. On June 7, 1837, she sent a letter to every New England female antislavery society, asking them to "afford every facility in your power to Sarah M. and Angelina E. Grimké, for the prosecution of their labours in the cause of emancipation." Chapman made the usual mention of the sisters' unique experiences with slavery, but she was equally enthusiastic about their commitment to women's duties and rights. For Chapman this was critical: if women's condition was not the main text, it must be the essential subtext of the Grimkés' lecture tour. "Let us help one another to refute the idea," she wrote, "that while the chief end of *man* is to glorify God and enjoy him forever, woman is sharer of the like glorious destiny but as it were in sort, or limitation."[17]

Angelina and Sarah emphatically agreed that women's right to speak out must be directly addressed in their lectures. On May 29, Angelina had written to Jane Smith that she felt "it is not the cause of the slave only which we plead, but the cause of woman as a responsible moral being." It was not suffrage, not economic opportunity, but the right to shoulder public moral responsibilities that women such as Angelina and Maria passionately espoused. Yet, as Angelina and Sarah would soon argue, the arenas could not be so neatly isolated. What was the relationship between women's right to crusade for moral causes and their economic dependency on husbands or fathers? How could wives and mothers balance the time required for domestic duties with the time required for organizational duties? Where was the line that separated advocacy of political and social change from the exercise of formal, political power? As individuals, Angelina and Sarah could avoid many of the dilemmas and restrictions faced by other women who wished to participate in public debate and influence public policy: they were financially independent and free of marital and maternal duties. But there were barriers set by social custom, organized religion, and ideology that confined them as sharply as any genteel woman. To gain support for abolition, they saw that they must break those barriers down. "What an untrodden path we have entered upon!" Angelina exclaimed to Jane Smith—and it would prove to be a rocky one as well.[18]

On June 6, the New England tour began. Henry C. Wright, a radical abolitionist who, like his friend William Lloyd Garrison, supported the equality of the sexes, peace principles, and temperance as well as abolition, served as the Grimkés' unofficial and self-appointed tour manager. But despite Wright's best efforts, the schedule proved grueling. The sisters traveled in bad as well as good weather, ate at irregular hours and in haste, and often had to make do with uncomfortable accommodations. Angelina did the bulk of the lecturing since Sarah soon developed a debilitating cough. The toll on Angelina was great, and Sarah worried about her sister's failing health. "I feel some fears least Angelina sh'd be doing more than is best," she wrote to friends, "she seems much exhausted after a Meeting and I think cannot continue to labor much longer."[19]

Throughout June, Angelina lectured almost daily to ever-increasing crowds in Boston, Brookline, North Weymouth, and back in Boston again. From the beginning, men slipped into the audience, drawn, she believed, more by curiosity than by commitment. On June 21, in Lynn, Massachusetts, Angelina faced her first truly "promiscuous audience" of more than a thousand white women and men. After the Lynn meeting, any pretense that the sisters intended to honor the tradition of exclusively female audiences was dropped. By the twenty-eighth of the month, Sarah Grimké could write to her friend and fellow abolitionist Gerrit Smith asking, "What will Brother and sister Smith say to our holding mtgs. irrespective of sex? One brother wanted to come and another thought he had a right and now the door is wide open. Whosoever will come and hear our testimony may come."[20]

The door was indeed wide open—but there were many who hoped to slam it shut again. A growing hostility to the Grimkés' rebellion against respectability was obvious, as ministers in the smaller towns closed their church doors to them and refused to publish notices of their meetings. Criticism began to appear in the press as well. The most painful attack came from Catharine Beecher, a woman whom Angelina had once admired and hoped to emulate. In June, during the early weeks of Angelina's lecture tour, Beecher published a book entitled *An Essay on Slavery and Abolitionism, with Reference to the Duty of American Females*. The essay's main thrust was an attack on the antislavery movement, for Beecher, like her father, was a staunch advocate of colonization. She considered abolitionists to be meddlesome and reckless troublemakers, and the essay's purpose, she explained in her preface, was to "assign reasons why [a gentleman friend] should not join the Abolition Society." But the last sections of the book were, as the title indicated, a reprimand to women such as Angelina Grimké who breached the boundaries of the domestic sphere. Having read Angelina's *Address* to Northern women, and hearing of her intention to recruit for the abolitionist cause in New England, Beecher felt compelled to condemn both Angelina's cause and her behavior.[21]

Angelina was angered by Beecher's public reprimand and appalled by the arguments Beecher put forward. "I do not know how I shall find language strong enough to express my indignation at the view she takes of *woman's* character & duty." But find the language she did. Despite the demands of the lecture tour, Angelina composed a series of letters to Catharine Beecher that began to appear on the pages of Garrison's *Liberator* on June 23 and the American Anti-Slavery Association's *Emancipator* in July. While the bulk of the letters focused on the positive effects of the antislavery movement, the last two letters contained Angelina's most radical statements on women's rights rather than women's duties. In them, she rehearsed many of the arguments that formed the basis for the first feminist movement. These arguments wove together, and arose from, her profound belief in the Christian tenets of universal moral capacities and the fundamental principles on which the American republic was founded. They provided a brilliant rebuttal to Beecher's idealization of domesticity and separate spheres and made an impassioned demand for the equality of the sexes. The arguments made in these two letters, written in July, would be more fully fleshed out in Sarah Grimké's *Letters on the Equality of the Sexes*, written at the same time.[22]

Angelina had taken on a formidable foe when she challenged Catharine Beecher. Beecher was the era's foremost advocate of separate spheres for women and men. Although she never married, she embraced the ideology that glorified marriage and motherhood. Ten years earlier, she had petitioned Congress in opposition to President Andrew Jackson's Indian removal policies, but by 1837 she argued passionately that women's moral power lay in persuasion and in example rather than in the invasion of the public sphere. At the same time, she was a vocal advocate of careers in schoolteaching for women, arguing that the education of children was a proper extension of domestic duties. In 1843, she would publish her most complete statement on the proper sphere of women, *A Treatise on Domestic Economy,* but the essay addressed to Angelina Grimké sets out her views on the distinctive roles of women and men.

Angelina's Letter XI, "The Sphere of Woman and Man as Moral Beings the Same," was organized as a dialogue between domesticity and feminism. She would, she wrote to Beecher, "quote paragraphs from thy book, offer my objections to them, and then throw before thee my own views." It was Beecher's contention that God had decreed one sex as superior and the other as subordinate, and therefore "the mode of gaining influence and exercising power should be *altogether different and peculiar.*" Angelina refuted Catharine's basic premise: that woman's subordination to man was decreed by Heaven. This, Angelina said simply, "is an assertion without proof." She refuted the notion of different modes of influence and power as well. "Does the Bible teach this?" she asked. Did Christ's doctrine of peace apply only to women? Beecher insisted that a man could press his points by shaming his opponents or by frightening or coercing them, but a woman could only appeal to kindly, generous, and peaceful principles. To this Grimké responded: "If so, I should come to a very different conclusion from the one at which thou hast arrived: I should suppose that *woman was the superior,* and *man the subordinate being,* inasmuch as moral power is immeasurably superior to 'physical force.'" Throughout her letter, Angelina challenged the notion of dual moralities, of the acceptance of motives such as greed or ambition or thirst for power in men but not in women. There was, she insisted, only one moral standard, set by Christ, and all who did not live up to it were held accountable by God.

Advocates of domesticity such as Beecher insisted that women's power lay in winning the respect and love of men, and in this way men would choose to yield to women's wishes. But Angelina exposed what were often the actual results of this romanticized arrangement: vanity and manipulation. "This principle may do as a rule of action to the fashionable belle, whose idol is *herself,* whose every attitude and smile are designed to win the admiration of others to *herself.*" But a true Christian, she wrote, recommends truth to others, "*truth* which she wants them to esteem and love, and not herself." And she challenged the equally romantic notion that women's dependence empowered them. Beecher had laid out the premise in its most appealing and idealized terms: "All the generous promptings of chivalry, all the poetry or romantic gallantry depend upon woman's retaining her place as *dependent* and *defenceless,* and making no claims and maintaining no rights, but what are the gifts of honor, rectitude and love." Angelina found such sentiment beneath the dignity of any Christian woman. A truly moral woman, she declared, "loathes such littleness, and turns with disgust from all such silly insipidities." The notion that woman must be defenseless and dependent was equally offensive, both to women and to God. "Did our Heavenly Father furnish man with any offensive or defensive weapons?" Christ instructed all his followers, regardless of sex, to go as sheep among wolves, not as wolves themselves. And, like men, women acquire their rights from God, not as gifts from men.

To Beecher's insistence that all women's moral goals could and should be accomplished within the confines of domesticity, Grimké could only reply, "Indeed! Who made thee a ruler and a judge over all?" The Bible, she reminded her friend, was replete with examples of women acting in "public stations"—Miriam, Deborah, and Huldah; the women who followed Christ from town to town; the women who were his disciples; the daughters of Philip who were prophets. "Did these holy women of old perform all their gospel labors in 'the domestic and social circle'?" Ironically, Beecher's own life was a contradiction to this philosophy of confinement, for she lived and labored outside the domestic sphere, teaching and running a school for teachers, publishing essays and instruction manuals, and even petitioning the government to expand the system of public education. In an oblique defense of her own life choices, she argued that women could respectably create associations with other women if it was for pious or charitable purposes. Teaching the youth of America, she would argue, fell under the umbrella of "appropriate offices of piety, charity, &c." But Angelina saw the essential difficulty of defining "appropriate offices." "What are they? Who can point them out? Who has ever attempted to draw a line of separation between the duties of men and women, as *moral* beings, without committing the grossest inconsistencies on the one hand, or running into the most arrant absurdities on the other?"

Beecher opposed the abolitionist campaign that encouraged women to

send or sign petitions to Congress on the issue of slavery. She found it especially inappropriate for these petitions to focus on the sexual abuse of slave
women. To bolster her position, Beecher applied a utilitarian yardstick to
such actions. Since these petitions have no "probable results," the practice
ought to be ended. Grimké returned to Scripture in her refutation. "I
thought the disciples of Jesus were to walk by *faith, not* by sight. Did Abraham reason as to the *probable results* of his offering up Isaac?" For anyone
to fail to act on moral issues because politicians might judge that person as
"obtrusive, indecorous and unwise" was to exchange the precepts of the
Bible for the opinions of mere men. Yet Grimké could not resist turning the
utilitarian argument back on Beecher. Many congressmen, even Southern
congressmen, she noted, had repeatedly conceded the impact of antislavery
petitions on the political life of the nation. Grimké went further, however,
pressing the issue of women's political rights. The men of the revolutionary
generation had waged a war because they were taxed without representa-
tion, she reminded Beecher, yet unmarried women continued to be governed in this fashion. "If, then, *we* are taxed without being represented [and
here, of course, "we" included the spinster Catharine Beecher], and governed by laws *we* have no voice in framing, then, surely, we ought to be permitted at least to remonstrate against 'every political measure that may
tend to injure and oppress our sex in various parts of the nation.' "

The core issue in this stinging exchange between Beecher and Grimké
was women's appropriate sphere. For Beecher, the public sphere was
fraught with dangers to the moral being; it was competitive, violent, a
breeding ground for sin and crime, and women preserved their moral
superiority and their nurturing natures only by remaining aloof and protected from that world. Within her domestic haven, a wife enjoyed power:
she could stand as exemplar of virtue to her sons; she could evoke the finer
instincts in her husband by her dependency upon him. When she stepped
gingerly into the public realm, it must be only to advance the cause of piety
and charity; to extend, carefully and without aggression, her moral influence for the sake of the poor and the young outside her own doorstep.
Beecher conceived of the moral power of women *as women;* Grimké conceived of the moral power of women as humans. She was not fearful that
women would be transformed by the sins of the outside world, for she
believed in the power of faith and the protecting hand of Christ.

In her final letter, Grimké elaborated her own position. She had learned
to understand her own rights, she began, by studying the rights of the slave.
She had come to realize that there are neither black nor white rights, nei-

ther male nor female rights—only human rights. "My doctrine then is, that whatever it is morally right for man to do, it is morally right for a woman to do. Our duties originate, not from difference of sex, but from the diversity of our relations in life, the various gifts and talents committed to our care, and the different eras in which we live." To Grimké, the notion of different natures and differing capacities for virtue based on sex was false; the argument that woman was created to be subservient to man was a corruption of the biblical text; and the idea that "romantic gallantry" was preferable to equality was dangerous. She did not shy away from the most radical, if only theoretical, implications of equality: "*If* Ecclesiastical and Civil governments are ordained of God, *then* I contend that woman has just as much right to sit in solemn counsel in Conventions, Conferences, Associations, and General Assemblies, as man—just as much right to sit upon the throne of England, or in the Presidential chair of the United States."

A generation earlier, England's Mary Wollstonecraft and New England's Judith Sargent Murray had declared that women had the mental and moral capacity to govern a society. Three decades later, the women who gathered at Seneca Falls would make a similar claim. But few expected such radical ideas to spring from the pen of a young South Carolina woman in 1837.

Six

"YOU HAVE HAD MY WHOLE HEART"

A Season of Surprises

SARAH'S *LETTERS ON THE EQUALITY OF THE SEXES* would not begin to be published until mid-July 1831, and Angelina's letters on women's rights would not appear until the autumn of that year. But as July began it was clear to both sisters that a storm was brewing. They found themselves magnets for the hostility to radical change and social disruption that the antislavery movement seemed to carry in its wake. More than the demand to end slavery, the demand for women to engage in public debate on the subject threatened the status quo of everyday middle-class life. Angelina and Sarah were dangerous not simply because they were advocates of women's rights but because each time they lectured, they were practicing what they so eloquently preached.

Angelina recognized the need to tread carefully. But in mid-July, she made a hasty and foolish decision. Perhaps it was exhaustion. Perhaps it was impatience or frustration. Perhaps, as Theodore Weld would later suggest, it was her old nemesis, pride. Whatever led her to make a spectacle of herself, she made a costly mistake. The trouble began in the small town of Amesbury, Massachusetts, where she was lecturing as usual. In the midst of her talk, two young men rose from the audience to protest her account of the horrors of slavery. They had spent time in the South, they said, and the slaves they had seen were not so badly treated as she claimed. Whether they were sincere or simply eager to embarrass Angelina, the two challenged Angelina to openly debate the issue. Social convention told her she should have demurred; instead, she agreed. On Monday, July 17, before an audience of the committed and the curious, the first public debate between a man and a woman ever witnessed in the United States began. Although the young men proved no match for the eloquent and by now experienced lecturer, and although her defenders described her demeanor as perfectly ladylike throughout the debate, Angelina knew the damage had been done. The specter of Fanny Wright had come to haunt her at last.[1]

If Angelina hoped against hope that the furor would die down, she was to be disappointed. The general association of Massachusetts Congregationalist ministers took the lead in the condemnation that followed. They circulated a pastoral letter calling on the state's Congregational clergy to close their pulpits to lecturers on controversial issues. They severely condemned women who overstepped the boundaries of acceptable female behavior. Echoing the sentiments of Catharine Beecher, the ministers declared, "The power of woman is in her dependence . . . when she assumes the place & tone of a man as a public reformer, her character becomes unnatural." No one in Massachusetts needed to ask whom the clergy meant when they spoke of women who "so forget themselves as to itinerate in the character of public lecturers."[2]

The attack on Angelina and Sarah was not the first made by New England clergy on the reformers, nor would it be the last. The ministers' hostility to the antislavery movement, and to Garrison and his followers in particular, had been obvious since 1834, when the Lane Seminary debates so severely damaged the colonization movement these clergy embraced. Since then, Quakers as well as Congregationalists in Massachusetts, Connecticut, and Rhode Island had closed their churches and meetinghouses to antislavery meetings and lectures, declaring that the abolitionist movement brought widespread disruption to society, not only dividing North and South but also breaking down the proper boundaries between men and women. Throughout the 1830s and 1840s, both clerical and lay opponents effectively used attacks on women abolitionists to discredit the movement and deflect its arguments about the evils of the peculiar institution.

But the pastoral letter was aimed directly at Angelina and Sarah. Neither sister was willing to be cowed by such condemnation. Angelina had always been ready to go against the current once she was certain she was right, and even in Charleston she had never allowed the opinions of others to silence her. She had stood her ground alone in those early years; this time, despite the many voices raised against her, she was not alone. Sarah stood firmly beside her, preaching the gospel of equality more forcefully and more frequently now that the clergy she so despised had condemned them for it. The women of the Boston Female Anti-Slavery Society stood with her, including her friend Maria Chapman, who poked fun at the clergy's outrage in a poem she entitled "The Times That Try Men's Souls." All across New England, women flocked to hear Angelina lecture each day, sometimes walking miles to do so. Even when notices of her meetings were torn down by opponents, women poured into local halls to listen to the notorious Miss Grimké.[3]

Angelina was exhilarated by the controversy. She was glad to see the issues out in the open, glad to have the opportunity to confront her critics directly. Her determination and excitement came through in a letter to Jane Smith: "Our *womanhood* . . . is as great offense to some as our abolitionism . . . the whole land seems roused to discussion on the *province of woman,* & I am glad of it. We are willing to bear the brunt of the storm."[4]

But Angelina was not as prepared for the criticism that soon came flooding in from within the abolitionist ranks. New York antislavery leaders such as the Tappans had always been leery of their organization's association with the Grimkés. Now, as news of the furor in New England reached them, conservative male abolitionists took steps to do damage control and, failing that, to distance themselves from Angelina and Sarah. They insisted that the sisters were abandoning the slave in favor of women's rights, and as proof they cited the well-intended but impolitic essay by the Grimkés' good friend and confidant Henry Wright. His "A Domestic Scene," which appeared in the antislavery press that month, was an intimate and admiring portrait of the sisters sitting in a parlor discussing women's rights. To many of Wright's fellow abolitionists, however, the piece was an exposé: the Grimkés' true cause, it seemed to say, was not the liberation of the slaves but the liberation of women.[5]

Efforts to pressure the sisters into renouncing their feminist radicalism came pouring in. The Reverend Amos Phelps, an ardent abolitionist, proposed publishing a statement from the Grimkés that they would no longer speak to mixed audiences. Angelina and Sarah rejected the idea at once. "Thy letter," they assured Phelps, "neither surprised us nor moved us, because we are prepared to find opposition & to meet with condemnation from the ministry *generally.*" Phelps's earnest request that they no longer discuss the sexual exploitation of female slaves met with no more success. If Phelps believed the sisters would bow to the wishes of the American Anti-Slavery Society's executive committee, he was sorely mistaken. "[W]hen we united ourselves to the A.S.S.," Sarah wrote, "we did not give up our free agency." Phelps, of course, was free to publicly declare anything he wished, but the Grimké sisters would not put their signatures to it.[6]

John Greenleaf Whittier took a different tack. Hearing of Angelina's and Sarah's essays and letters on women's equality, he pleaded with the sisters to cease debating women's rights in the press. "[Y]ou are now doing much and nobly to vindicate and assert the rights of woman . . . why then, let me ask, is it necessary for you to enter the lists as controversial writers on this question." For Whittier, as for many white and black American males before and after the Civil War, gender inequality seemed trivial when set beside racial injustices. "Does it not *look,* dear sisters, like abandoning in some degree the cause of the poor and miserable slave . . . for the purpose of arguing and disputing about some trifling oppression, political or social, which we may ourselves suffer?" It was an argument later feminists would face again and again.[7]

To Angelina's great dismay, Theodore Weld seemed likely to join the ranks of those distancing themselves from her. On July 22, he sent a long letter with an apologetic, organizationally self-serving explanation of the sisters' relationship to the American Anti-Slavery Society. "Your relation to the Executive Committee seems rather a relation of Christian kindness—a sort of *cooperative* relation recognizing harmony of views and feelings, with common labors, joys and trials in a common cause, rather than *authority* on the one hand and a *representative* agency on the other." In plain English, Weld, acting as the spokesman for the society, was disavowing any official connection between the sisters and his organization. It was in the context of Quakerisms, not abolitionism, he argued, that the sisters' feminist radicalism should be understood. "In short the relation which you sustain to the Ex. Com. no more attaches their *sanction* to your public holdings-forth to promiscuous assemblies than it does to your 'theeing and thouing.' " Yet, stepping out of his official capacity, Weld assured the sisters that he did not personally wish to see them abandon their commitment to equality. Promiscuous audiences seemed no more shocking to him now than they did when Angelina was in New York City. "If the men wish to come, it is downright *slaveholding* to shut them out. *Slaveholders* undertake to say that *one* class of human beings shall not be profited by public ministrations." As for him, if he was ever in "the vicinity of your meetings I shall act on the principle that he that hath ears to hear hath a right to *use* them." Like the Grimkés, he wrote, he believed that the mind had no sex and moral obligations fell equally on men and women. Trying to soften the blow of the letter's disclaimer with folksy humor, he added, "Why! folks talk about women's preaching as tho' it was next to highway robbery—eyes astare and mouth agape."[8]

Angelina replied on August 8, 1837. Assuming Weld's support, she wrote frankly: "We are placed very unexpectedly in a very trying situation, in the forefront of an entirely new contest—a contest for the *rights of woman* as a moral, intelligent and responsible being." She readily conceded that the timing of this new struggle was unfortunate. "I cannot help feeling some regret," she told Weld, "that this sh'ld have come up *before* the Anti Slavery question was settled, so fearful am I that it may injure the blessed cause."

But she was confident that God, not her or her opponents, had set the time for the subject to arise. "WHO will stand by woman in the great struggle?" she asked the man she deeply admired and who had befriended her.[9]

Over the next few months, Weld sent conflicting signals: he offered support and criticism in equal measures. He seemed driven to defend his credentials as a supporter of women's equality. He declared himself an "ultra," a term used to denote men and women who held a broad spectrum of radical social views. His ultraism, he insisted, went farther even than Angelina's; he suspected both she and Sarah would be shocked by his belief that women should have the right to court men for marriage. Yet he also felt compelled to add a reprimand to Sarah: "I do most deeply regret that you have begun a series of articles in the Papers on the rights of woman." Like Whittier, Theodore believed women's rights to be an issue less pressing and less important than abolition. "Now can't you leave the *lesser* work to others who can do it *better* than you," he asked Angelina, "and devote [yourself] to the *greater* work." Though he might call women's rights the lesser work, Angelina Grimké's estimation of Theodore Weld seemed to loom more important to him with every passing day.[10]

Weld's chiding infuriated and distressed Angelina. On August 20, she wrote a letter addressed to both Theodore and John Greenleaf Whittier, a letter marked by impatience and frustration. As she saw it, the pastoral letter, not the actions or opinions of the Grimké sisters, was responsible for the controversy. Could they not see that she and Sarah had done nothing more or less than they had done when their opponents challenged their right to speak against slavery? She was appalled that these two men seemed ready to endorse the crippling notion that for women, "silence is *our* province, submission *our* duty." Weld's claim to "ultraism" did not excuse him, and given the circumstances, his views on courtship were irrelevant. The issue was moot as long as "the men of Mass. stoutly declare that women who hold such sentiments of *equality* can never expect to be courted."[11]

Theodore could not let the matter of his feminism die, but his letters— tortured combinations of reassurances and reprimands—only made matters worse. On August 26, he wrote to the sisters, acknowledging that most men—but *not* Theodore Weld—"habitually regard [women] as *inferior* beings. I know that the majority of men regard woman as *silly*. The proposition that woman can reason and analyze closely is to them an absurdity." But, he assured the Grimkés, there was hope, for encounters with intelligent women would change male minds. It was a backhanded compliment to their intellects. If only he had stopped there, Angelina might have been appeased. But Theodore pressed on. The sisters should stop writing about equality and live the principle—this would be enough. And then Weld, who had abandoned other crusades for the sake of abolition, lectured them: moral reform, he declared, never succeeded unless its advocates stuck to the main issue. The demand for women's rights, therefore, was a drain, a distraction, and a danger to the far more important cause of abolition. Such sentiments did little to heal the breach with Angelina.[12]

The battles with her supposed supporters exhausted Angelina far more than those with her avowed enemies. "I expected to meet with trials, *personal* trials, & I (vainly perhaps) *think* I could have borne THEM," she declared to Theodore Weld, "but all this unsettlement & complaint among the *friends* of the cause is so unexpected that I don't know how to bear it." The criticism from Theodore had been especially difficult, for their relationship had deepened over the spring and early summer. He had written frequently since Angelina left New York, although he usually addressed his letters to both sisters. These letters had contained a mixture of advice, instruction, news, and concern for their health and well-being, leavened by occasional flashes of humor that evoked witty retorts even from the staid Sarah. Angelina had once viewed him only as a mentor but had quickly come to count him an intimate friend and confidant. His approval was important to her, but she had always welcomed his honest criticism as well. The patronizing and dismissive tone of his recent correspondence disappointed and saddened her. At the end of August she wrote a brief but telling addendum to Sarah's letter to their friend Henry Wright, whom the Executive Committee had removed from their side and ordered to Pennsylvania. "I am too depressed," she confided, "to feel I am doing any good at all."[13]

Also at the end of August, Angelina wrote once again to Theodore, asking for a clarification of the sisters' relationship to the American Anti-Slavery Society. Were Angelina and Sarah listed as agents of the society? She had assumed they were since they received copies of the society's newspaper, *The Emancipator,* without charge. She devoted the rest of her letter to a defense of the campaign for women's rights—and to a rebuttal of his argument that successful reform required a focus on a single issue. The prophets, she chided him, had preached not against single sins but against all sins. Weld was no more persuaded by her reasoning than she had been by his. In his reply, he reiterated that the Grimkés were not and had never been officially appointed agents of the society, only "*helpers.*" He was, he declared, in the same position as the sisters: neither salaried nor commissioned, a helper only. Then he returned to their deadlocked dialogue about the place of women's rights in their reform crusade. He dismissed her argument sharply: "I do so abhor a *self justifying* spirit," he wrote, adding fuel to the fire of disagreement between them.[14]

By mid-September, Angelina's anger seemed wholly focused on Theodore Weld. She told Jane Smith that his behavior was exasperating. "Brother Weld," she wrote, "was not satisfied with writing us *one* letter [about Sarah's *Letters on the Equality of the Sexes*], but whilst at Ashburnham we received two more setting forth various reasons why we should not meet the subject of woman's rights at all." Writing on September 20, Sarah was forced to explain to Weld that "Angelina is so wrathy that I think it will be unsafe to trust the pen in her hands to reply to thy two last good long letters." Taking up her "wrathy" pen, Angelina scratched out "good" and wrote "bad" above it. At the end of Sarah's letter, Angelina added: "Sister seems very much afraid that my pen will be transformed into a venomous serpent when it is employed in addressing thee . . . and no wonder, for I like to pay my debts, and as I received $10 worth of scolding I should be guilty of injustice did I not return the favor." "Well," she exploded, "*such* a lecture, I never before received. What is the matter with thee?" What followed was a torrent of complaints and defenses: she had a right to answer Catharine Beecher; she and Sarah missed Henry Wright and resented the Executive Committee's purposely removing him from their company; she resented Weld's unkind criticisms of Wright. The following day she added yet another postscript to the letter, accusing him of being frightened that she might accept a recent invitation to speak in Boston on women's rights.[15]

Theodore replied in early October, this time with obvious frustration. It was clear that he felt misunderstood and was anxious not to offend further. Letters, he wrote, were a hopeless means of communication. He was certain that the two of them had totally misread each other's meaning and intent. Yet he canceled out his attempt to placate Angelina by declaring that her "habits of reasoning greatly expose you to *fallacies*." The remainder of his letter must surely have seemed far more patronizing than placating. "Another subject," he began, "Angelina's last letter! Why dear child! What is the matter with you? Patience! Rally yourself. Recollect your womanhood my sister, and put on charity which is the bond of perfectness." He wanted no misunderstanding of *this* letter: "I speak just what I mean and in no spirit of ralliery when I say there are some things in that letter which you ought to be ashamed of and to repent of." The "some things" turned out to be Angelina's accusation that the Executive Committee had been dishonest about its motives for removing Henry Wright as the sisters' arrangements manager.[16]

Like a dog with a bone, Theodore continued to gnaw away at what he considered Angelina's unfounded accusations. Only a few days later, on October 16, he wrote again, in a letter addressed solely to Angelina this time. He defended the Executive Committee's decision to relocate Wright as a purely practical measure and expressed shock at her claim that the committee had disowned the sisters. He was, he said, utterly amazed at what he called her "wild claims," and declared the letter in which she made them "so ludicrous I could laugh aloud." Sounding ever more distraught, he added his doubt that she would ever understand him and his fear that the friendship could not be mended. "I suppose what little of me was left in your estimation before will be utterly annihilated when I tell you that to this day I have never read . . . the Appeal . . . with this very small exception: I read perhaps twenty lines . . . and saw its drift and *loathed* it." He ended with the harshest of judgments on her: "To KNOW and to RULE ones own spirit is the rarest and most difficult of human attainments, *that* in which deception is most *frequent* and fatal . . . you have studied everything more than the *moral* elements of your own spirit." Such a judgment, laid upon a woman who had spent agonizing hours, days, and even years examining her principles, forging her moral sense, and shaping her actions in accordance with both, seemed likely to end the relationship.[17]

Theodore's apology came that November. As always, it was ambiguous, giving and taking away comfort in equal measure. He apologized for his "unguarded letter," which he realized, in retrospect, must have pained her as it now pained him. Yet he felt cause to rejoice, for learning and self-knowledge came with pain. "Ah, my dear sister A," he wrote. "You have sore and long and multiform conflicts yet to wage with the powerful and subtle and endlessly ramified pride in your heart . . . SELF conquest is the *last* and yet the first and only *real* conquest." It was as if her young journal-keeping self were talking to her once again.[18]

Angelina, who had spent the fall lecturing from town to town—from Northbridge to Woonsocket Falls, Effingham, Uxbridge, Mendon, Holliston, and Franklin—lacked the energy to reply. She had fallen ill at the end of October, a victim of too many months of anxiety and work without rest. On October 31, she was forced to leave a lecture unfinished in Hingham, and by nightfall she was running a fever. The next morning the sisters traveled by stage to Boston, where Angelina's fever continued and a debilitating headache began. The sisters made their way to the welcoming home of

Samuel Philbrick in Brookline, where Sarah hoped a regimen of rest and calm would help her sister recover. But almost a month later, Angelina's fever had not abated. Sarah wrote grimly to their friend Sarah Douglass that Angelina's improvement was slow. "I fear her nature has been so over-tasked and her whole system is prostrated." Angelina was so weak she could not even read a letter.[19]

Learning of Angelina's illness, Theodore Weld set aside his criticisms of her intellectual and moral failings and concentrated on giving advice regarding her health. Sounding more like a mother hen than a somber moralist, he warned her not to go out in the New England cold. He urged the sisters to go as far south as Philadelphia for the winter. "You are children of the *sun*," he reminded the two South Carolina natives, and ill suited to the harsh winters of Massachusetts. As always, his concern for Angelina seemed to go awry, twisting a compliment into criticism: "I have little confidence in the predominance of Angelina's cool judgement over her feelings when *any personal sacrifice* may seem to be called for, that I tremble for her, lest she should begin to speak again before she is fully up." When rumor reached him that Angelina's lungs had been damaged by her extended illness, he was beside himself. Sarah hurried to reassure him that the rumor was false. As for wintering in Philadelphia, this was impossible. "Our abolition has deprived us of a home there," Sarah wrote. "I know of but one family who would receive us."[20]

By Christmastime, Angelina was recovered enough from what was probably typhoid fever to take up old arguments, and begin new ones, with Theodore. Yet the tensions between them seemed to have eased. Her old concern for his health and well-being returned as well. She worried, she wrote, that he lived the life of a hermit, without the relief of a close communion of minds with anyone. Theodore conceded that he had true rapport with no one in the New York antislavery movement. His only genuine confidant, he admitted, was the British abolitionist Charles Stuart. "I can hardly trust myself to speak or write of him; so is my whole being seized with love and admiration of his most unearthly character." Angelina took pains to tell him that she understood; she had no one except her sister Sarah and her friend Jane Smith—and, she added gently, him.[21]

That Weld's friendship meant a great deal to Angelina was clear. "Let me tell you how often I have thanked God for such a friend as you have proved to me," she wrote in late January 1738, for "you dear brother have, I must acknowledge, dived deeper into the *hidden* sins of my heart than any one ever did before." For men and women like Angelina and Theodore, the language of intimacy took its vocabulary from evangelical religion; to know the motives and thoughts of another was to discover their hidden sins and to hope for their purification. Yet Angelina still felt the bite of her friend's criticism: "I think in some things you wronged me in *that letter never to be forgotten,* but never mind, YOU DID NOT HURT ME, even that did me good."[22]

On February 8, Theodore sent a private letter to Angelina that contained a rambling apology for hurting her. The thought that he had inflicted "abiding pain" with his reproofs had utterly unnerved him. "Have I indeed done this to *you,* Angelina?" he asked. "I *would* explain the mystery of the *seeming* unkindness and cruelty of my spirit toward you in reproof, did not higher considerations than *inclination* or self interest forbid me to do it, until I have *first* fulfilled an obligation which I am *now* convinced should have been discharged long ago." The obligation was nothing less than the "sacred duty" to confess, at long last, his love for her. "I know it will surprise and even amaze you, Angelina, when I say to you as I now do, that for a long time, *you have had my whole heart.*"

Being Theodore Dwight Weld, he could not stop with a simple declaration of love, and so he poured out the history of his growing affection for her. From the moment he had read her letter in *The Liberator,* his spirit had been drawn to her. "I read it over and over and over," he confessed, and found in its author a spirit and soul congenial to his own. So strong was the connection, Weld wrote, "I forgot utterly that you were not of my own sex!" But it was this realization that complicated the relationship at once. The bond with Charles Stuart had been emotional and intellectual, an affection like that formed between brothers or between surrogate father and son. But a woman! Here was a different matter, Theodore explained, and a Quaker woman at that, one who no doubt would refuse to marry outside her faith. Despite this unsettling reality, "my heart turned toward you," he wrote, and though he struggled against it, he was in fact in love. "*Less* I cannot say, and *more* I need not"—yet more he did say. The dam had burst for this eccentric, passionate, and charismatic man who had struggled against his feelings for so many months. He wanted to tell her "*without reserve all that is in my heart toward you.*" Once he had done that, his confidence seemed to collapse on the very pages of the letter, a surging insecurity taking its place. "I have," he declared, "*no expectation* and almost no *hope* that my feelings are in *any degree* RECIPROCATED BY YOU." He knew she respected him, yes; but love? "I have no reason to believe, and as little assurance that the knowledge of my own feelings toward you may give birth to

such feelings." Weld was love-stricken, but he was a man of often exhausting integrity, who placed heavy demands upon himself to face the truth, no
matter how painful. In his moment of agony, that relentless pursuit of
truth and self-knowledge asserted itself: "If your heart, Angelina, does not
reciprocate my love, I charge you before a risen Lord not to shrink for a
moment thro fear of giving me pain from declaring to me the *whole truth.*"
And, with that, he subjected Angelina Grimké to the same unmodulated
standard of honesty that he so regularly applied to himself.[23]

It was, even for a nineteenth-century reformer whose fear of sin and dis-
trust of the ego were hallmarks of his personality, a remarkable declaration
of love. Angelina's reply was less tortured and more openly romantic. On
February 11, nine days before her thirty-third birthday, she wrote: "Your
letter was indeed a great surprise, My Brother, and yet it was no surprise
at all." He had hidden his feelings well, she told him, and thus she had hidden hers also. As society permitted only him and not her to initiate a
courtship—despite any "ultraist" philosophy he might espouse—she could
not help wondering why he had "so purposely and perseveringly" smoth-
ered his feelings. But it no longer mattered; they were, she wrote, "two
halves of one whole," and that was enough.[24]

Throughout the winter, the letters between the two lovers bore the
expected stamp of confession, the unburdening of feelings long held in
check. They blurted out their faults and character flaws, eager to expose the
worst for fear that later discovery might turn love to disgust. Theodore
was manic in his effort to paint the most dismal and disturbing picture of
his true self: he was selfish, prideful, "proud as Lucifer," in fact; he was
impatient of contradiction, bad-tempered, irritable, gloomy, intolerant,
indolent, indulgent, and sarcastic. Confessions of failings large and small
poured ceaselessly from his pen: "I hate to get up in the morning" was followed almost immediately by "I have a stupid and mulish preference for
my own notions and my own way." Angelina could not hope to match his
catalog of imperfections, for, as she solemnly reminded him, he had
already pointed out most of her failings already.[25]

No romance between Angelina Grimké and Theodore Weld could be
anxiety-free, of course. They both worried that their love threatened to
divert them from their devotion to God. They were, after all, committed
Christians in the aftermath of the Second Great Awakening, the most
intense religious revival of the century. True, they attended no church, had
made no pledges to one Protestant sect or another. Angelina had shed her
commitment to the Society of Friends several years before, even if her

name had not yet been removed from the Arch Street rolls. Theodore had been born again, finding salvation through the ministrations of the evangelist Charles Finney, and Angelina too had made her own pilgrimage of faith and embraced Christ. They were both strong-willed and rigid in their certainties, but they saw themselves as Christians who submitted humbly to His will. They spoke gratefully of Christ's personal aid and comfort, and Angelina believed she was able to lecture, despite the terror she felt in anticipation, because Jesus stood beside her. Both Angelina and Theodore saw a heresy in their longing for each other and in the intense attachment they felt. "Am I sinning, am I ungrateful," Angelina exclaimed, and asked him to tell her: "*Am I an* IDOLATOR?" It was a question that a secular soul could not have framed and one that the nineteenth-century religious soul felt compelled to answer.[26]

There were other concerns, however, that were more gendered. Angelina had formed a view of courtship and marriage that seemed to weave together her experiences with Charleston beaus and a profoundly rewritten recollection of her courtship by Edward Bettle. The views themselves were more typical than she realized. Nineteenth-century genteel ideology held as a truism that men were ruled by sexual passions while women were passionless. It was the absence of sexual appetite that enabled women to develop their higher natures and defined them as more moral than the opposite sex. When Angelina exclaimed, "How my womanhood has been outraged, by the base and mean and trifling arts to win my favor, how I have been tempted to think marriage was *sinful*, because of what appeared to me almost invariably to prompt and lead to it," she was closer to Catharine Beecher's sensibility than she might have imagined. It was animal passion that held most men captive, she declared, not the higher, nobler sentiments, and it was this that made a sham of a sacrament. "How I have feared the possibility of ever being married to one who regarded *this* as the *end*—the great design of marriage."[27]

But if Angelina feared the animal passions in others, Theodore, as a nineteenth-century Christian man, feared them in himself. Like many middle-class men of his generation, Weld had been raised to believe that sexual restraint was the mark not only of a civilized man but also of a healthy one. From medical writers and diet reformers alike came the warning that excessive sexual activity and excessive sexual stimulation—from masturbation to frequent intercourse—damaged the body and the mind as well as blemished the soul. For Weld, almost surely a virgin at thirty-five, the sudden rush of passion he felt for Angelina carried him into uncharted and disturbing waters. He did not dare see her yet, he wrote, now that they had declared their love, for he needed time to master his emotions. Until now, "I had striven and resisted almost unto blood against my love for you," he wrote, "I had seized it and with violent hands had struggled to throttle it." Now he acknowledged he was human, after all, with "a deep void, an aching *want.*" He could only speak of that want in the disembodied form of "ceaseless responsive communings," but his passionate language suggested much more.[28]

In the end, they elevated their pledge to marry to a plane that made moral sense to them both. Theodore put it into words that resonated for Angelina: "We marry Angelina not *merely* nor *mainly* nor *at all comparatively* to ENJOY, but together to do and to dare, together to toil and testify and suffer, together to crucify the flesh with its affections and lusts and to keep ourselves and each other unspotted from the world, to live a life of faith in the son of God, pilgrims and strangers ready yea rejoicing, called to it and each other."[29]

Seven

"WE ABOLITION WOMEN ARE TURNING THE WORLD UPSIDE DOWN"

Triumphs and Retirement

ANGELINA'S DEEPEST EMOTIONS HAD BEEN stirred by Theodore's profession of love, but the upheaval in her private life did not alter the pace of her antislavery work. In fact, in the midst of their impassioned exchange of letters, Angelina was preparing for the most important public appearance of her life. She and Sarah had been invited to address a committee of the Massachusetts State Legislature on February 21 and 22 on the subject of antislavery petitions. The invitation signaled a sharp break with tradition: no woman had ever testified before a formal American lawmaking body. Yet it seemed fitting as well, for though Lydia Maria Child spoke for many middle-class women when she declared that petitioning was "the most odious of all tasks," 70 percent of all the petition signers in 1838 would be women. Angelina suspected her decision to accept the Massachusetts invitation would be controversial among the New York abolitionist contingent. At the close of a letter filled with further declarations of love to Weld, she pressed him for news of their reaction. "I must now say a word to you about my speaking before the Legislative Committee which has the charge of petitions. . . . I have no answer as to whether the Anti-Slavery Committee will sanction it. If *not,* I feel that I must bear my own burden entirely and speak on my *own* responsibility alone, for woe is unto me if I speak not." Even with organizational support, Angelina admitted the prospect of such an historic public appearance was daunting. "It is a great undertaking for a *woman,*" she confessed to Theodore, but one she could not refuse.[1]

Sarah now added her comments on the upcoming testimony before the legislators. After that exceptional letter to Angelina marked "Private," the correspondence between Weld and the Grimkés had returned to its usual form: he addressed his correspondence to "S. and A. Grimké" and they responded, in turn, in a single letter. "We feel calm in the prospect," Sarah told Theodore, "and altho' it has cost much deep exercise of mind, yet we are settled in the belief that the Lord requires this sacrifice." The sisters had settled on their subjects for both the Wednesday and Thursday appearances. "Mine," Sarah explained, was to be the "dangers of slavery & the effect of abolition movements on the South; A's are laws of the District and compensation." If Theodore had any useful information on these topics, Sarah told him, she hoped he would send it immediately.[2]

Theodore had still not mastered his emotions enough to see Angelina in person, and he made no plans to attend the legislative sessions. Angelina, whose anxiety soared before each public appearance, was relieved that her most severe critic would not be there to pass judgment on her performance. On the evening of February 21, however, she wrote him a long and detailed description of this first session. The day had begun in crisis. Sarah, who had been scheduled to give this first lecture, had succumbed to a violent cold and could not speak at all. Angelina was forced to testify in her place. She was frankly terrified. "The novelty of the scene," she wrote, "the weight of responsibility, the ceaseless exercise of mind thro' which I had passed for more than a week—all together sunk me to the earth." Fortunately, Maria Chapman was there to provide her with comfort. She stood nearby, and as Angelina rose, Maria whispered, "God strengthen you my Sister." And, Angelina declared, God did indeed give her courage. As always, once she began to talk, all fear and tension fell away. Her heart ceased to pound—and she spoke for nearly two hours. Lydia Maria Child observed the transformation of a pale and anxious woman into a charismatic figure: "For a moment a sense of the immense responsibility resting on her seemed almost to overwhelm her. She trembled and grew pale. But this passed quickly, and she went on to speak gloriously, strong in utter forgetfulness of herself, and in her own earnest faith—in every word she uttered."[3]

Angelina's own evaluation of her performance was more critical. She had not excelled in intellectual argument or in the power of language, she told Theodore, and yet when "my heart broke over the wrongs of the slave, the deep fountains of sympathy were broken up, and many were melted to tears." If her intellectual argument had been wanting, her ability to convey who she was and what she stood for had not failed her. In a few simple sentences, Angelina Grimké offered the clearest statement of the ethical and moral code she lived by and the high price she had paid for her convictions. "I stand before you," she had declared that day, "as a southerner, exiled from the land of my birth by the sound of the lash and the piteous cry of the slave. I stand before you as a repentant slave holder . . . I stand before you as a moral being."[4]

The next evening, Angelina wrote once more to Theodore, describing the scene at the state capitol. News had apparently spread of the unusual testimony being presented, and on this second day of the hearings, the hall was packed. Angelina, the still-ailing Sarah, and their friends were squeezed through the doorway and had to walk over the seats to reach the table placed opposite the Speaker's desk. When Angelina rose to speak, a chorus of loud hisses rose from the crowd who filled the doorway. It was a potentially dangerous situation; violence had dogged the abolitionist movement since its inception, and there had been more than 150 mob actions against them in the North between 1834 and 1837. The memory of Boston's antislavery riots and of the recent murder of Illinois abolitionist editor Elijah Lovejoy surely crossed the minds of many in the room. But, Angelina told Theodore, "I never felt more perfectly calm in my life." Still, the noise continued, so loud that Angelina was forced to stop speaking while the officials tried to restore order. She rose to speak three times and was interrupted each time. She remained calm. Finally, a committee member asked Angelina to cross the hall and stand closer to the committee so that they could hear what she had to say over the din. She moved to a spot in front of the Speaker's desk but still could not be heard. The committee then asked Angelina to stand in the Speaker's desk and invited Sarah to sit in the Speaker's chair. It must have been a remarkable sight: two women in drab Quaker dress, occupying the place of one of the most powerful political figures in the state of Massachusetts, lecturing members of the state legislature on the constitutionality of antislavery petitions, the evils of slavery, and the appropriate political policies with regard to slavery in the District of Columbia.[5]

The crowd grew silent as Angelina once again began to speak, and it remained silent throughout her two-hour address. "I felt," she told Theodore, "as if I could stand up in the dignity of my moral being and face a frowning world, if need be." As always, her words touched many in the audience. Before she was done, she saw tears fill the eyes of the committee chairman, a man rumored to be an abolitionist himself.[6]

Angelina gave a similar account of the day's events to Sarah Douglass, one of her few remaining Quaker friends. She was convinced, she told Douglass, that God had stilled the crowd and given her the courage to speak. "I feel that when I am speaking I am surrounded by a body guard of hearts faithful and true and by an atmosphere of prayer." She could not judge the effect of her argument, either on legislative policy or on the opinions of the crowd. She expected no miracles; she knew that many who listened to her speak on the plight of the slave and the "elevation of woman" despised both her and her views. And yet, she wrote, she was confident of one thing: "We Abolition Women are turning the world upside down."[7]

No miracles came to pass. Angelina's arguments did not bring an end to the congressional "gag rule." Slavery was not abolished in Washington, D.C., or Florida as a result of her testimony. She had not destroyed, in one dramatic moment, the prejudice against women speaking out in public on controversial issues. As Lydia Maria Child dryly noted, "The sound part of the community (as they consider themselves) seek to give vent to their vexation by calling her Devil-ina instead of Angelina, and Miss Grimalkin instead of Miss Grimké." The press continued its attacks on Angelina as well, labeling her an old maid, a crank, an "orator in Petticoats," and a radical with the secret agenda of racial amalgamation. Nevertheless, she was correct that abolitionist women were "turning the world upside down." Thousands of ordinary middle-class women had been mobilized by the antislavery cause, and they would continue to go door-to-door on petition campaigns, organize fund-raising campaigns, write antislavery literature, and, in the coming years, speak out in public just as Angelina and Sarah did now. The Grimké sisters had laid the groundwork for the next generation of women, setting out, in simple but powerful terms, an argument that feminists would embrace: women were moral beings, equal to men in their ability to judge their society's political as well as social behavior and equally entitled to work for its reform.[8]

Angelina had only a few weeks to catch her breath after the statehouse appearances, for on March 22, the Grimké sisters were scheduled to begin a series of weekly lectures at the Odeon, the largest venue in Boston. These lectures would keep them in Massachusetts until late April 1838. Knowing this, Angelina pressed Theodore to come to Boston right away. It had been almost three months since his admission of love, and almost a year since the two had seen each other. "Now Dearest," she prodded gently on March 11, "if you do not come *this* week I cannot see you until after I go to Phil'a, for once I begin to feel the burden of my lectures, I know it will be *best* for me not to see you."[9]

Theodore's mind had turned, at last, in the same direction. Even before Angelina's letter arrived, he declared himself ready to see her. On March 12, he wrote that he would leave New York on Thursday, spend Friday with his brother in Hartford, and head to Boston on Friday evening by train. "I will be with you on Saturday evening," he promised Angelina. "You" in this case did not mean both sisters. "When I meet you," he pleaded, "let me meet you

ALONE. For a little while I MUST be *alone* with you." Sarah might be his "dear sister" as well as Angelina's, but he was in love with only one of the Grimkés.[10]

While they were separated, Angelina and Theodore had confessed to myriad failings and character flaws, large and small. But now, in anticipation of their reunion, Angelina felt compelled to confess one more thing to her lover: her former romantic involvement with Edward Bettle. Weld's response was extraordinarily generous. He urged her not to apologize for this relationship or drive it from her memory; if Bettle had been worthy of her love, then Theodore loved him, too. As for him, he had no such intimacies to reveal, for Weld was an innocent in matters of the heart.

On March 17, Theodore Weld arrived at Samuel Philbrick's home. He was greeted by Sarah and the Philbrick family and together they ate dinner. Angelina remained closeted in her room. When at last everyone but Weld left to attend a lecture in Boston, Angelina joined Theodore in the parlor. He had what he wished—time alone with her—but he was immediately overwhelmed by his emotions. He was so overcome with passion each time they embraced that he frequently fled from the room.[11]

Theodore's visit was brief, for he and Angelina agreed he should leave before the Odeon lectures began. With no distractions, Sarah and Angelina could make final preparations for what was to be the high point of their public career. The sisters' plan was for Sarah to give the first lecture. That evening, three thousand people crowded the Odeon—most of them hoping to hear Angelina. Whether the audience was disappointed is unclear, but rumor quickly spread to Theodore Weld that Sarah had alienated supporters and won no converts to the cause. From his brother's home in Hartford, Weld wrote a devastating letter to Sarah Grimké. Insisting, as he had done so often with Angelina, that perfect honesty was the hallmark of true friendship and love, he prepared her for "things which will be certain to grieve and mortify and disappoint and even afflict" her. On a train ride from Brighton to Worcester, he wrote, he had overheard a number of abolitionists express their dismay over the first Odeon meeting. "Our supporters were disappointed that Angelina did not rise to speak while our opponents rejoiced that you took the stage." The brutal truth, he told Sarah, was that she was uninteresting; "your manner is monotonous and heavy."[12]

Theodore's letter crushed Sarah. Its impact was as devastating as the order from Quaker elders to sit down as she spoke at the Arch Street Meeting. In that moment, all her cherished hopes of becoming a minister had been dashed. Now, an abolitionist elder was telling her to sit down as she spoke out against slavery. "It seemed as if God rebuked me in anger for daring to set my feet on hallowed ground," she told Theodore. Yet rather than challenge his assessment—formed, after all, out of hearsay on a train—she accepted his injunction to silence. Sarah had often turned her anger inward and swallowed her disappointments, but surely in this instance her tenuous future played some role in this meek acquiescence, for the impending marriage of her sister and Theodore Weld placed Sarah Grimké in an awkward position. If Theodore and Angelina set up housekeeping without her, her future would be bleak indeed. She was a confirmed spinster, an exile from the land of her birth, a Christian without a church, and a woman with limited capacity for friendship or intimacy. Her most intense emotional attachment had always been, and remained, to her Nina. Although she had assured Theodore that she was willing to give Angelina up to him, she could not help worrying what her own future would be.[13]

Angelina gave the remaining five Odeon lectures. Thousands came to hear and were moved by her. Decades later, the memory of her performance remained fresh in the minds of friends and allies. She had, wrote one, a "serene, commanding eloquence, a wonderful gift, which enchained attention, disarmed prejudice, and carried her hearers with her." The renowned abolitionist Wendell Phillips said she "swept the chords of the human heart with a power that has never been surpassed, and rarely equaled." Her most outstanding trait, he declared was "her serene indifference to the judgment of those about her. Self-poised, she seemed morally sufficient to herself."

As a young woman in Charleston, Angelina Grimké had been rebellious, certain of what values she rejected but uncertain of those she would embrace. In Philadelphia, she had clothed herself in conservative Quaker values just as she adopted Quaker attire, and though the clothing suited her, she soon found these values did not fit her well. In the end, she had forged her own moral identity and chosen the battles she would fight, whether together with others or alone. When she rose to speak at the Odeon in 1838, she was indeed "morally sufficient to herself."[14]

While Angelina was thrilling the crowds at the Odeon, news of her impending marriage to Theodore slowly spread through the abolitionist community. For many months, he had carefully hidden his relationship with Angelina from friends and associates. He did not reveal his plans to marry to his immediate family until that March. The couple were fully aware that the news would be controversial—and that many would be surprised by Theodore's willingness to marry the most notorious woman in America. As Theodore told Angelina, "Nine tenths of the community verily believe that you are utterly spoiled for domestic life." One man, he continued, confided that he "did not believe it possible for a woman of your *sentiments* and *practices* as to the sphere of woman to be anything but 'an obtrusive noisy clamorer' in the domestic circle 'repelled and repelling.' " No one, the man had declared, would ever marry her. Lewis Tappan expressed his grudging admiration for Weld, who had shown the courage to propose to an outspoken advocate of women's rights. Friends of Angelina were equally amazed. As Anna Weston put it: "A great many will go to hear you and may admire you, Angelina, yet I have believed you had thrown yourself *entirely* beyond the ordinary lot of woman, and *no man* would wish to have such a wife."[15]

For some, the news of the marriage came as a betrayal. Angelina heard rumors that her abolitionist friends in Boston were "almost *offended* that I should do such a thing as get married. Some say *we* were both public property and had *no right* to enter into such an engagement. Others that I will now be good for nothing henceforth and forever to the cause." After reporting all this to Theodore, she asked: "Are thy friends mourning over thee as mine are over me?"[16]

The extraordinary accomplishments of Angelina and Theodore had, in fact, made them public property—and they knew it. "We are very prominently identified with the great moral movements of the age," Theodore reminded Angelina, and he was correct. They had identified themselves with temperance, abolition, women's rights, Sylvester Graham's controversial diet regimen, and educational reform, not to mention "the battle with factitious life and aristocracy and thralldom of fashion, the great question of diversity of sects, anti Bible, etc. . . . This is the *crisis* age of the world," Theodore declared, and marriage—perhaps he meant *their* marriage—was "the crisis of the age."[17]

Like their friends, Angelina and Theodore believed that their public and private lives were inseparable. Their wedding, therefore, must be as much an abolitionist and feminist statement as it was a commitment between a woman and a man. From the wedding invitations to the guest list to the ceremony itself, they would defy tradition and challenge the status quo.

The invitations, composed and handwritten by Angelina, arrived on stationery adorned with a black-and-white engraving of a young slave kneeling in chains. The guest list, some eighty people in all, included several African American friends and acquaintances. Among them were Sarah

Douglass and her mother as well as Betsy Dawson, a former house slave of Judge Grimké, who attended with her daughter. The presence of these black women surely strained the hospitality of a conventional woman like their hostess, Angelina's sister, Anna Frost. And news of this mingling of black and white guests at a social affair gave credence to suspicions that Angelina Grimké was a racial amalgamationist. Far away, in Charleston, Mary Smith Grimké suspected that her youngest daughter would not conform to established rules of conduct. Both Angelina's mother and her sister Anna agreed that the guests assembled were "a motley crew."[18]

A motley crew it was, and not simply because of the racial mix. The stellar figures of every contingent of the antislavery movement were there, including Weld's Lane Seminary friends Henry B. Stanton, Amos Dresser, and George A. Avery; New York's Gerrit Smith and Lewis Tappan; and William Lloyd Garrison himself. Quakers and Presbyterians, ministers and anticlerics, all were invited to mingle in Anna Frost's Philadelphia parlor that day. At every turn, these guests encountered both symbolic and legal rejections of their society's institutional status quo.

The ceremony itself signaled a defiance of insular religious institutions and a suspicion of the virtue of the clergy. Angelina's marriage to a non-Quaker and Sarah's willingness to witness their vows were acts in clear violation of the rules of the Society of Friends. In committing these infractions publicly, the Grimké sisters were declaring their final break with the Arch Street Meeting. Loyal Quakers such as John Greenleaf Whittier carefully left the room when the ceremony began in order to avoid suffering the same expulsion the sisters would surely face. The guests who remained would witness a ceremony conducted by the couple themselves rather than a clergyman, for Theodore and Angelina had agreed to forgo any presiding ministers. Instead, they asked twelve guests to sign the marriage contract, making the marriage legal under Pennsylvania law. The couple spoke their vows extemporaneously, each saying what was in his or her heart. When they were done, bride, groom, and guests all knelt to pray. Despite the couple's refusal to have a minister officiate, they asked an African American minister and then a white clergyman to lead the room in prayer. Before prayers ended, Sarah Grimké rose to speak, offering up a prayer of thanksgiving. Silenced in the church and banished from the lectern, she reclaimed her voice at Nina's wedding.[19]

The guest list and the ceremony were socially radical, challenging racial and religious norms. But Angelina and Theodore's radicalism went further than this when they rejected the legal inequality of women in marriage.

Under both English and American law a husband was entitled to full control of his wife's property, even the clothes on her back. As a *feme covert*, or "woman covered" by the protection of her husband, a married woman could not keep the wages she earned, buy or sell property, or provide for heirs in a will. Theodore renounced this power over Angelina, signing a prenuptial agreement that ensured her full control of her own wealth after their marriage. This renunciation of tradition was radical in practical as well as symbolic terms, for Theodore Weld was a man of few financial resources and Angelina enjoyed a comfortable inheritance.[20]

Friends who gathered to celebrate the marriage of Theodore and Angelina Grimké Weld did not doubt the affection these two shared. But they continued to harbor doubts about the impact of the marriage. Many of those doubts reflected traditional male or female perspectives. Theodore's friend Lewis Tappan had already voiced his admiration for anyone willing to marry a woman "like that." Angelina's mother, on the other hand, expressed her great relief that her daughter had, at last, found a "protector." Mary Grimké hoped that, as "a Matron," her controversial daughter would "desire to retire from the busy scene of publicity, and . . . enjoy that happiness which I hope your home will yield you." But what a mother wished, many activists dreaded. In the end, the most pressing question for Angelina's friends was this: would Mrs. Theodore Weld retire into private life, abandoning the public stage she had occupied as Angelina Grimké?

The immediate answer seemed to be no. The day after the wedding, Sarah and Angelina made their way to the brand-new Pennsylvania Hall to attend the third Female Anti-Slavery Convention. Angelina was chosen to serve as a vice president and invited to speak. Under a banner that read, "Virtue, Liberty and Independence," the delegates conducted a series of debates on science, temperance, slavery, and the rights of workingmen. But the mood soon turned grim. Trouble was brewing outside the hall, for the racially integrated meeting had attracted angry protestors. The crowd's hostility was further fueled by rumors that Angelina and Theodore's recent wedding had included African Americans in the wedding party itself.

A sense of foreboding filled the hall on the evening of May 16 as the public meeting began. Both men and women, white and black, had gathered to hear Angelina, Maria Chapman, and Lucretia Mott address them. Angelina rose to speak, a voice of calm against the tumult growing outside the hall. Her speech wove into one seamless cloth an account of her personal odyssey and the journey of the abolition movement itself. Looking out at the nervous crowd, she raised a question that she had often asked herself and her closest confidants: why did women and men, white and black, throng to hear her speak? "What came ye out to see?" she asked. "Is it curiosity merely, or a deep sympathy with the perishing slave?" She was weary of addressing crowds who viewed her as an oddity, of audiences less interested in what she had to say than in seeing for themselves the controversial Miss Grimké. Tonight their commitment would be tested, if not by her then by the crowd gathering outside to do them harm. As the noise increased, she urged: "Hear it—hear it! Those voices without tell us that the spirit of slavery is *here,* and has been roused to wrath by our abolition speeches and conventions." Angelina believed that Northern racism was only another face of slavery, just as she believed that the people in that hall were the only ones who could combat it. The burden lay on their shoulders, for "the great men of this country will not do this work, the church will never do it." Like William Lloyd Garrison, she had no faith in the nation's political leaders; like her own sister Sarah, she had abandoned all hope that the clergy would lead their congregations into battle against racial prejudice and slavery. Over the roar outside, she reminded those who listened to her of her own intimate knowledge of slavery. "I have seen it! I have seen it!" she exclaimed, and they knew that this was no empty claim. "I know it has horrors that can never be described. I was brought up under its wing." Those who claimed that slaves were happy did not tell the truth. Perhaps they did not know it. They traveled to the South and were entertained by gracious planters and their wives who sheltered them from the horrors of the slave quarters and the scars upon slaves' backs. They "know nothing of the dark side of the picture," the side, Angelina said, that she had witnessed. "I have *never* seen a happy slave," she continued; although "I have seen him dance in his chains," it was mirth, not happiness, that moved him. It was his expression of despair, for when there was no hope, there was only the behavior that declared, "Let us eat and drink, for tomorrow we die."

As bricks and stones began to hit the windows, shattering the glass, Angelina showed no sign of fear. "What is a mob?" she asked. "What would the breaking of every window be? What would the leveling of this Hall be? Any evidence that we are wrong, or that slavery is a good and wholesome institution?" She tried to bring meaning to the violence threatening the anxious audience inside. The violent protest was a testament, she said, to the effectiveness of abolition, to the impact of antislavery agitation upon the nation. Just as she had witnessed slavery, she had seen and felt the rising tide of its opposition. As a young woman living in Charleston, she confided, she had wept alone over the evils of slavery. "I knew none who sympathized in my feelings," and knew of no one working to end the oppression of the enslaved. She had fled north to Pennsylvania, believing she would find others who felt sympathy for the slave, but "I found it not." The men and women of Philadelphia's orthodox Quaker community were kind and hospitable to her, but she came to realize that "the slave had no place in their thoughts." Yet in recent years, her despair had lifted, replaced by hope as the abolitionist movement took wing. An angry mob might threaten them tonight, she conceded, but there could be no doubt that, in the end, "liberty and good will to man" would triumph in America. "There is nothing to be feared from those who stop our mouths," she assured the anxious gathering of women and men sitting before her, for "the current is even now setting fast" against the threatening mob.

Angelina had used her personal journey from despair to confidence to ease the anxiety of the audience, to set their frightening moment within a larger and triumphant framework of history. She was nearly done. But it was never solely her mission to bring consolation or to reassure. Rather, her goal was always to instruct—and demand. On this spring night in 1838, Angelina Grimké Weld exhorted her entire audience just as she had exhorted audiences in New York and New England: learn what slavery is; read the books that will tell the truth; give their money to the cause rather than waste it on luxuries. But her final message was to the women in the hall. Her onetime friend Catharine Beecher had written of the "peculiar duties" of woman, but on this evening Angelina defined a very different set of obligations. "It is . . . peculiarly *your* duty to petition," she declared. The "men who hold the rod over slaves [and] rule in the councils of the nation" may deny us the right to petition and to "remonstrate against abuses of our sex and of our kind." But Angelina Grimké had long ago found a higher authority to guide her sex. "We have these rights," she assured the women in Pennsylvania Hall, "from our God." It was the last speech Angelina would give until 1863, and perhaps her best ever.[21]

When the speeches were over, the abolitionist women left the hall arm in arm, black together with white—just as women had done in Boston in the face of rioting three years earlier. The women were safe, but the hall was not. The mob broke in, setting fires, ransacking the antislavery offices on the first floor, hurling books and papers into the flames. Philadelphia firemen appeared at the scene but did nothing to save Pennsylvania Hall. Not satisfied with the total destruction of the building, rioters headed toward the homes of known abolitionists. William Lloyd Garrison, always a likely target of mob hatred, was rushed to safety, away from the City of Brotherly

Love. Still the violence continued. The following night, a mob set fire to a "shelter for colored orphans" run by the Quakers. Although local citizens condemned the violence, many believed that the abolitionists had brought it on themselves. Men—and especially women—who preached radical doctrines could not expect the community's protection or sympathy.

In the end, it would not be the violence of angry mobs or the indifference of those who found satisfaction in the status quo that persuaded Angelina Grimké Weld to abandon the public stage. By 1838, cracks in the unity of the antislavery movement had begun to appear and mainstream politicians were poised to take up the issues that had once been the province of the reformers. It was a sign of the times, perhaps, that Angelina, Sarah, and Theodore now decided to turn their energies toward the domestic sphere.[22]

Eight

"I CANNOT TELL THEE HOW I LOVE THIS PRIVATE LIFE"

Angelina and Domesticity

THE SOUNDS OF A VIOLENT AND HATE-FILLED CROWD echoed in Angelina's ears long after the fires that consumed Pennsylvania Hall had gone cold. But as the summer began, the newly married Mrs. Theodore Weld had other challenges on her mind. Although she and Theodore had been amused by the dire warnings that followed news of their engagement, for Angelina, the question still hung in the air: was she, as many said, "utterly spoiled for domestic life"? Could she prove by example that a woman could exercise her public voice without sacrificing her domestic identity? She was determined to demonstrate to the world that a woman could have private happiness and public service—and that the man she married would not be filled with regret. "May the Lord Jesus help me for thy sake," she wrote to Theodore a few weeks before the wedding, "and for *woman's* sake to prove that well regulated minds can with *equal* ease occupy high and low stations and find *true happiness in both.*" But could she occupy both "high and low stations" at the same time? Friends who feared that Angelina would withdraw from an active role in the antislavery movement had reason to worry, for the life Angelina Weld chose to live was not the life Angelina Grimké had chosen.[1]

By 1838, Angelina may have welcomed any reason to withdraw from the public eye. Life on the lecture circuit had been exhausting, and Angelina's health had suffered. Her advocacy of women's rights had brought criticism down upon her head from abolitionists, and although she had stood up bravely in the face of their attacks, the need to constantly defend herself had taken a toll. She knew that the women's rights issue threatened to splinter the abolitionist movement, and a sense of responsibility for the growing tensions no doubt troubled her as well. Shortly before they married, Angelina confessed to her new husband that she longed to be relieved of a life of public service. "O! how I should rejoice," she wrote, "if the Master should say '*It is enough.*' It is an increasing trial to me and most gladly would I retire from public view and sink down into *sweet obscurity.*"[2]

Both she and her new husband chose to believe that God had indeed said, "It is enough." And so Angelina and Theodore turned with relief to the details of setting up their first home. Although they had vowed to live by a code of marital equality, Theodore's wishes on major questions immediately took precedence. Angelina had spent her life in cities, but Weld pressed for a house in the countryside. He had been raised on a farm and was no stranger to planting crops, mending fences, and other rural manual labor. She acquiesced, knowing he had little love for urban life. After much searching, Theodore found a small house in Fort Lee, New Jersey, with a lovely view of the Hudson, rural enough to be affordable but close enough for him to commute to the offices of the American Anti-Slavery Society, where he still worked. Discussions of furnishings occupied them all spring. In these matters of decor and decoration, Theodore did seek his wife's opinion. Did Angelina prefer cane or flag-bottom chairs? What kind of knobs should they have on the dressers? What style bed? Should he buy the mattress in New York? To this last question, she replied no, for the only ones sold there were made from cotton produced by slaves. Should he buy mahogany dining tables? No, she said; tables made of cheaper cherrywood were "good enough for me." Should he purchase a stove? No, she said once again; they wouldn't need one in the summer, and they would be better able to tell what size they needed once they had settled in and knew "how many would be in our family."[3]

Angelina and Theodore had talked of inviting their two best friends— his mentor, Charles Stuart, and her confidante Jane Smith—to live with them. Although neither friend joined them, there was certain to be at least one other person in the household: Sarah Grimké. Despite Sarah's fleeting anxiety over her future, neither Angelina nor Theodore ever considered excluding her from their home. It was common enough for spinster or widowed sisters, orphaned children, aunts, nephews, cousins, and aging parents to find a home under a couple's roof, but the bond between Sarah and Angelina ran deeper than mere family obligation. From the beginning, Theodore Weld had tacitly accepted that he was joining the Grimké sisters' intimate circle rather than starting a new one of his own. Writing to Angelina on April 4, he had gently reminded her, "you and dear Sarah and I are a strange trio, different from all the world beside I do believe."[4]

Angelina worked hard to ensure that Sarah felt welcome. When she realized that Sarah's bedroom in their first house would be a small one, she wrote her husband-to-be, proposing—perhaps not fully in jest—that Theodore take the small room while she and her sister made themselves comfortable in the larger rooms of the master suite. Reading this, a cautious Sarah immediately added a postscript to the letter, assuring Theodore that Angelina was not serious. "I am afraid," she wrote, "thy tender heart will be wounded at her bantering about our having the suite of apartments so I enter my protest at once to let thee know I have neither part nor lot in the contrivance." But drawing the boundaries of Sarah's place in this complicated emotional triangle would, in the end, prove more difficult than simply measuring the size of a bedroom.[5]

Although knobs could be chosen and mattresses could be found, these were only the trappings of domestic life. It fell to Angelina to transform the Welds' house into a home. In part, Angelina had chosen this role, embraced it, for she sought to prove to the world that she was fit to be a wife and mother. But in part it became her burden by default; neither Theodore nor Angelina considered the possibility that domestic chores could fall to husband as well as wife. The truth was, however, that Angelina was ill-equipped to take up a woman's traditional domestic duties. At thirty-three, she had absolutely no experience in managing a home and none of the requisite skills. She had been waited on by slaves in Charleston and had lived as a guest in the homes of Quakers and abolitionists since coming north. Neither she, nor the forty-five-year-old Sarah for that matter, knew how to cook, garden, or clean. A staff of efficient and experienced servants might have solved Angelina's problem, but, to her mother's astonishment and dismay, she refused to employ any household help. More was in play than Angelina's stubborn determination to prove herself in the realm of the "true woman." Finances were also a factor. Theodore Weld was far from a wealthy man, and although Angelina had voluntarily turned her own inheritance over to him, economy and simplicity were financial necessities as well as moral imperatives.

Together, the sisters struggled to master the complicated tasks of boiling potatoes, sweeping and dusting, and baking bread. They celebrated their small successes and strove to learn from their mistakes. In the kitchen, they relied on the prescriptions of William Andrus Alcott's 1838 *The Younger Housekeeper; or Thoughts on Food and Cookery.* Much like Dr. Spock's guide to baby care for young mothers in the twentieth century, Alcott's book offered advice and instruction for inexperienced homemakers. But for Alcott, as for many of the food reformers of the antebellum era, diet was a matter of more than physical health: what a person ate had moral implications. "We are to do good," Alcott declared, "even by our eating and drinking." Each chapter of *The Younger Housekeeper* was a homily on the moral qualities of a food: Chapter 23 praised the apple as "one of the Creator's noblest gifts," while Chapter 34 reassured readers that the "evils of the cucumber" were overrated. The true virtue of a simple diet, one that did not require too much preparation time, was that it freed a woman to spend more time in the moral education of her children. Alcott thus condemned butter and cheese not only because they were fatty foods, bad for the digestion, but also because the time a woman spent churning and processing could be more profitably spent instilling proper values in a son or daughter. Ironically, Alcott's moral prescriptions echoed those of Angelina's bête noire, Catharine Beecher.[6]

In fact, Angelina's life had taken on something of the cast and character of a Beecher disciple's. As a spinster, she had fought doggedly to break down the gender barriers in public life. But she entered marriage determined to make it as conventional as her single life had been radical. Neither she nor Theodore had ever denounced the traditional divisions of labor within the household. In the Weld home, just as in any respectable middle-class American home, the kitchen, the parlor, and the nursery were a wife's domain; the office and the workshop were a husband's. To the outside world, the Welds appeared a traditional middle-class couple as he went off to work each day while she remained at home.

Those who followed Angelina's writings on gender carefully would not have been surprised. Her goal, after all, had never been to reorder domestic roles but to prove that women were capable of excelling in *both* the public and private realms. Fifty years after Angelina and Theodore wed, the American feminist Charlotte Perkins Gilman would propose the liberation of women from the home by turning over household chores and child care to paid, professional experts, but Angelina would have found this notion shocking. She had battled to *add* to women's duties, not to reduce them, and she would never suggest that the right to participate in the public sphere absolved women from the duties of the domestic realm.[7]

Angelina saw her acceptance of domestic duties as the best rebuttal to her critics. She and Sarah, she wrote to Anna Weston, "keep no help, and are therefore filling up 'the appropriate Sphere of woman' to admiration, in the kitchen with baking pans and pots and steamers, etc., and in the parlor and chamber with the broom & duster." Yet Angelina recognized that her success might be a pyrrhic victory: she had proven that she could operate in both the public and the private realms, but not at the same time.

"Indeed," she added in slightly self-mocking tones, "I think our enemies would rejoice could they look in on us from day to day & see us in our domestic life, instead of lecturing to *promiscuous* audiences." It was the "instead" that still distinguished the life of an antebellum woman from the life of a man.[8]

Although invitations to lecture continued to reach Angelina, she turned them all down. No amount of prodding could persuade her. "When shall we hear thee and Sarah again orally pleading the cause of the oppressed?" asked a Quaker friend in early 1839, adding, "Ought such talents to be rapped in a Napkin or such lights hid under a bushel?" And Lydia Maria Child gently scolded, claiming that Angelina had lost her individuality and become one of those matrons who declared, "Please ma'am, I don't live nowhere now; I'm married." Abby Kelley, now on the lecture circuit herself, pleaded with Theodore Weld to encourage the sisters to speak out once again. "I often think," she wrote, "that had I the qualifications of Sarah and Angelina, I could not wait another day, when the cry from the South is grating so harshly on our ears."[9]

But if others urged her to return to the public stage, Theodore encouraged her to say no. Even an appeal from Sylvester Graham, the diet reformer whose teachings Weld—and thus his wife—embraced, did not alter his conviction that Angelina should continue in retirement. Weld advised his wife to wait for a clear sign from God that this was what He wanted for her. But no such sign seemed to come. Instead, Angelina tried to find satisfaction in the daily grind of housework, refusing to turn over any of its chores to an outsider. With each passing day, however, she relied more heavily on Sarah to share the burdens.[10]

Soon after they moved to New Jersey, Theodore enlisted his wife and sister-in-law to assist him on a book project: a collection of accounts of the brutality of slavery drawn from Southern sources. It was a project tailor-made for Weld, who had always demanded that hard facts and solid evidence serve as the basis for abolitionist arguments. And so, in 1839, the Grimké sisters began to pore through Southern newspapers and to write letters asking Southerners of both races to send them stories. The resulting book, *American Slavery as It Is,* proved a massive undertaking. Years later, Theodore recalled that the sisters spent six months, averaging six hours each day, sifting through the pages of thousands of newspapers to find evidence of abuse and cruelty. When the project was done, the three researchers made an attempt to count the number of papers the sisters had scanned. When they reached twenty thousand and saw that there were many more stored in their attic, they stopped counting. *American Slavery as It Is* sold a hundred thousand copies when it was published in 1839. Only Theodore's name appeared on the title page; Angelina's and Sarah's contributions remained hidden from the eyes of the reading public. Yet to everyone in the Weld household the book seemed to be proof that the compromise between reform and domestic life was working for Angelina and Sarah. Sarah declared that the project had brought the sisters as much satisfaction as their New England tour. "I do not think we ever labored more assiduously for the slave than we have done this fall and winter," she wrote, "and although our work is of the kind that may be privately performed, yet we find the same holy peace in doing it which we found in the public advocacy of the cause."[11]

In the midst of the exhausting work of soliciting, editing, verifying, and organizing the many accounts they received, Angelina discovered she was pregnant. She was now juggling a number of roles that taxed what Sarah had earlier called the "peace [that] flowed sweetly" through her soul. She was an expectant mother, but she was also a researcher, writer, housekeeper, and hostess for the steady flow of houseguests and visitors who came and went in her modest New Jersey home. Angelina welcomed the company of Jane Smith and Sarah Douglass despite the additional strain on her time and energy that guests entailed. She was equally happy to see Abby Kelley, the young and dynamic abolitionist who seemed to be Angelina's successor on the antislavery lecture circuit. When other abolitionists criticized Angelina for abandoning the movement, it was Kelley who offered up a realistic defense. Mrs. Theodore Weld, she said, was simply too exhausted from housework and pregnancy to become active in the cause once again. Proving she was not "spoiled for domestic life" had become more tiring for Angelina than lecturing had been.[12]

On December 14, 1839, Angelina's first child was born. The nine-pound boy, named Charles Stuart Weld in honor of Theodore's mentor, delighted Angelina. But she was no more experienced in motherhood than in housekeeping. She relied heavily upon the child care instruction of the diet reformer Sylvester Graham, whose food regimen Theodore had introduced to the household. Graham was a Presbyterian minister who designed and proselytized for a vegetarian diet. The centerpiece of the Graham system was a whole-wheat bread made from unsifted and unbolted flour, free from the chemical additives used by nineteenth-century bakeries to render their loaves white. Today, Graham is remembered only through the graham cracker, but in the antebellum era of reform, his injunctions against alcohol, refined sugar, and chemical additives—and his insistence that unhealthy diets stimulated excessive sexual desire—won many converts. Unfortunately, the Graham diet was ill-suited to the needs of a growing baby or its mother. Because an infection made it impossible for Angelina to breast-feed Charles Stuart Weld, the rigid feeding schedule Graham demanded was followed. Poor Charles Stuart thus began life as an under-fed, listless, fretting child. Sarah watched Angelina struggling to maintain both the Graham regimen and her own calm for several months. At last, when Angelina made a brief trip away from home, Sarah seized the oppor-tunity and began to give her nephew the bottle on demand. Angelina returned to find a happy, cheerful baby—and, despite Weld's objections, Graham's rules were permanently discarded.[13]

Angelina at last softened her rule against household help as well. That winter, a former slave of the Grimké family, set free by Anna Frost, came to live with the Welds. Although Angelina still cooked the Spartan dinners of "rice and asparagus, potatoes, mush and Indian bread" that kept the family in a state of mild but persistent malnutrition, Betsy Dawson would relieve the sisters of some of the most exhausting household chores.[14]

Soon after Charles Stuart Weld was born, his father decided his family should move to a real farm. Using most of Angelina's money, and the fixed contributions Sarah made to the family finances, Weld purchased fifty acres in Belleville, New Jersey, on the Passaic River. With it came a fifteen-room colonial stone house, framed by weeping willows and a yard filled with flowers. Like all old houses, however, the Belleville home needed con-stant repairs. Theodore also needed money for seed, farm tools, the repair of fences, and the construction of chicken coops. The family's finances would have been severely strained under any circumstance, but the situa-tion was made worse by poor management from Isaac Lloyd, who handled both Sarah's and Angelina's inheritances, and by the fact that Theodore's meager salary was irregularly paid.[15]

The ramshackle condition of the Welds' new home did not prevent guests from arriving on their doorstep. With more rooms to accommodate friends and family, Angelina found herself cooking and cleaning for a steady flow of company. "Oh how I long to have our little family alone to sit down without any strangers at our meals," she exclaimed—but neither she nor the far less naturally sociable Theodore Weld seemed able or willing to turn people away.[16]

Although Angelina expressed a longing for quiet and isolation, she could not escape disturbing news from the outside world. Both she and

Theodore had watched with despair as the tensions within the antislavery movement increased. They had seen cracks in the unity of the movement even as Garrisonians and New York abolitionists mingled at their wedding—and Angelina knew that her advocacy of women's rights had contributed to the damage. Since then, the situation had grown worse. Writing to Gerrit Smith in October 1839, Weld had exploded in anger at the rancor within abolitionist circles. "The spirit of the Massachusetts belligerents on both sides is absolutely ferocious," he declared. Theodore saw little hope of reconciliation, for "their calling each other *dishonest hypocritical* double tongued false witnesses, etc. is probably what each *really believes* of the others."[17]

The issues destroying the solidarity of the movement involved both principles and strategies. The Garrisonian wing of the movement had openly embraced women's rights, while the more conservative wing, led by the Tappans, had dismissed them as a distraction at best and a questionable goal under any circumstances. The Garrisonians insisted that the antislavery movement must remain a moral crusade, its members ready to bear witness and to challenge the legitimacy of any political institution that tolerated slavery in its midst, including the federal government. While the editor of *The Liberator* remained a purist, his conservative opponents came to see him as a hindrance rather than a help to their cause. These New York–led abolitionists saw themselves as realists, and they had begun to consider the efficacy of forming political alliances with influential mainstream leaders, including the clergy.

The final break came in the spring of 1840. That April the news Theodore and Angelina had dreaded reached them: an open split had occurred at the annual antislavery convention. The Garrisonians had gained control of the convention and demonstrated their support for women's rights by electing three women—Lydia Maria Child, Lucretia Mott, and Maria Weston Chapman—to the executive committee of the American Anti-Slavery Association. It was a slap in the face to the Tappan faction that could not go unchallenged. Lewis Tappan declared that "to put a woman on the committee with men is contrary to the usages of civilized society," and then led the more conservative members out of the association. Together with his brother Arthur, James Birney, Gerrit Smith, and others, he formed a rival organization, the American and Foreign Anti-Slavery Society. The new organization adamantly refused to support women's rights and began at once to enter national politics through membership in the newly formed Liberal Party. When that party nominated abolitionist spokesman James

Birney for president, it was the Garrisonians' turn to be appalled. The movement could never again be made whole.[18]

The splintering of the antislavery movement produced a paralyzing crisis of loyalties for both Theodore and Angelina. Theodore had close ties with the Tappan faction and was critical of the personality cult that had developed around Garrison. Although he had no desire to become involved in formal politics, he thought that the new organization's willingness to work within the political system made sense. At the same time, the Tappan faction's hostility to women's right to speak out on moral issues deeply offended him. To his dismay, his dearest friend, Charles Stuart, agreed with the conservatives, voicing open contempt for the participation of women in the leadership of the movement. Women, Stuart wrote, should not be "intruded, as delegates, debaters and managers, into mixed Societies of men and women," for this was an "insane innovation."[19]

Angelina found the choice between the two factions equally difficult. She had found her way to the antislavery movement through Garrison and *The Liberator,* and she was grateful that the Garrisonian wing was solidly behind women's rights. She harbored unpleasant memories of the criticism and lack of support shown to her and her sister by the New York group during their New England tour. Nevertheless, she favored political action that went beyond petitioning and approved of efforts to influence political candidates. How could she possibly choose between a group that supported women's rights but turned its back on political action and a group that was willing to enter the political fray but was determined to exclude women from public participation? Neither Angelina nor Theodore nor Sarah knew which way to turn.

For Angelina, the solution was to turn fully inward, to the small and intimate community she had made with Theodore, Sarah, and her growing family. Elizabeth Cady Stanton tried to rally her, writing that Angelina's old friend Lucretia Mott "thinks you have both been in a state of reticency long enough, and that it is not right for you to be still, longer; that you should either write for the public or speak out for *oppressed* woman." Yet Angelina remained silent.[20]

On January 3, 1841, Angelina's second son, Theodore, was born, and she turned herself over to motherhood once again with relief. In typical fashion, she subjected her maternal feelings to analysis. She worried that perhaps she might love her second son more than her first, for she had been unable to breast-feed Charles but now formed that bond with Theodore. After some soul-searching, she concluded that her affection for her eldest child was strong enough to endure the competition. An attraction to the underdog still dominated her emotional preferences, and the deprivation Charles suffered from her inexperience and the Graham system led her to conclude, "I love Charles the better of the two still, for towards him my soul was drawn out in sympathy and sorrow and suffering."[21]

By the time Theodore was born, Charles was a healthy, active boy. But "sorrow and suffering" now plagued his mother. In the delicate language of avoidance common to their nineteenth-century circle, Theodore later described his wife's physical problems in vague but ominous terms. "Early in her married life," he wrote, "she was twice severely injured. These injuries, though wholly unlike, were in their effect a unit, one causing, the other intensifying a life-long weakness. Together they shattered incurably her nervous system. The one was wholly internal; the other caused a deep wound which never healed." Theodore never elaborated, but Sarah Grimké, more blunt perhaps, and more comfortable with a discussion of the female body, declared that her sister had developed a prolapsed uterus, aggravated by repeated pregnancies at close intervals. The problem was severe enough that at times Angelina's uterus protruded outside her body. What the second injury was is unclear. Although Angelina, like many women who bore children, suffered from hernias, the pain, though unpleasant, was not extreme enough to "shatter her nervous system."[22]

Perhaps the explanation for Angelina's poor health was simpler than Weld was willing to admit. Years of grueling and tiresome housework, cooking for guests, and giving birth to and caring for babies, as well as extreme diet restrictions and a life unrelieved by any indulgence or luxury, were enough to exhaust even the most determined wife and mother. A profound disappointment in the collapse of a movement she had labored for, and an aching sense that she bore some responsibility for that collapse, had dealt the final blow.

In 1842, the burdens of domesticity facing Angelina grew rather than abated, for that year Theodore Weld reentered public life. By June, much to the joy of friends in the movement, he was once again speaking at local antislavery meetings. That winter, he accepted a position as an antislavery lobbyist in Washington, D.C. The job did not pay a salary, although Congress agreed to cover his modest living expenses. To make ends meet, Theodore was soon borrowing money from the Tappans.[23]

While Theodore settled into the lively and, he admitted, satisfying life of political discussions and antislavery strategy sessions, Angelina remained cloistered at home. She had encouraged her husband to take the Washington assignment, telling him that he had been wasting his talents planting potatoes and beans. But the joys of private life were no longer so evident to her, either. She conceded, hesitantly, that the "restless, ambitious temper" she had acknowledged in herself so many years before had not abated. She still craved, she confessed, a life of "high duties and high attainments." Both Theodore and Sarah condemned Angelina's desire to do great and worthy things as sinful pride—and she accepted their judgment. "I have at times thought this ambition was motive to me to do my duty and submit my will." To remain in the domestic sphere was now an act of penance rather than of defiance.

Nine

"INNUMERABLE, HORRIBLE, UNSPEAKABLE, EARTHY, SENSUAL AND DEVILISH DISTORTIONS OF MARRIED LIFE"

The Crisis Years at Home

THROUGHOUT THE WINTER OF 1843, Theodore Weld sent Angelina accounts of life in Washington. He described, and deplored, the decadence of American society that he saw in the nation's capital—"the lust of eye and the pride of life, the vaporing, and vain glory, and struggle for supremacy in worldly splendor going on all around me"—a decadence that he and the sisters had tried to insulate themselves from in their rural home. Yet he could not deny that the cause he had labored for had at last found allies among the country's political leaders. A struggle to end the gag rule, led by John Quincy Adams, was being waged, and suddenly the "most mobbed man in America" was being consulted by congressmen. Indeed, he reported to Angelina with delight and uncharacteristic humor that the members of Congress sharing his boardinghouse treated him and fellow abolitionists "as though we were not fanatics."[1]

Every letter from Theodore gave evidence of his satisfaction in doing meaningful work once again. But Angelina could not match her husband's enthusiasm in her reports from home. The drudgery of domestic life weighed ever more heavily on her, and she seemed to have lost a sense of herself. In desperation, she turned to religious fanaticism. As a young woman, she had entertained an apocalyptic vision of a battle between the armies of Christ and those of "Gog and Magog." Now, in Theodore's absence, she became fascinated with the apocalyptic visions of a Baptist farmer named William Miller. Miller had pored over the Bible, finding clues in the books of Daniel and Ezekiel and Revelation that he used to determine the Messiah's return. Based on his calculations, he predicted that the second coming of Christ and the establishment of the millennial kingdom could be expected sometime in 1844, leaving his ardent followers to pinpoint October 22, 1844, as the exact date of the messianic return. Miller's promise of the Kingdom of God on a troubled earth galvanized many Americans who had been participants in the religious revivals of the 1820s and 1830s. As the date approached, perhaps a hundred thousand Millerites abandoned their homes and farms, left their jobs, and began to preach the coming of the end of history. When October 22 came and went uneventfully, Millerites were distraught. Many returned to their previous lives, but the most devoted continued to believe despite what they called the Great Disappointment, simply fixing a new date for Christ's arrival.[2]

Angelina never went so far as Miller's acolytes. But her flirtation with the promise of this apocalyptic vision seemed to mirror the battle between a sense of doom and a hope for relief being waged within her. Theodore must have known something of the unrest and confusion she felt, for he confessed that, for more than two years, he too had "ceased to know myself." His warnings against a continuing involvement with Millerism suggested that, on some level, he understood her deepening sense that she was caught in a trap of her own—and his—making. "The study of prophecy has great witchery over minds of a certain cast," he wrote from Washington in early 1842. "It powerfully stimulates curiosity, love of the marvelous, the element of superstition, the spirit of adventure, the desire for novelty." If Angelina had a desire for novelty or a thwarted spirit of adventure, Theodore recognized that she had little chance to satisfy either. "I know your crowd of cares and labors and responsibilities in my absence," he wrote a few days later, "with the children the housekeeping, company, letter writing, etc." He prayed that her infatuation with Miller's prophecies would pass. In the meantime, he could only urge her not to add to her duties by writing to him so often.[3]

But a year later, little had improved. Theodore sympathized, yet a touch of impatience could be read in his letter the following January: "The fact of your having had ever since our marriage an overburden upon your physical strength, exhausting it, drinking up our spirits and corroding your mind, has been to you *and to all of us*, in its effects, deplorable" (italics added). Somehow, Angelina's physical weakness had become one with a weakness of character. Sarah, Theodore declared, had shown "greater powers of endurance" and thus had emerged the stronger of the two.[4]

Theodore's concern for his wife was genuine. Yet by 1843, he had formed an image of Angelina as a frail woman whose nervous nature made it necessary to avoid "deep mental excitement." "Your indisposition," he wrote that January, "is I think rightly attributed by both of you to mental excitement. The mere fact of reading or *studying* much of the time would not I am sure be injurious if unaccompanied with *deep mental excitement*."[5]

Theodore's fear that Angelina's interest in Miller's millennialism strained her capacities showed how much things had changed since their marriage. In 1838, Angelina's passion for emancipation, her deep mental excitement at the cruelty of slavery, her sustained reading of abolitionist literature—these had been positive driving forces behind her brilliance as an orator. Now, an "*absorbing* interest"—combined with her habit of picking up her sons when they fell down—was seen as perilous.

Angelina suspected that other factors had imperiled her. By 1842, she had begun to fear she had lost herself in the "strange trio" of husband, sister, and self that was the core of the Weld household. Boundaries among the three had certainly blurred: Theodore seemed to belong as much to his "dear sister" as to his wife, and Angelina noted with alarm that Charley had come to think of Sarah as his mother, much as she herself had once done so long ago in Charleston. In her private letters to friends, Sarah echoed this collapse of boundaries. Writing to turn down an invitation for a visit in 1842, the older Grimké explained: "I cannot leave my children, ie, T., and A. and my babies." Sarah's intense desire to be needed had combined with Angelina's willingness to rely upon her sister to create an odd domestic circumstance: Angelina was neither fully wife nor mother nor even mistress of her own household. Yet for over a decade Angelina did not confront her sister or take steps to redefine the complicated relationships that had evolved. Instead, her reliance on Sarah grew rather than diminished during these years. With her husband so often far away in Washington, whom could she turn to in 1843 when she suffered a miscarriage or when she found she was pregnant once more only a few months later?[6]

Angelina's world did not end in 1844 as the Millerites had predicted. Instead, she brought new life into it that April when her daughter, Sarah Grimké Weld, was born. Yet even the arrival of a healthy baby could not lift the gloom that had settled over the Weld household. Theodore, who had been lecturing once more on a small, local scale when he was not in Washington, lost his voice again that February. He became preoccupied throughout the spring and summer with his own health, pursuing every avenue that promised to restore his ability to speak. He tried water cures, rest cures, and several of the many quack remedies that flourished in the antebellum years. Abolitionist friends urged him to find his voice on paper if he could not recover it in the lecture hall, but he stubbornly refused. Instead, he filled his days by tending his fruit trees and working in his garden. Angelina knew her husband was frustrated and unhappy, and she urged him to pursue something that would give him true satisfaction. "I entreat you," she said, "no longer to kick against the pricks of conviction and condemnation that are tearing and wearing your spirit *all* the while."[7]

Angelina had little time to consider the wear and tear on her own spirit. By 1844, Belleville had become a refuge for their extended family's sick, elderly, poor, and incompetent. Theodore's ailing parents, his invalid nephew, and his mentally ill sister had joined them in New Jersey, along with Angelina's widowed sister, Anna Frost, and her daughter. Although their finances were stretched thin, the Welds periodically supported Theodore's elderly aunt and uncle as well. Pressed for money, and without any paid employment, in 1851 Theodore turned to teaching. That October, he established a boarding school at Belleville, opening the doors to twenty students as well as his own sons, Charley and Theodore (called "Sody" by his family). Angelina and Sarah were enlisted to teach, but their duties did not end with the classroom. The sisters also did all the cooking, washing, and cleaning for the school. Within a year, Angelina was close to collapse. She traveled to Brooklyn to take a water cure, but the baths did little to restore her. At the same time, Sarah suffered a bout with pneumonia. Frustrated and depressed, Theodore admitted defeat, closing the school only a year after it was founded.[8]

The dark clouds that seemed to hang over the Weld household had appeared on the national horizon as well. From the sidelines, Angelina and Theodore watched as sectional tensions mounted. In 1850, the last of the patchwork of compromises between slave and free states that held the nation together was engineered. That year, the "Great Compromiser," Kentucky's Henry Clay, put together an omnibus bill that gave something to both sides. California was to be admitted into the Union as a free state, but in the remaining territories, the settlers would have the right to decide whether slavery would be acceptable. This policy of "popular sovereignty" would not prove to be a panacea, for in only a few short years it would lead to bloodshed and violence as men in the Kansas territory took up arms over the issue. Clay's proposal also included the abolition of slavery in the nation's capital, something abolitionists such as Angelina had advocated for over a decade. But what the antislavery movement gained from one hand, it would have had taken away with the other: the compromise also included a new and more effective fugitive slave law that allowed slave-catchers to travel north to capture and return escaped African Americans to their owners. Clay's omnibus bill failed, but the artful Senator Stephen A. Douglas saved the component parts by arranging for them to be approved individually. The resulting Compromise of 1850 demonstrated how divided the nation was, for it did little to decrease sectional tensions. Southern leaders feared that the balance between free and slave states in the Senate had been destroyed; Northern leaders faced growing pressures to ensure that western territories remained a haven for farm families rather than slave labor. The abolitionist cause was, at last, a part of the national political agenda, but its peaceful victory now seemed less likely than ever before.

In 1852, as Angelina washed linens for the students at the Belleville school, Harriet Beecher Stowe, the younger sister of Catharine Beecher, published a sensational novel that drew heavily upon Theodore Weld's *American Slavery as It Is*. *Uncle Tom's Cabin,* Stowe's tale of patient slaves and sadistic overseers, roused antislavery sentiment in the North and planter ire in the South. Two years later, in 1854, Congress debated the Kansas-Nebraska Act, which would reopen the issue of the extension of slavery and lead to the violence known as "Bleeding Kansas." At the same time, a new political party emerged, built entirely along sectional lines. This Republican Party was formed by a coalition of interested groups. Former Whigs, disgruntled with their national party's compromises with the slave interests, joined, as did Free Soilers, whose concern was to keep the western territories free for small farmers. Antislavery Democrats also helped organize the new party, abandoning the last of the connecting political threads that held the two regions, North and South, together. Angelina now gave up all hope that slavery would vanish without bloodshed. The antislavery societies she had spurred others to join in the 1830s seemed increasingly irrelevant in the turbulent 1850s. "It seemed," she wrote, "as tho' the bloody scenes of the Revolution *must* be reenacted before Slavery could be abolished."[9]

In the midst of this growing national crisis, the Weld family moved farther away from the decadence and sin and looming disaster that they believed defined the nation. They left Belleville for one of the many utopian communities that sprang up before the Civil War. The Raritan Bay Union was a newly formed cooperative experiment located in New Jersey where the Raritan River emptied into the bay of the same name, twenty-five miles from New York City. By borrowing money from Sarah, Weld was able to purchase $1,000 worth of shares in the community's stock. Although Raritan Bay proved to be a gathering place for visiting intellectuals and reformers, the communal arrangement promised to provide Angelina and Sarah with little relief from their domestic burdens. Sarah predicted a crisis coming for the family if they joined the commune. She wrote frankly that her sister and Theodore should abandon the path they had doggedly committed themselves to; although God may have called them, as Sarah put it, "to the living out of our anti slavery principles in every day life," the plain truth was that Angelina "was no more designed to serve tables, than Theodore to dig potatoes."[10]

Angelina was no longer sure what she was designed for. But she was certain that she was no longer meant to be part of that "strange trio" she had formed more than fifteen years earlier with Theodore and Sarah. The proposed move from Belleville brought to a head the personal crisis that had been brewing for almost a decade in Angelina Grimké Weld. In 1854, she demanded that the Welds' finances be separated from Sarah's—and, by implication, that Sarah separate herself from the Welds. Angelina argued that the separation would liberate Sarah from the chains of domesticity and free them all from the pain and unhappiness that had dogged them for a decade.[11]

If Angelina believed she was offering Sarah her freedom—a freedom she herself could not seize—Sarah believed she was being cast out into a world for which she was no longer suited. "I have for so long been cooking, sweeping and teaching the abc of French and the angles and curves of drawing," she wrote, "that I seem to have lost the mental activity I once had." Sarah's bitterness at the life she felt she had been forced to endure came pouring out. "In childhood," she declared, the powers of her mind "were repressed by the false idea that a girl need not have the education I coveted. In early youth by wrong views of God and religion, then I was fairly ground to powder in the Quaker Society." Since she left the Society of Friends, her life had not improved, for she had suffered from "the overwhelming superiority of those whom I have been in contact." Now, she asked, "what can I expect in old age?"[12]

No harder blow could be dealt to Sarah Grimké. Now sixty years old, she made a feeble effort to take control of her life. She went to Washington, D.C., in the winter of 1853–54, with vague hopes of establishing herself as an advocate for the rights of children. She considered other projects as well—revising her *Letters on Equality,* compiling the laws covering women in the various states. But she quickly abandoned every plan. Her life, she wrote, had been a life of "deep disappointments, of withered hopes," and so it would always be. The only joy she had ever known, she said, was the "innocence and earnest love of Theodore's children." Charley, Sody, and Sarah—Theodore's children, not Angelina's; her children, Sarah believed, after all.[13]

Lonely and without purpose, Sarah wrote to Angelina after the Welds had settled into their new Raritan Bay quarters, offering to join them and take up her housekeeping and child care role once again. Angelina said no. Yet Sarah's obvious distress ate away at her younger sister, and a sense of guilt battled with the relief she felt at Sarah's exile. "There are times," Angelina confessed soon afterward to Sarah, "I feel humbled in the dust, because I never have been willing to share my blessings with you equally. Often, very often, when I look at all the sorrow and disappointment you have met with in life and all that you have done for me I feel ashamed and confounded at my ingratitude and selfishness." Yet surely, Angelina continued, was she so wrong? "It seems unnatural that a wife and Mother should ever thus be willing to share of the affection of her dearest ones with any human being and my heart refuses its assent and struggles on in darkness and death for I know these feelings wither and blight and keep me from growth and yet it seems impossible for me to overcome them." It was an old struggle for Angelina: how to distinguish selfishness from what the self deserved, how to separate what one wanted from what one ought to want. She had waged it when she was a young woman in the dark and silent room with her mother, again when she was courted by Edward Bettle, and yet again when abolitionists demanded that she abandon the public call for women's rights and racial equality. But she was almost fifty now, in poor health and with meager resources, financial or emotional, that she could draw upon. This battle was too much for her. "I often feel weary of a conflict which has lasted 15 years," she told Sarah, "and wonder when and what will be the end of it." The dilemma was insoluble because she faced no real enemy, only someone who loved her. "You never meant to do me any wrong. You have only lived out your own (in many respects) beautiful nature. I would not, I could not blame you, altho' . . . the conflicts thro' which I have passed have been terrible."[14]

Come home, she wrote at last to Sarah. "We all want you with us." And Sarah came home. Only death would separate the strange trio again.

Ten

"THIS IS NOT AN *IN MEMORIAM*, IT IS A WAR-CRY"

The Last Years of Angelina Grimké

"WE HAVE JUMPED OUT OF THE FRYING-PAN into the fire in point of leisure," Sarah Grimké wrote soon after the family settled into the Raritan community. The Raritan Union was not radical enough to challenge traditional divisions of labor between men and women, and thus the cooperative living arrangements did little to ease the sisters' domestic burdens. The women of Raritan cooked and cleaned for the community, just as they had cooked and cleaned for their individual families. But the sisters had other duties as well, for Theodore wasted little time in establishing a new school, the Eagleswood School. Like Belleville, this was a family operation. Angelina taught history, handled medical care and first aid for the students, and managed much of the correspondence for the school. Sarah taught French, and although she never enjoyed teaching, she was happy to play the role of housemother to the students. Like Charley and Sody, the boys and girls of Eagleswood came to "Aunt Sai" for comfort rather than to Angelina. Sarah was more emotionally responsive; Angelina, ironically like her own mother, was too reserved. The school bore the distinctive mark of Theodore Weld, with a curriculum that included manual labor as well as academic study and a student body of boys and girls, black and white. Anyone who watched as the gangly middle-aged man with the long white beard and uncombed hair danced and played with the children would have realized that Theodore Weld was happy once again.[1]

Unfortunately, Eagleswood, like Belleville, proved unprofitable—and short-lived. By the end of the year, both it and the cooperative community it was a part of were dead. Most members of Raritan abandoned the site, but a few purchased property and built homes of their own. The Welds were among those who chose to stay. By 1856, Theodore had organized a new school, and the three aging companions settled into a busy routine once again.

The Raritan experiment had failed, but by 1856, the larger community outside seemed to be failing as well. In rapid succession, a series of events unfolded that persuaded Angelina the crisis of disunion had come at last. That year, the newspapers carried the disturbing news of a cycle of violence, murder, and retribution in the territory of Kansas. Proslavery and antislavery factions in the territory had vied with each other to determine how the state would enter the Union, and outsiders flooded into Kansas to tip the balance one way or another. Among those who arrived in 1855 was a Connecticut farmer named John Brown. Brown was no newcomer to the antislavery cause; he had helped finance the publication of both David Walker's *Appeal*, which had called on African American slaves to rebel, and Henry Highland Garnet's equally provocative "Call to Rebellion" speech. Since 1849, Brown and his large family had lived in the black community of North Elba, New York, a hamlet founded by Angelina and Theodore's old friend the abolitionist Gerrit Smith. But as Kansas turned into "Bleeding Kansas," Brown traveled south, ready to kill or be killed for his cause. In 1856, as an act of retribution for an attack by proslavery men, Brown led his followers into a proslavery town and brutally murdered five settlers. For Angelina and Sarah, who had always advocated peace and deplored violence even in self-defense, Brown represented the new and disturbing trajectory of the abolitionist movement.[2]

Yet as the decade ended and both the courts and the presidency seemed to be firmly in the hands of the slaveocracy, Angelina reluctantly concluded that violence might be the only answer. In the same year that John Brown cut a bloody swath across Kansas, a slave named Dred Scott made a final, futile bid for his freedom, not by running away but by suing in the courts. Scott's story captured the twisted logic of compromise between slavery and freedom. The family who owned him had moved to St. Louis in 1830, part of the steady migration of Americans into the new slave states of the Mississippi Valley. Here, they sold Scott to a military surgeon stationed at the Jefferson Barracks, just south of the city. For the next twelve years, Scott accompanied his new master to posts in Illinois and in the Wisconsin territory, where slavery was forbidden under the rules of the 1830 Missouri Compromise. During these years as the servant of Dr. John Emerson, Dred Scott became a husband and a father of two children. In 1842, while John Quincy Adams was waging his battle against the gag rule, Emerson returned to St. Louis, bringing Scott with him. The following year, the doctor died, but his widow continued to hold the Scott family in bondage. In 1846, however, Scott and his wife sued Mrs. Emerson for their freedom, insisting to the St. Louis circuit court that their years of residence in states and territories that forbade slavery established their freedom. The court did not agree. When Scott's lawyers appealed the case to the U.S. Supreme Court, the entire country knew that more was at stake than the fate of one black family.

In 1857, Chief Justice Roger Taney and his Court ruled that, despite his residence in free territory, Scott remained a slave. As a slave, he was not a citizen of the United States, and was thus ineligible to bring a suit in federal court. But Taney went further, in the misguided belief that he could settle the dispute over slavery forever. He ruled that the provision in the Missouri Compromise permitting Congress to prohibit slavery in the territories was unconstitutional. The Constitution, the Supreme Court declared, guaranteed the protection of private property to all its citizens, no matter where they took that property within the nation's borders.

The repercussions of the Dred Scott decision were clear at once. It was a stunning victory for the slave states and for slave owners eager to settle in the West. It threatened to unravel every compromise that had held the Union together since 1830. It was a death blow to "popular sovereignty," and a litmus test for every politician who had tried to avoid a head-on conflict between Southern and Northern interests. The newly formed Republican Party now gathered under its wing all those who could not accept the legal spread of slavery into every corner of the nation, and the Democratic Party was permanently severed in two.[3]

While the country was still reeling over the Dred Scott decision, John Brown reappeared on the national scene. This time, he was prepared to strike at the heart of the slave society: the Old Dominion itself. On October 16, 1859, Brown led thirteen white men and five African Americans into Virginia. His goal: to provoke a general uprising of slaves that would signal a war against slavery. Brown's men seized the federal arsenal at Harpers Ferry, hoping that local slaves would rush to join them. Instead, local farmers and militiamen surrounded the arsenal, and at daybreak on October 18, West Point graduate Robert E. Lee stormed the engine house where Brown's men were waiting. Within thirty-six hours, Lee had captured or killed most of the raiders. Five of Brown's followers, including his son Owen, escaped, but a wounded John Brown was captured and taken to Charlestown, Virginia. Here he was tried, convicted of treason, and sentenced to death. Addressing the court, a defiant John Brown declared: "I believe to have interfered as I have done . . . was not wrong, but right. Now, if it be deemed necessary that I should forfeit my life for the furtherance of the ends of justice, and mingle my blood further with the . . . blood of millions in this slave country . . . I submit; so let it be done." On December 2, 1859, Brown was hanged. In that moment, his martyrdom was ensured. And Angelina Grimké Weld, who had once condemned the abolitionist printer Elijah Lovejoy for defending himself against the violence of an angry mob, now mourned John Brown as a hero.[4]

When war came in 1861 it divided the Grimké and Weld families as it did thousands of other American families. Angelina's brother John and her sisters Eliza and Mary remained staunch defenders of slavery and loyal to the Confederacy despite the poverty that enveloped them during the war. Angelina sent them what little aid she could spare and took Eliza in briefly after the war. Her immediate family in Raritan was divided as well. Her own son, Charles, refused to join the Union army and fight for what he declared an "unjust cause." He rejected not only this cause but all causes; raised in a household of reformers, he wanted nothing to do with temperance, abolition, or women's rights. The only evidence that he was, after all, a Grimké and a Weld was that he pursued a life as a writer and teacher. Yet the ties to his mother and aunt must have been strong, for he did not marry until both Angelina and "Sai" were dead.[5]

Charley had turned his back on the antislavery cause, but Angelina and Theodore had not. The war reinvigorated these two aging abolitionists, who immediately joined the crusade to press President Lincoln and his party to make emancipation as well as union their goal. By November 1862, Theodore was in Boston, using his powers of persuasion once again as he spoke out against the continuation of slavery. Finding his voice remarkably restored, he set out on a speaking tour, urging the Union to support universal emancipation. When he spoke before a crowd of thousands at a reunion of the Lane Seminary rebels in 1863, he found himself surrounded by old comrades in the antislavery movement, differences forgotten, friendships renewed. Everywhere he went, he was greeted with respect. Theodore Weld was no longer a fanatic but a pioneer in the battle for equality.[6]

Angelina and Sarah, too, seemed revived by the war. Even in her darkest days during the 1840s, Angelina had not totally abandoned her activism. She had supported local temperance laws while living at Belleville, and though she had not attended the women's rights conventions of that decade, she had occasionally sent written statements on women's issues to the gatherings. But when war came, she returned at long last to the public arena she had abandoned. Along with Elizabeth Cady Stanton, Susan B. Anthony, and others who had taken up the cause of women's rights,

Angelina turned her energies to the war effort. She was one of the organizers of a Womans Loyal National League, which held its first convention in May 1863. Angelina attended, registering then as she had done so long ago in 1838, as a delegate from South Carolina.

In their resolutions, the League women pressed the nation to go beyond the Emancipation Proclamation to a complete end to slavery and to racism as well. There had been tacit agreement to set aside the issues of women's rights in this, the hour of the slave. But as always, Angelina reminded the convention—and the world—that the oppression of the slave and the oppression of women were part of a seamless web of inequalities. "True," she declared, "we have not felt the slaveholder's lash; true, we have not had our hands manacled, but our *hearts* have been crushed." After much debate, the convention agreed: the issues must remain linked. Their final resolution read: "There never can be a true peace in this Republic until the civil and political rights of all citizens of African descent and all women are practically established." Twenty-five years after Angelina and Sarah Grimké had raised their voices for women's rights, the old issues remained alive and the old techniques were suddenly made new: by 1864, a League's petition campaign to end slavery had collected 400,000 signatures.[7]

Angelina's daughter, Sarah Grimké Weld, had attended the League's founding convention with her mother. Alone among the three Weld children, Sissie had caught the reform impulse from her parents. What Charles rejected and Sissie embraced, Sody ignored. Sometime in his youth, Angelina's second son developed a strange illness that left him in a state of near-constant apathy. Whether it was physiological or psychological no one knew, but Theodore Weld's namesake spent the rest of his life sitting motionless for hours, often in a wheelchair, not working, not studying, and seemingly indifferent to the world around him. His distraught father feared that masturbation had brought on the disorder, an explanation that fit the nineteenth-century conviction that a man's energies could be sapped by excessive spilling of his seed. But the numerous physicians who examined Sody could offer no diagnosis. It was for Sody's sake that the family gave up their school, left Raritan, and moved to Perth Amboy in 1862. The move did little to improve Sody's condition and, reluctantly, Angelina and Theodore sent him to live on a farm in upstate New York under custodial care.[8]

Angelina had not been back to Massachusetts since 1838, when she made history in the statehouse. But before the war ended, she was settled into a new home in West Newton, Massachusetts. It was not the family's final move; soon afterward, they relocated to another town outside Boston, known as Hyde Park. They had made a contact with a homeopathic doctor, Dio Lewis, who had treated Sody. Their son had not improved, but Dr. Lewis was impressed enough by Weld to ask him to join the staff of a new girls' boarding school in Lexington. The position was not ideal, but the salary was good and so, for the fourth time, the trio became teachers. The war was now over and Angelina thought it was fitting to teach a class on the history of slavery. Her interest in the welfare of African Americans was still strong, and in addition to teaching, Angelina was busy raising money and collecting clothes for the newly freed men and women. Her sympathies for the problems facing the former slaves prompted her to make her first, and perhaps only, public speech on their behalf since she had married. No longer the charismatic and impassioned lecturer, the middle-aged Angelina was still impressive. "There was," wrote one of the audience, "a refinement and dignity about her, an atmosphere of gentleness and sweetness and strength, which won the way to the heart."[9]

It had been many decades since the young Angelina Grimké had challenged her family to renounce slavery and the degradation it brought upon both servants and masters. Now her mother and most of her brothers and sisters were dead, but the legacy of their lives as South Carolina slave owners was not. In 1868, Angelina and Sarah were surprised to read about a young student at Pennsylvania's Lincoln University who carried their family name. The news item roused Angelina's curiosity, not least because Lincoln was a school for African Americans. She suspected that her own family held the same secrets as other planter families, and she was correct: the young Archibald Grimké was indeed a relative. In her lectures and in her antislavery writing, Angelina had never flinched from the topic of the sexual exploitation of slave women—and the living consequences of that abuse. Now she was faced with the fact that one of her own brothers was guilty of sexual exploitation. Without any hesitation, she made contact with Archie and asked him to tell his story. He told her that he was the son of her brother Henry and a slave named Nancy Weston. Henry had never freed Nancy or the three sons she had with him. Late in life, however, his conscience compelled him to ask in his will that Nancy and his illegitimate children be treated like family. His son Montague ignored his wishes. Archibald fled to freedom. His younger brother Frank tried to run away but was captured and sold. John, the youngest, also was held in slavery. At the end of the war, Archibald returned, Nancy Weston's family was reunited, and a local church sent Archibald north to college, paying his tuition.

Angelina responded to the news with kindness and honesty. "Dear young friends," she wrote the brothers, "I cannot express the mingled emotions with which I perused your deeply interesting and touching letter. The facts disclosed were *no* surprise to me. Indeed had I not suspected that you might be my nephews, I should probably not have addressed you." She asked them to join her in forgetting the past and attending to the future. "I will not dwell on the past," she declared, "let that all go—it cannot be altered—our work is in the present." For her, that present was full of promise and even forgiveness. "I am glad you have taken the name of Grimké," she wrote, "it was *once,* one of the noblest names of Carolina, a purer patriot never lived than my brother Thomas S. Grimké. I charge you most solemnly by your upright conduct, and your life-long devotion to the eternal principles of justice and humanity and religion to lift *this name* out of the dust."

Angelina had always believed that principles must be acted out in daily, ordinary life. It was for this reason that she had welcomed African Americans into her circle of friendship, attesting to their humanity and refusing to see them simply as an abstract cause. It was for this reason that she turned to household duties with such earnestness, hoping to prove that she could practice what she had proclaimed to be true. And it was for this reason that she acknowledged and embraced Henry's sons as full members of her family. She and Sarah proved the strength of their convictions: they provided financial and emotional support to Nancy Weston's sons. When Archibald graduated from college, Angelina proudly attended the commencement exercises and stayed to get to know the brothers personally. Although John returned to the South, Archibald went on to Harvard Law School and his younger brother Frank to Princeton Theological Seminar.[10]

After the Civil War, the reins of race reform were turned over to the men who sat in Congress and to the black leadership that arose during Reconstruction. The era of the abolitionist had passed. Still, there was work to be done in the grassroots movement of women's rights. At the age of seventy-nine, the indomitable Sarah Grimké set out on foot across the New England countryside to sell copies of John Stuart Mill's feminist critique, *Subjugation of Women.* In 1870, when the Massachusetts Woman Suffrage Association was founded, both Angelina and Sarah agreed to serve as vice presidents. Like the female antislavery societies of the 1830s and 1840s, such suffrage organizations understood the value of public drama. Thus in the winter of 1870, a group of these Hyde Park feminists gathered to hold a caucus and select a ticket for the upcoming local election. Spurred on by a stirring speech from none other than Theodore Weld, the women planned a demonstration for Election Day. On March 7, 1870, forty-two women gathered in a Hyde Park hotel. Armed with bouquets of flowers from their male supporters, the women made their way through a heavy snowstorm to the nearby polling place. Here, a special area had been designated where they would cast their votes. A large crowd had gathered to watch the spectacle. It was a scene all too reminiscent of the Grimké sisters' past: before them were the curious and the hostile, mingling with the few who sympathized, a crowd ready to jeer at a cause that disturbed them and at its advocates. But as Angelina and Sarah led the procession into the hall, the crowd grew quiet and opened a path for the women to pass. The women placed their votes in a special ballot box and departed, leaving the scent of roses in the air. The demonstration did not change Massachusetts's voting laws; it did not make converts of every man who watched, even those who politely removed their hats as the women moved by. Only two years later, in 1872, Susan B. Anthony would be arrested and fined for attempting to vote in the presidential election in Rochester, New York. But on this cold March afternoon, Angelina Grimké Weld was satisfied with what she had done. Perhaps more than most of her companions, she understood that reform did not happen overnight.[11]

On December 23, 1873, the strange trio lost its first member. At the age of eighty-one, Sarah Grimké died. "You know what I have lost," Angelina wrote to a friend, "not a *sister only*, but a mother, friend, counselor,—everything I could lose in a woman." She had also lost one of the few remaining links to her past. The old generation was vanishing, as Lydia Maria Child gently reminded her friend Angelina. Did it seem strange to Angelina, Child asked, "that those exciting and eventful years, that so tried our souls and taxed our energies, have passed away into history?" The following summer, Angelina Grimké Weld began her own slow journey into history. She suffered the first of several paralyzing strokes. As her husband helped to dress her, Angelina made light of her condition. "Well, here I am a baby again," she said, "have to be dressed and fed, perhaps lugged round in arms or trundled in a wheel-chair, taught to walk on one foot, and sew and darn stockings with my left hand. Plenty of new lessons to learn that will keep me busy." Other strokes followed, and Angelina died six years later on October 26, 1879, at the age of seventy-four.[12]

Old friends from her antislavery days gathered at Angelina's funeral. In their eulogies, they brought to life, for a moment, the struggles of a bygone era. Elizur Wright, who had first recruited Angelina to the American Anti-Slavery Association, recalled how she had faced angry, howling mobs and the disapproval of men in positions of authority and power. Her principles had led her to renounce all that "the high position of her birth" had to offer, and to speak out against "the seductive system" of slavery. Lucy Stone declared that young women owed a debt of gratitude to this pioneer in women's rights. But it was Wendell Phillips who best captured the sense of history, saying, "this life carries us back to the first chapter of that great movement with which her name is associated." "We were but a handful," Phillips recalled, "and our words beat against the stony public as powerless as if against the north wind. We got no sympathy from most northern men. . . . At this time a young woman came from the proudest State in the slave-holding section. . . . No man at this day can know the gratitude we felt for this help from such an unexpected source." Phillips, more than any who mourned her that day, seemed to recognize how difficult the path was that Angelina had chosen. "Her own hard experience," he said, "the long, lonely, intellectual, and moral struggle from which she came out con-queror, had ripened her power," he reminded his friends, and out of these struggles had come her eloquence, "her wondrous faculty of laying [bare] her own heart to reach the hearts of others." She had swayed thousands, but, perhaps most important, Phillips observed, she had inspired those in the movement to persist and endure. "It was when you saw she was open-ing some secret record of her own experience, that the painful silence and breathless interest told the deep effect and lasting impression her words were making on minds that afterwards never rested in their work."[13]

Angelina was buried beside Sarah at Mount Hope. Theodore Weld sur-vived for seventeen more years, living with his son Charley and surrounded by friends and admirers. He was eager to see the story of the Grimké sis-ters told, and that task fell to Catherine Birney, the daughter-in-law of abolitionist James Birney. When *The Grimké Sisters: Sarah and Angelina Grimké, the First American Women Advocates of Abolition and Woman's Rights* appeared in 1885, Birney borrowed a quote from Florence Nightin-gale to eulogize Angelina. "This is not an *in memoriam*," Nightingale had declared as she spoke over the grave of a woman who, like Angelina, had devoted herself to humanitarian reform. "It is a war-cry such as she would have bid me write,—a cry for others to fill her place, to fill up the ranks, and fight the good fight against sin and vice and misery and wretchedness as she did,—the call to arms such as she was ever ready to obey." It was a fitting eulogy for Angelina Grimké Weld as well.[14]

TWO

Varina Howell Davis

Varina Howell Davis.
Courtesy of Louisiana State University Special Collections.

Eleven

"THE HAPPY FIRESIDE"

The Deep South Before the Civil War

BY THE 1830S, COTTON HAD SPREAD its tentacles to the banks of the Mississippi River. Mississippi and Alabama, Tennessee and Louisiana had become magnets to men from nearby Georgia and Kentucky and as far away as New Jersey and Maryland. Many came with the dream of rising from farmer to planter, just as young men from New England or the Hudson Valley flocked to the seaport cities in search of their fortunes. Only a few found the wealth they dreamed of, but their rise to the ranks of America's elite kept the dream alive for all. Before the decade was out, Alabama had almost two hundred thousand white residents, and frontier settlements such as Natchez had grown into bustling cotton towns, with gracious homes perched on the river's cliffs. Riverboats such as the *Magnolia* carried supplies and passengers down to the Deep South's most elegant city, New Orleans, passing docks along the way that served vast plantations with fanciful or lovely names like The Hurricane and Locust Grove in what became known as the Cotton Belt. To work the fields and clear the woods, the ambitious men who settled the Deep South brought—or purchased— thousands of slaves, wrenched away from their own families in an internal Middle Passage no less disorienting and tragic than the Atlantic crossing had been for their grandparents and great-grandparents. The 1830 Alabama census counted more than 117,000 African American slaves; by 1840, following the establishment of the state's first cotton gin factory in 1833, the number had risen to more than 250,000. Small wonder that the Cotton Belt was also known as the Black Belt.

The men and women who created the Cotton Kingdom in the 1830s and 1840s were cut from the same optimistic cloth as their Northern counterparts. As much as New Yorkers and Bostonians, they considered themselves patriotic Americans whose grandfathers had fought in the Revolution and their fathers and brothers in the War of 1812. They were ready to raise their glasses in a toast to territorial expansion, and when the Mexican War broke

Jefferson Davis.
*National Portrait Gallery, Smithsonian
Institution/Art Resource, NY.*

out in 1845, the sons of Mississippi and Louisiana would be among the first to volunteer. The great orators of the Old South and the Deep South sang the praises of the American Constitution and the liberties and rights it ensured just as the orators of Massachusetts and Pennsylvania did, although even the most distracted listener could not fail to note the differences in emphasis on exactly what those rights might be.

The cotton planters who sat in Congress were Whigs or Democrats, just as their Northern neighbors were, and until the 1850s, they could not envision a political party that did not function to knit the sections together. Despite increasingly bitter arguments over the expansion of slavery into the territories, tariffs, internal improvements, and the protection of human property, not even the most radical abolitionist or states' rights advocate contemplated an end to the Union in the days before the Republican Party came to power.

The men of the Southern elite viewed themselves as better-mannered and more chivalrous than their Northern brothers, although, as gentlemen, they rarely made the claim anywhere but in the privacy of their own homes.

Valor and honor were their guiding principles, and not a few young men mistook Sir Walter Scott's romantic fiction for their reality. Yet they found common ground with Yankees in their assumption that the natural order made politics, law, and the marketplace male domains and the parlor, the chapel, and the nursery the proper sphere for women. As a Mississippi planter and politician named Jefferson Davis once declared, "Woman's part in the social economy, as she had been made beautiful and gentle, should be to soothe . . . her true altar is the happy fireside." If woman's role was more idealized and her sphere more restricted in the South, still it was recognizable to Americans of any region. From the dizzy heights of their imaginary pedestals, Southern plantation mistresses sewed clothes for their family and their slaves, planted and weeded their gardens, tended their orchards, nursed their children, supervised their staff, and prepared to serve as gracious hostesses to the steady stream of guests and relatives who broke the rhythm of their days. Poorer women and black women—denied a place on the pedestal—suffered the limitations placed on them by gender ideology without even the pretense of reverence for their femininity. Like the Irishwomen who worked in Northern factories or as domestic servants, these women were invisible within the American "cult of domesticity."[1]

Yet the differences between Yankee and planter society were as obvious as the similarities. As slavery breathed its last gasp in Northern states—still clinging on in some of the newer states such as Minnesota—it planted deeper roots in the newer Southern states with every wave of forced migration across the Appalachians. Institutions familiar to Northerners took on unfamiliar shape, as the family, the church, law, and local government were drafted into service to sustain the system of slavery. While the free states devised segregation patterns and laws to isolate their smaller black populations, the Southern planter class found themselves expending great energy to keep the two races in the intimate but exploitative relationship that would later come to be known as the "peculiar institution." And while Northern entrepreneurs busied themselves with the commerce and manufacturing enterprises that created first the market revolution and later the industrial revolution, the South's ruling class remained wedded to staple crop production and enslaved labor. There was perhaps no more telling sign of the differences in economic and social trajectory than the completion of the Erie Canal in 1825 in New York and the burning of abolitionist literature in Charleston, South Carolina, in 1835.

Cultural differences, less obvious perhaps than economic ones, could also be discerned. The reform impulse grew weak as it approached the

Mason-Dixon Line, for there were few energized middle-class zealots eager to alter the eating and drinking habits of their neighbors and few utopians anxious to create model societies. Although religious revivals swept through the poorer white communities of the South, the quest for salvation and perfection did not prompt the creation of reform organizations like those that attracted the Grimké sisters and Theodore Weld.

Looking back, we can marvel that Americans of the 1830s and 1840s did not tremble with anticipation at the coming of the "irrepressible conflict" known to us as the Civil War. Omens abounded; signs were everywhere; the fire bell in the night had, it seems in retrospect, been ringing for decades. Yet the men and women of the South were no more prescient about their futures than we are about our own. In 1850, as in 1830, even the man who became the first and only president of the Confederacy did not predict the conflict that would change his life, and the life of all Americans, black and white, forever.

When the war ended, generals and political leaders on both sides of the conflict put their memories on paper, hoping not only to vindicate their role in the crisis but also to impress upon posterity a version of events they believed to be true. Surely one motive for their memoirs was to lay to rest the raw images of death, destruction, searing rage, and hatred, and to honor the touching scenes of kindness, bravery, and decency they had witnessed or been part of. But women, too, had witnessed the rising political animosity, the brilliant political debates, the broken friendships, the enthusiasm of young men who donned their uniforms and the tragedy of their maiming and death, the inflation and deprivation born of civil war, and, in the end, the humiliation of defeat or the satisfaction of victory. Their versions of the long decades between 1830 and 1876 offer insights that arise from a different angle of vision, a lens imposed by the era's notions of womanhood. Most of these observer-participants recorded their thoughts in diaries, private musings not intended for strangers' eyes, or in letters to family and friends. But Varina Howell Davis, wife of Jefferson Davis, became a public figure in 1861 and found a public voice, first as an adviser to the president of the Confederacy, then in the struggle to win her husband's freedom after the war, in her ambitious memoir designed to vindicate his character and his cause, and finally in her brief but liberating career as a journalist and patron of the arts in New York City.

Twelve

FROM THE BRIARS TO THE HURRICANE

Varina Banks Howell and Jefferson Davis

THE HOWELL HOME, THE BRIARS, sat high on a bluff near Natchez, Mississippi. The ground beside the house sloped on the west to a dry bayou where pines, oaks, magnolia trees, and the wild roses that gave this attractive home its name grew in profusion. The Briars was, by Varina Howell Davis's own admission, a large old-fashioned house, and in many ways the thirteen Howells who eventually inhabited it were a large and old-fashioned family. William Burr Howell, the master of the house, grew up in the shadow of a highly successful and socially prominent father, Major Richard Howell. Major Howell was a Revolutionary War veteran and showed his patriotic colors early by destroying a cargo of tea that loyalists had dared to unload at Greenwich, New Jersey. Though he had been born in Delaware, after independence was won Major Howell practiced law in New Jersey and rose to become chancellor and later governor of his adopted state. He married Keziah Burr, a Quaker, who could count as her distant relative the infamous Aaron Burr. Their son William served in the War of 1812, and when it ended, the restless, optimistic spirit of the postwar Era of Good Feelings carried him far from his birthplace. He settled in Natchez, where he met and married Margaret Louisa Kempe. It was a somewhat irregular match, for William was a young man with an uncertain future and Margaret was the daughter of one of this Mississippi River town's most distinguished citizens. William's pedigree assuaged all fears, however. To help the young couple out, the bride's father financed the construction of The Briars; as things turned out, William Howell would need assistance from his family for the rest of his life. But what William lacked in luck or effectiveness, he made up for in charm and an easy, open affection for his many children. Margaret Kempe Howell remained devoted to her hapless husband, making do when the business ventures he hoped would secure his fortune came to nothing.[1]

On May 7, 1826, Margaret and William's second child and first daughter
was born. They named her Varina Banks Howell, and as she grew up they
gave her what Natchez's social elite considered the proper education and
training for a young girl. At the age of ten Varina was enrolled in Madame
Grelaud's school in Philadelphia, where she studied for two terms. During
the same year, another Southerner gone north to Philadelphia, Angelina
Grimké, published her *Appeal to the Christian Women of the South*, but
Varina surely knew nothing of this or any other abolitionist propaganda.
By the following year, Varina had returned to Natchez, her formal education ended. Fortunately for her, however, a family friend took up where
Madame Grelaud ended and for twelve years Varina's natural intelligence
was honed through the study of Latin, French, literature, and moral philos-
ophy with her family's bachelor friend, Judge George Winchester.

Throughout her life, Varina acknowledged the powerful influence of
this mentor, whom she called "Great Heart." He taught her more, she
wrote, than the proper conjugation of French irregular verbs; he taught her
"the pure high standard of right, of which his course was the exemplar."
Winchester's devotion ensured that Varina Banks Howell would be something of an intellectual, often more vice than virtue in the world she
expected to inhabit. But if the judge trained her mind, it was her grandmother Kempe who passed down to her the quick and sometimes biting
wit and the keen amusement at human foibles that won Varina both admirers and enemies.[2]

Varina passed many of her childhood days in the garden, her nose
buried in books, for "Great Heart" was a demanding teacher. When she was
seventeen, however, she was excited by an invitation to spend the Christmas holidays at the home of her parents' close friend Joseph Davis. Davis
was one of Mississippi's success stories: a lawyer and a planter, he had
amassed more than five thousand acres, many of which he had doled out to
his children in a manner befitting a family patriarch. Davis's connection to
the Howell family was intimate: it was Joseph who had introduced William
to Margaret, and the young couple had named their firstborn in his honor.
Although his wealth and prestige made him a formidable man in Mississippi society, to his godson and namesake, and to all the Howell children
who followed, he was simply "Uncle Joe." Varina adored him, but the
appeal of the invitation, no doubt, was its novelty. Varina set out eagerly
with Judge Winchester as her chaperone for the boat trip up the Mississippi. Her first stop was the home of Davis's oldest daughter, a plantation
known as Diamond Place, thirteen miles north of Uncle Joe's elegant
home, The Hurricane.

A few days after her arrival, Uncle Joe's younger brother, Jefferson, stopped on his way to Vicksburg, carrying the message that all was ready for Varina at The Hurricane. Varina was both impressed and bewildered by the attractive Mr. Jefferson Davis, for he cut a graceful, youthful figure on horseback, yet she could not determine if he was young or old. She wrote to her thirty-seven-year-old mother about the problem: "He looks both at times; but I believe he is old, for from what I hear he is only two years younger than you are." The observation may have been tactless, but in the 1830s and 1840s, it was not entirely unreasonable. In the early nineteenth century, the signs of age came quickly, even to elite women. Frequent pregnancies not only destroyed girlish figures but also leached calcium from women's bodies. By the age of thirty a planter's wife might have made the painful visit to the dentist many times to have teeth extracted, and her body would show the wear and tear of repeated childbirth.[3]

Margaret Howell might have been amused by her daughter's letter but not surprised that Varina found Joe Davis's brother an attractive man. On this, mother and daughter agreed. Some eighteen years before, when she was pregnant with Varina, Margaret had met Jefferson Davis. He was a young West Point cadet, full of boyish charm and mischief, with a decided preference for whiling away the hours in the local tavern rather than the library. Like her daughter, Margaret was impressed with the young man's "graceful strong figure." But the Jefferson Davis who fascinated Varina was no longer an immature young man; he was a thirty-five-year-old planter and budding politician. He was also a widower with a tragic past.[4]

Sometime in 1832, Lieutenant Jefferson Davis met the first, and many still believe the only, love of his life. He was stationed at Prairie du Chien, assigned to the staff of the commanding officer, Colonel Zachary Taylor. Here he fell in love with the colonel's daughter, Sarah Knox Taylor. In Knox, as she was called, Davis believed he had found his soul mate, the "beautiful and gentle" woman who would soothe him and share his fireside. "Often I long to lay my head upon that breast which beats in union with my own," the young suitor wrote in December of 1834. Knox returned his ardor. But Colonel Taylor was determined to prevent the marriage of his daughter to a career soldier, for he knew well the difficulties his own wife had endured. Although the colonel liked Davis personally, he refused to give his blessing to their marriage. In fact, Taylor took the precautionary step of forbidding his daughter to see Jefferson.[5]

But Jefferson Davis was equally determined to make Knox his wife. While Knox continued to plead with her father for his blessing, the couple carried on their courtship in secret, enlisting friends to help them arrange trysts and "accidental" encounters. Months-long separations while Jefferson was on duty seemed only to intensify their attachment. For two years, Jefferson Davis waited and worried; Knox pleaded and cajoled. The circumstances were trying, but they were also romantic; every effort to frustrate the young couple's wishes seemed to deepen the attraction. In June 1834, Jefferson took the desperate step of resigning his military commission, hoping to eliminate the colonel's major objection to their marriage, but to no avail. In the end, they defied her father and married without his consent.

The ceremony was held in Kentucky, at the home of Knox's aunt. Neither of her parents attended and no one from his family was present, for Jefferson's father had been dead for over a decade, his mother was infirm, and the wedding was held on such short notice that none of his brothers and sisters had time to attend. But the groom was eager to show his new bride to his family, and thus the couple soon headed to Mississippi and Joe Davis's Hurricane plantation. Perhaps as a wedding gift, brother Joseph turned over plantation land to Jefferson.

But a bright future turned quickly grim. It was chill and fever season on the Mississippi, and although Jefferson took the precaution of making his next stop his sister's less disease-prone plantation, Locust Grove, both he and his wife were stricken with malaria. The family believed that his case was more severe, and as a precaution, they nursed the couple in separate rooms. It was Knox, however, who soon became delirious. (It was said that as her fever rose and her condition worsened, she began to sing one of her favorite songs, "Fairy Bells," but this family story is unlikely: "Fairy Bells" was written in 1839, four years after Knox's death.) Jefferson struggled to her bedside, only to find her dying. On September 15, 1835, only three months after he had wed, Jefferson Davis became a widower. He returned to Mississippi, and to life as a virtual recluse on his plantation, Brierfield. Those who had known him as the sociable, sometimes raucous cadet at West Point would not recognize the somber, solitary figure the widower had become.[6]

It had been eight years since Knox's death when the now thirty-five-year-old Jefferson Davis carried his message to the seventeen-year-old Varina Howell. It was not their last encounter, however; they would meet again at The Hurricane.

Thirteen

"THE DESIRE I HAVE TO BE WITH YOU
EVERY DAY AND ALL DAY"

The Courtship of Jefferson Davis and Varina Howell

THE HURRICANE BORE EVERY SIGN of a Mississippi planter's successful quest for gentility. The house stood in the midst of acres of oak trees draped with Spanish moss. The main section of the house had three floors, including the attic, each with four rooms apiece. A guest, entering through a wide hall, could see a drawing room and a tea room to the right; to the left lay a bedroom and an office. If the rooms on the right bore the mark of the Davis women, the office was a decidedly masculine domain. Here, for eight years, Jefferson Davis had sat with his brother Joseph, discussing everything from crops to the law, politics, and literature. Wide galleries ran around most of the house, both upstairs and downstairs. On the west side, Joe Davis had added an annex of two large rooms: the lower one served as a dining room, while the upper was known as the music room.

The music room was the gathering place of the younger members of the Davis family and their guests. In it they sang, played charades, and gave spontaneous concerts. Joe Davis clearly relished his role as patriarch of the large and extended family that lived at or visited The Hurricane, for next to his bedroom he kept a small storeroom stocked with treats for his many young nieces, nephews, cousins, and grandchildren. A barn and a stable with thirty horse stalls stood on the east side of the house. An impressive garden of rare roses and plants filled the area directly behind the house, and beyond this, the Davis family and their slaves had cultivated eight acres of peach, fig, and apple trees. Half a century after she first saw the house, Varina could remember every detail of The Hurricane, down to the family portraits on the music room wall.[1]

Varina joined easily into the boisterous holiday activities at The Hurricane. She played charades and other games in the music room and accompanied the singing on the piano. She took her turn reading aloud to Uncle

Joe and Jefferson when the two men grew tired of reading themselves, and she won compliments on her pronunciation and translation of the French and Latin phrases she encountered. When the Davises, loyal Democrats all, teased Varina about her family's Whig affiliation, she met their taunts with good humor—and not a little curiosity. How, she wondered, could a respectable family support a political party known to cater to the lower classes? In the Howell household, Kentucky's Henry Clay, founder of the Whig Party, was revered as the advocate of forward-thinking programs to develop the national economy and as a champion of the entrepreneurial classes. Yet here was Uncle Joe, praising the party that carried the banner of universal white male suffrage, and here was the younger Mr. Davis, just back from his first Democratic caucus in Vicksburg. For the moment, however, political differences seemed to matter far less than the strong attraction growing between Varina and Jefferson.

Had Joe Davis invited Varina to The Hurricane in order to draw Jefferson out of his long period of mourning? Had Jefferson Davis decided on his own that it was time to find a wife and start a family? On this, the record is silent. Yet one thing was clear: the timing proved to be perfect. Jeff Davis had already shown signs he was on the mend; he had, after all, made a tentative entrance into Mississippi politics. All that remained, it seemed, was for someone to revive his long-dormant emotions. Varina did just that. To Jefferson Davis, the seventeen-year-old Varina Howell seemed a perfect combination of beauty and intelligence. She was more than physically attractive, although she was surely that. She was tall and graceful, and her thick dark hair framed her face well and accentuated her strikingly large, dark, and deeply set eyes. But, as Jefferson came to appreciate during their long, engaging conversations, she also had "a fine mind."[2]

A courtship began that was both intense and serious. It was pursued, in large part, on horseback, during daily rides that provided the couple a measure of privacy from the prying eyes of family and friends. They could be glimpsed riding across The Hurricane's landscape, he with his military erectness and surprising grace, she with her plumed hat, sidesaddle upon the dark bay from Joe's stable. By the time her visit ended in February, the couple were engaged.

That month, Varina returned home to share the news with her parents, but the engagement was not greeted as warmly as she had hoped—or expected. Her mother was wary. Not only was Jefferson twice her daughter's age, but his tragic first marriage was likely to cast a long shadow over their relationship. Varina, her mother feared, would always be second in a heart that had been given first, and fully, to the bride of his youth. There were social objections as well: although the Howells were not wealthy, their family tree included governors on one side and Virginia elites on the other. When William and Margaret had announced *their* engagement some two decades earlier, a friend had remarked, "What a clutch of trueblues there will be between the blood of Kempe and Howell!" The same could not be said of a Howell-Davis union: though Joe Davis had prospered and Jefferson was likely to succeed as well, they could boast no "trueblues" in their lineage. Their attachment to the Democratic Party seemed telling proof of their ordinary background.[3]

For Jefferson Davis, history thus seemed about to repeat itself. He had met with parental objections before, but this time the all-too-familiar hesitations and doubts did nothing to heighten his desire or intensify the romance. He was a grown man, not a youth, and he would not battle to prove his worth. His impatience and carefully contained resentment showed through in his letter to Varina on March 8, 1844: "But why shall I not come to see you. In addition to the desire I have to be with you every day and all day, it seems to me but proper and necessary to justify my writing to you that I should announce to your parents my wish to marry you." Varina's reply is lost, but in the end, quite different family circumstances delayed Jefferson's visit. His brother-in-law, Judge David Bradford, was ambushed and killed by a disgruntled plaintiff, and Jefferson had to bring his grieving sister Amanda and her seven children to The Hurricane to live. By the time a trip to Natchez was possible, Varina's mother had apparently relented.[4]

Yet Margaret's misgivings about a widower's devotion to her daughter made a lasting impression on Varina. No sentimental novel of the era could ask for a more compelling plot than Jefferson Davis's romantic past, with its challenging courtship and its tragic death of a young bride. Long after her husband's death, Varina would warn a friend against his daughter Belle marrying a widower. "I am not pleased," she wrote, "with the widower prospect. It is as you know but a burnt out vessel offered to a fresh young creature like Belle after a successful love has been identified with one's soul life, and removed by death. I gave the best & all of my life to a girdled tree, it was live oak, & was good for any purpose except for blossom & fruit, and I am not willing for Belle to be content with anything less than the whole of a man's heart." For Varina, Knox Taylor Davis proved to be a ghost that decades of marriage could not dispel.[5]

Haunted by the thought of Knox, Varina seemed to require endless reassurances from her fiancé. Jefferson failed to appreciate the depth of her concern or to take it seriously. Instead, he attributed her insecurity to an anxious and overemotional nature, to the high-strung character that he believed often marked the female sex. He indulged her need, yet his affirmation carried a hint of impatience: "If after the unlimited declarations I have made to you of my love I could neglect you, it would not become you to give me another thought."[6]

"I send you my deepest, truest, purest love," Jefferson Davis wrote that September. This love for Varina was genuine, but in 1844 Davis was no young lieutenant on the frontier, recklessly in love; he was a grown man, a planter with financial concerns, a number of slaves to house, feed, and clothe, obligations to an ever-expanding extended family, and a promising presence on the Mississippi political scene. He intended to make her his wife, but he had competing priorities. He was busy campaigning for the Democratic presidential candidates until late November and so did not press for a spring or summer wedding. Varina, on the other hand, had no external concerns to distract her from romance and no family or occupational obligations to compete with her expectations of—and fears about—marriage. As the months passed, she vacillated between a pride in her fiancé that bordered on hero worship and a rising anxiety about the impending momentous change in her life. By summer, she had suffered a nervous collapse.[7]

Varina's response to the impending marriage may have been extreme, but her anxiety was not irrational. Marriage was the most important decision facing any young American woman in the 1840s, just as it had been for their mothers and grandmothers before them. Where they would live, and in what comfort or neediness they would live, depended upon the husband they chose. Many a young bride and expectant mother found herself far from family, church, and friends, carried west by a restless husband or a career soldier. And many a young wife discovered too late that her husband was unambitious, incompetent, unlucky, or profligate. In a society where divorce was rare, if it was allowed at all, even a girl of eighteen understood that her future was ransomed to another on the day she said "I do." Whatever her future as Mrs. Jefferson Davis might bring, one thing was certain: Varina's life would change dramatically. She would be leaving a lively, cultured community for a life of rural isolation. She would be exchanging a comfortable, attractive home for the relatively crude and architecturally flawed house Davis had designed and built for himself. She would be separated from a warm and loving family and thrust into an intimate relationship with a man twice her age.

Varina's anxiety was born of the grand expectations, deep fears, and as-yet-untested abilities of youth—emotions and conditions foreign to Jefferson Davis. He did his best to bolster her confidence, assuring her, in somewhat patronizing tones, of his confidence that she would prove "fully competent to meet the exigencies and yield to the necessities our fortune imposes." It was a far from rosy view of the future, but it reflected the stoicism his own experiences had produced and that sustained him in later years. Varina may have accepted this stoicism as wisdom, but when he reminded her it was "well however to be prepared for the worst which is within the range of probabilities as blessed are they who expect nothing, for surely they shall not be disappointed," such a dismal view could not have been comforting for an eighteen-year-old Southern girl.[8]

November came and went and then December, and still the engagement dragged on. Almost a year had passed since the couple had met when Davis penned a terse, formal note, written as he returned home from a visit to Natchez. Because Varina's letters from the year are lost, it is unclear whether some crisis had developed, and if so, what was its cause. Yet by February it had resolved itself. Jefferson made another trip to Natchez that month and within a few days of his arrival, on February 26, 1845, it was decided that the couple should marry immediately. A minister was called to the Howell home, two bridesmaids were summoned, and a wedding dinner was prepared. Varina, thin and pale from her months of on-and-off illness, wore a simple white embroidered India muslin dress trimmed with lace. In her thick hair, she wore one rose, and her only jewelry was the necklace, brooch, and pendant earrings of cut glass that had belonged to her grandmother Kempe. For Jefferson, this impromptu ceremony must have brought a sense of déjà vu; it was the second time he would marry without a single member of his own family present to wish him well.[9]

Almost immediately, the couple left Natchez, boarding a riverboat that would take them to Bayou Sara, Louisiana, where one of Jefferson's sisters lived—and where Knox Taylor Davis had died. Here, Jefferson Davis and his new bride visited the grave of his first wife. Varina looked on while her husband placed flowers upon the grave. What should Varina have made of this pilgrimage? Had they come at her suggestion, an act of generosity on the part of a devoted wife? Had Jefferson insisted upon it, revealing an inexcusable insensitivity? Was it an act of unthinking cruelty—or a moment of closure? Or was this visit to the cemetery of a piece with the sentimentality of the era and the recognition that early death was a frequent reality of life along the Mississippi? We will never know, for neither Varina nor Jefferson left any explanation of this strange beginning to their honeymoon journey.[10]

Fourteen

"CALMER, DISCREETER, HAPPIER & LOVELIER"

The Months at Brierfield

AFTER BAYOU SARA, JEFFERSON AND VARINA made their way down the Mississippi, visiting other members of the extended Davis family as they headed to the final stop on their honeymoon journey: New Orleans. Here, perhaps the memory of the disturbing visit to Knox's grave was softened by the elegance of their rooms at the St. Charles Hotel and the company of the sophisticated and interesting people they encountered in this most cosmopolitan of Southern cities. From New Orleans, the couple made their way, at last, to Brierfield.[1]

Varina was charmed by her new home, despite the oddity of the house itself. Brierfield was an experiment in architecture gone wrong, with its oversize doors that made the house shake when they were opened, its chest-high windowsills, and its cavernous hearth that seemed more suited to the seventeenth century than the nineteenth. But here the couple's isolation from the rest of society helped re-create the intimacy of their courtship. Together, they worked in the garden, rode, and shared their views on books and politics. In her memoirs, Varina recalled these months as an idyll, but Jefferson's letters to Margaret Howell suggest that his wife was far from recovered from the exhausting anxiety of the previous year. In March 1845, he reported, "Varina has not been entirely well for many days together, though she says her health has been better than heretofore, she is much thinner than when she left you and appears sometimes very languid." With unexpected and appealing humor, he added that her condition was probably due to "the company she habitually keeps, being your corresponding son and a mongrel puppy, in both of whom by a power of vision peculiarly her own she sees highly valuable and loveable qualities." Jefferson himself seemed more content than he had been in many years. Although they lived "humbly," he was confident that he and Varina could not be more happy "if the walls of a castle sheltered us." Indeed, despite

Varina's fragile health, he reported to her mother that his wife grew "calmer, discreeter, happier & lovelier with each passing day."[2]

Over the years, Varina's health was often a matter of concern. It was generally agreed that she suffered from a congenital heart ailment that produced periods of weakness, discomfort, and lethargy. For this, nineteenth-century medicine could offer little relief and no cure. Yet Jefferson attributed much of his wife's health problems to her emotional makeup. Like many nineteenth-century men and women, he looked to temperament and "humours" to explain the body's failings. His wife, he believed, was a victim of her own tendency to "nervous excitement," and thus a "calmer, discreeter" Varina would surely be a healthier Varina.[3]

Perhaps Jeff's contentment in the early months of his marriage blinded him to one cause of his wife's lapses into both "languid" states and "nervous excitement": homesickness. The simple fact was that Varina missed her family terribly. Unlike him, she had not spent years in solitude, growing accustomed to separation from others. And, unlike him, she did not have an extended family close by. Her only connection to the Howells was the erratic and unpredictable mail service. If the river rose too high, the mail boat would not stop, and weeks might go by without word from her mother or father. When letters did arrive, they sometimes prompted "crying spells," brought on by good news and bad. Baskets of flowers sent by her mother brought on tears; reports of illnesses or accidents did the same. "I took such a crying spell at the thoughts of Father's accident," she wrote in the same year her husband declared their contentment, adding that word of her younger brother's sickness "swelled the torrent of my tears." The news, she confessed to her mother, had made her head ache and her stomach queasy. Jeff might report with satisfaction on her improving health, but Varina's own letters revealed the difficulty of adjusting to life as a wife—even a happy one—rather than a daughter or sister.[4]

Although he did not look to his "humours" to explain his own illnesses, Jefferson's health was as precarious as Varina's. The malaria that killed his first wife lingered throughout his life, subjecting him to recurrent bouts of fever, chills, and exhaustion. He endured painful and damaging eye inflammations that threatened to leave him blind. War wounds would cripple him for many months, and his brutal imprisonment following the collapse of the Confederacy would leave him frail and physically broken for the rest of his life. And, if Varina suffered from "nervous excitement," her husband's carefully maintained calm took its toll as well. In times of severe stress he became an insomniac, and the lack of sleep combined with a depressed appetite often incapacitated him.

There were, in fact, few periods of respite for the Davises from poor health—whether physical or psychological in origin. But there were few periods of robust health for most of their friends and acquaintances either, especially those who lived in the humid, hot incubator for malaria and dysentery known as the Cotton Belt. Even in the healthier climates of the North, epidemics could still rage through crowded cities. Doctors did their best, but early-nineteenth-century medicine was limited and, to our modern minds, almost barbaric. What scientific medicine there was in Varina's day was heroic medicine, based on a conviction that all diseases resulted from an excess of fluids. The cure was to diminish this excess by bloodletting, purging, and cupping (placing heated glass cups over small incisions made in the skin). Most diagnoses rested on little more than pulse, skin tone, and urine color, and there were few medicines available to the ailing patient in this century before "wonder drugs" and antibiotics. A patient suffering from syphilis might be given mercury; malaria was treated with quinine; ipecac was prescribed for amebic dysentery and digitalis for heart failure. Changes of scenery and ocean voyages were recommended for a variety of illnesses from depression to heart palpitations. Medical advancements were virtually nonexistent during the antebellum years, when romanticism and evangelicalism produced a bias against empirical research. Even among the American elite, quackery reigned as the solution to physical ailments of all types, and water cures, electric wraps, radical diets, and vegetable compounds and concoctions were the preferred medical treatments of the day. Small wonder that the letters to and from family members usually contained reports on health and illness.[5]

Varina's separation from the Howells might have been easier if she were busy starting a family of her own. But in this she was disappointed. Despite Jefferson's steady presence, she had not become pregnant. Her mother had pressed for news of a grandchild by offering to send Varina a "comfortable" dress, but Varina advised her it was not necessary. "My dear Mother," she wrote that July, "I do not need a 'comfortable' dress, and think I shall probably never *require* one." She conceded that both she and Jefferson regretted their "being condemned to live in *single blessedness*" but assured Margaret Howell that they would get over it. It would be several years before their "single blessedness" ended with the birth of a son. In the meantime, the Davises slowly began to fill their home with Howell children. Varina's older brother Joseph had arrived by July, and for the rest of their lives, a parade of

Howell boys and girls, young men and women, would become members of their household. They would keep her company during her husband's many absences.[6]

The first of those absences, brief though it was, began that fall when Jefferson Davis was elected to the United States House of Representatives. Varina was proud, but less than enthusiastic. The life of a politician—and a politician's wife—was a bitter one, she feared; "it meant long absences, pecuniary depletion from ruinous absenteeism, illness from exposure, misconceptions, defamation of character; everything which darkens the sunlight and contracts the happy sphere of the home." If it was a bleak view, it would prove all too true for the Davises.[7]

Despite her misgivings, Varina had to admit that their political life began triumphantly. The junior representative from Mississippi received the honor of introducing the leading Democrat of the day, John C. Calhoun, who was scheduled to arrive in Vicksburg for a rally soon after Davis's election. Jefferson set out on horseback for the state capital at once. Varina was left behind to pack their belongings and close up the house; she would join him in Vicksburg later, arriving with Jefferson's twenty-year-old niece, Mary Jane Bradford, or "Malie," and her own brother Joseph, both of whom would accompany the Davises to Washington.

That November, Joseph described their Vicksburg adventure in an enthusiastic letter to his mother. They arrived, he wrote, to a city in which cannon were firing and drums were beating all day. "The whole town was in a commotion," he wrote, and "every body seemed excited, some with liquor, others with politics, among the most conspicuous of whom was my Brother Jeff." The source of the excitement was obvious: Calhoun, the champion of states' rights, was coming to town. Jefferson's introduction was, Joseph reported, "a beautiful and appropriate address." After Calhoun spoke, an elegant reception was held, at which, Joseph was pleased to report, there was old-fashioned dancing. Nineteen-year-old Varina sat on the sidelines, carefully playing the role her husband expected of her: the proper matron. Yet she did not fade into the background that evening, for Calhoun was instantly charmed by the beautiful and intelligent young woman whom Mr. Davis introduced as his wife. The guest of honor spent the entire evening by her side. Proudly, Joseph wrote to his mother, "He told me just before he left that . . . although she was so young he had never met a lady with whose manners he was more pleased or whose talents he had a higher opinion."[8]

In her memoirs, Varina recalled the evening vividly. Her Whig background prepared her to dislike the great "Nullifier," yet she was immediately won over by the old man. "I felt," she wrote many decades later, "like rising up to do homage to a king among men." During the course of their conversation, she confided to him that she missed her mother; he replied that he had a daughter her age whom he loved deeply. With this exchange of confidences, a lifelong friendship began and Varina's Whig prejudice began to fade.[9]

Fifteen

"HOW GRAND AND *BLASÉ* THE PEOPLE ALL LOOKED"

The First Washington Experience

THE TRIP FROM VICKSBURG TO WASHINGTON was as memorable as their triumphant evening with Calhoun—but far less pleasant. Today, Mississippi is only a few hours away from the District of Columbia, but the transportation revolution in the 1840s had gone no further than steamboats and railroads. To get to Washington, the Davis entourage would have to travel by conventional boat up the Mississippi and then head east, by boat where possible or by stagecoach or wagon. Cold weather had set in, and ice and wind soon forced the travelers to abandon the river and board a rough wood sled to continue the journey. They huddled together atop their luggage as the sled carried them along a narrow road covered with frozen snow. As they were making the steep and dangerous ascent up the side of a mountain, the sled tipped over and they found themselves falling down a twenty-foot bank below the road. No one escaped unscathed. By the time the party reached Wheeling, West Virginia, Jefferson Davis's feet were frozen. The next leg of the journey was taken in a stagecoach, but the snow was so deep its wheels frequently slipped to the edge of the many precipices along the way. They subsisted entirely, Varina recalled, on meals of wurst covered in maple syrup. After three weeks, they finally entered Washington, "more dead than alive."[1]

Even by nineteenth-century standards, Washington was still a small town in 1845. While New York City boasted almost four hundred thousand residents, the nation's capital had only about thirty-three thousand people during the months when the Congress was in session. The number dropped dramatically during congressional recesses, and during the humid, rainy months of summer, many Washingtonians fled to the seaside or countryside or to rented homes and local hotels in the cooler climates of New England. Yet there could be no denying the electricity in the air of the Pierre L'Enfant–planned Federal City. Many, if not most, of the country's brightest, most powerful, and distinguished citizens gathered here to make laws, lobby for office and funding, and debate the major issues of the day. The city was a magnet for the wealthy, the sophisticated, and the influential, and despite her social triumph in Vicksburg, Varina Howell Davis felt like a naive girl from the countryside. "How grand and *blasé* the people all looked to these weary country girls," she recalled in her memoirs.[2]

Within a few weeks, the Davises had settled in and joined one of the congressional "messes," groups of like-minded politicians and their families who took their meals together. In their mess were two Mississippi representatives and their "pleasant kindly wives," George Jones (who was, like Jefferson Davis, an alumnus of Lexington's Transylvania University), and several Northern representatives. While meals were lively, Varina had few other opportunities to test herself in social situations, for her husband immediately threw himself into the study of the issues and policies likely to be debated in the upcoming session of the House. Many evenings, he worked until the wee hours of the following morning. Varina quickly realized that this was a mistake—and one he would make for the rest of his political career. Her husband, she knew, never understood the role of Washington's social life in greasing the wheels of its political life. In this, he might have learned a useful lesson from the founder of his party, Thomas Jefferson, who was a master at solidifying loyalties, winning support for legislation, and mounting campaigns against his political enemies over intimate private dinners. But Davis refused to throw himself into the whirl of dinners, receptions, and parties that occupied the evenings of many of his more astute colleagues. Instead, he approached politics much as he seemed to approach life after Knox's death: as a moral and intellectual endeavor, a test of individual intelligence, individual honor, and what the founding fathers might have called "disinterested patriotism." While he would earn the respect of many political allies—and enemies—for his intelligence, his honesty, and his devotion to the principles of the Constitution as he understood them, his avoidance of both the Washington social scene and later that of Richmond would lead many to consider him aloof and rigid.[3]

Varina worried about the demanding schedule her husband insisted on keeping. When he would not go out, she brought entertainment into their home. She persuaded him to co-host a "little hop," a dancing party to which she and a group of other wives invited "some sweet looking girls, some intelligent looking young men." Everyone had a delightful time, she reported to her mother, "at least every body but me." Her husband remained in the next room, with "the hottest fever I ever felt," and though she managed to dance twice, she had to excuse herself to nurse her sick husband.[4]

Despite Jefferson's distaste for social life, Varina believed he had a natural charm that eluded her. "Wherever he went," she told her mother, "he left a smiling face," while she, on the other hand, presented an "embarrassed, angry-looking" face to the world. Although later in her life some women would describe Varina as haughty, most of the men she met in Washington seemed to enjoy her intelligence and wit as much as John C. Calhoun did. The eccentric intellectual George Bancroft relished her company, making her feel brilliant, she wrote, just because he talked to her. Vice President George M. Dallas and Charles Ingersoll, two of Washington's leading Democrats, spent an evening in serious conversation with Varina, debating the relative merits of Byron and Wordsworth and of Dante and Virgil. In her memoir, Varina remembered the evening with pleasure, calling it the "most delightful evening of my early youth." Although she continued to believe her husband was more socially gifted than herself, Varina's own sophistication grew steadily. Jeff might feel it necessary to intervene when President Tyler spoke to her—excusing her in patronizing terms by declaring, "My little wife is trying to be a statesman"—but Varina's astute judgment of both politics and political figures would have made her tutor, Judge Winchester, proud.[5]

Varina was quick to appreciate the intelligence and talent of the nation's leadership in the 1840s—and equally quick to critique their character. Gathered in the Senate were the likes of the Massachusetts lawyer and orator Daniel Webster, who shared leadership of the Whig party with Henry Clay; the Missouri Democrat Thomas Hart Benton, whose long career included newspaper editor, lawyer, and author; Benton's bitter enemy, the impressive architect of the "American Plan," Henry Clay; Lewis Cass, war veteran, former minister to France, and critic of slavery; the obese but brilliant Dixon H. Lewis of Alabama; Tennessee planter John Bell, whose defection from the Democratic Party during Andrew Jackson's presidency earned him the sobriquet "the Great Apostate"; the towering Sam Houston of Texas; and the aging former president John Quincy Adams. Of Webster she wrote, "No words can describe the first impression he made upon me"; his "massive, overhanging forehead" and his "great speculative, observant eyes full of lambent fire" awed her as much as his oratory. She declared Benton a man of "rare personal dignity," despite the fact that later in his career his unruly behavior on the floor of Congress almost merited him a censure. Whatever temper he may have had, Benton won Varina's affection because of his devotion to his paralyzed wife. Every day, she wrote, he would leave the Senate to take his wife outside for fresh air and pick a bouquet of flowers for her. She described Lewis Cass as "a very large, fleshy person," as "blunt as he was big," but discovered he was "one of the kindest-hearted men in the world." The even more obese Dixon Lewis weighed close to five hundred pounds and sat in a chair especially constructed to hold his bulk. She did not like Sam Houston, for despite his good looks, she judged him nothing more than a shallow flirt. When introduced to a woman, Varina recalled, the Texan would present her with a little wooden heart, carved by his own hand during the Senate debates. The gift was accompanied by the too bold appeal, "Lady, let me give you my heart."[6]

Despite the luster of Washington's political leadership, Varina was confident that Jefferson Davis was a match for most of the men in Congress. She sent her family copies of his speeches, accompanying them with her own praise for his eloquence and erudition. Yet she was deeply concerned that her husband would not survive the grueling regimen he set for himself. He had not been in the government two months when she shared her growing anxiety about his health with her mother. "I feel so fearful—so uneasy—he has not been well since we arrived here," she confessed to Margaret Howell. "I feel as if he would not stand it another year. I had fearful enough anticipations of what a public life would be but they were nothing like the reality. Jeff is not away from me, but he is not so happy as he used to be. His mind," she declared, "wants rest."[7]

But rest was not likely to come, for his first session of Congress was marked by political crises. In 1845, President Polk had drawn a line in the sand against British claims to Oregon territory, insisting on a U.S.-Canadian border that ran along the 54'40" line. There was a good deal of bravado-laced rhetoric in the House over the issue, although it was fairly quickly agreed to resolve the problem at the bargaining table rather than on the battlefield. The problem of Texas was less easily resolved. The recent annexation of Texas had increased the tensions between slaveholding and nonslaveholding states. Although both the South and the North embraced the notion of "Manifest Destiny," each push westward seemed to heighten the anxiety over a balance between slave and free states within the national government. In his first speech on the floor of the House, Jefferson Davis placed the blame for these rising tensions squarely upon the shoulders of abolitionists. "When ignorance, led by fanatic hate, and armed by all uncharitableness, assails a domestic institution of the South," he declared,

"I try to forgive, for the sake of the righteous among the wicked." But internal tensions were not the only problem; a war with Mexico over the Texas-Mexico boundary loomed on the horizon. And this, even Davis would have to concede, was not the result of abolitionist propaganda.[8]

In December 1845, Congress passed the joint resolution that made Texas the twenty-eighth state of the Union. In it, they established the Rio Grande as the new state's southern border. But the Mexican government rejected this boundary; indeed, despite the Texas revolution, Mexico continued to consider Texas a Mexican province. President Polk made some attempt to settle the Texas border dispute through negotiation, but he dispatched American troops to Louisiana—to settle by arms what might not be settled by diplomacy. The president also made the provocative pledge that his government would support any effort by citizens in California to establish their independence from Mexico. By April 1846, Mexico had declared war.

Americans were deeply divided over this conflict, and the divisions followed both sectional and party lines. Southerners and Democrats embraced the war; New Englanders and many Whigs opposed it. Abolitionists warned that the war proved the country was dominated by the same "Slave Power" that had ensured passage of the gag rule and that now risked the lives of American soldiers in order to see slavery move farther west, while Southerners sprang to the defense of Texas—and its slaveholding citizens. In the House, congressmen debated how best to wage a winning war.

Jefferson Davis took the floor to argue the need for more professional soldiers and better military education for those who made the army their career. To drive home his point he asked his fellow representatives whether they thought a blacksmith or a tailor could achieve the same results as a professional soldier. For Davis, the choice of civilian occupations was random, but to Andrew Johnson, who had once earned a meager living as a tailor, the words stung. The Tennessee congressman rose from his seat to demand an apology for the insult from this member of an "illegitimate, swaggering bastard scrub aristocracy." A somewhat bewildered Davis tried to make amends. In the midst of crisis, the odd exchange seemed little more than a by-product of the tension war produced. But, looking back, an aging Varina would mark the moment as fraught with serious consequences in her husband's life.[9]

In May 1846, however, Johnson's rage was less significant than the honors Mississippi was about to bestow upon Jefferson Davis. The state legislature called upon Varina's husband to lead its troops into war against

Mexico. Jefferson's enthusiasm was equaled only by Varina's despair. She pleaded with him to refuse the commission. For a brief moment, Varina believed she had won her argument, for Jeff promised he would not don the uniform. But he could not—or would not—honor his promise; duty to country and the political rewards of military heroism trumped the desire to calm the fears of an anxious wife. Six months after she had arrived in Washington, Varina was back in Mississippi and her husband had gone to war.[10]

Sixteen

"THE HEART AT LAST, IF IT IS WELL GOVERNED, MAKES THE HEAVEN"

War, Injury, and Domestic Discord

JEFF DAVIS CONSIDERED THE OPPORTUNITY to lead the Mississippi troops "a real compliment." Varina considered it a possible death sentence. On June 6, she wrote to her mother of her first major marital conflict—and her sad defeat. "Today I am so miserable I feel as if I could lay down my life to be near you and Father. It has been a struggle between Jeff and me, which should overcome the other in the matter of his volunteering, and though it was carried on in love between us, it is not the less bitter. Jeff promised me he would not volunteer, but he could not help it I suppose and you have by this time seen *The Sentinel* in which it is published. . . . I found out last night accidentally that he had committed himself about going. I have cried until I am stupid, but you know there is 'no use crying, better luck next time.'"[1]

Jeff had apparently been surprised by Varina's heated opposition to his decision. Searching for the cause of her behavior, he concluded she must be pregnant. "Jeff thinks there is *something* the matter with me," Varina told her mother, "but I *know* there is not." Against his maddeningly calm and patronizing manner, however, she could not prevail. For Varina, it was a painful reminder that marriage was not an equal partnership; "no use crying, better luck next time" was a declaration of women's reality.[2]

Jeff had made his decision. The only choice left to Varina was where to stay during their separation. She could remain alone at Brierfield, or move in with Uncle Joe's family at nearby Hurricane, or she could go home to Natchez. For Varina, the choice was clear. If the worst should come to pass and Jeff were to die in battle, she told her mother, "no earthly power shall persuade me to live with anyone else but you." She was driven not only by a desire to be with her family but also by an aversion to being with his. It was no secret that Varina and Joe's wife, Eliza, had little affection for each other. And, as Jeff made clear to his favorite sister, Lucinda, it was also no secret that he laid the blame for the friction on his wife. Varina, he declared, was a difficult person to grow fond of, even if her weakness sprang "from a sensitive and generous temper" rather than a selfish one.[3]

Such comments made it obvious, in 1846, that neither Jeff nor his family considered Varina an ideal wife. Jeff made it abundantly clear that he disapproved of her willfulness, her stubbornness, and what he considered her unfeminine insistence on independent judgment. All these character flaws he said, reflected poorly on him. He loved her, he assured her, but warned that she must learn to be a proper wife. Varina certainly wished to live up to his expectations and to his demands. Indeed, throughout her marriage she would demonstrate a devotion to Jefferson Davis that seemed to arise from a mixture of genuine admiration and a gnawing fear that she was somehow failing him. Yet even in our modern era of egalitarian marriage, their characters would not have easily meshed. He was too cerebral, guided by the absolute virtues of duty, responsibility, and self-sacrifice; she was too human, guided by affection, friendship, and family loyalties rather than abstractions. She was an astute observer of people and accepting of their foibles; he demanded men and women live up to principles and often saw them as abstractions. He sometimes tolerated her weaknesses; she often denied his. But in this first year of marriage the conflict was simple: she was struggling to be recognized as an adult, and he was determined to turn her into a dutiful wife.

It did not help that Jeff's letters from the war were a mixture of affection and patriarchal sermonizing. His declarations of love were followed by lectures on the behavior he expected of his wife. His reputation, he declared, now rested in part on her conduct. "My love for you placed my happiness in your keeping, our vows have placed my hono[r] and respectability in the same hands." Doubt seemed to hang over their relationship: could she ever become the calm, useful, temperate, and obedient woman he demanded in a wife?[4]

The answer seemed to be no. Indeed, by the fall, an insecure and lonely Varina had become so depressed by his absence that Jeff Davis arranged a sixty-day leave of absence from the battlefield. The couple spent two weeks together at Brierfield—and then Jeff returned to Texas once again. This time, Varina chose to remain at their plantation, preferring its solitude to the noisy and less than hospitable Hurricane. She conceded that her relationship with Joe Davis and his family had grown more strained during Jeff's absence. She bridled at Joe's attitude toward her husband, for the elder Davis brother continued to behave as if Jeff were one of his many dependents.

Perhaps it was a misplaced empathy on Varina's part for her own father, who had been dependent upon his in-laws and was now moving to dependence upon her husband. Perhaps she did not want Jeff to feel a sting of dependency similar to what she felt at that moment in her marriage. Perhaps she resented Joe's continued treatment of her as a child rather than a grown woman. Most likely it was all of these things, and more. Sometime before or during his military service in the Mexican War, Jeff had drawn up a will. In it, he made provision for the childless Varina to reside at Brierfield during her lifetime, but she was to share the income from the plantation with his two widowed sisters and two orphaned nieces. To Varina, the will not only negated her primacy as Jeff's wife but also served as a testament to the entire Davis family's image of her as a child rather than an adult.[5]

Jeff's letters from the battlefront continued to be filled with patronizing lectures. He showed little sympathy for her desire to be treated as a woman rather than a girl. "[R]emember," he wrote with a hint of smugness, "to be responsible for ones conduct is not the happy state which those who think they have been governed too much sometimes suppose it." He took pains to once again lay out his standards for a wife's behavior: she might see social conventions for what they were—arbitrary, foolish, even oppressive—but she should adhere to them for the sake of avoiding collisions with others. The criticism that would follow if his wife did not behave properly would "render me as *husband* unhappy."[6]

Varina sincerely wanted to please her husband, yet she continued to wage small battles against her dependence. In January 1847, she wrote a long letter to her mother in which she enclosed money for the education of her brother William. "*The money,*" she insisted, "*is my own.* I have refused a piano because I wanted to apply the $450 to a better use. Don't consider it as anything from Jeff," she declared, eager to make the point that this was her decision, her choice. And yet a sense of fairness compelled Varina to admit that Jeff was always generous to her family. "Even if it were from him," she added, "he would send it with a son's affection." This was true. Over the next few decades, Jeff Davis would assume the burden of many Howell children's education, room, and board. Varina's family, like Varina herself, was caught in a web of dependency.[7]

But Varina had more on her mind at the moment than the care and keeping of her sisters and brothers. She was twenty, alone, far from people who loved her for who she was and sympathized with her plight. She wanted her mother's sympathy for her predicament, but at the same time she also wanted to elicit praise for her resourcefulness. "I spent my New Years at home entirely alone," she boasted to Margaret, "putting down and stretching carpet. I sung as loud as I could every thing I could, not forgetting 'ni-ni-na.' It was a brave sight I tell you. . . . I have got my parlour and dining room fixed." As if to show her superhuman housewifely activity, she added, "Now as to pumpkin pies! I made twelve myself." But her blasé and brave front slipped as she ended her letter home and she confessed her anxiety over the fate of her husband. "I spend my days here pretty much as I do everywhere—projecting immense improvements, thinking of Jeff, and wondering if I ever shall see him again."[8]

While Varina was busy laying carpet, the American army was preparing for a decisive battle with the army of Santa Anna. That February, the Mexican general marched north to meet the U.S. forces under General Zachary Taylor. During the Battle of Buena Vista that followed, Jeff Davis's Mississippi Rifles served as Taylor's escort onto the field. Davis emerged as one of the heroes that day, for despite a serious wound he remained on the field until the Mexicans retreated.

Jefferson had been hit by a ball that pierced his ankle and sent slivers of his brass spur deep into his flesh. Blood had filled his boot, and there was a serious danger of infection. His military service had come to an end, and by May he was on his way home. Knowing how upset Varina would be by the news of his injury, he minimized the damage, telling her simply, "I cannot walk yet am steadily recovering." It was far from true. Although his foot was not amputated, the splintered bones left him nearly crippled and in pain for several years.[9]

Jefferson Davis, hobbling on crutches, was greeted with a hero's welcome when he arrived in New Orleans. In Natchez, a dozen young ladies crowned him and his officers with wreaths. But at home in Brierfield he faced a different kind of warfare: the escalating conflict between Varina and his brother Joe. The heart of this conflict was who would be first in Jeff Davis's affections. But the immediate issue was the design for a new home to be built on the plantation. The plan called for a house with two kitchens in order to allow Joe's widowed sister Amanda and her seven children to settle permanently at Brierfield. Varina had briefly given in to this notion of a shared living space, but now she rebelled. The problem was not Amanda; in fact, Varina and her widowed sister-in-law were quite friendly, and Amanda's daughter Malie often spent the night with Varina. The problem was the arrangement itself: Varina could not be mistress of her own household if an older, more experienced Davis woman resided at Brierfield. It is not clear if Joe and Jeff understood Varina's concerns at all. Nor would it have mattered. As men, their role was to protect and provide for family members in need; before this duty, all other wishes ought to give way.

In the end, Varina carried the day. Brierfield would have one kitchen—and one mistress. But the victory was pyrrhic: Jeff's vocal disapproval of Varina's behavior stung her deeply. Jeff laid the blame for the conflict squarely on her. Why did she have to argue with his brother? he asked. "You had an opportunity when I came to you cripple," he told her, "to quarrel with me as much as would have satisfied any ordinary person."[10]

Despite their open hostility, Varina and Joe could not avoid each other. She rarely went to The Hurricane, but Joe and his family came to Brierfield almost every day to visit her husband. Varina confessed to her mother that the situation gave Jeff "more pain if possible than I expected." He was not acting, she said, "like himself," but she consoled herself by arguing that, in the end, his injury was more to blame than her feud. She was eager to be useful to him, and was pleased anytime he allowed her to dress his wound. Yet the events of the past year had taken their toll on Varina. She was no longer a young girl full of hopes for the future. The future, she concluded, was neither predictable nor secure, and marriage seemed to create as many problems as it solved. "I do not think circumstances can make any one happy," she declared to her mother that summer; "the heart at last, if it is well governed, makes the heaven."[11]

Seventeen

"THE SOUTHERN RIGHTS CAUSE
IS THE LOSING ONE NOW"

The Return to Washington, D.C.

CIRCUMSTANCES MIGHT NOT MAKE ONE HAPPY, but circumstances were certain to change. That fall Varina reported to her mother that her own health was excellent—"only having two chills . . . and they were slight"—and that Jeff, too, was on the mend. His appetite had returned and he was walking fairly well with only one crutch. He was ready, Varina thought, to head to Washington once again.[1]

Jeff's reputation as a military hero made him a prime candidate for political office; the only question was what office he would fill. The death of Mississippi senator Jesse Speight presented the right opportunity, and the governor was quick to appoint Jeff Davis, former commander of the Mississippi Rifles and former congressman, to serve out the remainder of Speight's term. By November, Jeff was on his way to the nation's capital, taking the northern route to Washington. He was far from fully recovered, and Varina worried about the effects of the long and usually uncomfortable trip, for he had developed a constant backache as a result of his wound. She was especially distressed that she could not travel with him, to provide what comfort she could, but, she explained to her mother, she was not yet equipped to reenter public life. Her wardrobe, suitable enough for the isolation of Brierfield, was woefully inadequate for the social obligations that would face her in D.C. "I had not one dress [in which] I could receive the visitors who would crowd to see Jeff."[2]

A meager wardrobe was not, however, the only thing keeping Varina in Mississippi. What Varina could not confess to her mother was that the domestic tensions and conflicts had taken their toll: Jeff had not invited his wife to join him in Washington. He had made his motives painfully clear: "I will be frank with you," he wrote from the capital: "with body crippled, even shattered, and mind depressed," he could not bear the thought of continuing strife. "I cannot expose myself to such conduct as yours when with me here," he declared. "I cannot bear constant harassment, occasional reproach, and subsequent misrepresentations." Varina must mend her ways, he warned, or it would be "impossible for us ever to live together." Jeff Davis loved his wife, but he meant to mold her to his preferred image—by instruction or punishment.[3]

Nothing Jeff said could diminish Varina's devotion or her concern about his safety and health, yet his stinging words had the desired effect. She filled her letters with expressions of appreciation for the man who had chosen her as his wife. "Much as I have loved and valued you," she wrote that January, "it seems to me I never knew the vastness of my treasure until now." And she urged him to take care of himself for the sake of "your thoughtless, dependent wife." Varina's characterization of herself as thoughtless and dependent was becoming as deeply ingrained as the image of him as stoic and oblivious to personal danger.[4]

Yet Varina's independence of mind always reasserted itself. In January 1849, while she was still in Natchez, she received a copy of one of the speeches Jeff had given on the Senate floor. In it, he responded to a challenge from a New Hampshire senator sympathetic to the abolitionist movement. The senator, John Hale, had introduced a bill, spurred, he declared, by the recent attack on the Washington office of an abolitionist newspaper. But slavery advocates insisted that the rioters had been provoked by what they considered the kidnapping of more than seventy slaves aboard the schooner *Pearl*. Davis had leaped to his feet to defend the constitutional right of Southerners to protect their property. Varina appreciated how important, and explosive, the issue was, but she did not entirely approve of her husband's sharply worded counterattack—and said so. "I saw your forcible little speech in partial answer to Mr. Hale's vituperations against slavery," she wrote. "It was a little too violent, more so than I would have liked to hear you be, however well deserved the censure might be."[5]

Having issued her criticism, Varina immediately wrapped the mantle of domesticity around herself. While he was debating important issues, she said, she was hard at work, molding herself to his expectations. She was reading Mrs. Ellis's *Guide to Social Happiness,* an advice book to women that she had confidence would "help 'Winnie,' " as her husband called her, "to be 'Wife.' " She closed her letter with the affectionate baby talk that became a regular part of her correspondence, using the nickname that reduced the regal name Varina to a diminutive: "Winnie is Husband's baby and baby is your devoted Wife."[6]

Varina's efforts to mold herself into a good wife had the desired effect:

domestic tensions eased and Jeff no longer forbade her to join him in Washington. But Varina could not make the trip in fall 1849, for poor health—or perhaps a miscarriage—kept her in Mississippi. Varina was certain that Jeff would engage in "flirting" while he was alone in Washington, for he had never denied his attraction to the company of beautiful women. But she did not voice any disapproval of such behavior. That society allowed a husband to express an attraction to the opposite sex with impunity though a proper wife could not was simply another of the "conventionalisms" that Jeff had directed Varina to accept gracefully.[7]

When at last she made her way to Washington that December, Varina's first task was to find proper housing. This proved a greater problem than expected, given the social snobbery that came as second nature to a descendant of the Kempes and Howells and a prosperous Mississippi planter. They had taken rooms at a Mrs. Wise's but felt forced to leave since the other boarders were "a mess of clerks, and that sort of people" who labored for the government. The solution was a joint venture with several other Southern Senate families, arranged by the wives. Along with the Burts of South Carolina, the Toombses of Georgia, and the McWillies of Mississippi, the Davises rented a house near the U.S. Hotel. The families also arranged to take their meals in a private dining room at the hotel. Varina was enormously pleased. "We have a right nice parlour," she told her mother, "and I hired an excellent piano, and we sometimes have music in abundance." She conceded the drawback of living "on the avenue" rather than in a quieter, more genteel spot, but she liked "the bustle."[8]

Varina felt more comfortable with "the bustle" this time around. In 1845, she had been a young bride, a teenage girl among a sea of strangers, awed by all she saw and often intimidated by the sophisticated men and women she met. She had held her own by sheer dint of will and intelligence, but she had worried about the impression she made. She had worried even more that she would embarrass her husband, later reflecting on the "woeful experiences" she now recognized as the fate of many novice political wives. But in 1850 she was twenty-three, no longer newly wed, familiar with many of the congressmen and their families, and savvy enough about the patterns of society in Washington to be at ease. As always, she shared her experiences with her mother, writing long, detailed descriptions of the clothes she wore, the people she met, the dinners and levees and parties she attended. "I wore my light brocade with a thread lace cape and cherry colored bows," she wrote on January 6, 1850, setting the scene for a lively account of a dinner party. She was still a country girl at heart, however, for she found it difficult to adjust to meals served as late as 7:00 p.m. and parties that did not end till nearly midnight.[9]

A few months later, she wrote to her mother that she was to have dinner with President Taylor. She did not look forward to going—"I think I had rather take a whipping than go," she declared—but whether it was entirely because this was the family of her husband's first wife or because the event also required her to spend money on a new dress is unclear. Two days later she reported on her evening at the White House. She had worn a new sky-blue silk with a train, she said, and in her hair and at her bosom had been scarlet rosettes. To her surprise, she had had a "sweet time," although she found the Taylors' youngest daughter, Mary Elizabeth Taylor Bliss, "less loveable than the rest of them" and not at all a cordial woman. Perhaps Varina's view of Betty Bliss was biased by the fact that the younger Taylor daughter bore a striking resemblance to her dead sister.

After dinner, Varina took the time to go upstairs and visit Mrs. Taylor. The president's wife never joined the formal entertainments hosted by her husband, and the role of hostess fell to the young Mrs. Bliss. It was rumored that Margaret Taylor had taken a vow during the Mexican War that if her husband was returned to her safely, she would never go out into society again. Her reclusive life had led to other rumors as well: this daughter of an elite Maryland family, schooled in every social grace, was transformed in gossip into a crude, pipe-smoking virago, unfit for society. Varina discovered instead a frail and ailing woman who "seemed so charmed to see me, said she felt so wretchedly lonesome, and chilly," that she kept the president's wife company as long as she could.[10]

Despite her accounts of social life in the capital, Varina and Jeff went out far less frequently than other congressional couples. He preferred to spend his evenings at home, working each evening. Once again, Varina played the role of amanuensis as he dictated letters to constituents back home. As they worked, husband and wife discussed both large political issues and specific proposed legislation. Varina knew that the growing sectional tensions, so evident in heated exchanges such as the one between her husband and Senator Hale, troubled Jeff deeply. She saw, too, that a rift was growing between Jeff and many of his Southern colleagues, especially since the death that March of John C. Calhoun. Men such as William L. Yancey and Robert Barnwell Rhett, later known as secessionist "fire eaters," were determined to uphold the doctrine of nullification that Calhoun had espoused; Jeff Davis held the Union far dearer. The Constitution, Varina observed, was his bible, and until events forced his hand, he believed that it would both guarantee his right to hold human property and limit his right to nullify its laws.[11]

In her memoirs, Varina Davis, like her husband, placed the blame for the escalating sectional tensions, and for the civil war that eventually followed, squarely on the abolitionists and their incendiary literature. Everywhere one turned, it seemed to her, abolitionists and their sympathizers were ready to rain down insults and criticisms on the South in the form of petitions to Congress to end slavery. "From the State legislatures, the press, the county meetings, the pulpit, the different societies, no matter what their object, the lecturers, and above all the abolitionists, came this downpour of petitions; yards of signatures were appended, and those who stood behind this mass of misrepresentation and invective presented it with insulting epithets and groundless accusations."[12]

For Varina, the morality of slavery never loomed large in the equation. She was comfortable with the racial arrangement she had known all her life, and remained blithely certain that the slaves of Brierfield shared her view of slavery as a benign institution. Her naiveté, or blind refusal to question the status quo, colored her perception before the war and her memories after it. "When our first child was born," she would write in her memoir, "every negro on the plantation, great and small, came up with little gifts of eggs and chickens and a speech of thanks for the birth of a 'little massa to take care of we, and be good to we.'" As one woman kissed the infant, Varina recalled her remarking, "Honey, you ain't never gwine work—your negroes gwine do all dat for you." Astute as she was in catching the nuances of white conversation and commentary, Varina remained entirely innocent of the resentment this slave clearly harbored. For the mistress of Brierfield, the adoring tableau unfolded exactly as it was meant to be.[13]

Angelina Grimké, raised in a slave society just as Varina had been, saw slavery in a different and far harsher light. She had rejoiced when thousands of New Englanders put their signatures on petitions to end the gag rule and debate the issue of slavery on the floor of Congress. And by 1850, she had approved the shift from protest to politics by the Tappan wing of the movement. But in Varina's eyes, all abolitionists remained Garrisonians, eager to dissolve the Union, reviling it "as a compact with hell." Their constantly escalating attacks upon the "patriotic, lawabiding, humane" gentlemen of the South would leave men such as Jefferson Davis, who admitted to "a superstitious reverence for the union," no choice but secession.[14]

Varina was wrong, of course. The abolitionists alone could not shape the nation's destiny. The commitment of Northerners and Southerners alike to national expansion was what ensured repeated sectional confrontations. If

Americans agreed it was their "manifest destiny" to extend their borders from ocean to ocean, they could not agree on which labor system would extend into the new territories they acquired. By 1848, the cry of "free soil, free land, free labor" had spawned a new third party, the Free Soil Party, which challenged the two national parties to take a stand on whether slavery, like the Constitution, would follow the flag. Both Zachary Taylor, the Whig candidate, and Lewis Cass, the Democratic candidate, had done their best to avoid the question: Cass put forward a doctrine of "popular sovereignty," which would leave the question of slavery up to the citizens in a territory, while Zachary Taylor had declared that no one had the authority to control slavery in the territories. Taylor now sat in the White House, but the issue of slave labor or free labor had not, would not, disappear even if every abolitionist from Garrison to Grimké were silenced.[15]

Years later, in her memoirs, Varina would mark the beginning of the "irreconcilable conflict" that came to be known as the Civil War with precision: December 20, 1848, the day the Senate debated whether a known abolitionist, a priest named Theobald Mathew, would be permitted to sit within the bar of the Senate during a visit to Washington. But this was only dramatic hindsight. In 1848 and indeed in 1850, the dissolution of the Union was on few Congressmen's agenda. And, like most white Americans at the time, Varina herself remained confident that the brilliant assemblage of statesmen in the House and the Senate could find a peaceable solution to the problems raised by the expansion of the United States and the resulting battle over the expansion of slavery. Here, after all, were Davis, the ailing Calhoun, Clay, Webster, Benton, Cass, Fillmore, Douglas, Seward, Chase, Butler, and the irrepressible Sam Houston. Indeed, that year a compromise was in the offing that promised to allay, if not put to rest, the tensions that kept Jeff Davis awake, pacing the floor, each night.[16]

This omnibus bill was largely the brainchild of Henry Clay, known to future generations as "the Great Compromiser." It was a remarkable attempt to give something to everyone but not tip the balance in favor of anyone. Under it, California—with its beckoning gold mines—would enter the Union as a free state, but all other territories acquired from Great Britain and Mexico would decide their status by popular sovereignty. To the abolitionists, the bill promised an end to the slave trade in the nation's capital city; to Southerners, it promised a new, more effective fugitive slave law. Like all efforts to please everyone, the compromise bill of 1850 pleased no one, and it was defeated. Clay left Washington tired and despairing, but Stephen A. Douglas of Illinois rescued the Kentuckian's efforts by proposing each element of the compromise as a separate bill. By September, the Compromise of 1850 was a reality.[17]

Varina witnessed the dramatic debates over Clay's proposal. She watched as her terminally ill friend John C. Calhoun made his way into the Senate, supported on the arms of younger colleagues. Other congressional wives and daughters filled the galleys and sat on the floor between the senators, keeping "still as mice, feeling themselves present there on sufferance." Varina was seated close enough to the South Carolina champion of states' rights to see that his eyes shone with fever, his breath came in short and painful gasps, and his tall, now emaciated body was closing in upon itself. During these critical days of heated discussion, she observed the friendship and respect that could develop between political enemies. Neither Thomas Hart Benton nor the volatile Daniel Webster, political foes of the South Carolinian, would raise his voice against the fragile Calhoun. When Jeff Davis's nemesis, Henry Foote of Mississippi, whom Davis considered little better than an abolitionist, rose to bait Calhoun, Benton exclaimed, "No brave man could do this infamy. Shame, shame!"[18]

Calhoun died only a few weeks later, and Daniel Webster gave his eulogy. "He is now a historical character," another of Calhoun's old rivals, Henry Clay, remarked. "He is not dead," Benton retorted. "There may be no vitality in his body. But there's plenty in his doctrines." Varina had grown politically sophisticated enough to recognize the truth of Benton's remark. In reporting on the funeral of her old friend, she noted astutely that it was a political as well as personal event. The funeral procession conveyed its political message: "Twelve white horses with a Negro at the head of each to lead them drew the hearse," she told her mother, adding, "The Negroes were substituted in the place of white men by the committee for the edification of the free soilers." Even in death, Calhoun would speak for the rights of slaveholders, the benign character of the "peculiar institution," and the sanctity of property, even the human sort.[19]

Many of the old guard would vanish over the next few years: Taylor, Clay, and Webster himself would soon be dead. In July 1850—only a few months after Varina had visited Margaret Taylor in her bedroom—the president lay dying. Varina wrote of the deathbed scene to her parents, describing how "poor Mrs. Taylor" sat on the bed, "chafing his hands, and telling him she had lived with him nearly forty years and he must talk to her, begging him to tell his poor old wife if she could do nothing for him." But Zachary Taylor could neither see nor speak. After he died, his grieving wife had to be forcibly pulled from the body, for she had continued to feel his pulse and put her ear to his heart, insisting that "he did not die without speaking to her." In fact, Varina recalled, the last words Zachary Taylor spoke were not to his wife but to Jeff Davis. Suddenly, without warning, the dying man had blurted out these cryptic instructions to his former son-in-law: "Apply the constitution to the measure, Sir, regardless of consequences."

What he meant was uncertain to Varina, but the sad scene had touched her deeply. "This morning when I waked up such a weight of thankfulness came over me when I thought I have Husband, and Father and Mother." Twenty-first-century readers might easily empathize with Varina's sense of good fortune, but the chasm between centuries would once again widen when they read her final thought. She was thankful to have parents and husband, the twenty-four-year-old believed, because she was "almost an old woman."[20]

It was Jeff, not Varina, however, who seemed both old and frail as the tumultuous decade of the 1850s began. Although her health was often poor and made worse by episodes of depression, her husband continued to suffer a punishing assortment of ailments: neuralgia, eye trouble, bouts of malarial fever, gastric problems, and the chronic insomnia that led to his late-night pacing and obsessing. Emotional stress seemed to prompt outbreaks of these ailments, and the death of Taylor and the ongoing political battle with Henry Foote had together produced considerable anxiety. Soon after the compromise legislation was passed, Foote had challenged Jeff to a race for the governorship of Mississippi, intending it to be a referendum on the state's commitment to the institution of slavery.

Jeff accepted the challenge, for there was nothing to hold him in Washington. The new president, Millard Fillmore, was neither a political ally nor a personal friend, and the Great Compromise of 1850 had done nothing to restore unity between moderates such as Jeff and radicals including Rhett. That summer, Jeff campaigned for his party's nomination throughout Mississippi, speaking to crowds so adoring that the *Vicksburg Sentinel* characterized his campaign as a "triumphal march." By September 17 his nomination was official, and less than a week later he resigned his Senate seat.[21]

Almost immediately after resigning from Congress, Jeff suffered a new bout with malaria. The gubernatorial campaign that fall brought on an inflammation of the eye that doctors feared would lead to an ulceration of the cornea. Varina hovered over her husband, applying chloroform to his eyes, massaging his head, dosing him with opium, quinine, and castor oil, all acceptable medicines of the day. Unable to stand the slightest ray of sunlight, Davis slept all day and worked feverishly on his stump speeches each night. With only three weeks left before the November election day, Jeff hit the campaign trail, wearing green goggles to protect his bandaged eye. When the votes were counted, he had lost the election by almost a thousand votes. Exhausted and humiliated, he returned to Brierfield—and to his wife.[22]

Varina was not surprised by her husband's failed bid for the governorship. Writing to her parents on October 28, she reminded them that the political climate had changed in Mississippi. Her husband, she wrote, "is just finding out what I predicted, and everybody but his friends knew, that the Southern Rights cause is the losing one now, whatever it may be when further aggressions have been perpetrated." Jeff's insistence that there was no contradiction in reverence for the Constitution and the protection of Southern rights was a middle ground that few Mississippi voters could accept. Varina was a realist in other ways as well. Life in the governor's mansion would be expensive, and she was happy enough to avoid the "outlay upon servants, silver, china, cutglass, table linen, bed linen, and carriage and horses" that would strain their financial resources. On balance, she wrote, she was "as contented as possible to remain where I am."[23]

Varina soon had even more reason to welcome her husband's return to private life. After seven years of marriage, the couple were about to have their first child. The baby would grow up in the Davises' new home, which, though less imposing than The Hurricane and not as elaborate as some of the mansions Varina had known in Natchez, was a dignified house befitting a former senator. Gone was the drafty old house, with its odd windows and doors; in its place was a spacious and comfortable home, with twelve Doric columns supporting the roof, floor-to-ceiling windows, multiple chimneys, and a fireplace in every room. Joe Davis condemned Varina's extravagances, including the white marble mantels in the parlor and dining room and the elaborate—and single—kitchen. Here was another reason, if he needed one, not to deed the property to his younger brother Jeff.[24]

But Joe's wrath could not destroy the mood of happiness and expectation that Jeff and Varina felt that spring. Jeff's health returned and he and Varina rode daily, just as they had done during their whirlwind courtship. Together they settled into the rhythms of life as a planter and his wife, installing trees and shrubs, overseeing the labor of slaves in their cotton fields and in the shops where the blacksmiths and carpenters worked. The idyll was intense but brief, for the world of politics could not be permanently shut out. Five days before Varina went into labor her husband was far away, campaigning in New York, New Jersey, and Pennsylvania for his old friend Franklin Pierce and against his old enemy Winfield Scott. Varina longed for him to return. After a few concise comments on the presidential race, she added a wistful postscript to a letter in late July: "Don't think me too selfish, but can you not come home—I so long to see you, and my resolution gives out." She showed herself resigned to her role as the wife of a politician, however, for she added, "Do come if you are neglecting nothing."[25]

On July 30, 1852, Samuel Emory Davis was born, and the procession of admiring slaves Varina later memorialized came to view her son. To mark the arrival of his long-awaited heir, Jeff Davis destroyed his old will and drafted a new one. In a quirky if well-intended ceremony, he built a fire on a warm July evening and burned the document that had so troubled his wife. In that same year, Harriet Beecher Stowe published *Uncle Tom's Cabin*, the book that would inflame the South and carry the country one step closer to war. The following year, newly elected President Franklin Pierce appointed Jefferson Davis secretary of war. For the third time, the Davises were headed back to Washington, D.C.[26]

Eighteen

"WE FELT BLOOD IN THE AIR"

Personal and Public Tragedies

JEFF DAVIS'S HEALTH WAS ALWAYS a good barometer of his satisfaction with his public and private life, and in 1853 his health was especially good. He was eager to take up the duties of the War Department, for he continued to see himself more as a military man than a politician. Varina's spirits were high as well now that she was, at long last, a mother. While Jeff took up temporary residence in the Washington home of his niece, Mary Jane Brodhead, Varina made the rounds of family and friends in Mississippi, proudly showing off her son, Samuel. Finally, in the summer of 1853, she made her way to the capital, with her younger sister Margaret, her ten-year-old brother Becket, and a baby nurse in tow.[1]

The Davis household was far less dour than it had been during Jeff's early years in the Congress. His enthusiasm for his work, his unrestrained pleasure in fatherhood, and the absence of any domestic strife made him far more open to entertaining than he had been before. Varina proved to be a good hostess, organizing pleasant dinner parties rather than lavish ones, for she knew her budget was more modest than that of truly wealthy planters' wives. Jeff, after all, did not even own the lands he planted, and though his cotton fields were profitable, she had brought more financial burdens than benefits to the marriage as the daughter of the hapless William Howell.

Despite her successes, Varina realized she would never be fully welcomed into the inner circle of women who dominated capital city society. She was neither rich enough nor feminine enough to meet their standards. She made no effort to disguise her preference for serious conversation with men rather than gossip with ladies. Her own guest list included more scientists, scholars, novelists, and poets than some felt seemly. While she formed lasting friendships with women such as the smart and well-read Mrs. Pierce and the insightful and sometimes caustic South Carolina diarist

Mary Boykin Chesnut, her intelligence, education, and thinly disguised contempt for the frivolous and the inane not only excluded her from some gatherings but also made her the topic of unflattering gossip. Many women would dismiss her as haughty and aloof—a judgment that echoed the complaint their husbands leveled against her spouse. It was ironic that members of the opposite sex were always more generous in their views of Varina and Jeff, drawn to her by the novelty of her frank intellectuality and to him by the aura of self-contained manliness and rationality.[2]

Varina and Jeff seemed content with life on the margins of Washington's most elite social circles. They could, after all, count the president among their closest friends, and they had the opportunity to meet distinguished visitors including the Pope and several Japanese princes. Their home reverberated with the laughter and camaraderie of army officers, cabinet members, and members of Congress. Northerners and Southerners were equally welcome, and Varina discovered that even the radical antislavery senator Charles Sumner, who would soon gain fame—or infamy—when a congressman from South Carolina beat him unconscious on the floor of the Senate, delighted in conversation with Southern women such as his hostess. During this brief but happy period, the Davises also met men who, later in their lives, would prove to be critical allies in times of need: among them were Charles O'Conor, the New York lawyer who would defend the imprisoned president of the Confederacy, and the diplomat and statesman A. Dudley Mann, who would throw in his lot with the Confederacy and provide support and assistance through the dark days after the South's defeat. Varina declared him "the perfect man" in every regard, observing that her husband and Mann were "like David and Jonathan, until extreme old age."[3]

The calm that settled over the Davis household in 1853 seemed mirrored in the larger political world outside. Nationalism appeared to have trumped sectionalism, at least for the moment: Mississippi's Jeff Davis served in the same cabinet with New York's William L. Marcy; Virginia's Robert E. Lee directed the affairs of the nation's military academy at West Point; Northern congressmen married Southern belles; and families from both regions engaged in genial conversation over dinner or mingled on the dance floor. But tensions, however muted, were not resolved. In 1854, the debate over, and eventual passage of, the Kansas-Nebraska Act revived sectional mistrust and reopened the divisive question of the extension of slavery.

The bill establishing the rules for the Kansas and Nebraska territories was the brainchild of the ambitious Stephen A. Douglas. It incorporated the principle of "popular sovereignty," permitting both territories to decide whether to enter the Union slave or free. Southern congressmen welcomed the bill, for it promised to lift the restrictions on slavery set by the Missouri Compromise. But the realignment of political loyalties that year were even more disturbing to those able to discern the consequences: by July, the two-party system that had knit the country together was unraveling. The warning signs were everywhere; indeed, as early as November 1853, Varina's brother Jeffy had written that the Whig Party in New Orleans had become "a decided myth, an obsolete idea, said to have existed, but utterly impossible to find now." In the North, anti-Catholic and anti-immigrant sentiment had revived the Know-Nothing Party; even more ominously, Free Soilers, dissident Northern Democrats, and antislavery advocates had united to create the Republican Party in 1854.[4]

By 1856, what would later be seen as a dress rehearsal for the Civil War would begin in the Kansas territory. Slavery advocates and abolitionists poured into the area, producing competing constitutions and resorting to violence in their struggle to bring Kansas into the Union as an ally. The resulting violence in "Bleeding Kansas" seemed to many to have no remedy. The presidential election that same year exposed to everyone the fragmented nature of the political party system. Gone was the Whig Party that Varina's family had once embraced; in its place were the two new sectional parties, Know-Nothing and Republican, both determined to challenge the party of Thomas Jefferson, Andrew Jackson—and Jeff Davis. When the votes were counted, the Democratic candidate, James Buchanan, had carried the day. But widespread support for the Republicans established sectionalism within the structure of politics itself.[5]

The cloud that hung low and ominous over the nation darkened the private world of the Davises as well. In June 1854, as the political parties made their final plans to convene, Varina and Jeff's beloved son, Samuel Davis, died. He was not yet two years old. Nineteenth-century American graveyards were filled with the tiny coffins of infants and children, carried away by diseases modern medicine can cure with a simple prescription. No mother assumed she could safely navigate her baby's way through the threat of dysentery, scarlet fever, or whooping cough. But Sam's death had been painful to watch. His mouth had swelled and blistered and bled. His eyes had turned bloodred. Sores spread over his entire face, and though Varina managed to cure them, it left his head "a perfect mat of scabs." He had stopped walking. Briefly, he seemed to be recovering—and then he was dead. In July, Varina wrote to her parents: "I have made several attempts to write to you since our loss, but could not. My child suffered like a hero," she declared. "A cry never escaped his lips until his death, but he would say 'Mamma, I tired, I wana walk, I wan bed,' showing restlessness, and suffering—and would hold up his mouth to kiss me to make me stop giving medicine." Varina was heartbroken, but Jeff Davis was devastated by the death of his son. His stoicism failed him, and Varina heard him walking through the house in the dead of night, a restless and inconsolable mourner.[6]

Varina may not have realized that, even as she buried one child, a second one was on the way. Her daughter, Margaret, was born nine months later, on February 25, 1855. After so many years of suspected infertility, Varina's pregnancies now followed one another in close succession. When her third child, Jefferson Junior, was born less than a year after Margaret, it was Varina's life, not his, that hung in the balance. The birth had been difficult and Varina was dangerously ill. Jeff sent out a call for a nurse, but it was January in Washington and the snowdrifts made the streets virtually impassable. News of the crisis reached William Seward, who was by then a vocal opponent of slavery and thus a political foe of Jeff Davis. Yet Seward set aside political animosity and ordered his own horses hitched to a sleigh that could carry a nurse to the Davises' door. In her memoirs, Varina recalled this act of kindness. "After all these long years of bitter feuds, I thank him as sincerely as my husband did to the last hour of his life."[7]

By February 1857, Varina could report to her worried mother that she was weak but had no disease. "I can sit up sometimes a half hour and walk into the nursery and back." Her new son, she added, "is really very pretty and looks smooth." Her daughter, Maggie, seemed to welcome the new arrival, although by summer Varina would report clear signs of what modern mothers know as sibling rivalry: she had found Maggie biting Jeff Junior's ears.[8]

By spring Varina had recovered, but life as the mother of two and the wife of a man whose health could never be taken for granted proved exhausting. When she at last returned to Brierfield that May, she poured out her discontent to her mother in a detailed account of her trials and tribulations. Although the letter read like a litany of complaints, every sentence revealed her sense of inadequacy. There had been ear infections to cure, maids and nannies to fight, stairs to climb a thousand times a day. Little Jeff had nearly strangled to death in his crib, and he was diagnosed with pneumonia. For two weeks his survival was in doubt, and Varina's only moments of relief came when a battalion of female friends took turns nursing him. She had proved her inadequacy as a mother, she declared, for "my milk gave out, and he cried from hunger as well as pain." In the midst of all this, Jeff had resigned as secretary of war, said his goodbyes to the outgoing president, Pierce, and left for Mississippi. She could not go with him, for little Jeff was still weak and Maggie had come down with the chicken pox. Maggie cried incessantly—and soon enough, the telltale blisters appeared on the baby as well. By the time she packed her family up and reached Brierfield, her nerves were raw from her children's constant crying. But more disappointment and trouble were in store. The house, abandoned for so long while the Davises were in Washington, was in shambles. "All the locks spoilt, sheets cut up for napkins . . . nothing even to cook." It was too much for Varina, and she admitted, "I just sat down, and cried."[9]

Varina's despair and exhaustion, her anxiety over the survival of her children, and her sense of inadequacy were no easier to bear because these feelings often defined motherhood in nineteenth-century America. Nor would it console her, if she stopped to consider that many women suffered more than she suffered, battling loneliness and isolation from female friends and relatives on the frontier, or grueling poverty in the immigrant slums of Northern cities, or forced separation from husbands and children at the hand of planters like her own husband. She took no comfort in the fact that neither wealth nor power could protect children from the diseases that struck so quickly and fatally; even President Pierce, after all, had buried a son.[10]

In June 1857, Jeff took his family to the Gulf Coast, hoping to revive the spirits of his weary wife. Although he soon returned to Brierfield, Varina and the children remained for the summer. Only a little more than a decade earlier, Jeff had relished the solitude of his life on the plantation, but now he admitted to a terrible loneliness. "Oh Winnie," he confessed to Varina, "you cannot know how dreary the house seems." He missed his "dear Daughty and sweet little Boy"; he missed the wife who made Brierfield a true home. His letters had often been a mixture of patronizing instruction and romanticism, but this one ended with an ardor more common in a young lover than a middle-aged married man: "In all hours bright or gloomy you are the unclouded object of your husband's love."[11]

In November 1857, the Davis family returned to Washington with two Howell children in tow. There was a new president in the White House and Jeff was once again a senator. Although Jeff would never feel the same warmth toward the elderly James Buchanan as he felt toward Franklin

Pierce, the two men were cordial friends and the Davises were quickly welcomed into Buchanan's intimate circle. The bachelor president was especially fond of Varina's wit; she, in turn, wholeheartedly approved of his personal character. He was, she noted, fastidious in his dress, quick-witted in his conversation, and refreshingly frank in his opinions—traits, in fact, that an observer might readily note described Varina herself.[12]

Buchanan's politics were in full sympathy with her husband's, and this formed the basis for their bond. But as a woman, Varina had always had the luxury of judging men by their personal character and their private actions, rather than their political loyalties. She knew what mattered to her and measured men by standards as firm and clear as her husband's were in his public life. Although she was fiercely, sometimes foolishly, loyal to Jeff, the attacks she waged on his enemies were as often about their character as their voting records. Stephen A. Douglas was, she knew, responsible for the elevation of popular sovereignty to a congressional policy, but it was Douglas's hygiene and personal morality as much as his politics that earned her condemnation. He was, she wrote her parents, a "dirty speculator and party trickster, broken in health by drink." He would be wise, she added, to "wash a little oftener." In the end, a good man was neither Southern nor Northern: nothing the Texan Sam Houston could do on the floor of the Congress could cancel out his superficial and forward behavior toward a woman, and nothing William Seward could say would diminish her respect for his generosity.[13]

But Varina had little time in 1857 and 1858 to dwell on the personal hygiene of enemies or friends, for soon after the Davises returned to Washington, Jeff collapsed. It was as if he had been struck down by the cumulative political and personal crises of recent years. He had lost his son, and he felt his country slipping away as well. In the last weeks of 1857, bouts of laryngitis and neuralgia left him bedridden and unable to speak; by February 1858, an inflammation of his eye brought on blazing pain and the very real threat of blindness. Varina cared for him night and day, just as she had done during his failed attempt at the Mississippi governorship. She rarely left his side, although her younger brother Jeffy (known to the family as Jeffy D.) lay in a nearby room battling scarlet fever. As Jeff lay in total darkness, William Seward once again reached across the divide that separated slave owner and abolitionist. Throughout the long weeks that Jeff lay silent and sightless, Seward appeared at his bedside, reporting on political affairs, recapping national news, and musing gently and with surprising insight on their very different political styles and philosophies.[14]

Outside the Davis home that winter and spring, Washington society did its best to drown out the sounds of political conflict with music and laughter at glittering social events. Indeed, the capital had never been as lively—or as tense. "The surface of society in Washington," wrote one astute Southerner, was "serene and smiling, though the fires of a volcano raged in the under-political world, and the vibrations of Congressional strife spread to the furthermost ends of the country the knowledge that the Government was tottering." The charming Miss Harriet Lane acted as President Buchanan's White House hostess; the sophisticated English ambassador, Lord Napier, and his patrician wife were lionized by everyone; and a new dance, called the lancers, became the rage. In April 1858, after the Davises' long and harrowing winter, Varina welcomed the distraction of the season's most glamorous social event: the costume ball thrown by Democratic senator William Gwin of California and his wife. "All Washington was agog," wrote Virginia Clay, the wife of Alabama's senator Clement Clay, as the wives of senators and congressmen flocked to costumers and scoured history books and novels for illustrations of their chosen characters. On the night of the ball, guests arrived as Gypsy fortune-tellers, Shakespeare's fairy queen Titania, playing-card queens, fictional heroines, real-life poets, ancient kings and warriors, milkmaids and barmaids, writers, and mythical goddesses. Varina chose to go as Madame de Staël, the French-speaking Swiss author who influenced literary tastes across Europe in the late eighteenth and early nineteenth centuries. It was a persona that fit Varina comfortably, for de Staël was brilliant, witty, and often acerbic. Throughout the evening, she kept up the illusion, speaking fluent French to those who knew the language and broken English to those who did not. Virginia Clay noted with delight that Varina annihilated "all who had the temerity to cross swords with her" that evening.[15]

When Congress adjourned, Jeff and Varina accepted an invitation from Alexander Dallas Bache to spend the summer in Maine. Bache, the great-grandson of Benjamin Franklin and a West Point graduate like Jeff, was a professor of natural sciences at the University of Pennsylvania. He had set up a survey station on Mount Humpback, and the professor and his guests spent several weeks on the mountainside, sleeping in tents and whiling away the evening looking up at the stars and listening to the latest Verdi opera on a music box. Decades later, Varina remembered the people of Maine fondly. They were kind and open and showered attention on her daughter and her husband, who was awarded an honorary doctorate of laws from Bowdoin College.[16]

Varina was relieved to see Jeff's health return and his spirits lift that summer. But she was overcome with an acute longing for home and family. From Humpback Station, she poured out her homesick longings to her mother. "Upon the whole I have had as nice a summer as I could expect," yet she confessed that she had been begging Jeff to let her go south with him in the fall—without her children and without the current batch of Howell children living under her care. Jeff had not said yes or no. But Varina knew that if he left for Mississippi before her brother Jeffy and her sister Maggie's holidays from school were over, her wishes would be thwarted. "In this weary pilgrimage I am never more to do as I please," she wrote, bowing to the reality of her maternal obligations.[17]

The trip back to Washington from Maine carried the Davises through Boston. Here, the Boston Democratic Party invited Jeff to speak at the city's historic Faneuil Hall. Benjamin Butler was among the most vocal political leaders urging the Mississippi senator and former cabinet member to accept the invitation. Two years later, Butler would don a blue uniform as a major general in the Union army; by 1862, the brutal humiliation of New Orleans citizens under his occupying forces would earn him the name "the Beast." But on a summer day in Massachusetts in 1858, Benjamin Butler and Jeff Davis stood together as loyal members of a fragile national party.[18]

The memory of the Maine idyll faded quickly. In August Varina discovered she was pregnant once again, news she greeted with trepidation. She struggled with the very real fear that she would die in childbirth. Her gloom deepened when, as she feared, Jeff left for Mississippi without her. That November, alone and pregnant for the fourth time in eight years, she poured out her frustration to her parents. In the midst of a letter to her father, filled with news of the Howell children's progress and her own children's health, she confessed: "It is getting to be a great many years now since I have ceased to do what I would, and been forced to do what I could, That is the lot of all flesh I suppose—But oh it would be lovely sometimes to cut duty, and go on a *bust*." Only a few days later, she would make a similar confession to her mother: "Oh, how I would like to be free of care for a few days if only to know how it would feel, if I should not have to lose the objects of those cares. Cares do wear out one's youth." She was thirty-two years old. Far away, in the New Jersey countryside, fifty-three-year-old Angelina Grimké would have understood Varina Howell Davis's lament over the price a woman paid for marriage and family.[19]

Jeff had his share of worries as well. Back home in Mississippi, he discovered that his appearance in Boston, a city infamous in the South for its abolitionist strength, did not sit well with local political leaders. They were not appeased by the fact that he had poignantly pleaded for an end to anti-slavery extremism, asking his Boston audience to "arrest the fanaticism" that threatened to tear the nation apart. Many Mississippi leaders seemed to be steeling themselves for a showdown between North and South; Jeff Davis's efforts to soothe the troubled waters between the Northern and Southern wings of his party had begun to look quixotic. For both Varina and Jeff, worse was to come.[20]

Nineteen

"EVERYBODY IS SCARED"

John Brown, the Fire Eaters, Lincoln, and Secession

BY MARCH 1859, VARINA AND JEFF were hundreds of miles apart, as they had often been in the past. He had returned to Mississippi once again, this time because of warnings that floods threatened to destroy their plantation. She remained in Washington, tied down by an advanced pregnancy and her role as surrogate mother to her brother Jeffy and her sister Margaret. She had no idea when Jeff would return and so, for her part, made plans to spend the summer in the Maryland countryside. "With plenty of books and work" to keep her occupied, she hoped to get through the months "comfortably, if not very cheerfully." As March turned to April, her anxiety over her impending childbirth increased. Writing to Jeff, who was witnessing the destruction wreaked by the Mississippi River on his plantation, she mused on the possibility of her own death. Yet, despite her concerns and her growing physical discomfort, Varina continued to perform the duties she had taken up when Jeff was a junior congressman. In the same letter that carried thoughts of death, she told him proudly that she had franked 2,780 envelopes for him. "It gives me pleasure," she wrote, "to be doing something which seems to bring us nearer to each other. I do so long to see you, my dear Husband. It saddens me to realize that there is so very much in one's being the first love of early youth. Often since you have been away this time I have experienced that queer annihilation of responsibility and of time, and gone back fourteen long years to the anxious, loving girl, so little of use, yet so devoted to you—and nothing but my grey head, swollen feet, and household cares awake me from the dream."[1]

Varina's worst fears did not come to pass. Although her feet had swollen so much that she could not walk, her sleep had been repeatedly interrupted by aches and pains, and she had run a fever before she went into labor, on April 18 she gave birth to a healthy baby boy. The delivery was not difficult, and a week later she could slyly joke about her son's resemblance to

Jeff's side of the family. "To tell you the truth," she wrote her mother, "he looks enough like his Uncle Joe to be his child. . . . However, I pray he may grow out of this resemblance." She was not amused, however, by the fact that the baby was named for his uncle Joe. She had hoped to name him William, in honor of her father, but Jeff had exercised his paternal prerogative to name him Joseph Evan Davis. Varina did not challenge her husband's right to name her child, but she confessed to Margaret Howell that she hated the thought of "paying . . . the highest compliment in a woman's power to a man whose very name was . . . suggestive to me of injustice and unkindness."[2]

Meanwhile, Jeff was struggling with real rather than symbolic worries of his own. Brierfield was underwater, the river rising to the very steps of the house. The garden and orchard were gone, and Jeff was "distressed and broken." Summer found Jeff still in Mississippi, while Varina headed to Maryland with their children. Varina knew that politics, as well as the ruined plantation, was keeping him away, and she gently chided him that July. "Do remember that you are part of a powerful party and therefore can be spared, but you are all to your wife and babes." But many members of the Democratic Party would not have agreed.[3]

The ability of the Democratic Party to hold the nation together was now unlikely. Although Buchanan was in the White House and Roger Taney sat on the Supreme Court bench, the party had been splintering even as a new, sectional party grew stronger in the North. Years of compromise and avoidance had not eliminated the problem facing the country: would human rights or property rights prevail? No matter how it was framed, this was the nation's Gordian knot. Abolitionists declared the issue a moral one. Politicians began by debating it as a question of the extension of slavery into the territories, yet both Southern leaders and Northern ones quickly recognized that American expansionism produced a race to control the national government and its policies. By the mid-1850s, the fate of slavery itself had become the subtext in every congressional session. Outside the halls of government, Northern condemnation of the evils of slavery was countered by Southern attacks on "wage slavery," and the vigorous defense of the "peculiar institution" had hardened into a test of loyalty for men such as Jefferson Davis. By 1857, legislators had seen their best effort at compromise fail: popular sovereignty had led to "Bleeding Kansas"; fugitive slave laws had spurred the creation of the Underground Railroad to aid runaway slaves. What the legislature could not accomplish, the courts had attempted to resolve. In 1857, as Varina was recovering from the birth of Jefferson Davis Junior, the Supreme Court ruled that neither Dred Scott nor any other African American could be a United States citizen. Thus Scott, who had sued for his freedom after residing in the free state of Illinois, had no right to sue in a federal court. Southerners rejoiced, abolitionists wept—and in October 1859, John Brown, a man Varina considered "violent, lawless, and fanatical," would ignite hatred and adoration in equal measure.[4]

The deep and unbridgeable divide between South and North was nowhere more evident than in the Thirty-sixth Congress, which convened in December. Here, Jeff Davis squared off against Stephen A. Douglas. The Mississippi senator demanded a guarantee that the national government would protect slavery in all federal territories; the Midwesterner resurrected the policy of popular sovereignty. Hovering over the debates was the specter of the next presidential election. Varina cherished few illusions about the situation: "The political outlook was gloomy, and threatening storms were lowering everywhere."[5]

On January 6, 1860, Franklin Pierce wrote to Jeff, urging him to become the standard-bearer for the Democratic Party. "Our people," he said, "are looking for 'the coming man'—One who is raised by all the elements of his character above the atmosphere ordinarily breathed by politician." That man, Pierce declared, was Jefferson Davis. Pierce saw clearly that the Democratic Party was fracturing in the North, with those who abhorred slavery pitted against those who put loyalty to the party above any "fanatical passion." The former president feared the worst. "I have never believed that actual disruption of the union can occur without blood," he wrote, and in his search for a savior of the Union, he turned to his old friend Jeff Davis.[6]

Others shared Pierce's hopes. Yet when the Democratic National Convention met at Charleston that April, Jeff was not there. He was in Mississippi, trying to persuade his home state not to rush headlong into secession. Despite his absence, the Massachusetts delegation—led by Benjamin Butler—voted for him for president in fifty-seven ballots. When Stephen A. Douglas was put forward, the delegates from the lower South bolted. In the end the party splintered. Douglas was nominated by the rump Democratic Party; the Constitutional Union Party—an amalgam of former Whigs, Know-Nothings, and disgruntled Democrats—put forward John Bell of Tennessee; and John Breckinridge became the Southern rights candidate. Jeff Davis threw his support to Breckinridge. Few Democrats held out hope for victory against the united Republican Party and its candidate, Abraham Lincoln.[7]

The world Varina and Jeff knew was falling apart. From Washington, Varina described the political mood to her absent husband in blunt and urgent terms. *"Everyone is scared,"* she wrote, "especially Mr. Buchanan." Southern leaders were obsessed with secession, she reported, some ardently proclaiming themselves for it, others more hesitant, and radicals such as Georgia's Robert A. Toombs "blathering about a resignation (in future)."[8]

The election went much as Jeff and Varina feared. Abraham Lincoln won 180 electoral college votes, enough to carry him into the White House. Jeff's candidate, Breckinridge, won 72 electoral votes and Bell 39. Varina had the small satisfaction of seeing that only 12 electoral votes had been cast for the man she despised, Stephen A. Douglas.

On December 20, 1860, the state of South Carolina seceded from the Union. On December 26, the United States sent Major Robert Anderson to fortify Fort Sumter, an action South Carolina read as an act of war. Other Southern states agreed. On January 9, 1861, Jefferson Davis's home state of Mississippi seceded. Before official word reached him, Jeff rose on the floor of the Senate to plead with his Northern colleagues, many of them friends, to allow the South to depart in peace. "If you will but allow us to separate peacefully since we cannot live peacefully together," he reasoned, "there are many relations which may still subsist between us, which may be beneficial to you as well as to us." With that, he went home, exhausted and ill.[9]

His doctor ordered Jeff Davis to remain in bed, but duty commanded him to return once more to the Senate. It was January 21, 1861. Crowds began to gather in anticipation, and by 9:00 a.m. the galleries were filled to overflowing. Years later, Varina recalled the scene vividly: "The ladies were assembled together like a mosaic of flowers in the doorway. The sofas and the passageways were full, and ladies sat on the floor against the wall where they could not find seats. There brooded over this immense crowd a palpitating, expectant silence." The silence was broken by Jeff, who rose to officially declare that Mississippi was no longer a member of the Union and thus he, Jefferson Davis, was no longer a member of that body.[10]

Varina alone knew the cost of this declaration to her husband. The prevailing mood of the crowd had been curiosity and expectation, but Varina, "who had come from a sleepless night, all through the watches of which war and its attendants, famine and bloodshed had been predicted in despairing accents," knew that beyond "the cold exterior of the orator" lay a deep depression, a mourning for the Union "in whose cause he had bled."[11]

Her husband gave an eloquent farewell address, but it was Varina who captured the personal sadness of the day in her memoirs. "To wrench oneself from the ties of fifteen years is a most distressing effort. Our friends had entered into our joys and sorrows with unfailing sympathy. We had shared their anxieties and seen their children grow from infancy to adolescence." For Jeff, the tragedy was the unraveling of the Union; for Varina, it was the severing of emotional ties.[12]

Twenty

"CIVIL WAR HAS ONLY HORROR FOR ME"

Varina Becomes the First Lady of the Confederacy

VARINA SAID HER GOODBYES TO THE CITY where three of her children had been born and where she had grown from a girl to a woman, from a young bride to a mature wife. The future seemed bleak to her; her husband still hoped for a reconciliation between South and North but, knowing war was likely, accepted a commission as a major general in the Mississippi army. He did not share the optimism of some that Lincoln and the Congress would allow the Southern states to leave peacefully if no compromise could be worked out. Varina feared he was right: independence would not be won without bloodshed. Yet neither of them suspected that Jeff would be called upon to lead the South in that struggle.

They were pruning roses at their home in Brierfield on February 10 when the message came that Jeff Davis had been chosen the first president of the Confederacy. Varina's immediate reaction was that this was a mistake. She did not think her husband had the political skills for the task. He might achieve greatness on the battlefield, but, even after all his experience in Washington, she feared he still did not know "the art of the politician." Yet she did not doubt that his sense of duty would force him to accept.[1]

Varina knew her husband well. Eight days later, as bands played the new tune "I Wish I Was in Dixie's Land" and Montgomery crowds cheered, Jeff Davis and his vice president–elect, Alexander Stephens, made their way to the Alabama state capitol to be sworn in. "The man and the hour have met," declared Alabama's William Yancey, but Jeff had no illusions that it would prove an hour of easy victory. Writing to Varina, who was still at Brierfield preparing the family for its next move, Jeff refused to paint a rosy picture of the future. "Upon my weary heart was showered smiles, plaudits, and flowers," he said, "but, beyond them, I saw troubles and thorns innumerable."[2]

As a former soldier, Jeff Davis grasped the challenges facing the Confederacy. War seemed more likely with every passing day, although the

Confederates' new president insisted that the South neither sought it nor wished to provoke it. "We seek no conquest, no aggrandizement, no concessions from the free States," Jeff Davis declared that April. "All we ask is to be let alone—that none shall attempt our subjugation by arms. This we will and must resist."[3]

Yet resistance would not be easy. Nor would aggression. The truth was that neither side was well prepared for a war. The Union boasted a population over twice the size of the Confederacy's, and a white population four times larger than its enemy's, yet it had only sixteen thousand men in uniform when Abraham Lincoln came to office. That army had lost some of the best and brightest of its officers, men who had resigned their commissions to don the Confederate gray. As the drums of war beat louder, President Lincoln found himself forced to rely on elderly generals such as the seventy-four-year-old Winfield Scott or on younger officers without combat experience. The Confederacy faced a different but equally vexing dilemma: Jeff Davis had many generals but no army, and from the beginning, men with military experience vied with men with family pedigrees for rank, honor, and command. Throughout the war, bruised egos and inflated ones created problems within the Confederate army.[4]

Providing soldiers with arms, ammunition, and supplies was an immediate challenge facing both the Union and the Confederacy. The Union had an arsenal, but the weapons it contained were old; the Confederacy had no arsenal at all, except what it might scavenge from the federal installations within its borders. In the long run, the North would have the advantage, for it had more than a hundred thousand factories that could be converted to wartime production, while the South had fewer than twenty thousand to rely upon. Although Jeff Davis quickly dispatched commissioners to Europe to purchase armaments, his nation could never produce the shoes, blankets, and uniforms the soldiers needed. Nor could it transport goods and men as effectively as the Union. As any traveler in peacetime could testify, the Southern rail system was both limited and inefficient. In the end, neither the bravest army nor the most brilliant generals would prove able to overcome the wartime problems facing a society that preferred the cotton field to the textile mill and the tobacco shed to the countinghouse.

The problems of mobilization were not the only issues that bedeviled Abe Lincoln and Jeff Davis. Neither president had forged an internal political consensus as the war approached, and neither would ever achieve that goal. Throughout the war, President Lincoln would face a fractured national politics, with radicals and moderates in his own party tugging in opposite directions while Northern Democrats and those who sympathized with the South openly criticized the president. Jeff Davis's problems were equally thorny. In 1861, newspapers might declare that "the mantle of Washington falls gracefully from his shoulders," but Jeff Davis knew that George Washington had taken the reins of a government with newly enhanced powers, while he had been chosen to lead one that rested on the principle of states' rights. In the Confederacy, state governments jealously guarded their powers, and when war began, each clamored for resources and military support. Perhaps even worse for the sensitive, thin-skinned Davis, his new nation had no tradition of party loyalty to provide a buffer against personal attacks on its president. For both Lincoln and Davis, the presidency would prove a lonely and exhausting command.[5]

Varina and her children arrived in Montgomery that spring and the family settled into a comfortable two-story house with a small garden. She saw little of her husband during their brief stay in the Alabama capital, for Jeff's days were filled with the demands of establishing a new government. There were swarms of office seekers clamoring to see the new president, cabinet meetings to attend, military commanders to appoint, mobilization plans to set in motion, commissioners dispatched to purchase arms from abroad. As usual, Jeff's health suffered and the steady hum of anxiety about her husband was added to Varina's difficulties as she struggled to define her role as First Lady of the Confederacy.[6]

Although she was not privy to cabinet meetings or Confederate political parleys, Varina could see the secession crisis deepen with every passing day. The path to war appeared, at last, inevitable. Most Northerners were enraged by the Southern threat to the national union, and Radical Republicans had begun to speak boldly of punishing all traitors to the United States and its binding Constitution. Many who cared little for the fate of African Americans now seemed eager to crush a "slaveocracy" that both abolitionist propaganda and mainstream newspapers portrayed as a power-mad aristocracy that had held the nation in its iron grip far too long. Southerners, even those who owned no slaves, seemed equally eager to do battle, for they viewed the North as a tyrannical force, running roughshod over the Constitution and depriving men of their inalienable right to private property. To Yankees, an insurrection needed to be crushed; to the men and women of Dixie, another war for independence had to be waged.

War advocates on both sides did not have to wait long. In his inaugural address on March 4, President Abraham Lincoln declared that the Union was "perpetual," and thus secession was impossible. South Carolina, he said, had set in motion an insurrection, not an independence movement. When President Lincoln announced his intention to send supplies to Fort Sumter, President Davis countered with orders to his newly appointed commander at Charleston to demand the fort's immediate evacuation. On April 11, 1861, Confederate batteries opened fire on the fort and the Union forces responded in kind. There were no casualties—but war had begun. Soon after Lincoln called for the mobilization of the militia to squash the rebellion, a second wave of secession began. Arkansas led the way, and North Carolina, Virginia, and Tennessee followed. By June, war was a stark reality.[7]

With Virginia's secession, the Old South and the Cotton South were now one. And in late May, the Confederate government acknowledged the importance of the Old Dominion by moving its capital from Montgomery to Richmond. For Varina, pregnant once again, this meant uprooting her household—which now included three young children and Varina's younger sister Margaret—for the third time in less than a year. The journey itself was a grueling "four nights and three days *constant* travel without sleeping cars," and the Richmond hotel that provided Varina and her family with temporary lodgings was noisy and crowded. Writing to her mother that June, Varina confessed the toll her nomadic life had taken on her. "I do get so tired & so weak sometimes," she told Margaret Howell. Far more grueling journeys lay ahead for Varina, but for now, Richmond, Virginia, would be her new home.[8]

The move brought new problems for Jeff as well as his wife. Although the flood of army volunteers who poured into that city cheered their president whenever he appeared before them, the newly elected Confederate Congress proved less uniformly supportive. To Varina's horror and disgust, criticism of her husband began almost at once. Jeff did have allies, but there was no established party loyalty to act as a buffer against the recriminations that seemed to follow every policy decision, every appointment, and soon enough every battle, whether won or lost. Even the celebration of the early Confederate victory at Bull Run, near Manassas, Virginia, in July 1861 was marred by criticism of the president when Southern troops failed to pursue the fleeing Yankees into the very capital of the Union. It did not seem to matter that Davis had, Varina insisted, ordered such a move but his forces had been in too great disarray to act.[9]

Varina vented her frustration at the criticism in a letter to her old friend Mary Chesnut. "How I wish my husband were a dry goods clerk," she declared. "Then we could dine in peace on a mutton scrag at three and take an airing on Sunday in a little buggy with no back, drawn by a one eyed horse at fifty cents an hour. *Then* Yankees or no Yankees we might abide here or there, or any where." But she was too much a realist to imagine that Jeff would abandon his responsibilities and return to private life. And she was not, after all, the wife of a clerk but the First Lady of the Confederacy. The real issue before her was how to help her husband mollify his critics. She tried to smooth over some of the tensions in the same way she and other political wives had done in Washington: by inviting disgruntled officers and congressmen to the Davis home and engaging in soothing flattery at social events. But Jeff simply grew more withdrawn. In her memoirs, Varina acknowledged the hopelessness of her strategy. "He was abnormally sensitive to disapprobation," she wrote, "even a child's disapproval discomposed him. He felt how much he was misunderstood, and the sense of mortification and injustice gave him a repellent manner."[10]

Jeff's fierce pride and thin skin were not the only problems facing Varina as she tried to calm the troubled waters surrounding her husband. Her own popularity was at issue, and the female support she desperately needed was difficult to come by. She knew that no matter where she went, she was not universally liked by other women. She had left a trail of critics and enemies everywhere, from Davis family women in Mississippi to congressional wives in Washington. In Montgomery, too, she faced female animosity. In the short time she had reigned as First Lady of the Confederacy in Alabama, she had taken her duties seriously, working to create an atmosphere that was free of pomp and excessive formality. Male commentators approved of her hostess skills. After one of her receptions, the English journalist William H. Russell reported to his readers: "There was no affectation of state or ceremony. . . . Mrs. Davis, whom some of her friends call 'Queen Varina,' is a comely, sprightly woman, verging on matronhood, of good figure and manners, well-dressed, ladylike and clever, and she seemed a great favorite with those around her." Yet Russell did not realize that the label "queen" was used by enemies as often as by friends. Once again, Varina's sharp wit and her unwillingness to hide her intelligence had translated for some into haughtiness and snobbery.[11]

The situation had grown worse rather than better in Richmond, though ironically, here much of the criticism was radically reversed. While Montgomery's social leaders labeled Varina haughty, the elite women of the Old Dominion condemned her as coarse and unpolished. To these women of impeccable genealogy, Varina represented the crass, nouveau cotton society. Mary Chesnut, whose husband was the wealthy South Carolina planter who served as President Davis's aide, marveled at the reversal of opinion both Davises seemed to suffer at the hands of local Richmond society. "In Washington when we left it," she noted in her diary, "Jeff Davis ranked second to none—in intellect—maybe the first from the south. . . . Now, they rave that he is nobody and never was. And she? Oh, you would think to hear them that he found her yesterday in a Mississippi swamp." Chesnut understood the undercurrent of resentment that ran beneath the criticisms of her friend, for Varina had usurped a position of prominence in Richmond usually reserved for local matrons. She struck many as a confusing mix of kindness and contempt, pride and democratic impulse, formality and informality, and wit that was at once delightful to some and devastating to others. Above all, she was comfortable in the company of men without being flirtatious, and openly acknowledged her role as a political and military confidante of her powerful husband. In the end, Mary Chesnut quipped, "even those who did not like V had to admit she was not dull."[12]

In private, Varina and her friend Mary mocked her critics, yet in her memoirs, Varina showed a surprising sympathy for these cliquish Richmond women. She understood them even if they misunderstood her. "I was impressed by a certain offishness in their manner toward strangers; they seemed to feel that an inundation of people perhaps of doubtful standards . . . had poured over the city, and they reserved their judgment and confidence, while they proffered a large hospitality. It was the manner usually found in English society toward strangers," she added. Difficult though these women were, Varina recognized the importance of establishing good social relationships with those who dominated society in the Confederacy's capital. As the war progressed and Richmond's women, rich and poor, faced the problems of scarcity, the immediacy of danger, and the haunting presence of military casualties, the "offishness" diminished.[13]

The Union capital and the Confederate capital now lay within striking distance of each other. Yet in the months after Bull Run, an eerie quiet seemed to settle over both cities. In the North, General George B. McClellan, the commander of the newly created Army of the Potomac, devoted his energies to turning his 185,000 new recruits into a well-trained and disciplined war machine. In Richmond, the Confederate government concentrated on taking the necessary precautions to protect its capital, creating three armies in Virginia. The first, under Joseph E. Johnston, was stationed at Harpers Ferry, the scene of John Brown's thwarted revolution; the second was under the Louisiana creole Pierre Gustave Toutant de Beauregard, who had left his civilian pursuits as a writer and inventor to command the army at Manassas; and the third, at Norfolk, was under Generals Benjamin Huger and John Magruder, whose dramatic gestures and stylish uniforms earned him the name "Prince John." As the war progressed, Johnston and Beauregard would become vocal critics of Jeff Davis. Johnston's animosity would soon prompt Mary Chesnut to declare that his hatred of the Confederate president "amounts to a religion." Long after the war, Varina would devote pages of near vitriol to Johnston.[14]

Varina had few illusions about the peril facing the South now that war had begun. She knew that the youthful enthusiasm of Confederate troops could not protect them from an enemy who was better armed and more numerous. "Their hordes," she had written soon after she arrived in Richmond, "are very near & their bitterness is very great." But as winter approached, her own thoughts had turned inward, for despite the certainty of bloodshed and death, the creation of new life was also a reality. On December 6, 1861, her fifth child, William Howell Davis, was born.[15]

Twenty-one

"THE PEOPLE OF OUR COUNTRY
ROSE IN THEIR MIGHT"

From First Lady to Refugee

EIGHTEEN SIXTY-TWO BEGAN GRIMLY FOR THE SOUTH. In February, Union general Ulysses S. Grant moved against the Southern strongholds in the Mississippi Valley. Kentucky fell to him and most of Tennessee came under Union control. On February 22, in a pouring rain that seemed to heighten the gloom of this military setback, Jefferson Davis was inaugurated for his second term. The rain-soaked crowds cheered, but Jeff knew that he lacked the support of many in his government and a growing number of his generals. Varina recalled the day sadly, describing her husband as he stood, pale and emaciated, looking more like "a willing victim going to his funeral pyre" than the leader of a new nation.[1]

In April, the horror of the war became a reality to both the North and the South. On the sixth of that month, Confederate General Albert Sidney Johnston led a surprise attack on Grant's forces at Pittsburg Landing, Tennessee, near a small meetinghouse called Shiloh Church. Victory seemed within the grasp of the Confederates, but Union reinforcements arrived, Grant counterattacked, and the Southern army was forced to retreat. The Union had its victory, but it came at staggering cost: the dead, wounded, and missing numbered in the many thousands for both victor and vanquished. A Confederate soldier put into words what those around him felt: "Death in every awful form, if it really be death, is a pleasant sight in comparison to the fearfully and mortally wounded." The carnage of the Battle of Shiloh was only the beginning.[2]

Grant's successes in the Mississippi Valley were part of a Union strategy called the Anaconda Plan, which aimed at cutting the Confederacy in two, much as the British general John Burgoyne had hoped to separate New England from the remaining rebellious colonies in 1778. But the general public in the North preferred a more direct strategy aimed at taking the Confederate capital. Bending to popular pressure, Abraham Lincoln gave greater priority to eastern campaigns in 1862. In Richmond, both military men and civilians braced for an assault on their capital city. When it came, it took the form of General William McClellan's Peninsular Campaign.[3]

McClellan bargained that by marching his Army of the Potomac up the peninsula between the York and James rivers, he could avoid the casualties certain to come from a march south to Richmond from northern Virginia. By April 4, Union forces were on their way north to Richmond. Fearing that the Confederate armies might not be able to protect the city, Jeff Davis insisted that his wife and children flee to the safety of North Carolina. By the time Varina left, the area around Richmond was in panic and many had begun to seek refuge in the city. "It was pitiable," she recalled, "to see our friends coming in without anything except the clothes they had on, and mourning the loss of their trunks in a piteous jumble of pain and worriment."[4]

Varina was not without her own "worriment." She had wept bitterly when news came that April of the death of General Albert Sidney Johnston at Shiloh. He had been a warm friend to her husband, and his death, probably from an errant Confederate bullet, removed one of the best and most loyal of Jeff Davis's commanders. Then word reached her that her parents had narrowly escaped from the Union occupation of New Orleans, fleeing to Montgomery by boat. Finally, she learned that the tentacles of war had reached deep into the Davises' own state—and their own future, for Brierfield had been ransacked, the library destroyed, the stock killed, and the slaves driven off the land. Jeff wrote of their personal loss in his characteristic stoic manner: "You will have seen a notice of the destruction of our home. If our cause succeeds, we shall not mourn over any personal deprivation; if it should not, why, 'the deluge.' "[5]

Varina was devastated. "I live in a kind of maze," she confessed to Mary Chesnut, "disaster follows disaster . . . this dreadful way of living from hour to hour depresses me more than I can say." In June, while she was still in Raleigh, North Carolina, disaster struck again. Her infant son, Billy, fell seriously ill. Exhausted by anxiety and child care, Varina suffered a return of the mysterious heart problem that had plagued her since her youth. Jeff, burdened with a seemingly endless stream of military and political crises, took the news of Billy's illness equally hard. Unable to control his emotions, he wrote: "My heart sunk within me at the news of the suffering of my angel baby. . . . My ease, my health, my property, my life I can give to the cause of my country. The heroism which could lay my wife and children on any sacrificial altar is not mine." The long separation, the anxiety over

Billy's survival, and the precarious condition of the nation they represented as president and first lady brought Varina and Jeff closer emotionally than they had ever been. They spoke frankly in their letters of their love
and their concern for each other. "My heart is with you," he wrote, while
she confessed that "we have been so much together of late years that my
heart aches when I can not kiss you good night." There was no hint of
patronizing in his letters and no sign of self-doubt in her replies. Her need
to assert herself and his need to restrain her seemed irrelevant in the midst
of the war raging around them.[6]

Despite Confederate general Joe Johnston's pessimism and his poorly
coordinated attacks on McClellan at Seven Pines and Fair Oaks, Richmond
was not taken by the enemy. Much of the credit for its survival was due
to the efforts of Robert E. Lee, who replaced the wounded Johnston. Lee's
daring strategy—splitting his forces and attacking McClellan's army from
all sides during a seven-day campaign—marked him as the Confederacy's
most valuable general. A telegram bearing news of Confederate success
reached Varina as she walked her sick son to and fro in front of her hotel
window. The telegraph office sat across a narrow alleyway from Varina's
room, and an anxious crowd waited below, hoping to hear a report from
the front. As the telegrapher shouted the brief message to the men and
women below, someone admonished the crowd: "Don't hurrah, you will
scare the sick baby."[7]

On her return to Richmond that August, Varina found the city air filled
with the odors of the battlefield. The women who had remained behind
had kept vigil on the roofs of their houses, she recalled, watching "the
smoke and gleam of battle" and praying for victory. The city itself seemed
diminished, war-weary, no longer the elegant gem of the Old South. Even
before the Peninsular Campaign, Richmond citizens had begun to feel the
pinch of scarcity and the painful presence of sick and wounded young soldiers in gray. The women of the city had done, and would continue to
do, what they could: they visited the wounded in the makeshift hospitals,
reading to the boys and often singing to them as well, and they knitted
socks and gloves and sewed shirts for the able-bodied men. "Our women,"
Varina wrote, "knitted like Penelope, from daylight until dark." The women
offered up their jewels, their silver, anything of value for the cause. Nothing
was deemed too sacred or cherished. "I tried," confessed one woman
guiltily, "and could not make up my mind to part with my wedding-ring,
and it was so thin from wear; else I think I could have given it up."[8]

"Making do" became as much a challenge to women's ingenuity and resourcefulness as a mark of patriotism. Varina admired the determination of the city's elite matrons to remain symbols of elegance. "The ladies . . . covered their worn-out shoes with pieces of silk and satin, drawn from old boxes long unused," she recalled; "old scraps of silk were cut in strips, picked to pieces, carded and spun into fine yarn, and silk stockings knitted from it. The most beautiful hats were plaited from palmetto, dried and bleached, as well as from straw. The feathers from domestic fowls were so treated that they were very decorative to their bonnets, and if one sometimes regretted that millinery should be a matter of private judgment, still, in their pretty homespun dresses they would have passed favorably in review with any ladies."[9]

But feathered bonnets and silk stockings could not hide the fact that the world these women knew was shattering. Household slaves, emboldened by the presence of Northern armies in Virginia, had begun to desert their mistresses. And a ripple that would later become a flood of refugee African Americans, driven from Virginia plantations, began to fill local cities. White Southerners such as Varina responded with mixed and contradictory emotions. She voiced disappointment and surprise when one of her own household slaves, whose loyalty and affection she had never doubted, ran away. She spoke with contempt of the "lazy, good-for-nothing vagabonds" flooding cities such as Alexandria. Yet she was appalled and saddened by the daily assaults upon blacks by white soldiers, and in 1863 she would rescue a young African American boy being abused by his master on the streets of Richmond. The problem was as difficult as it was simple: there was no code of behavior to guide white Southerners such as Varina, no social conventions to fall back on, and no acceptable ideology to embrace as African Americans made their claim to be people rather than property.[10]

For the rest of the year, military victories and defeats seemed to come in equal measures. That summer, Memphis, Baton Rouge, and the state of Missouri fell into the hands of the Union. But in August, the Second Battle of Bull Run ended as the first had ended, with Confederate success. Only a month later, a Southern army was defeated at Antietam in Maryland. The grim mood that settled over Richmond that fall lifted suddenly that winter when reports came of a crucial victory at Fredericksburg, Virginia. Looking back, Varina spoke with pride of the Confederate army's tenacity and resiliency. "The disasters of the early part of the year," she wrote, "had been redeemed. The whole world paid homage to the military prowess and genius that the Confederates had exhibited." Yet, in this roller coaster of successes and failure, the loss of life was so staggering that claims of victory must have seemed hollow to many. Twenty-three thousand men died at Antietam in only three days of fighting and more than seventeen thousand fell at Fredericksburg, where dying men were left on the battlefield all night.[11]

If 1862 ended on the high note of victory at Fredericksburg, 1863 began with the news of Abraham Lincoln's Emancipation Proclamation. Varina believed that this attack on property, rather than disheartening Southerners, would produce a new, steely determination among Confederate troops. For her part, Varina turned to music and song in an effort to bolster the morale of Richmond society. She brought the city's most talented musicians and singers to the executive mansion for "matinee musicales" perhaps reminiscent of the sing-alongs in The Hurricane's music room that had delighted the Davis family so many years before. She also hosted large receptions and intimate breakfast parties in the elegant home that was known as the Confederate White House, hoping to divert her neighbors' attention from the war, if only for a moment.

It came as no surprise to Varina that these social events brought equal measures of scorn and approval. She had learned to greet criticism of her behavior with both resignation and a measure of amusement. When curious—or, more accurately, nosy—matrons pestered Mary Chesnut to reveal what was done and said at the breakfast parties, Varina's friend and confidante shocked them by declaring that everyone danced on tightropes. Varina was clearly amused, but she warned Mary to "have mercy," for her enemies were all too ready to believe the worst. "They will believe you," she said, for "you do not know this Richmond. They swallow scandal with such wide open mouths . . . next winter they will have the exact length of our petticoats, and describe the kind of spangles we were sprinkled with."[12]

The forced gaiety of Varina's musicales did little to soften the news coming off the battlefront. Every Confederate victory seemed to contain some cause for sorrow as well as rejoicing. Success at Chancellorsville, for example, cost the South dearly, for it was here that one of the South's most beloved leaders, Thomas Jonathan "Stonewall" Jackson, died from what modern Americans would call "friendly fire." News of the tragedy reached Richmond almost immediately: Jackson had been reconnoitering with members of his staff when he was struck by three .57-caliber bullets. Despite frantic efforts to save his life, the young general died on May 10. In her memoirs, Varina remembered Jackson as others had described him: a man with a heavy dark beard and war-weary eyes, his dignity undiminished by his fondness for sucking lemons.[13]

Musicales could not soften the growing desperation within the Southern capital, either. Varina knew that, like herself, the women of Richmond had done their best to maintain a façade of hopefulness and optimism. While their husbands, sons, brothers, and friends fought their desperate fight, not only against the federal armies but also against "cold, heat, starvation," these women "choked back their tears, tried to forget their bare feet, their meagre fare, their thousand alarms by night, and all the grinding want that pressed them out of youth and life, and wrote of the cheer our victories gave them, of their prayers for success, and their power to endure unto the end."[14]

Yet not even the sacrifice of youth and life could stop the downward spiral of circumstances in Richmond. Repeated military campaigns had devastated the farmlands that supplied the city, and much of the produce that remained went to feed the army. Basic necessities grew scarce and spiraling inflation made it difficult for Richmond's poorer population to feed their families; the situation was aggravated by the rising number of refugees who entered the city that year. On April 2, 1863, a group of desperate women took matters into their own hands. They marched to Capitol Square and confronted Virginia's governor, demanding relief from the high cost of food. The governor had no solution to a problem caused by war rather than state policies. Frustrated, the growing crowd that some say reached over a thousand men and women began to smash windows and loot local food, clothing, and jewelry shops. Richmond's Bread Riot had begun.

Despite the potential danger, Jeff Davis went out to address the angry crowd. No circumstances, he told them, no matter how extreme, justified acts of lawlessness. He was unbending in his condemnation of their actions, yet he sympathized with their suffering. Before he left, he reached into his own pockets and emptied them, offering what money he had and his own watch to the crowd. Then he ordered them to disperse—or be fired upon. Whether it was his generosity, his threat, or both that moved the crowd, they slowly returned to their homes.[15]

News of the Richmond Bread Riot was carried in both the Southern and Northern press. The differences in the reports were telling. The *Richmond Examiner* told a tale of lawlessness perpetrated by "prostitutes, thieves, Irish and Yankee hags," none of them true Virginians but "gallows-birds from all lands but our own." The *New York Herald* told a more sympathetic tale of desperate women who had "begged in the streets and at the stores until begging did no good" and whose battle for survival drove them to violence and looting. The Richmond paper laid the blame for this riot—and others like it in Mobile, Alabama, and Atlanta, Georgia—on outside agitators who were agents of the Northern government; the *Herald* portrayed the riot as evidence of the widespread deterioration of Confederate circumstances and morale.[16]

Varina was not there to witness the riot or her husband's risky appearance before the mob. News had come to her that her father was fatally ill, and she had left for Montgomery in March. When she returned to Richmond in April, she found that Jeff, too, was ill, his fever, pain, and inflamed throat and eyes all telltale signs of the stress he was under. Events that summer did little to alleviate his worry: the South suffered a major defeat in the mutual slaughter at Gettysburg, with its fifty thousand casualties in only three days of battle, while at the same time Vicksburg was falling to General Grant. Hundreds if not thousands of Southern mothers, fathers, sisters, and brothers mourned the loss of loved ones—and Jeff Davis was no exception. His sister Lucinda's son died on the Gettysburg battlefield. More than thirty-four thousand other boys wearing the blue or the gray would die that fall in the Battle of Chickamauga, a Southern victory in the war to control Tennessee. That fall, Union forces under General Grant managed to break the Confederate siege of Chattanooga and drive the Southern army as far as Atlanta. During the campaign, Confederate officers had called for the removal of their commanding officer, Braxton Bragg, and in October 1863 Jeff Davis was forced to visit the camp to see if he could resolve this damaging internal conflict. He failed, and the Confederate defeat that followed only increased the already vocal criticisms of the president. Depression hung over the Davis household. But worse was to come.[17]

Rumors of another attempt to take Richmond were rife as 1864 began. In March, Varina wrote a long letter to her brother Jeffy, a midshipman in the Confederate navy. In it she recounted with seeming good humor the extraordinary plan she and her sister Maggie had devised should the Yankees invade. They intended to run, wearing every stitch of clothing they could possibly manage. In a practice run, she noted proudly, "I had on seven petticoats, 3 chemises, 3 pair of stocking on my legs and six pair buckled round my legs in my garter." Varina had no illusions about the likelihood of a successful escape, especially since she was almost six months pregnant at the time: "The Yankees would have caught us certainly, for we were so heavy we could hardly walk, running would have been impossible." But Varina's effort at humor could not hide the undercurrent of hysteria brought on by "this dreadful war." She wanted it over; she wanted all her family members out of harm's way. "I sometimes feel nearly wild," she confessed, "but pray continually to God to keep all of mine and me in the right way or I would be a maniac."[18]

It was not a Yankee bullet or cannon fire that took another member of her family away the following month. It was only an unguarded moment in the life of a harried family. On April 30, Varina left her children with an Irish nurse while she carried a lunch to her busy husband at his office. While the Davises stole a welcome moment together, word came that their five-year-old son, Joe, had fallen from a balcony onto the brick pavement below. Varina and Jeff rushed home, but their son never recovered consciousness. He died a few minutes after his parents arrived.

Varina was heartbroken, her husband dazed. "I saw that his mind was momentarily paralyzed by the blow," she wrote. Throughout the night, family and friends such as Mary Chesnut could hear "the tramp of Mr. Davis's step as he walked up and down the room above." For a brief moment the demands of office were forgotten; the president of the Confederacy needed time to mourn for his son.[19]

The death of their child erased, for the moment, all the rancor and hostility of Jeff's critics. In a city that had grown almost immune to news of death and suffering, men and women grieved over the Davis family's intimate tragedy. A procession of schoolchildren and Confederate dignitaries followed Joseph Evan Davis's small coffin up a hillside to the Hollywood Cemetery. Each child carried flowers or a leafy bough to toss on the grave. On May 8, Varina wrote to the widow of Brigadier General Richard Griffith, thanking her for her letter of condolence. "One week ago I should have been able to tell of my most beautiful and promising child. Now I can only tell you that I have three left—none so bright, none so beautiful, but all infinitely precious." Even as she wrote, Varina said, alarm bells were ringing in the streets of Richmond and Robert E. Lee was struggling to ensure that the city would not fall to the enemy.[20]

On June 27, with the sound of the guns in Petersburg audible in Richmond, Varina gave birth to her last child, a daughter and namesake, Varina Anne Davis, known as Winnie. By now, the blockade of the capital had reduced Richmond's citizens to desperate measures, and the Davises were no exception. Jeff sold every horse he could spare; Varina sold her best clothes, her carriage, and her jewelry "to get the necessities of life." Jeff worked night and day, ignoring meals and sleep. "Darkness," Varina later wrote, "seemed now to close swiftly over the Confederacy.[21]

Yet Varina made every effort to maintain a normal life for her children and for the several Howells who seemed always to be with them. Maggie and Jeff's days were filled with school or dancing lessons. When Christmas came, the news that Savannah had fallen to Sherman did not prevent a holiday celebration. No one was forgotten: Varina organized a toy collection for children in a local orphanage, and Jeff made sure that the White House guards received pieces of cake on Christmas Eve. Varina filled the house that evening with the laughter of some twenty young people who decorated the tree with apples and popcorn, drank eggnog, and feasted on homemade gingersnaps and lady cake. The Davis children's Christmas stockings were stuffed with molasses candy, fruit, and warm woolen gloves, and every household servant received a gift. That year everyone's gifts were modest, but Varina managed to provide them for all nonetheless.[22]

It now seemed only a matter of months, or perhaps weeks, before Richmond would be lost. In March 1865, the day she dreaded but expected arrived and Varina said her goodbye to her husband. Though ailing and feeble, Jeff was going to the field; Varina and the children were going to seek refuge in Carolina. "I have confidence in your capacity to take care of our babies," Varina recalled her husband saying, "and understand your desire to assist and comfort me, but you can do this in but one way, and that is by going yourself and taking our children to a place of safety." He made no effort to assure her that all would be well, for she was a grown woman and understood, perhaps better than most, that the Confederacy was crumbling. "If I live," he said, "you can come to me when the struggle is ended, but I do not expect to survive the destruction of constitutional liberty."[23]

Varina had made her own preparations for flight, small though they were. She had purchased four barrels of flour to exchange for food or lodgings along the way south. It was a small precaution, but one Jeff would not allow. The families remaining in Richmond needed these supplies more than his, he insisted. Yet he did give Varina a small sum of gold—and, on the day before she left, a pistol. He showed her how to load it, aim, and fire. It was a desperate measure that reflected the chaos that was spreading in the hours of defeat. There were roving bands of troops, both Yankee and Confederate, in the countryside. Should she be attacked, Jeff told Varina, "you can at least, if reduced to the last extremity, force your assailants to kill you."[24]

The next day Varina was on the run, hoping to reach a port from which to sail to Texas or a foreign country. But travel was excruciatingly slow as she, her children, her sister Maggie, and Jeff's private secretary, Burton Harrison, made their way south from Richmond by train. Burton did his best to protect Varina from the hostility of army deserters who shouted obscenities as their coach pulled into Charlotte, North Carolina, but he could not protect the family's clothes and bedding from being drenched by the steady rain that entered the leaky baggage cars.

For a brief moment, Charlotte seemed a welcome refuge. Varina had found not only decent lodging but also a sympathetic host. "I have carpets, some curtains, some window shades and three pictures and some lovely volumes of books," she wrote to her husband on April 7, adding that she was "very kindly treated" by the owner of the house. It was a measure of her diminished expectations that the first lady of the Confederacy was grateful for kindness and window shades.[25]

Even these small luxuries, however, were not destined to be long enjoyed. Before a week was up, Varina was on the move once again, this time headed for Chester, where she hoped to leave the children in the care of Mary Chesnut. Even this was not to be. Rumors of a raid on Chester set her in flight once more. "I am going somewhere," she wrote to Jeff, "perhaps only to Abbeville." Much depended on how long the children could endure the hardships of the road. Varina's own weariness showed through as she tried to explain her situation to her husband. "I am wordless," she confessed, "helpless . . . May God have mercy upon me."[26]

But if words failed her, her determination did not. Varina persevered. No longer able to rely on the rail lines, she and her family took to the country roads. Along the way, she had found an old ambulance, or wagon, for her family to ride in. When the muddy roads became virtually impassable, Varina got out and walked. One evening found her trudging five miles through the mud, her baby in her arms, while the ambulance remained stuck in the mire. Feeding her family was also a constant problem, for provisions were scarce and expensive unless she was welcomed into the home of a friendly Confederate. A glass of milk could cost Varina a dollar, a biscuit fifty cents. On April 19, she wrote to Jeff once again, this time from Abbeville. She was at her wits' end, she declared, constantly worrying "what ought I to do with these helpless little unconscious charges of mine." That she did not know where Jeff was or how he was doing added to her anxiety and sense of desolation. "I am so at sea," she wrote—yet there was nothing she could do but pretend to her children that all would be well.[27]

Perhaps worst of all, bad news seemed to follow her everywhere she went. The Petersburg line had failed; the Confederate army was in retreat; Richmond had fallen; Lee had surrendered at Appomattox. In the end, it was not her muddied shoes, her hunger, her lack of sleep, or the shock of hostile, jeering strangers that unnerved Varina. It was the news of Lincoln's assassination. She understood that this was both a personal tragedy for his family and a political crisis for the crumbling Confederacy. "I burst into tears," Varina recalled, "the first I had shed, which flowed from the mingling of sorrow for the family of Mr. Lincoln, and a thorough realization of the inevitable results to the Confederates, now that they were at the mercy of the Federals." Varina had cause to worry, for "with malice toward none" was far from the watchword of the new president, Andrew Johnson, nor of the Republicans who dominated Congress. In fact, Jeff's old Senate foe, the onetime tailor from Tennessee who now sat in the White House, issued a statement declaring Jeff complicit in the Lincoln assassination plot. A $100,000 reward was offered for his capture. Varina's husband was now a criminal as well as a traitor in the eyes of many of his enemies.[28]

By early April, Jeff, too, was in flight from Richmond. For several days the two Davises moved, out of sync, through the Carolinas and into Georgia, with Jeff trailing behind his wife as they moved from town to town. Anxious, depressed, exhausted, the couple found some relief in the exchange of tender—and revealing—letters. For Jeff, his inability to protect and provide for Varina was a sign of personal failure. "Dear Wife," he wrote ruefully on April 23, "this is not the fate to which I invited you when the future was rose colored to us both." But for Varina, the future held a promise of intimacy that compensated for the loss of power, fortune, and fame. "It is surely not the fate to which you invited me in brighter days," she conceded, but "you must remember that you did not invite me to a great Hero's home, but to that of a plain farmer. I have shared all your triumphs, been the *only* beneficiary of them, now I am but claiming the privilege for the first time of being all to you now these pleasures have passed for me."[29]

Jeff reached Washington, Georgia, a few days after Varina had departed. Hoping to catch up with her at last, he decided he could move more quickly if he shed much of his military escort. Fellow Confederate leaders who had fled with him now scattered. Judah Benjamin headed for Florida; John Breckinridge went west, hoping to draw off pursuing federal troops and ensure Jeff Davis's safety. Determined to catch up with his family, Jeff now pushed himself to the limit, riding three days and nights, traveling thirty miles in one day, and recklessly riding ahead of his few remaining men in order to rendezvous with his wife. At last, near midnight, he found Varina outside the small village of Dublin. It had been six weeks since they had said goodbye.

On May 9 the two Davis parties made camp together just north of Irwinville, Georgia. They were only fifty miles from the Florida state line. Jeff had promised Burton Harrison that he would ride on to safety, but rumors that a band of marauders were planning to attack the camp convinced him to stay. Fearing the worst, Jeff went to sleep that night beside

Varina, fully dressed. When the attack came at dawn the next day, it was led not by marauders but by federal troops. It began in confusion: two regiments, the Fourth Michigan and the First Wisconsin, had approached from opposite directions and, in the dim light of morning, had begun firing at each other. Hoping to take advantage of the situation, Jeff tried to make his escape. In the chill morning air, he headed toward the nearby woods, wearing a water-repellent cloak and a black shawl that Varina had thrown over his shoulders. But his effort proved futile. Fifty-one months after they had become the First Family of the Confederacy, the Davises became prisoners of war.[30]

Now a new journey, northward, began. Along the road to Augusta, Union troops jeered and taunted the president of the Confederacy and his wife. At Augusta, the Davises were put on a small steamer that carried them, along with Clement and Virginia Clay, General Joseph Wheeler, and General John Ralls, downriver to Savannah. Burton Harrison, too, was among the prisoners, for he had refused to abandon his charge—and was now to pay dearly for his loyalty. At Savannah, they were transferred to the *William P. Clyde* and headed out to sea. On board Varina and Jeff discovered other prisoners, including Alexander Stephens, the vice president of the Confederacy. The small group did their best to preserve their dignity and the dignity of their president: each evening at dinner, they stood until Varina and Jeff were seated.[31]

The *Clyde* reached Hampton Roads, Virginia, on May 20. Now the prisoners were scattered, taken in small groups by tugboat to prisons. Jeff and Clement Clay, who had also been implicated in the Lincoln assassination, were the last to go. "Try not to weep," Jeff told Varina when they at last spirited him away; "they will gloat over your grief." Varina did her best. In her memoirs, she cast the moment, and her husband, in the language of myth and legend. "As the tug bore him away from the ship," she wrote, "he stood with bared head ... and as we looked, as we thought, our last upon his stately form and knightly bearing, he seemed a man of another and higher race."[32]

With the men gone, the women prisoners on board the ship were rudely treated by the Union officers. Varina's trunks were rifled by the soldiers, who took both the children's clothing and the shawl she had draped over her husband's shoulders on the day of his capture. Their heavy-handed treatment sparked Varina's old rebelliousness; as one of the officers who confiscated her possessions walked away, she taunted him, insulting his manliness by calling him "Puss-in-boots!"[33]

For the moment, Varina's own fate and the fate of her children were uncertain. But she feared that her separation from her husband would be long and challenging. She was correct. For the next two years the former president of the Confederacy was held without charges and without trial; while he was in prison, Varina would labor tirelessly for his release.

Twenty-two

"I NEVER REPORT UNFIT FOR DUTY"

Varina Begins Her Campaigns for Freedom

FOUR YEARS OF PENT-UP ANGER, worry, suffering, and sacrifice on the part of Union soldiers and their families seemed to find their release in a hatred of Jefferson Davis. This alone might have made political leaders wary of showing respect or dispensing leniency toward their most notorious prisoner. But there were larger political stakes, for Jeff was a pawn in the growing conflict between the Democrat from Tennessee who now sat in the White House and the Radical Republicans who controlled the legislature. And there were legal issues to consider: Should Jeff Davis be tried for treason? If so, should the trial take place in a civil or military court? Would such a trial, whatever its venue, open the door for a constitutional vindication of secession? While politicians, military officers, lawyers, and judges debated these thorny issues, Jeff Davis languished in prison.[1]

Varina was determined to get her husband out, but first she had to win her own freedom and ensure her family's well-being. Neither task was easy. She had been sent back to Savannah and placed, in effect, under town arrest. Here she rented rooms in a hotel for herself, her four children, her sister, and a former Davis slave, Robert Brown. She had little money and few possessions, for her clothes and her children's clothes had been ruined, confiscated, or lost; her furniture, plate, and other household possessions were scattered in Richmond. Much of what she valued at Brierfield— including their library—had been looted or destroyed. The possibility of a life of poverty weighed heavily on her mind. She worried even more desperately about her children's health. She was certain that the humid, hot climate of the Deep South would add to the dangers posed by childhood diseases. She worried, too, about the emotional scars that her children might suffer. To her horror, occupying Union soldiers thought it was amusing to teach her three-and-a-half-year-old son, Billy, the lyrics to a song entitled "We'll Hang Jeff Davis on a Sour Apple Tree."[2]

The only solution, Varina decided, was to send her children far away, to Canada, where they would be safe from taunts, deprivations, and disease. She enlisted her widowed mother, Margaret Howell, to take everyone but baby Winnie to Montreal. Thus, in mid-July of 1865, Varina said her good-byes to Maggie, Jeff, and Billy.

To the outside world, Varina seemed the strong, even haughty woman who had once been the first lady of the Confederacy. But over the ensuing months she confessed her deepening despair to her closest friends. "As for me," she wrote to Mary Chesnut, "I have nothing—but my one little ewe lamb—my baby. . . . I will not go through the weary form of telling you how I have suffered . . . you know how I bled inwardly—and suffer more because not put in the surgeon's hands as one of the wounded." Yet as long as Jeff was imprisoned, as long as her family was scattered, Varina felt she could not enjoy the luxury of giving up the struggle. "I never report unfit for duty," she would write to Mary—an observation filled with equal parts of despair and pride.[3]

"Duty" meant more than protecting her children from illness or insult. It meant more than defending her husband's honor and preserving his rep-utation. For Varina Howell Davis it meant waging a campaign to free her husband and herself from their respective imprisonments. Soon after she arrived in Savannah she had begun a letter-writing campaign, and now, with her children out of harm's way, these letters flew fast and furious from her pen. Hoping to at least win an improvement in Jeff's living conditions and freedom of movement for herself, she reached out to all and any who she believed might champion their cause. She drew upon friendships she had fostered years earlier as the wife of a United States congressman and senator; she wrote to powerful men she did not personally know but thought she might persuade to be useful; she contacted influential men who seemed, on the surface, to be enemies to her husband's cause and crit-ics of his past deeds as a slaveholder and a leader of secession. She wrote to the newspaper editor and antislavery reformer Horace Greeley; to the con-quering General Ulysses S. Grant; to Missouri Republican senator Francis Blair, who, like Jeff, had studied at Transylvania University and served in the army during the Mexican War; and ultimately to President Johnson himself.[4]

Varina's letters were sometimes long, impassioned, and rambling, and their tone ricocheted between the expected feminine voice—humble, help-less, and pleading—and the bold, demanding voice that was a masculine privilege in her society. Demands that her husband receive humane treat-

ment were followed by pleas for mercy on a wife and mother who had suffered much and desired little but a reunion with her husband and children.
Although she frequently repeated the story of flight, suffering, and mistreatment that cast her as a helpless female victim, she also aggressively
denied the rumors now circulating that Jeff Davis had disguised himself as
a woman in hopes of evading capture. An intelligent mind's contempt for
unreasoned behavior showed through even as she pleaded for chivalrous
assistance: "What have I done," she asked Blair, "that I am a prisoner at
large with my family in a strange place surrounded by detectives who
report every visitor? Have I transgressed any rule of your government since
I have been under its dread tyranny? Why am I kept in a garrisoned town
bereft of home, friends, Husband, and the means of support?"[5]

Varina was not alone in throwing off all notions of proper female behavior for the sake of a husband's welfare. Virginia Clay, whose husband was
also imprisoned at Fortress Monroe, was equally active in seeking his freedom. But this aggressive role, this active engagement, seemed ironically
suited to Varina's character. Though she vacillated between supplication
and demand, her relentless and resourceful campaign seemed to reflect
Queen Varina writ large. No longer presiding at the dinner table or in the
parlor, Varina Howell Davis had turned her considerable abilities to influ-
encing the public world of the newspaper editor, the lawyer, and the politician. Though she found it physically and emotionally exhausting to take
Jeff's place as the head of the family, the independence that came with this
role resonated to her earliest inclinations. The reliance on her own judgment after so many years of deferring to her husband was surely sometimes
satisfying.

Even if Varina had vowed to keep a proper feminine silence, there were
those who were eager to thrust her into the public eye. Both Northern
and Southern newspapers rushed to publish articles on the most famous
prisoner in the country—and, by association, his wife. Personal letters
between Jeff and Varina soon appeared in the press under headlines such as
"Glimpses into Jeff Davis' Desk. Interesting Correspondence." Varina's outrage at this invasion of her most intimate relationship erupted in letters to
William Seward and the attorney George Shea. "The precious records of
my few happy hours" were being used, she wrote, to satisfy the "excitement"
of strangers.[6]

There had been few "happy hours" in the early summer of 1865. Varina
was still forbidden to write to or hear from her husband. Rumors that Jeff
Davis was critically ill reached her, however, and newspapers suggested he

might be dying. Yet she could not go to him, nor could she go to Canada to see her children. At last, in late July, the authorities gave Varina permission to relocate to Mill View, the home outside of Augusta of her old friend George Schley. The Schleys did everything they could to make Varina and her baby, Winnie (whom Varina often called "Pie Cake"), welcome, but nothing could erase her sadness at the diaspora of her family and the uncertainty of her husband's survival. At Mill View the dog days of early August passed in a strange combination of anxiety, rage, boredom—and flashes of humor. "I lead a very humdrum life," she wrote to a friend. She ate, sewed, and slept little as she looked "drearily at my diminished well thumbed greenbacks and with a pathetic sigh mount the family carriage and hie me home talking platitudes with my tongue & with my heart following my soul's laboring in some dread extremity." And yet Varina saw the dark humor in the authorities' assumption that she was a dangerous figure. She joked to the wife of a former Confederate: "Think what a roaring lion is going loose in Georgia seeking whom she may devour, one old woman, a small baby, and nurse; the Freedman's bureau and the military police had better be doubled lest either the baby or I turn again and rend them."[7]

There was no irony to be found, however, in the ban on communication between Jeff and Varina. Until late August 1865, Jeff was not allowed to communicate with anyone except his unresponsive jailers and guards and the doctor who ministered to his many ailments. When, in June, Varina learned the physician's name—Dr. J. J. Craven—she had immediately written to him. "Through the newspapers I learn that you are the Surgeon of the post and thus in attendance upon Mr. Davis," she wrote on June 1, 1865. "Shocked by the most terrible newspaper extras issued every afternoon, which represent my husband to be in a dying condition, I have taken the liberty, without any previous acquaintance with you, of writing to you." Varina knew that proper protocol did not allow a woman to write to a strange man, but her concern for her husband overrode all fears of disapproval. "Would it trouble you too much to tell me how he sleeps—how his eyes look—are they inflamed?—does he eat anything?—may I ask what is the quality of his food?"[8]

Despite her pleas that he take pity on her and answer her questions, Craven did not reply. He was not allowed to. Still she persisted, and when the newspapers reported the doctor's acts of kindness toward Jeff, she poured out her gratitude to him. "Thanks to God," she declared on July 2, 1865, "that He has raised you up a 'present help' in my husband's time of trouble." Even the smallest kindnesses deserved her thanks, she said, for she had read with horror that her husband had been manacled for several days, that a light was kept burning day and night in his cell, and that his health and spirit were failing him. All of this was true, yet despite inflamed eyes, rashes, carbuncles, and bacterial infections, Jeff survived.[9]

If the letters to Dr. Craven did not gain Varina the information she craved, they were perhaps useful in other ways. She hoped that the doctor would convey to her husband the reassuring information she provided about his family. She hoped, too, that he would share with Jeff the account of her life since their separation. For this reason, she took care to stress her positive experiences in Georgia. She offered anecdotes that showed the loyalty of her black servant Robert Brown as he defended her against the rudeness of black waiters at the hotel. She recounted the hospitality of Savannah's citizens, saying, "Had I been a sister long absent and just returned to their home, I could have received no more tender welcome." And, being Varina, she trained her sharp wit on the foibles of a military underling to the commanding officer of occupied Savannah, "whose animus was probably irreproachable, but whose orthography was very bad." Her critique of the military commander was sharper and more damning. He "did himself justice, and verified my preconceived opinion of him," she noted, by refusing to allow her to telegraph to Washington or write to the heads of departments there (or, in fact, to anyone) without approval. The only thing the commander readily allowed, she added, was her right to pay all her expenses.[10]

When the ban on writing was finally lifted, Jeff's letters were subject to censorship and hers were read by military personnel. Varina filled her letters to her husband with news of the children and assurances that both she and they were well. Her greatest pain, she wrote, came from her inability to provide him consolation. "Can it be that your nights of pain are passed without one loving hand to touch you?" she wrote that September. "I wake and weep, watch and pray to be granted strength to wait, to possess my soul in patience . . . and be strong." But patience was not among Varina's virtues; she admitted to Jeff that she had begun a campaign to win permission to see him, waged in letters to the president, to the attorney general, and to others.[11]

Jeff, completely cut off from the outside world, filled his letters with outpourings of love and gratitude. During the long months of imprisonment, she was his lifeline, his reminder that family, friends, and supporters remained outside the walls of Fortress Monroe. "Shut out from the ever changing world," he confessed to Varina, "I live in the past . . . all the years of our love rise before me and bear witness how very dear you are to your Husband." In the solitude of his cell, all memories of her "willfulness," all the times that she had displeased him faded and were replaced with a history of their past together that made her the perfect wife he had always desired—and demanded. "Need I say," he wrote, "that every pang reminded me how often your soft touch and loving words had soothed me in like times of suffering." And as the year was drawing to a close, he thanked her for her care that "protected me from many ills, your hand [that] assuaged suffering, your voice [that] told of happy things and breathed the music sweetest to my ears." There was unabashed tenderness in these prison letters, but Jefferson Davis was cut from nineteenth-century patriarchal cloth: the sum of Varina's life was, and would always be, a catalog of what she did for him, not who she was herself.[12]

Although she was not locked in a cell like her husband, Varina's confinement in Georgia took its toll on her. In November she wrote to Jeff of "the dreary, dreary days, and weeks, and months" she had spent waiting for a reprieve. "I grow hard & sullen with sorrow," she confessed, and her health was suffering. The humid, hot summer had made it difficult for her to breathe, and what she called a nervous excitability left her sleepless and weary. As winter began, she felt a loss of confidence in her ability to make the right decisions for her family. "If you only could know what an awful responsibility I feel, without your counsel, your decision." In this moment of self-doubt and depression, she longed for a return to her life as "Wiffe": "Twenty-one years of happy dependence upon the wisdom and love of another so much better and wiser," she wrote, "does not fit one to stand alone."[13]

Although the months of inactivity and isolation brought Varina these moments of despair, she never lost her saving wit. "Here I am," she wrote to Jeff that December. "Here will I remain until the great end of the constitutional government of a great and free country be answered by my restriction like yourself." Nor did she lose her pride and anger. She had written to President Johnson, asking to visit Jeff. When news came back to her that Johnson had dismissed her to others as a "woman of strong feelings and strong temper," the insult cut deep. The failure of her supporters to press her case angered her more. "If to despise moral cowards and to loathe a man capable of insulting a defenseless, sorrowing woman to unresisting listeners, is to justify this characterisation," she declared in a letter to Armistead Burt, "I acknowledge its justice." Not even on Christmas Day could she find it in her heart to forgive their enemies. Writing to Jeff she exclaimed: "You tell me you think I do not understand the kind of forgiveness which we are to exercise. I do not if it is required of me to pray for those who despitefully use you ... because you are in their power." For these people, she could not find a prayer in her heart. "It is a great sorrow to hate, and a very intense feeling when the object so detested is powerful and the sufferer powerless"—but hate she did.[14]

At long last, in January 1866, Varina received permission to visit her children in Canada. But eager as she was to see them, she did not head north immediately. Instead, she traveled west, to Mississippi and Louisiana, escorted by a strong and devoted black man who refused to accept payment for his services and by the recently released Burton Harrison. She was going to visit family and friends and to see "what had been left to us" at Brierfield. The journey proved both heartening and sad. Everywhere she went, she was greeted warmly by Southern men and women whose criticism of Jeff Davis when he was in power had been replaced by sympathy now that he had been brought low. From New Orleans, Varina wrote to Jeff that it was "impossible to tell you the love which has been expressed here for you—the tenderness of feeling for you." A defeated nation, she declared, "is mourning your suffering with me." Yet everywhere she went she saw the sad outcome of that nation's defeat: General Joseph Wheeler, working as a hardware clerk in New Orleans; "Col Whittle's brother, whose empty sleeve was buttoned to his coat"; and her old nemesis, "Uncle" Joseph Davis, living in near poverty in Vicksburg.[15]

Varina's reunion with "Uncle Joe" was cordial, for a thousand years seemed to have passed since a young bride and a planter patriarch had locked horns over kitchens, inheritances, and the affections of Jefferson Davis. Joe Davis was no longer a formidable foe; he was eighty-two and almost completely deaf, no longer the patriarch of a large family of dependents both black and white. Before she left, Varina gave the man she now called "Brother Joe" $400 and a dressing gown. The war, and time, had healed this family breach.[16]

Together Varina and Burton Harrison headed north by steamboat from Vicksburg to Cincinnati and then by train to New York City. Here she met with Jeff's lawyer, Charles O'Conor. O'Conor had volunteered to take the case soon after Jeff was arrested, and his participation was considered a coup for the Davises. The son of an Irish immigrant, O'Conor had quickly built a reputation as a brilliant lawyer, and he had served as a U.S. district attorney in the 1850s. His interest in Jeff's case was intense, for he was a fiercely committed states' rights Democrat who had opposed efforts to coerce the South to remain in the Union. In 1872, he would be drafted by the South's "Bourbon Democrats" to run for the presidency; though he declined, he received more than twenty thousand votes.

Although O'Conor would ultimately win Jeff his freedom, Varina came away disheartened by their first meeting. An indictment for treason had been handed down in the U.S. Circuit Court in Virginia that June, but no steps had yet been taken to try the case. Within the Johnson cabinet there was strong disagreement about what course to follow, and debates raged over whether Jeff Davis should be tried in a civil court or a military one. For the time being, any effort to gain Jeff's release on bail—or Varina the right to visit him—was futile. There was nothing Varina could do but wait.

Realizing she could do nothing more for the moment, Varina headed to Canada for a reunion with her children. It had been a year since she had seen them. She found them well, though living in a dreary boardinghouse. The older children were enrolled in Catholic schools and only young Billy remained at home with Varina's sister and mother.

Varina had been in Montreal only a few days when rumors reached her that her husband was dying. Panicked, she telegraphed President Johnson: "Is it possible that you will keep me from my dying husband?" It was not. Although the rumors of Jeff's imminent death proved false, the president granted Varina permission to visit the prisoner at Fort Monroe.

Twenty-three

"I SAW MR. DAVIS'S SHRUNKEN FORM AND GLASSY EYES"

The Reunion at Fortress Monroe

VARINA ARRIVED AT THE FORT before daybreak on May 10, 1866, a day she later remembered as cold and raw. She sat for several hours in a small waiting room, anxiously awaiting someone to take her to her husband. It was past 10:00 a.m. when a young lieutenant appeared and asked Varina to sign a parole that she would not take deadly weapons to the prisoner. Then he escorted her to her "quarters," a casement room, which, like the casement where Jeff had been kept, was covered by some fifteen feet of earth on one side and earth and masonry on the other. When at last the twenty-six-year-old commander of the prison, General Miles, came to see her, he curtly informed her that "Davis" was in good health. Varina was stung by the intentional insult to her husband, for the general had pointedly refused to refer to Jeff as Mr. Davis. Next, an officer came and walked her to Carroll Hall, on the far side of the fort.

Varina vividly recalled the scene:

> There were three lines of sentries, which each required a password of the officer, and at last we ascended a stairway, turned to the right, and entered the guardroom, where three young officers were sitting. Through the bars of the inner room I saw Mr. Davis's shrunken form and glassy eyes; his cheek bones stood out like those of a skeleton. Merely crossing the room made his breath come in short gasps, and his voice was scarcely audible. His room had a rough screen in one corner, a horse-bucket for water, a basin and pitcher that stood on a chair with the back sawn off for a washstand and a hospital towel, a little iron bedstead with a hard mattress one pillow, and a square wooden table, a wooden-seated chair that had one short leg and rocked from side to side unexpectedly, and a Boston rocker, which had been sent in a few weeks before.[1]

Varina entered the cell—and the door was locked behind her.
Over the next days and weeks, Varina wrested more humane treatment

from General Miles. He would not allow her to spend the evenings with Jeff
or accompany him on his now daily walks within the fort, but he did
extend the length of each of her visits. Miles defended his treatment of the
prisoner vigorously to Varina, laying the blame for the decision to briefly
manacle Jeff on the secretary of war and insisting that he had provided Jefferson Davis with "all that a gentleman should require." To this, Varina
replied sharply that "perhaps some gentlemen were more exacting than
those he knew." The general's only defense was that Jeff had not asked for
more. "Davis would not beg," he said; he was "a sullen prisoner, and when
he wanted any favor, if he asked for it, it would be given to him."[2]

Miles balked at every effort Varina made to ameliorate Jeff's circumstances. A confrontation was inevitable between this stubborn and determined wife and the young and insensitive officer. It came when she brought
white napkins, silverware, and treats that friends had provided to brighten
Jeff's evening meal. Miles raged that "this fort shall not be made a depot for
delicacies, such as oysters and luxuries for Jeff Davis." He informed Varina
of his intention to check all future packages she carried with her as she
entered the cell. Varina replied just as heatedly: *she* was not his prisoner, she
reminded him, and she would not submit to such a search. It was a battle of
wills the young officer was destined to lose.[3]

Although the new attending physician, George Cooper, assured Varina
that her husband's health was poor but not dangerously so, she was convinced Jeff would not last through the summer. She decided to take matters
into her own hands once again, and left for Washington, D.C., to demand
an interview with the president. Although Jeff and Andrew Johnson had
been in the government together for almost fifteen years before the war,
Varina had never met her husband's old adversary. She knew the story of
his confrontation with Jeff over the "tailor" comment well, however, and so
was not surprised when he sent her a curt reply to her request for an audience: talk to the Republican senators, he told her, rather than to him.[4]

Varina was undeterred. She appealed to a former member of President
Zachary Taylor's cabinet, Reverdy Johnson, who was serving as a Democratic senator from Maryland. Johnson, along with Delaware senator Willard
Saulsbury, who had been a harsh and blunt critic of Abraham Lincoln,
pressed her case with the president. Andrew Johnson had to be pressured
into seeing Varina, but another influential Northerner, Ulysses S. Grant,
proved far more willing to help. The general who defeated the South
offered to meet with Varina and to assist her in any way.[5]

When it came, the meeting with the president was both frustrating and revealing. He was helpless to do anything for Jeff for the moment, he said, for public opinion was still too negative for any show of leniency. Varina would not let this statement pass unchallenged. She reminded Johnson that the public might never have grown so hostile if he had not implicated Jeff in the assassination of Abraham Lincoln. He had known better, she declared, and he did not deny it. His only defense, he admitted, was that drastic measures were demanded at the time. Whatever Varina thought of this excuse, Johnson continued to plead his own helplessness in the face of both Republican and popular animosity. She left, frustrated but, as she wrote, oddly sympathetic toward his "miserable state."[6]

Varina readily conveyed her own "miserable state" in her appeals to men who might respond with sympathy and chivalry. Writing to Horace Greeley, for example, she appealed to the reformer's empathy for the downtrodden and oppressed. "May I come to you again in the bitterness of my sorrow . . . for light and help," she asked. "For thirteen months, I have prayed and tried to cheerfully grope through the mist to find the end, and now it seems no nearer. . . . And now I appeal to you who always sympathise with the weak to help me." Just as Angelina Grimké had solicited signatures for her antislavery petitions, Varina Howell Davis now called on the former abolitionist Greeley to add his name and others to her own petition. "*Will you not procure* signatures enough to that paper which Mr. Shea has," she pleaded, "to arrest Mr. Johnson's attention?"[7]

But if she was indeed anxious, and often felt helpless, Varina was not content to remain passive or patient. She simply refused to accept the president's claim that Jeff "must be left to the Republicans." To give in to this was to ensure that her husband would spend the rest of his life in prison, for, as she explained to her mother, "it is in the power of the judge to postpone his trial from one time to another and this they have done."[8]

Back at Fort Monroe that fall, Varina received welcome news that the arrogant General Miles had been replaced by Brigadier General Henry S. Burton. Burton granted Jeff the freedom of the fort during daylight hours, and this meant not only that Varina could walk and talk with him but also that friends could visit. The news spread quickly, and a train of old friends and the sons of old friends made their pilgrimages to the fort. Several came to dinner in the casement, sitting on candle boxes or the few rickety chairs, reminiscing about happier days, silently toasting the war dead and talking somberly about the future. Soon General Burton provided Varina with four rooms and a kitchen at the end of the fort's Carroll Hall and gave permission for Jeff to stay there with her. Now the number of visitors increased; they came from Baltimore, Norfolk, and Richmond, bringing wine and delicacies to stir Jeff's appetite. The bishop of Montreal, unable to come in person, sent bottles of chartreuse to the Davises. Every evening, after their company departed, Varina read aloud to her husband. By summer, they had settled into a tolerable routine.[9]

That fall, Varina wrote a long letter to William Preston Johnston, the son of Jeff's dear friend and favorite general, the late Albert Sidney Johnston. "We are about as usual here," she explained. "Nothing new, nothing certain—all as misty and anxious as ever—shuffling and truckling seem to be the order of the day." The dreadful mix of tedium and anxiety led her to engage in useless activities, meant only to pass the hours. She read, she told Johnston, but could not remember what she had read when she was done; she sewed a bit but ripped it out, knitted a little but unraveled it; she talked a little "but unsaying everything." She had made a friend in Mrs. Burton, who was Mexican and hated the Yankees for their treatment of her people. "We get together quietly," she confessed to Johnston, "and abuse them."[10]

Twenty-four

"THE BUSINESS IS FINISHED"

Jefferson Davis Goes Free

ALTHOUGH TIME DRAGGED HEAVILY FOR VARINA, she was not as idle as she suggested in her letter to William Johnston. Her husband's case was stalled. Jeff had been indicted for treason by a grand jury in the Virginia circuit court, but Supreme Court Justice Salmon P. Chase had refused to issue the writ of habeas corpus O'Conor had requested on the grounds that Virginia was still under martial law. The U.S. circuit court judge, John Underhill, had refused to set bail for Jeff, arguing that he was technically a military rather than civil prisoner. While O'Conor pressed for a speedy trial, influential men pressed for Jeff's release on bail.[1]

As usual, Varina pressured them all. She wrote to Greeley again on November 21, 1866, no longer stressing her helplessness or her need for a champion. Instead, she laid out a strategy the newspaper editor could pursue, and pressed him to act. While she appreciated the editorial in his *New York Tribune* that had urged Jeff's immediate release, she wrote, she believed he could do more. "Can you not," she asked, "will you not get some such pressing recommendations for my Husband's release as will move Mr. Johnson?"[2]

By early December, Varina had conferred once again with Charles O'Conor in New York. When O'Conor advised her to go to Washington, to lobby old friends and possible allies, she set out immediately. "I am going down to Baltimore Monday evening," she wrote to Jeff on December 8, to see the governor of Maryland. From Baltimore she intended to head to the capital to do what good she could. "I do not know my dearest . . . that I can do anything," she admitted, but nothing could prevent her from trying.[3]

A rain of criticism had fallen on Varina for her bold attempts to "do something" about Jeff's imprisonment. Her critics included Southern matrons such as Nannie Yulee, the daughter of onetime governor of Kentucky Charles A. Wickliffe, who believed that Southern women ought to "submit and be placid" rather than attempting to influence events. God, she declared, was punishing Varina, as much as Jeff, by keeping Jeff in prison. The Lord's purpose, she told Varina, was "to influence your character, and when you please Him He will change his condition." Varina turned a deaf ear to this "pharisaical talk from a really good selfish woman," as she did to all such suggestions that she had breached the boundaries that defined the "true women" of her era. That April she could be found lobbying once again for Jeff's release on bail.[4]

Varina's effort that spring brought promising results. She had won the support of John W. Garrett, president of the Baltimore and Ohio Railroad, who agreed to press Secretary of War Edwin Stanton into removing his objections to Jeff's parole. Varina was, for the first time, genuinely hopeful. Her letters to Jeff were a touching mix of optimism about the future and resignation about her own physical decline. For when she had traveled to Baltimore in early 1867, she had gone with two purposes: lobbying and extensive dental work. On March 18, she wrote to Jeff: "At last I am on my way to the Dentist, pale with fright, but plucky to all outside appearances." Despite the impending oral surgery, she did not fail to make a report on her lobbying efforts. "Governor Pratt called yesterday and [I] went over this morning . . . and I trust that we may know what can be done tonight." Two days later, Varina reported that she had managed to speak to one of Jeff's supporters despite the fact that the pain she was suffering at the dentist's hands—"the killing nerves, and punches and pluggings"—had left her hardly able to think. A few weeks later she reported once again on both the progress of efforts for his release and her dental appointments. "Mr. Garrett seems to think that the Sec. of War is now favorably inclined to your release," she told her husband on April 9, 1867, adding, "I am to go with Prof Smith tomorrow and have seven or eight teeth extracted by the use of chloroform to give me courage." Later, she reported with typical Varina humor: "[M]ost of my decayed teeth are out, and I live to tell this wondrous tale." Varina attributed her loss of teeth to "the ravages of time," and tried to make light of the disfigurement that resulted. She now had "but three upper teeth," she wrote, "but I can live just as well without them, however unlovely I shall appear." Her musings on lost beauty and her reports of the pain she endured were not prompted by any questions on Jeff's part. With characteristic self-centeredness, he had never inquired about her ordeal.[5]

Weeks later, Varina was still mixing reports on politics and dental work, sometimes in the same sentence. "[T]he last operation, pulling seven teeth, was a very severe one," she admitted to Jeff, and then, with no transition, not even a period or comma, she continued, "and our advisors seemed to think I must wait until Congress adjourned before I put myself hors de combat." She knew her days of battle might be coming to a close, however. Garrett's pressure on Stanton had produced favorable results, and Massachusetts senator Charles Wilson had moved for Jeff's release. As the ordeal seemed to be ending, Varina grew suddenly cautious. She admitted to her husband, "I have had so many disappointments that I am greatly stirred up but not hopeful, where others seem to feel certain."[6]

In the end, the optimism of her friends and lawyers proved correct. On May 11, 1867, Jeff Davis at last left the confines of Fortress Monroe. Varina, the fort's commander, General Burton, the physician, Dr. Cooper, and Burton Harrison accompanied him as he boarded the *John Sylvester* and sailed up the James River to Richmond. Here a civil court awaited him. Two years before, Varina had stood beside her husband as crowds in Augusta jeered the captive Confederate president; now as she entered Richmond beside him, crowds gathered at the river landing with flowers and applause. In the city streets men removed their hats out of respect for their former leader, and women waved their handkerchiefs from their windows. Friends poured into the Spotswood Hotel, where Varina and Jeff were given the same rooms they had occupied on their arrival in the Confederacy's new capital in 1861. Burton Harrison captured the mood in a letter to his fiancée: "Everyone has called, bringing flowers and bright faces of welcome to him who has suffered vicariously for the millions." All the criticism of Jeff's handling of the war and all the harsh judgments heaped upon his administration had indeed faded from the memory of the men and women who were already turning the shame of defeat into the romance of the lost cause.[7]

The courtroom formalities were brief: bail was set at $100,000, and promptly provided by a number of supporters including Horace Greeley, the abolitionist Gerrit Smith, and the railroad magnate Cornelius Vanderbilt. No trial date was set, and there seemed to be no enthusiasm for one on the part of the government. Jeff's attorney, Charles O'Conor, declared that "the business is finished. Mr. Davis will never be called upon to appear for trial." Although the matter dragged on until the end of 1868, O'Conor's prediction proved correct. As news of Jeff's release spread, letters of congratulations poured in from family and friends including Joe Davis, Texas

Democrat John H. Reagan, and General Robert E. Lee. "Your release has lifted a load from my heart," Lee wrote—sentiments that Varina surely shared. But for Jeff Davis, his release was yet another bitter defeat: by freeing him, the government had denied him both the chance to vindicate secession and the martyrdom he sought.[8]

Twenty-five

"OUR ONCE HAPPY HOMES"

Varina's Postwar Odyssey

IN 1861, WHEN POLITICAL CRITICISMS of her husband began to grow, Varina had dreamed of a life far from the public eye. She wished, she had confided to Mary Chesnut, that her husband was not in politics, not president of the Confederacy, but an ordinary man no more in the spotlight than a "dry goods clerk." By 1867, that wish born of frustration had become her reality. Jeff Davis's political career was over. She was at long last the wife of a private citizen—but the circumstances proved more ordeal than idyll. For the next two decades, Varina's life was filled with an anxiety and uncertainty far different from what she had known as a politician's wife, but it was anxiety and uncertainty nonetheless.

While Jeff was imprisoned, Varina had focused all her energies on his release. Although it was far from pleasant, the battle to win his release carried a drama and purpose that seemed to evaporate when he walked out of the courtroom that day in May 1867. Now the problems facing Varina were both mundane and overwhelming: Where would they live? What resources did they have to make a new start? How would they educate their children? What work could fill Jeff's days and give his life focus? What role would Varina play after so many years as a powerful and influential man's wife?

For the moment, all decisions were postponed. Jeff was still, technically, on parole rather than a free man, and despite O'Conor's assurances, Varina knew that her husband would take few decisive steps until his legal situation was resolved. The most pressing need, both Varina and Jeff agreed, was for the children to see their father and mother once again. So the Davises headed north to Canada, where Maggie, Jeff, Billy, and Varina's widowed mother had been since Varina's detainment in Savannah. Confederate refugees in Canada greeted them warmly and expressed their hopes that the Davises would settle in "a country freed from the *tyranny* and brutality now dominant, at our once happy homes."[1]

Whatever tonic Varina hoped the family reunion would provide, she was disappointed. The Canadian trip served only to emphasize the scars that political and military defeat and two years of prison life had left upon her husband. He was now hypersensitive to noise and craved quiet and solitude. The busy streets of Montreal disturbed him, and even the babble of his children and the cheerful confusion of a large household grated on his nerves. His dependence upon the charity of supporters and friends embarrassed him, and he refused to socialize with those who aided him. To Varina, he seemed to have closed in upon himself. She did what she could to draw him back into the world: she took his letter book and other documents from the bank vault where she had placed them for safekeeping and urged him to begin a history of the Confederacy. But Jeff refused. "I cannot speak of my dead so soon," he told her. And Varina understood. "All the anguish of that great struggle came over us," she recalled, "we saw our gaunt, half clothed, and half-starved men stand vibrating with courage to their finger-tips, their thin ranks a wall of fire about their homes; we saw them mowed down by a countless host of enemies, overcome, broken in health and fortune, moving along the highways to their desolated homes, sustained only by the memory of having vindicated their honor." She was describing others, but she might have been speaking of her husband and herself.[2]

Jeff was clearly scarred by his ordeal, yet Varina, too, seemed exhausted, drained, finally "unfit for duty." Nothing could be counted as certain, not her husband's health nor his safety nor his ability to support his family. Despite all her ministrations, Jeff remained weak, and in June he collapsed, falling down the stairs with Winnie in his arms and breaking two ribs. News reached them in Canada of a plot, organized by African Americans, to kill Jeff when he reentered the United States. Even if the rumor was false, it drove home the point: the future was too clouded for Varina to be optimistic. No ray of hope could be found. Their former home, Brierfield, was in ruins, and neither Canada nor the Reconstruction South seemed a welcoming site to lay down new roots. She had no money of her own and no inheritance; indeed, her parents had long relied upon Jeff to provide for their family. Now her husband had no source of income and no experience in the world of commerce and business in which contented "dry goods clerks" labored. His only immediate job offer, a college presidency, carried a salary far too meager to support a family. In her memoirs, Varina admitted to the deep depression that enveloped her: "[I] could not think clearly or act properly, difficulties seemed mountain high, the trees and flowers sheltered and bloomed for others, I knew they were fair, but they were not for me or mine."[3]

The search for a home, a steady income, and appropriate schools for their children produced a nomadic life for Varina and Jeff over the next decade. Together, they traveled from Canada to Havana, where funds were rumored to have been deposited by a former Confederate agent on behalf of the Davis children. None were found. From Cuba, they went to Mississippi, where "the desolation of our country" deepened Jeff's depression and persuaded both Varina and Jeff that they must look elsewhere to begin their life anew. Varina noted her husband's growing desperation in a postscript to a letter from Jeff to their friend Howell Cobb: "Mr. Davis looks wretchedly, and I think much of his indisposition is induced by his despair of getting some employment which will enable him to educate our children." To Cobb's wife, Mary Ann, Varina spoke more openly of her own exhaustion and despair. She wished the two could meet again face-to-face so that she could "give you some of my cares to share with me." But no such meeting was possible, for by July 1868 Jeff and Varina were aboard a ship bound to London, where Jeff hoped to turn vague business connections into a viable career. Nothing materialized; even his efforts to turn a profit from a Canadian copper mine he had invested in proved fruitless.[4]

Varina's cares did not vanish with the crossing of the ocean. In a long letter to Mary Ann Cobb that October, Varina recited a litany of cares. The family's poverty, she explained, forced her to live like a hermit in England, unable to either travel or socialize. "It costs so much to dress even decently, that I have decided not to try and I never accept any invitations to go anywhere to dinner, or elsewhere, not even to an exhibition, except such as are free, for I feel hourly the necessity of pinching at every turn." Far worse, she almost lost her son Billy to a form of typhoid fever. She had rushed to his school to find him delirious, his lips black. Although the doctor predicted the boy would die, Varina would not allow it; she nursed him back to health, pouring brandy down his throat when he ceased to be able to swallow. As for Jeff, she confided that his health was "permanently broken," and she feared he would "never be able to do much again." All she could do was watch over him at all times, and "pray to go first if it must be that we are to be parted."[5]

By January 1869, the Davises were in Paris. Jeff considered settling in the French capital, where his close friend, the diplomat A. Dudley Mann, had taken up residence. While her husband did some desultory house hunting, Varina returned to England. In the end, Jeff rejected Paris; Parisian morals were too lax, he discovered, and the city's women too indecent. Writing to Varina in early February, he declared himself "thankful my wife was reared beyond the contact of [what the French considered] refinements." Eager to protect their oldest daughter from French mores, Varina and Jeff decided to enroll the fourteen-year-old Maggie in a convent school. Jeff, their oldest son, was placed in school in Liverpool. Once again, parents and children were separated.[6]

In September 1869, Varina and Jeff were also separated. He headed back to the United States to pursue his hopes for a job with the Southern Pacific Railroad—and a more realistic possibility of a position with an insurance company. Varina remained in England, near the children. Her own hopes lay with the insurance company, which, she told Jeff, "seems to promise more of a home than anything else." Reluctantly, Jeff was forced to agree. When the railroad post did not materialize, his choices narrowed to relying on the charity of friends or accepting the job with the insurance company. "Soberly, indeed sadly, looking at my needs as well as those of others near and dear to me," he wrote, he was inclined to say yes. In this fashion, the sixty-one-year-old former president of the Confederacy became the president of the Carolina Life Insurance Company. In both cases, his term in office lasted a little over four years.[7]

The insurance company headquarters were in Memphis, a city that held no appeal for Varina. The humid summers there would bring a recurrence of her vaguely diagnosed heart trouble. It was perhaps a measure of his sense of failure as the family patriarch that Jeff did not command her to join him. Instead, he left the decision up to her. "Choose freely," he wrote—and, for the first time, Varina did. She was no doubt tired of "floating uprooted," as she had once described her postwar life to a friend. And she did not want to go south at all—at least until the Union's policies of Reconstruction ended. Hateful though the Radical Republican regime seemed to her, much of her contempt was reserved for the people of the South, by which she meant white men and women. She damned them for their complicity and acceptance of military occupation and political domination. Instead of casting her lot with cowards and accommodationists, she would remain in England, perhaps moving from London to Liverpool as an economy measure. She faced such a move to a smaller community with trepidation, for she saw a distinct advantage in the anonymity of London. "How soon solitude and the habit of isolation becomes a pleasing vice. . . . Now it seems like a cold plunge to go among those who are happy and at home with a tolerably certain future before them." Yet she dreaded a return to

America far more: "I turn sick with the thoughts of what you will undergo," she wrote Jeff, "while you see the ideal people of your life's long love change into a mere temporizing people of expedients." Reports from friends hardened her resolve to avoid her defeated homeland. "*As long as you can bear the separation*," Mary Ann Cobb wrote, "*remain in England*. You know not what may be in store for you and yr children in this country. . . . There will be no peace to the country during the Radical rule, and there is much cause for apprehension that things will grow worse than better." Varina needed no more uncertainty in her life: she remained in London.[8]

Varina's own depression and exhaustion—"this death in life," as she described it—absorbed her. The promise she had made to Jeff to "be all to him" as they fled Richmond could no longer be kept. But Jeff's need for the encouragement, approval, and attention of a woman was strong, and in Varina's physical and emotional absence, he sought new confidantes. Sometime in 1870 he began a short-lived but intimate correspondence with Virginia Clay, wife of the former Confederate cabinet member and fellow Fortress Monroe prisoner Clement Clay. While Clement was consumed by tuberculosis, Jeff began to reveal his soul to Ginnie. The affair was emotional rather than physical and had about it something of the romance of the age of chivalry. He worshiped her from afar, with words rather than deeds. "In writing to you, I find it hardest to stop," he confessed to Mrs. Clay, and continued in a somewhat stilted language of love: "It is as if to leave you so near does the act of addressing you bring you to me." It would not be the last time Jeff Davis's need for the attention of a sympathetic, adoring female confidante carried him away from his wife.[9]

Whether Varina knew of this impassioned yet apparently pristine exchange between her friend and her husband is unknown. She surely knew of the lurid accusations of adultery, or attempted adultery, that appeared first in the Louisville newspaper and then in Cincinnati newspapers that July. The story, embellished as it spread, was that Jeff Davis had been seen boarding a train with an unidentified married woman, had booked two berths for the evening, and then had been caught climbing into bed with his companion. Jeff denied the story, and after a month, reader interest faded. In this case, Jeff was probably guilty of little more than the accepted chivalry of the day: gentlemen frequently agreed to chaperone respectable women who were traveling alone. Such acts of gallantry fit Jefferson Davis's image of himself as the protector of women; public displays of lust and adultery did not. Knowing her husband well, Varina probably dismissed the alleged adultery. But she also knew he remained as capable of flirtation with beautiful women as he had been so many years before when he was alone in Washington, D.C. Varina knew her own beauty had faded. She was forty-five years old, and if she had once been shapely and lithe, she was now heavyset, slow in movement, more dowdy than majestic. The shape of her face had altered with the loss of her teeth, a succession of closely spaced pregnancies had taken their toll, and the deaths of so many she loved showed in her eyes. Small wonder her sixty-three-year-old husband, who in her mind's eye was still erect of bearing and elegant, was willing to serve as escort to another woman.[10]

Varina's own letters say nothing on the subject of her husband's emotional or physical fidelity that year. She filled her correspondence to him with accounts of the children's bouts of chicken pox and flu, reports on her own aches and ailments, and news of the unexpected, and disappointing, decision of her sister Maggie to marry an Alsatian businessman living in Liverpool. Maggie had lived with the Davises since childhood, and though the relationship between the sisters had sometimes been strained, Varina cared deeply for her. She was convinced the marriage was a mistake, although she conceded to her husband that Karl Stoess had good manners and irreproachable morals: "he neither drinks, smokes nor gambles." He also seemed devoted to Maggie and considered it "a great privilege to marry her" despite her lack of any fortune at all. Stoess was a widower whose first wife had died in childbirth, and thus, Varina explained, Maggie would become the stepmother to what appeared to be a well-mannered seventeen-year-old boy. What, then, was Varina's objection? Her complaints seemed to focus on the cost of providing a trousseau for her sister, but perhaps there were other reasons, hidden from her own consciousness. Karl Stoess was twenty years older than Maggie—only three years more her senior than Jeff Davis had been to Varina. And his first marriage had ended tragically—just as Jefferson Davis's marriage to Knox Taylor had ended. Varina skirted the issue, saying only that she did not believe Maggie loved her future husband. "Having married young I suppose I idealised more than she does," Varina added, reassuring both her husband and herself. As the wedding drew nearer, Varina grew more distressed. "The whole affair nearly drives me mad," she told Jeff. Despite all her misgivings, Varina stood in place of her absent husband and gave the bride away.[11]

In August 1870, Jeff set sail once again for England, this time to bring his wife home to Memphis. Varina bowed to his wishes, although she feared the effect of the heat and humidity on her own fragile health. Slowly the children were settled in schools in America, and in 1871 the Davis family celebrated their first Christmas together since the fall of Richmond. The last time the Davises had enjoyed such a holiday celebration was in 1865, when Varina had labored to create a joyful atmosphere in the midst of scarcity and in the shadow of military defeat. Looking back on the years since she had distributed treats to the soldiers guarding the president's home and presents to the family and friends gathered inside would have been a melancholy experience for Varina. Her father, her mother, and Uncle Joe Davis were now dead. Two sons were buried in small graves hundreds of miles apart in Mississippi and Virginia. She and Jeff were beset with illnesses, both chronic and new. Their budget provided few comforts, and they had been reduced to a rented "old shackled-down" house in a less than fashionable section of town. What Varina did not know was that more death, sickness, and disappointment lay ahead.

Whatever hope Jeff's job and the New Year held, it could not be sustained. In October, Varina's adored son William Howell Davis, namesake of her father, died suddenly of diphtheria. With Billy's death, Varina had buried three of her four sons. It was more than Varina could bear, and she crumbled. Months went by and she remained depressed. Her body seemed to fail her—she suffered sudden attacks of numbness in her arms and legs, and the violence of these attacks grew rather than diminished as a new year began. The outside world mirrored the violence of her illness as the Panic of 1873 swept across the nation, destroying individual fortunes and leaving wrecked businesses in its wake. The Carolina Life Insurance Company was one of its victims, and by August 1873 Jeff had resigned as its president. His salary stopped at once. The family had no other source of income.[12]

Jeff had been a reluctant capitalist, and now he conceded that he was a failed one as well. "The tide of my fortune is at lowest ebb," he confessed to Varina in September, and he had no prospects in sight. In desperation, he took up a battle to recover Brierfield, filing a lawsuit against a niece who had laid claim to this part of Joe Davis's estate. The dispute drove a wedge between him and Davis family members. "The last link that bound me to happy childhood is broken," he wrote as 1873 ended. Saddened, he turned once again to Varina for solace. Writing from New Orleans, he expressed his hope that he would "hear often from the love of all my mature life." Forgetting—or suppressing—his ventures in emotional intimacies with other women, he lauded Varina as "the partner of all my great efforts, and more than equal sharer of all my trials and sorrows." Their history together lent credence to this claim. He now expressed deep concern about her health, for the thought of losing her was unbearable. "Oh my beloved Winnie," he wrote in his characteristic mixture of affection and selfish need, "how dark would be the future if deprived of your helpful, hope giving presence." He needed her "sweet assurances and wise counsels" more than ever.[13]

Varina was quick to respond, not with a demand for "sweet assurances" about her own trials and sufferings but with the suggestion that he take an ocean voyage for his emotional and physical health. Jeff reluctantly agreed. He would go, he declared, but only in order to pursue the slim possibility of employment with an English company. He booked passage on the USS *Alabama*, and after several visits to his doctor in New Orleans for ailments of his own, he prepared to set sail for England. At the last minute, an ailing Varina traveled to New Orleans to see him off. Jeff's reluctance to undertake the journey was obvious, and though he had often chosen to travel without his wife, this time he appeared to feel the looming separation keenly. From on board the ship he wrote: "Long and wistfully did I look after you when the carriage bore you from my sight."[14]

Whatever hopes Jeff had of finding employment with an English company, nothing materialized. British firms, he wrote Varina, were fearful of giving the former president of the Confederacy a position. "How far dread of the Yankees may render it impossible for me to get any thing in this country is doubtful," he observed that February. "I cannot run round begging for employment, less still can I promise to conciliate the meanest, basest, but not the wisest of mankind." By summer he was home, but despite his distaste for "begging for employment," he continued to search for a way to support his family.[15]

Eighteen seventy-five arrived with a new set of disappointments and tragedies. That fall word came that Varina's favorite brother, "Jeffy D" Howell, had died at sea in an attempt to rescue an elderly passenger aboard the ship he commanded. Not even the marriage the following year of her older daughter, Maggie, to a handsome and responsible young bank cashier, J. Addison Hayes, could take Varina's mind off the parents, sons, and brother she had lost. More bad news came on the heels of tragedy: her husband lost his Brierfield lawsuit, and she greeted with no enthusiasm his insistence on appealing the decision. (Jeff would finally win possession of Brierfield in 1878.)[16]

Trapped in a seemingly endless downward cycle of disappointment, anxiety, and loss, Varina gave up all hope. The same cycle afflicted hundreds of Southern families, white and black, as Reconstruction came to an end, not with a bang but a whimper. All around her were the legacies of war and defeat: mutilated veterans of war, widowed women with children, planters without land, freedmen and -women forced into a new form of bondage known as sharecropping, renewed racial violence, and the embrace by former Confederates of a paralyzing nostalgia for a past that had never really existed. Few of the Davises' friends had made fresh starts; the successes in Europe of the resilient Judah Benjamin and the politically savvy Dudley Mann were exceptions to the rule of generals turned hardware salesmen, and planter patriarchs like Uncle Joe gone gray and humiliated by poverty. Jeff might have been describing his region's ailments when he diagnosed Varina's condition: "The symptoms you describe all belong to the effect on the nervous system produced by a severe concussion on its centre, and clearly indicate the propriety of both bodily and mental rest." His only prescription was a trip abroad.[17]

Jeff himself was preparing to go to London once again. He had, at last, been offered a position as president of the American Department of the Mississippi Valley Society, a group that hoped to encourage immigration and investment from abroad. There was no fixed salary attached, but he anticipated at least $6,000 (one-half of his former salary from the insurance company) and traveling expenses. His first fund-raising trip would carry him to London. Couldn't Varina be persuaded to join him?[18]

At the last moment, Varina agreed. Thus in May 1876, Jeff, Varina, and Winnie set sail. But neither the ocean voyage nor the return to England revived Varina's spirits or her health. She suffered a severe attack of her heart trouble soon after she arrived. Jeff believed that simple despair had brought his wife low. But modern doctors would conclude that Varina Howell Davis had suffered a nervous breakdown. Two years before, she had written Jeff an uncharacteristically bitter and self-pitying commentary on her life. It was prompted by her sister Margaret's failure to send a condolence after Billy's death, but its anger and disappointment seemed to encompass all those whom she had cared for and sacrificed her own desires to for so many years. "I have worked for them all, prayed, and denied myself the joys, the best of youth, and sacrificed the little vanities of life to them every one and not one thinks of me, and I am done. I am done. I ceased to hope & then to care, and then to wish—How bitter this has been to me I can scarcely say even to you." Her conviction that this was true, more than all the tragedies in her life, seemed to have defeated Varina Howell Davis at last.[19]

Twenty-six

"IN THE COURSE OF HUMAN EVENTS I SHALL PROBABLY GO DOWN TO MR. DAVIS'S EARTHLY PARADISE"

Separation and Reconciliation

JEFF RETURNED TO AMERICA ALONE, his efforts to commit English investors to the Mississippi Valley Society a failure. Surely he and Varina sensed what proved to be true: he would never work again. His thoughts turned to the long-delayed project of writing the history of the Confederacy and to making a home beside "the rolling waves of the Gulf." He had visited what was then called Mississippi City (now Biloxi) in the fall of 1875 and found "a sense of rest and peace" on its beaches that now beckoned him. Varina had no such longings. Too sick to travel, she remained in Liverpool when her husband sailed away. She would not return to America until October 1877.[1]

By January 1877, Jeff was in Mississippi City, enjoying the hospitality of an old acquaintance and avid admirer, the widowed Mrs. Sarah Anne Ellis Dorsey. Sarah had been a childhood friend of Varina's in Natchez, and like Varina, she enjoyed the conversation and company of intelligent men over the gossip of women. Like Varina, she had escaped the provincialism of her hometown, not through a husband's political career but through a "good" marriage to a cotton planter and a literary career. She had been educated in Europe, where she had hobnobbed both with British nobility and with leading literary figures such as the Rossettis. She had published four books using the nom de plume Filia. Far more important to Jeff, Sarah Dorsey was still an attractive woman: olive-skinned, petite, and charming. She had embraced the Confederate cause wholeheartedly and had openly expressed her view that Jeff Davis was "the noblest man she had ever met on earth." Such admiration was no doubt balm to Jeff's battered ego.[2]

Sarah offered Jeff the refuge he was seeking: a cottage on her beautiful coastal plantation, Beauvoir, and the chance to begin his work on the history of the Confederacy. He moved in, along with his body servant, the now free but loyal Robert Brown. The acquaintance he had hired to help him collect the necessary documents, Major Walthall, found lodgings nearby. For Jeff, the situation was ideal, but he recognized that his wife might find it less than appealing. "This arrangement involves no permanent decision," he assured his daughter Maggie that February, and he was prepared to make a change if Varina did not find it satisfactory. Still, he could not hide his own contentment. "The soft air, here," he added, "is delicious."[3]

Meanwhile, Varina had moved closer to her youngest daughter, Winnie, who was in school in Karlsruhe, Germany. She was struggling to regain her strength, venturing out on a half-mile walk to a local church. She spoke of returning soon to America, for she was eager to see her daughter Maggie's newborn son. "Oh how I do long to see the baby and its Mother!" she wrote and with an enthusiasm that had long evaded her. But by May it was clear her health was still too poor to undertake the voyage, and by July her grandchild was dead.[4]

Ill health was not the only thing keeping Varina an ocean away from her husband. Sarah Dorsey was the other. Rumors had reached her that the widow Dorsey had insinuated herself into Jeff's history project, taking up the role of amanuensis that had for so long been one of Varina's wifely duties. She sensed how satisfying it was for her husband to have an adoring, sympathetic woman seeing to his comforts, listening to his anecdotes, helping him organize his papers and his thoughts. That August she wrote: "I have so often hoped though so far away that you would find it necessary as a matter of sympathy to tell me of [your book's] plan and scope and of its progress—but I know I am very far off—and—'and things.' " There was, in this letter, a complex mixture of wistfulness, regret, and accusation.[5]

By September, it had become widely known in England as well as America that Jeff's history of the Confederacy was now a collaboration with the mistress of Beauvoir. Varina's confusion of feelings soon crystallized into anger at both the usurper and her husband. To Jeff's prodding that she send a note of thanks to Mrs. Dorsey for her hospitality to him, to his son, and to the visiting Hayes family, she replied: "I am sorry not to have written Mrs. Dorsey—but I do not think I could satisfy you and her if I did & therefore am silent." If Jeff missed her point, she made it crystal clear: "I do not desire ever to see her house—and cannot say so and therefore have been silent." As for the open invitation from Sarah to join them at Beauvoir, she was equally clear. "Nothing on earth would pain me like living in that kind of community in her house. I am grateful for her kindness to you and my children, but do not desire to be under any more obligation to her." Varina's hurt and embarrassment poured from her pen: "When people here ask me what part of your book she is writing, and such like things, I feel aggravated nearly to death. Of course she must have given out the impression, as it could not so generally prevail, no one would have known she wrote at your dictation, even still less would it have come out in the newspapers."[6]

Jeff might well have seen the situation differently. He had undertaken a challenging project and one that threatened to revive the horrors of war and the painful recollections of his own errors of judgment, frustrations, and inadequacies, as well as the stinging criticisms that clouded his years as the leader of his nation. He was nearing seventy, a frail, bone-thin man with failing eyesight, diminished in body and mind by almost two decades of pitting his own principles against more powerful political and social forces. His views of women's role—as comforters and supporters of men— were consistent and unchanging, and his reliance on Sarah Dorsey in the continuing absence of his wife could not have seemed an inappropriate departure. Indeed, her presence must have been a welcome relief to his spirits. Yet for Varina, this was a betrayal, made more painful by the fact that the history he was writing was *her* history as well as his, her experiences as much as those of her husband. It was as if her autobiography were being stolen from her.

It was time, Varina decided, to come home—though where that home would be remained uncertain. She did not share her itinerary with Jeff, but her destination was definitely not the Gulf Coast. She arrived in Memphis in late October, and Jeff came to visit her at their daughter Maggie's home. When it became clear Varina would not leave with him, he returned to Beauvoir.

On November 7, Varina explained her situation to a friend, in prose revealing that her sharp wit had not abandoned her. "In the course of human events," she began, drawing a parallel to a more famous declaration, "I shall probably go down to Mr. Davis's earthly paradise temporarily." But, she declared, she could not reconcile her own need for sociability with his inclination to the " 'gentle hermit in the dale' style of old age." If she had once proclaimed a desire for solitude, she now wished to be surrounded by people. No compromise seemed possible between her husband and herself, "so behold we are a tie—and neither achieves the desired end."

In the game of wills between Varina and Jeff, a "tie" seemed a victory to a woman who had so often submitted to her husband's wishes.[7]

Varina's family knew that the conflict was deeper than a clash between sociability and the life of a "hermit in the dale." The thorn in Varina's side was Mrs. Dorsey, whom Varina viewed as a usurper—and the humiliation her husband's connection with his admirer continued to cause her as his wife. Maggie, at least, took her mother's side. "I never liked Mrs. Dorsey," she had written her mother in June 1877. "I think she is mannish and her conduct to you extremely ill bred to say the very least. . . . I told Father what I thought of her when he was here. I said I did not think you would enjoy being her guest. She assumes a superiority over all other women which is very disgusting to me." This condemnation, as Varina surely knew, echoed the criticisms once leveled at "Queen Varina."[8]

When Jeff finally requested Varina's help on the book, she agreed, but she sent her recollections on important events and her perceptive comments on Confederate personalities by mail. Her analysis of his difficulties with past and recent critics revealed how well she knew and understood him, and them. "You have not been a conciliatory man in your manners always, and the vain and dishonest men who could not bend you to their wills, do not like you." This, too, was a commentary that could have been applied to Varina and her female enemies as well.[9]

Jeff made an effort to show his appreciation for her advice. In a sense, he was courting her, hoping to soothe her hurt feelings and her sense of betrayal. When she recommended he ignore an attack by a current enemy, he hastened to tell her that other friends agreed with her advice. "So you see your opinion is not singular," he told her; yet he added, "But if it stood alone it would be worth more than all the rest in deciding my course."[10]

Jeff continued to hope that Varina would come to the Gulf Coast, if only for a visit. Varina remained unwilling to budge. When a guest arrived at Maggie's house that April, Varina preferred temporary quarters in a boardinghouse to a visit to her husband's "earthly paradise." Yet in the spring of 1878, her attitude softened. On April 7, she began to lay the ground for a trip to the Gulf Coast. "It is very kind of you to invite me to meet you in New Orleans," she wrote to Jeff. The idea appealed to her because, as she continued to explain, "I very much desire to have my teeth attended to as they now are stretching my upper lip in a most disfiguring degree." Her continuing dental problems aside, Varina conceded that the long separation from Jeff was wearing on her. "[T]he five months that we have been apart, now verging as it does on to six, and the year that preceded it, broken by ten days of your companionship when you met me here, seem a long absence." She missed him, and her sentimentality emerged as she told him that seeing roses at a nursery brought back memories of her wedding day. "The tears," she confessed, "sprung to my eyes."[11]

Varina's dental needs became the opening for a rapprochement both she and Jeff desired. With some humor, he urged her to visit a dentist at once, for "the poorer we are the more need for teeth and nails to bite and scratch our way through the world." He promised to be waiting for her when she arrived in New Orleans. Diplomatically, he addressed the future: "As to your coming here, you must do as you please & we can talk of that here- after." He took pains to add that "my circumstances here are well suited to my present engagements, but are not indispensable; so if you will not stay on the coast I have been willing to change my abode until we have a *home*." The message was clear: Varina was more important to him than Mrs. Dorsey or her lovely home.[12]

In July 1878, Varina arrived at Beauvoir. Perhaps to Varina's surprise, but certainly in a balm to her sense of propriety and justice, Sarah Dorsey turned over all assistance on Jeff's book to her. By September Varina had decided that the Gulf Coast suited her after all. Thus the Davises enjoyed a rare moment of contentment together, broken abruptly by the terrible news that their only remaining son had "died quietly and peacefully at five this afternoon." The yellow fever epidemic that took the younger Jeff's life in October took many Memphis residents that fall. But for Jeff and Varina, the loss was especially severe. "The last of my four sons has left me," Jeff wrote his son-in-law, Addison Hayes, and "I am crushed under such heavy and repeated blows." He reported that Varina had collapsed and lay helpless in her bed. It was Sarah Dorsey who "nursed her with unwearied care," and Varina openly acknowledged her former rival's generosity of spirit and her nursing skill.[13]

Sarah Dorsey's generosity extended beyond her willingness to nurse Varina back to health. She had developed breast cancer in 1877 and, prepar- ing for the worst, she took steps to turn Beauvoir over to the Davises before she died. In February 1879, she proposed to sell the estate to Jeff Davis for a modest sum, but before payment could begin, Sarah's condition worsened. She moved from Beauvoir to New Orleans, where she died on July 4, 1879. Jefferson Davis was at her bedside as her life ended.

Jeff made no excuses to Varina for his vigil at the side of another woman. "I should be as mean as some of her kin," he wrote, "if I did not feel grate- ful for many kindnesses and deeply grieved at her death." Among her kindnesses was this: she left Beauvoir, as well as two other plantations, to her friend Jefferson Davis. Sarah's will made it clear how deeply devoted to the Confederacy's leader she was: "I do not intend to share in the ingratitude of my country towards the man who is in my eyes the highest and noblest in existence." Varina and Jeff had a permanent home at last—and the fear of poverty that haunted them for a decade had ended. The worst was over.[14]

Twenty-seven

"OTHER REFUGE HAVE WE NONE"

Life and Death at Beauvoir

VARINA HOWELL DAVIS WAS NOW fifty-three years old. Her husband was seventy-one. She had grown fatter; he had grown frailer. Together, they had been honored and suffered humiliation, lived well and then frugally, welcomed children into the world and lost many of them. Whatever their quarrels, whatever their disappointments in each other and their life together, whatever injuries each had inflicted on the other, one thing was true: their history together stretched over almost four decades. Now, in what would be their last decade together, they settled into that comfortable companionship that had eluded them for so long. "You and I have lived long enough to know that 'other refuge have we none,'" Varina had wisely observed in 1875, when the future looked bleak and an ocean separated them. At long last, that refuge was enough for Jeff. Together, the aging couple tended Beauvoir's roses, picked strawberries, planted and harvested their vegetable garden. And together they labored over his history of the Confederacy, with Varina assuming her familiar role as her husband's amanuensis.

Varina understood how difficult the stir of memories was for both her husband and herself, but she believed Jeff owed this book to the world. "The weary recital of the weary war" weighed heavily on them both, she confessed to her daughter Winnie, still in school abroad. But this "splendid but heartbreaking record of cherished hopes now blasted, brave warriors bleeding and dying, and noble men living, yet dead, in that they are hopeless" was Jeff's gift to the world. "While he writes," she continued, "the graves give up their dead, and they stalk before us all gory and downcast, but for all that a gallant, proud army, ready if they could again put on their fleshy shield to do battle for their rights." The image was touching, but it was also telling: for Varina and her husband, the war remained, as it had always been in their eyes, a conflict over the constitutional rights of white

Southern citizens, not a war of liberation or oppression of a race of enslaved men and women.[1]

The first volume of *The Rise and Fall of the Confederate Government* appeared in June 1781. It produced barely a ripple in the historical consciousness of the nation. The *New York Herald* printed a negative review, written by General James Longstreet, a man who had fought for the Confederacy but was now a member of the Republican Party. Most other Northern papers ignored it. Jeff received some favorable reviews from English papers, but Judah Benjamin had warned Varina that an edition in England was unlikely. "Public interest in our struggle," he noted, "has now quite died out in England." The publisher, Appleton, did little to advertise either volume. Jeff's disappointment was obvious, but he took solace in the fact that he had, at last, been able to make the argument he had intended to make at his trial: secession was a constitutional right, not rebellion or treason. Not once in the 1,500 pages did Jeff Davis ever doubt that his view was correct.[2]

Despite the lukewarm reception given the history, the mere act of its publication reminded Southerners that their "Lost Cause" and Jeff Davis were, after all, synonymous. As nostalgia and myth rewrote the war, only his most bitter political and military enemies refused to abandon their criticisms of Jeff's brief and troubled administration. Thus, throughout the 1880s, visitors made their pilgrimages to Beauvoir, eager to pay their respects to the president and first lady of the Confederacy. Northerners such as the newspaper magnate Joseph Pulitzer and Englishmen including the eccentric Oscar Wilde came too. Jeff began to accept invitations to speak—in Montgomery; Atlanta; and Savannah, Georgia, where monuments to Confederate heroes and heroism were erected; and Macon, Georgia, where Confederate veterans gathered. His hosts sent a special train to carry him from the Gulf Coast, and with it an honor guard. Along the routes, crowds gathered to cheer him as they had once done in more optimistic days. Virginia Clay, now Virginia Clopton, marveled at the adoration she saw offered to the elderly Jeff Davis by Confederate widows, "shrouded in black," who fell at his feet. The Davises' younger daughter, Winnie, home from Europe and now an attractive young woman, traveled with her father on many of these occasions. She soon became known to all as the "Daughter of the Confederacy."[3]

Both Varina and Jeff welcomed the return of public affection, but a reentry into public life proved too great a strain on the aging Jefferson Davis. In 1887, he suffered a heart attack at Macon. When he recovered,

he returned to his sanctuary, Beauvoir. Two years later, on a cold, rainy
November day, he boarded the *Laura Lee* at New Orleans, on his way to
visit the Brierfield plantation. He caught a cold and the cold turned to
bronchitis. By the time he reached his destination, Jeff Davis was seriously
ill. Sick and nearly delirious, he wrote his last note to Varina. "Nothing is as
it should be," he said, and though he seemed to be speaking of his plantation, it was his own body that had gone awry. When news reached Varina,
she rushed to him and took him back to New Orleans. She hoped to nurse
him back to health in the city where they had honeymooned, just as she
had done so many times before. It was not to be. Jeff died on December 6,
1889. In death, he became a central figure of Southern mythology, a "hero
of the Lost Cause."[4]

Twenty-eight

"HER CONVERSATION
IS SUPERLATIVELY INTERESTING"

Varina's Years of Independence

AS A YOUNG WIFE WHOSE HUSBAND had gone off to the Mexican War, Varina had battled desperation and despair by keeping busy. She had cleaned rugs, baked pies, mended clothing. Now, a widow at sixty-three, she turned to a project grander and more challenging than these domestic chores: a biography of Jefferson Davis. She began to gather records and correspondence, determined to vindicate Jeff completely, vanquishing his critics at last, and in the process adding her own amen to his interpretation of the Civil War. Although she may not have realized it, she was also writing her autobiography.

Varina threw herself into the project, aided by one of Jeff's grandnieces. As the biography grew into a two-volume memoir, its villains and heroes emerged clearly: Jeff stood at the center of a circle of loyal and honorable men, while his old nemeses Joe Johnston and Pierre Gustave Toutant de Beauregard and his prison keeper, Nelson Appleton Miles, stood condemned.

The memoir was one of Varina's final gestures of fidelity to her role as Mrs. Jefferson Davis, a gesture she believed her husband would have expected of her. But it did not achieve what Varina hoped. *Jefferson Davis, Ex-President of the Confederate States of America; A Memoir by His Wife* proved a literary and financial failure. Varina laid the blame on her publishers, the Belford Company, rather than on the book itself. They had not promoted the book, she declared; the book was too long, they replied. Perhaps both sides were correct. The memoir rambled, and the publisher, whose company soon failed, did not have the budget to publicize the books widely. A lawsuit followed, initiated and eventually won by a very angry and frustrated Varina. She received close to $10,000 in damages—and the almost two thousand unsold copies of the book.[1]

Varina could not acknowledge what others might have seen clearly: even if it had sold widely, Varina's wordy and highly partisan tribute to her husband would not have silenced his critics or vindicated his career. But if she had failed him in this regard, she took pains to control and shape his legacy in other ways. She insisted on supervising all monuments erected in his memory and tried to play the role of censor with any speech or article written about him. Her protectiveness knew no bounds, and even friends began to chide her. She could not control public opinion, could not force history to view Jeff Davis as she wished him to be known. "History, patriotism, fidelity," her old friend William Preston Johnston told her, would ensure her husband's immortality.[2]

There was a driven quality to Varina's efforts to celebrate her husband's life. In her memoir, in her efforts to oversee what was said about him and what monuments were erected in his honor, in her long battle to ensure that Beauvoir was preserved as a shrine to Jeff Davis, and in her decision to change her name to Varina Jefferson Davis, she combined two contradictory impulses: to remain in his shadow and to make certain she would not be "hidden in death."

There were other signs that Varina was emerging from that shadow and escaping from that death in life she feared was her fate as a widow. An astute observer might have noted Varina's frank assessment of her husband's faults, sprinkled throughout a memoir devoted to lauding his virtues. Throughout her marriage she had pointed out these faults in letters to him, urging him to be less dogmatic, to master the art of politics as well as the ability to articulate its issues, to learn to win men over with good food and drink as much as with the force of his intellect. Now she had told the world the same things. Even if few read her memoir, she had broken the silence expected of a good wife. These were small acts of rebellion on her part, but telling ones.

More signs of independence followed. Less than a year after Jeff's death, she reversed her husband's dictum against Winnie marrying the Northern lawyer who loved her. Fred Wilkinson was not just a Northerner but the grandson of an abolitionist. Jeff had blanched at the idea of the "Daughter of the Confederacy" wedded to a descendant of the antislavery movement and had sent Winnie to Europe in order to separate the two. But in April 1890, Varina announced the couple's engagement, prompting exactly the furious outcry among white Southerners that Jeff had feared. It was not public opinion that finally prevented the marriage, however; it was the discovery that Fred was unable to support a wife. Love alone could not conquer all, and Varina was unwilling to see her daughter suffer the poverty she herself had known. By the fall of 1890, the relationship had ended. And though the Confederacy's favorite daughter did not marry her Yankee, it would be many years before this betrayal of the cause by the Davis women would be forgiven.[3]

More surprises were to come from Jeff Davis's widow. In death, Jeff had become a much sought-after symbol of the Confederacy, but which state would have the honor of serving as his final resting place? He had been interred in a temporary grave in New Orleans, but multiple claims were immediately pressed for his remains. Requests came from Mississippi, his home for much of his adult life; from Kentucky, his birthplace; from Alabama, where the first capital of the Confederacy was established; and from Virginia, the site of the second Confederate capital. The choice lay with Varina.

Although many people expected Varina to favor Mississippi's bid, she did not. Instead, she decided to bury her husband in Hollywood Cemetery beside her son Joseph. She announced her decision in a public letter that stung Mississippi's pride, as much because of the weak justification she offered—that the prospective Mississippi burial site was below sea level— as the choice itself. The snub opened a breach between Varina and the people of her home state that was slow to heal.[4]

But perhaps nothing shocked white Southerners more than Varina's unexpected desertion of Southern soil. In 1891, Varina packed up her belongings and, together with Winnie, moved from Beauvoir to New York City, where a job writing for Joseph Pulitzer's newspapers waited. Varina's expatriation enraged many Southerners, especially Mississippians. It was one thing for other former Confederates such as Burton Harrison and his wife to migrate to New York and create a thriving expatriate community there, but the first lady and the "Daughter of the Confederacy"—never.[5]

Varina defended the move. Writing to a friend, she explained, "I do not remain in the north because I have ceased to dearly love my own people and country, but suffer from a weak heart which a warm day or two depresses so that I breathe with great difficulty." But more than health concerns surely prompted her to abandon Beauvoir and the region of her birth. She was fed up with criticism, tired of the wrangling over her husband's memory and his remains. Most of all, she wanted to surround herself with admirers who valued her for herself rather than as the widow of Jeff Davis. She was forging a career for herself as a writer, and she suspected that New Yorkers would take her ambition more seriously than the men and women who were content to view her as the great man's widow.[6]

Thus, in her seventies, fat and white-haired, looking far more like Queen Victoria than a Southern belle, Varina Howell Davis began a new life. She never achieved the fame she might have wished for as a writer; indeed, most of the articles and reviews she churned out for her salary at Joseph Pulitzer's *Sunday World* never appeared in print. And most, like her sketch "Christmas in the Confederacy," were what modern observers would call fluff. But Varina wrote steadily, turning out essays on manners and child rearing as well as a tale of an Indian war that implied that all wars—even the great Civil War itself—were both foolish and futile.[7]

Though she was at last the old woman she had felt herself to be at the age of thirty, her new life seemed to energize her, to restore a long-lost joie de vivre. In New York, she found a world of constant stimulation: opera, theater, art galleries, and long conversations with intellectuals and university professors. Writing to her son-in-law, she compared her deliverance from "the torments I had endured at Beauvoir" to the release of the Israelites from their bondage in Egypt. She had once declared to Constance Harrison, "I dearly love people," and in New York she had at last found people who could hold her interest and match her intellectual curiosity. When she moved into the Gerard Hotel, Varina created her own informal salon for artists, actors, playwrights, and journalists. She charmed and dazzled the young men and women who visited her, just as once, long ago, she had charmed senators and presidents. To these friends and acquaintances she was not Jefferson Davis's wife but a dynamic personality in her own right. "Her powers of conversation and description were superior to those of any other woman I have ever known," wrote a friend, the historian John Burgess. Another admirer put it succinctly: "She was a great talker."[8]

Her new surroundings slowly changed Varina's perspective on the war and the sectional hatred that had fueled it. By the 1890s, she had come to appreciate the cost of the war to the North as well as to her own region. She now recognized that loyalty to the Union had spurred the same heroism as loyalty to the Confederacy. In her years as a senator's wife, she had observed men whose politics were antithetical to her own and her husband's but whose character she admired. Now she was able to do the same. It was this understanding that she brought to her chance encounter with the widow of General Ulysses S. Grant in 1893.

Meeting at a Hudson Valley resort hotel, Varina Howell Davis and Julia Dent Grant felt a kinship that knew no regional boundaries. Pulitzer's *Sunday World* recognized the symbolism of these widows sitting down to dinner together. "Eternal Peace Now" read the headline, "Mrs. Ulysses S. Grant

and Mrs. Jefferson Davis Shake Hands." Four years later, Varina attended
the dedication of Grant's Tomb in New York's Riverside Park and acknowledged that heroes wore the blue as well as the gray. "The soldiers of the
Confederacy," she wrote, "who bore their own beloved leader from New
Orleans to his last resting place in Richmond . . . would be the last to cavil
at the enthusiasm of the North for their dead hero."[9]

But if the North seemed to embrace Varina, many Southerners still
viewed her with hostility and suspicion. One Virginian went so far as to
deny that Varina was a true daughter of the South. "She wasn't a Southern
woman," she insisted, "and while we may admire her loyalty to her husband
and her adopted cause and country, we realize it was self-interest rather
than simon-pure patriotism that actuated her." In 1894, Varina responded
to attacks like this one with an idiosyncratic defense of her behavior after
Jeff's death that she called her "anti mortem letter." Whether she meant this
justification to be shared only with the man it was addressed to, a good
friend and confidant, or hoped it would be made public is unclear. But
there was a more intriguing ambiguity: had she meant to say "ante," as in
before her death? Or was this a defense *against* death, an effort to prevent
being erased from the memory of the South? No one, perhaps not even
Varina, knew. But this was the first and most ferocious battle Varina would
fight for her own reputation and her own vindication rather than Jeff's. To
her friend Mary Hunter Kimbrough, she expressed a hope that *her* struggles in the postwar years would be appreciated by those who now spoke ill
of her. "Some day in the future the hard battle I have fought with disease
and poverty will I hope suggest itself to the people of the South, and the
effort I have made to sustain myself in dignified independence may be
acceptable to them as not unworthy of my position."[10]

As the century ended, Varina and the South seemed at last to mend their
relationship. In 1896, Varina and Winnie made a pilgrimage to Richmond
to attend a Confederate reunion and observe the laying of the cornerstone
of her husband's monument. Together the two Varinas, mother and daughter, sat on the balcony of a hotel named for Jefferson Davis, listening to
bands play songs such as "Dixie." In 1902, now seventy-six years old, Varina
returned to the Cotton Belt cities of her youth and her married life: New
Orleans, Jackson, Natchez, Vicksburg, Memphis. She was welcomed in
each. Admirers in Memphis, where she had once found a moment of
respite from the postwar troubles in her "old shackled-down" home on
Court Street, presented her with a diamond-and-ruby brooch. The pin was
shaped like a crown, an acknowledgment perhaps that she remained

"Queen Varina." And when Winnie Davis died of a stomach ailment in 1898, the grieving Varina chose to bury her in Richmond's Hollywood Cemetery beside her brother and father, yet another sign that Varina's own war with the South was ending. Southerners responded in kind, according the Daughter of the Confederacy full military honors at the funeral.[11]

The loss of her thirty-four-year-old daughter was a serious blow to an aging mother who had now seen five of her six children precede her in death. Only Maggie and her children remained. Varina tried to do for Winnie what she had done for Jeff—write her biography—but she abandoned the project as too painful. Yet despite her age, her illnesses, and her sorrows, Varina still cut an impressive figure. In 1903, a reporter described a gathering in her hotel room: "It looked for all the world like a miniature court. In the middle sat Mrs. Davis, holding our unwavering attention, not by prerogative of rank, but by the power of her extraordinary intellect which compels attention to all she says. Whether composed of the veriest commonplaces, or reminiscent of the turbulent times of which she was not only an eye witness but a foremost participant, her conversation is superlatively interesting."[12]

Three years later the woman who presided over this "miniature court" was dead. Varina Howell Davis died of pneumonia on October 16, 1906. She was eighty years old. She had lived, she once wrote her daughter Maggie Hayes, "to see Lucifer matches introduced . . . the telegraph, the telephone, the audiphones, the sewing machine, gas-& kerosene oil as well as many of the minor inventions," and she had witnessed the beginning years of modernity. But Varina's last comments to her daughter, as Maggie stood at her dying mother's bedside, suggest how deeply etched in Varina's character the old patriarchal rules of the previous century remained, despite her own odyssey to independence. "Don't you wear black," she told Maggie. "It is bad for your health, and will depress your husband."[13]

THREE

Julia Dent Grant

Julia Dent Grant.
Courtesy of the Library of Congress.

Twenty-nine

THE WINDS OF CHANGE,
THE SHELTER OF TRADITION

MODERN-DAY PUNDITS AND COMMENTATORS applaud or lament the rapid-fire changes taking place in our society. New technologies, new ideologies, and new concerns—from global warming to terrorism—seem to ensure that instability is the only certainty in our world. Yet nineteenth-century Americans might challenge our uniqueness. Within their lifetimes, two centuries of enslavement of Africans and African Americans abruptly ended and with it the world of privileged white masters and exploited black women and men. The unified nation they had proudly, and aggressively, fought to expand in the 1840s was splintered in the 1860s, and only a bloody civil war secured its survival. But along with these political and economic upheavals came changes in the way men and women perceived women's proper sphere. The ideology of domesticity that defined middle-class marriage and pronounced "true women" as angels of the hearth and guardians of the home was challenged by a women's rights movement that called for full citizenship and broadened economic opportunity. The winds of change were everywhere—and many white women stood clearly in their path.

For some of these women, these winds of change stirred introspection and a questioning of custom and tradition that was both disturbing and liberating. Angelina Grimké engaged in a painful, often tortured internal dialogue that led her to abandon her family's way of life and renounce the values and social arrangements on which it was based. Varina Howell Davis wrestled with the social expectations that demanded the bending of a woman's will to her husband's and the suppression of her independent spirit and her intellect. Yet many middle- and upper-class American women held fast to traditional beliefs and customs as if they were a port in the storm raging around them. As challenges to their domestic role grew, they wrapped themselves tighter in the familiar notion that male and female

Ulysses S. Grant.
Courtesy of the Library of Congress.

character, temperament, and social destinies were distinctive and that their appropriate spheres were separate.

For these women, life remained encompassed by family, friends, personal enemies, and the mundane details of daily life. Even the large, catastrophic, or awe-inspiring events happening around them took on meaning only, or at least primarily, when their consequences were felt in the small circle of ordinary life that defined them. It was as if all the new -isms and -izations, all the military and political victories or defeats on the grand scale, had to be pared down in order to be comprehended, personalized in order to be recognized. For those who lived in the particular rather than the abstract, for those whose daily focus was not on trends and prognostications but on dinner and a child's illness, the seemingly quickened pace of life and its high stakes entered their consciousness in more manageable bits and pieces. In some, perhaps this was a means of escaping changes that they could not control and whose trajectories they could not hope to chart. But in others, a genuine complacency reigned, a complacency with the mainstream role they were expected to play and with the mainstream ideas and values that defined it. Home and hearth were their domain; society had assigned them a domestic role that largely shielded them from the outside world, and only rarely did they find its narrowness confining.

Julia Dent Grant was one of these women. Her marriage to Ulysses S. Grant carried her to the heart of the struggle to preserve the Union, to the vital center of power in its aftermath, to national fame and national disgrace, to poverty and wealth and once again to financial ruin. But her compass never failed: her true north was her role as wife and mother. She sat calmly in the maelstrom of history, a model of genteel domesticity—and a reminder of the rewards of the unexamined life.

Thirty

"ONE LONG SUMMER OF SUNSHINE"

Growing Up in Missouri

MISSOURIANS SUCH AS JULIA DENT often spoke of themselves as Westerners, but the Dent family home, White Haven, gave testimony to the fact that many lived as Southerners after all. The house was an elegant showcase for a prosperous gentleman and his family, from the impressive front piazza where Colonel and Mrs. Dent greeted guests to the fruit-filled orchards of peaches, apples, apricots, nectarines, and cherries and the bright blooming garden beds that surrounded it. In building White Haven, the Dents had successfully transplanted plantation life to the northernmost outpost of Dixie.

The master of White Haven was "Colonel" Frederick Dent, a Maryland merchant who made his fortune in the Mississippi River town of St. Louis and then cemented his respectability by acquiring an eight-hundred-acre estate in 1820. The Colonel was a short man with white hair and a beardless face who dressed, as his youngest daughter recalled, "in the sober black long coat [and] dark trousers" that were the mark of a gentleman in the 1820s and 1830s. Dent quickly retired entirely from the world of business, relishing his new role as country gentleman. It was his opinion, he later told his daughter, that commerce had been ruined by the influx of Yankees who had "come west" and "reduced business to a system." Dent was intelligent but decidedly opinionated, a man who loved to argue and loved even more to win his point. He considered himself a Democrat "of the old school" and remained an ardent Southerner despite several years spent in Pennsylvania and his move to what was then considered the West. His wife, Ellen Bray Wrenshall Dent, was not a Southerner by birth. She had spent her childhood in Pittsburgh, a city that only a few decades earlier had been the nation's frontier. Ellen's father was a Methodist minister, strict in the manner of the Wesleyan school. Grandpa Wrenshall, Julia noted, considered it a sin to dance "or to enjoy yourself in any way." Ellen grew up to be a beautiful and delicate woman, small in stature and slender, with gray eyes and a gentle voice. In marriage, she rejected her father's stern view of life. As the wife of a prosperous planter, she left most of the household management to trusted slaves, preferring to engage in just the sort of enjoyment her father frowned upon—reading poetry and playing music.[1]

Julia Boggs Dent was the fifth of Ellen and Frederick's eight children, born on January 26, 1826, in nearby St. Louis, where the Dents maintained a second home. It soon became clear that their daughter inherited none of her mother's good looks. Julia's sister Emma would later put it bluntly when she wrote, "she was not exactly a beauty," and, as Julia recalled, even the family's slaves declared, "Oh, young Missus, you never will come up to old Missus in looks." If these young women were tactless, they were honest: Julia grew into a short and stocky woman, with a prominent nose and a noticeable cast in one eye. Throughout her life, her only positive features were her lustrous hair and her tiny, elegant hands.[2]

Yet if Julia lacked the beauty desired by most Southern girls, she never lacked a beautiful woman's confidence. Indeed, from the moment she was born, she was enveloped in a warm cocoon of affection and indulgence that ensured her a sparkling smile and a lively personality. Her earliest memory was of her father stepping out on White Haven's piazza to catch her up and hold her high in the air, inviting her to see that "the very trees were welcoming me." After four sons, Colonel Dent was clearly thrilled with his daughter, and though more daughters would follow, Julia knew—and accepted without guilt—that she would always remain her father's favorite, his pet.[3]

Julia remembered her childhood as one long idyll, filled with carefree afternoons spent picking strawberries, fishing for minnows, riding, and enjoying the laughter and music that filled the Dent household. "Life," she wrote, "seemed one long summer of sunshine, flowers, and smiles to me and to all at that happy home." Indeed, Julia was certain that all those around her were as happy and contented as she. Although the family owned more than a dozen slaves, she never shared Angelina Grimké's insight into the tragedy of bondage or Grimké's sensitivities to its cruelties. Like Varina Howell Davis, she drew a picture of slavery in pastel shades. Her father, she wrote, was the "kindest of masters to his slaves, who all adored him." He made sure his slaves were well fed, purchasing "great barrels of fish" and providing them with molasses, tobacco, and even whiskey. The men and women Julia called her black "uncles" and "aunts" were welcome to share in all that the farm produced—vegetables, bacon, beef, and poultry. On their wedding days, Colonel Dent provided fine suppers for his slaves, and at corn shuckings, she remembered him providing feasts. Julia's memory of contentment among these enslaved people was as naive as it was vivid; in old age she could still picture White Haven's slaves gathered around a celebratory bonfire, engaging in "the wild, plaintive, and to me, pathetic music" she associated with their race. "It brings up a most pleasant memory," she wrote, certain that any of the slaves would recall it with equal fondness. Looking back on the days before emancipation, she could confidently declare that "I think our people were very happy," although, as the Civil War began, she confessed some of the younger slaves might have grown less content with their place in the edenic world that was White Haven.[4]

Julia's family members were not the only ones who indulged and spoiled her. Her nurse, "dear old black Kitty," saw to all her needs, and she was followed wherever she went by "a dusky train of from eight to ten little colored girls" who were both her playmates and her servants. Her slave "uncles" made every effort to delight her, bringing her pet rabbits and squirrels and the prettiest of the birds' eggs they found. Outside White Haven, she was treated as much like a princess as she was within its sheltering walls. While other children in the little local schoolhouse sat uncomfortably in backless chairs, Julia was seated in a comfortable armchair, sent to the classroom by her mother. And if the schoolmaster was harsh in his punishment of other children, he never used the switch or rod on little Julia. She escaped without penalty if she failed to do her work or master an assignment. By her own admission, she was an indifferent student and found many subjects, including mathematics, too dull or too difficult. She saw little reason to master "those dreadful roman numerals," for example, and could not reply when she was called upon to identify them properly. But rather than a scolding or worse, Julia received gentle encouragement. "Never mind," she recalled her teacher saying, "don't trouble your little head about it any more now." Though he comforted her with the certainty she would eventually learn Roman numerals and their usage, Julia admitted freely that she never did.[5]

When Julia was nearing eleven, she was sent to a boarding school in St. Louis, where she remained for almost seven years. Despite the rigorous curriculum advertised by the Mauro family's Academy for Young Ladies, Julia managed to study only what she liked. When the two sisters who ran the school attempted to discipline Julia—a move that probably surprised as much as offended her—she held her ground. "I, feeling that they had been a little, or very, unreasonable, did just as I pleased, declining to recite again in English grammar and absolutely refusing to look at the multiplication table." She spent much of her day reading romance novels. Although she was able to excel in the subjects she liked—philosophy, mythology, and history—"in every other branch I was below the standard, and worse still, my indifference was very exasperating." The exasperation was not her own and she did not see it as her duty to ease it in others.[6]

Despite, or perhaps because of, her lackluster performance, Julia was happy at the Academy. Every other weekend she was allowed to invite a classmate or a teacher home with her, riding together with them in the roomy carriage with its driver and footman that her family sent to carry them to White Haven. Here, she and her friends were warmly greeted and treated to a fine meal prepared with artistry by the family's "mammy, black Mary." Few who entered the warm and sheltering world of the Dent household could fail to see how fortunate Julia was.[7]

Julia's school days ended in June 1843, and her introduction to society began that winter in the bustling town of St. Louis. The St. Louis of Julia's youth may have been the gateway to the still-young nation's frontier, but it was not a new settlement. Mississippian Mound Builders had left their mark on the site, and traces of their culture could be found long after this Indian civilization vanished. The city itself had begun as a small Catholic mission in 1703 but had grown into a trading post with the arrival of an enterprising group from New Orleans in 1763. In that same year, France ceded all the territory east of the Mississippi River to the British, leaving St. Louis, which sat on the western bank of the river, to mark the eastern edge of the French empire in North America. In 1768 the Louisiana Territory was turned over to the Spanish, but by 1800 a secret treaty made it French once more. In 1803, President Thomas Jefferson's representatives abroad took advantage of Napoleon's focus on the conquest of Europe to purchase the vast Louisiana territory for $15 million. The Louisiana Purchase transformed St. Louis into the expanding nation's gateway city to the West. The complex history of the city could be read in its multiethnic and racial population: in Julia's day, Indians still occasionally appeared on city streets, French and Spanish could be heard spoken in its shops, and an influx of German immigrants added yet another language and new customs to the mix.

For Julia, raised in the countryside and sheltered from the life of the city by her schoolmistresses, these months in St. Louis were her first grand adventure. With her father's second cousin, the beautiful and sophisticated

Caroline O'Fallon, as her chaperone, Julia had her first taste of parties, days spent shopping, and the art of flirtation with eligible young men. Though she was a bit shy at first, the presence of young officers from nearby Jefferson Barracks soon put her at ease. Not a few of them had been guests at White Haven, arriving with her oldest brother, Frederick, who was stationed there. Julia was accustomed to the sight of men in uniform and familiar with the cadence and character of the language of these soldiers. Indeed, she showed a marked admiration for the military. At her boarding school, she had declared to friends that she intended to marry a soldier, "gallant, brave, [and] dashing." Now, at the parties and dances, she was surrounded by these dashing gentlemen. Among them were Julia's fourth cousin, the handsome and popular James Longstreet, and his barrackmates Richard Garnett, Sidney Smith, George Sykes, and Charles Hoskins. No one among this carefree crowd, least of all Julia, would imagine that Smith and Hoskins would soon meet their death in the Mexican War. And none of these officers and friends could envision that within two decades, Sykes would serve as a general in the Union army while Longstreet and Garnett would command Confederate troops. For the moment, there was nothing to dampen the spirits of St. Louis's gallant young men and charming young ladies.[8]

Thirty-one

"BUT ONE SWEETHEART IN HIS LIFE"

The Courtship of Julia Dent Grant

"PETE" LONGSTREET, AS HE WAS THEN KNOWN, had been a frequent visitor to White Haven while Julia was at school in St. Louis. When he arrived, Pete often had his best friend, Ulysses S. Grant, in tow. Ulysses—or Sam, as his fellow officers sometimes called him—was a favorite of Julia's younger sisters. Emma considered him "pretty as a doll," with his porcelain complexion and rosy cheeks. "[H]is hair was fine and brown, very thick and wavy," she recalled, and "his eyes were a clear blue." At five-eight, Grant still towered over the Dent girls, and though he was slight of build and almost painfully slender, Emma thought him graceful, especially on horseback.[1]

In the spring of 1844, Lieutenant Grant made one of his regular appearances at the Dent home, and this time, seventeen-year-old Julia Boggs Dent was among those who greeted him. She had not encountered him during the winter festivities in St. Louis, for unlike Longstreet's other friends, Grant was quiet and socially retiring; he was a young man who did not dance and decidedly did not flirt. A fellow cadet at West Point had once commented, "He had no facility in conversation with the ladies," and by his own admission, he was just short of terrified to speak to women.[2]

This silence and emotional restraint were as much a part of Ulysses's character as a ready smile and open expressions of affection were a part of Julia's. His father, Jesse Root Grant, was a hard-fisted, proud man, born in poverty, who had pulled himself up by his own bootstraps and assumed that anyone with a backbone could do the same. Jesse's mother had died when Jesse was only a boy, and his father was at a loss how to manage a family of six children on his own. Jesse left home at the age of eleven, unskilled and illiterate. He learned to read while working for a judge in Youngstown, Ohio. But he learned something equally valuable at the same time: observing the comfort and ease of the judge's life, Jesse decided that having money was far better than having none. The rest of his early life was devoted to acquiring a sizable fortune. He apprenticed himself to a tanner in Ohio, then moved to Kentucky to complete his training with a half brother who practiced the craft. By the age of twenty-six, the determined Jesse Root Grant had become a partner in an Ohio tannery. The next year, he took a wife. In marrying Hannah Simpson, Jesse had climbed the social ladder, for her parents were prosperous landowners in the Ohio Valley, as pious as they were respectable. Hannah, too, was pious, but her true nature was stoic. She spoke little; she focused her energies on the practical and the necessary; she rejected exuberance and even the smallest displays of pleasure and delight as firmly as she rejected signs of self-indulgence. She was the quintessential American Gothic, a woman of unrelenting character and limited joy. She taught her son duty and uncomplaining endurance; all else was folly.[3]

For that son, the atmosphere of the Dent home was as inviting as it was foreign. Laughter and music filled the air; the effects of comfort and indulgence, and an unshakable sense of entitlement, were evident in the character of every member of the family. Ulysses Grant felt the welcome wash over him each time he entered White Haven's doors. But it was the welcome from Julia Dent that would now bring him back almost daily in the spring of 1844.

Only a year before, seventeen-year-old Varina Howell had met and fallen in love with a former soldier, Jefferson Davis. Together, they had taken daily rides through the nearby fields and woods, just as seventeen-year-old Julia Boggs Dent and her soldier-suitor, Ulysses Grant, were now to do. But if Jeff Davis had been attracted to Varina Howell's intelligence and wit, the younger, more awkward Ulysses Grant was drawn to Julia's simple ability to make him feel comfortable. In her presence, he did not feel tongue-tied; as they rode or puttered in the gardens, he found to his amazement he could talk to her much as he did to her brothers. Later, Ulysses would declare that he had had "but one sweetheart in his life" and that sweetheart was Julia Boggs Dent.[4]

Perhaps Julia's homeliness put Ulysses more at ease than he would have been with a beautiful woman such as Varina. Perhaps her conscientious churchgoing struck a familiar chord in Hannah Grant's son. But most likely it was her openness and her willingness to carry the conversation with amusing anecdotes and uncomplicated humor that made her the object of his desire. Before April was out, he was urging Julia to accept his class ring. But to his great disappointment, she refused. "Mamma," she declared, "would not approve of my accepting a gift from a gentleman."[5]

There things might have remained were it not for Ulysses's persistence and Julia's superstitious nature. Throughout her life, Julia would believe in premonitions, omens, and the foretelling of the future in dreams. For her, these magical, mystical glimpses into the future were rarely ominous. Instead they acted to reassure her that she was on the path to happiness and that pleasant events were just around the corner. The very evening after Ulysses had asked her to wear his ring, she lay in her newly decorated room, in her brand-new bed—and dreamed of him. Although he was thought to be on his way the following morning to visit his family in Ohio, Julia saw him clearly in her dream: he came to her home dressed in civilian clothes and declared that he was going to try to stay for a week. Julia was certain of the predictive powers of her dream, for it was well known that one's first dream in a new bed came true. And so it did.[6]

The next morning, Julia's maid came to tell her that Mr. Grant had arrived with her father—and he was not in his military uniform. To everyone's amazement but Julia's, he announced his plans to stay for a week. It was clear to Julia that Ulysses meant to press his suit. Alone with her on a buggy ride, he stated his intentions: he loved her and wanted to marry her. Julia greeted his proposal with a counterproposal: they could be engaged, which she observed would be "fun," but the engagement must remain a secret.[7]

If this seemed a flippant response to a serious proposal, Julia did not intend it so. She was neither cruel nor a coquette who toyed with her suitor's affection. She was simply unprepared to move from the role of daughter to the role of wife. Barely eighteen, she was still more girl than woman, her understanding of love and marriage garnered more from romance novels than from experience. She was charmed by the attentions of a handsome soldier, and perhaps already loved him, but she was not yet ready to leave her father's household. An engagement was acceptable to her, for her dreams confirmed that her fate was intertwined with his. But marriage, and with it the passage into adulthood, was more than she could contemplate at the moment.

Julia was surely aware that the secrecy and uncertainty troubled Ulysses, but he had accepted her terms and she was content. The situation grew more complicated, however, for soon after his declaration of love, he was shipped off to Camp Salubrity in the Louisiana Territory, not far from Nachitoches. During his months there, Ulysses wrote long letters to Julia, love letters that must have required him to overcome his deep-seated emotional restraint and verbal terseness. By his own frequent admission, he missed her terribly. She was the singular source of warmth and open affection in his life.[8]

For Julia, the separation was less tragic. While she delighted in receiving ardent expressions of love from her soldier-suitor, she failed miserably to hold up her end of the correspondence. Surrounded as she was by family and friends, she did not share his loneliness. Even if she had suffered as much as Ulysses, she found writing a chore rather than a chance to express herself. Her frustration at trying to capture strong emotions with paper and pen was obvious, for Julia had little literary talent and was largely unaccustomed to probing or articulating her innermost feelings and thoughts. Her most sustained enthusiasm came when she recorded her dreams or, in later years, described her adventures abroad. And her strabismus, the problem of eye coordination that plagued her all her life, made it difficult to focus long on the written page. Finally, Julia lacked the discipline that was second nature to Ulysses. Over her lifetime, she left a trail of unfinished projects and projects conceived but never begun. During their long marriage, Ulysses saw many such projects taken up and then abandoned. It is possible that in 1844, many a letter begun was never finished.

Still, the absence of letters from his "dear Julia" disheartened Lieutenant Grant. Insecure and lonely, Ulysses found himself pleading, cajoling, and chiding her, always hoping she would realize that her letters alone broke the tedium of military life. "Be as punctual in writing me Julia," he urged in July 1844, "and then I will be compensated in a slight degree,—nothing could fully compensate—for your absence." By the end of August, he confessed, "I have waited so long for an answer to my three letters . . . that I began to dispare of ever recieving a line from you."[9]

Despite his pleas, Julia's letters remained sporadic. Without a steady stream of reassurances, Ulysses came to fear that he was losing Julia. Although he had promised to keep their engagement a secret, he decided to press the matter. That September, he wrote to Colonel and Mrs. Dent, asking permission to marry their daughter. Unsure of himself, he told Julia he had sent this letter "unsealed that you may read it before delivering it." Despite his fervent hope that consent would be given, Ulysses conceded that there were reasonable objections. "Youth and length of acquaintance" would, he feared, be brought against them. But he hoped Julia would make their case: "the longest acquaintance, or a few years more experience in the world could not create a feeling deeper or more durable" than their love.[10]

No answer came from the Dents. On April 1, Ulysses received a month's leave, and headed to St. Louis to ask in person for Julia's hand in marriage. The Colonel's reply was blunt: Grant was too poor to provide for his daughter, and she was wholly unsuited for the life of a soldier's wife. Here were objections Ulysses had not expected. The Colonel drove home his point: if Ulysses wanted to marry Julia's younger sister, he would give his blessing, for Nellie could adapt easily to the requirements of military life. But Julia? Impossible.[11]

Colonel Dent no doubt thought he was protecting his favorite daughter from unfamiliar hardship just as Margaret Howell had hoped to protect Varina from heartbreak. But like Jefferson Davis, Ulysses Grant held firm. It was Julia and Julia alone he wanted, he declared. There things stood, two stubborn men determined to have their way, when Grant received orders to join gathering military forces in Texas. War with Mexico darkened the horizon in 1845, and Ulysses S. Grant, like Julia's brother, Frederick, Pete Longstreet, Jefferson Davis, and hundreds of other American soldiers, was being sent west to serve his country.

With Ulysses off to war, the Colonel wasted no time trying to distract Julia from thoughts of her absent fiancé. Julia and her younger sister Nell were taken to St. Louis, where they could enter the lively social life of the city—and meet available eligible men. Julia's father clearly hoped she would abandon plans to marry the man she called "her Lieutenant" once she was caught up again in the whirl of dances and parties St. Louis's young people enjoyed. Julia proved more than willing to enjoy herself, but she remained stubbornly committed to Grant. She might delight in serenades sung outside her window by local bachelors, but she had no intention of turning her back on what she considered her destiny.[12]

From Corpus Christi, Matamoros, Monterey, and Tacubaya, Mexico, Ulysses once again showered Julia with letters, this time written on the eve of battles and during the long and tedious days of inactivity. And once again, although she loved reading the "sweet nothings" contained in every letter, her output fell far short of his own. Since Ulysses did not save Julia's letters, their contents remain lost to us. But if we hear only one voice in this lovers' conversation, it is revealing. Grant took each letter he received as an affirmation, an assurance, of Julia's continuing affections, and there was gratitude and relief in his every response. "Your letters," he wrote only a short time after his departure from White Haven, "always afford me a greatdeal [*sic*] of happiness because they assure me again that you love me still." For his part, he wrote, there was no sacrifice too great to make for her—"I . . . would sacrifice evrything Earthly," he assured her that September.[13]

By October 1845, Julia and Ulysses had been engaged for almost seventeen months and Ulysses had run out of patience. He pressed Julia to take the next step. It was a promising moment, for he had received a promotion, and a career in the military now looked like a good choice. But he was willing, he quickly added, to resign his commission if her parents continued to object. He had been offered a professorship in math at an Ohio college and he would take it if necessary. The Colonel's continued resistance amazed him. "How can your Pa continue to disapprove of a Match which so much affects the happiness of both?" Surely her father must yield. If not, Julia must defy him. "You know my views my Dear Julia on the subject of the interference of parents in matters of such vast importance." Years later, he was to feel the sting of these words himself, as his own most beloved daughter entered a marriage Ulysses knew would end badly.[14]

Julia's temperament was unsuited to confrontation or rebellion. She would never marry without her parents' blessing, nor would she argue the pros and cons of her choice in husbands with her father. Pressed on both sides by strong-willed men, Julia chose to persevere. She had made her decision, and she could not be moved to change it; she would simply wait until her father's disapproval turned to resignation. In the end, both men wanted her happiness, and one had already compromised; the other, she believed, would ultimately follow.

Julia was correct. As 1846 came to a close, the Colonel grudgingly gave his blessing. Nothing Ulysses had said or done had swayed Frederick Dent, but the doting father could no longer hold out against his daughter's desires. Julia's younger sister Emma understood the family dynamic: "when Julia wanted a thing of my father she usually got it."[15]

Still, the months went by without any hope of a reunion. Although the peace treaty ending the war was signed in February 1848, it was not until June that Ulysses could write with any confidence that he would soon be home. "The thought of seeing you so soon is a happy one dearest Julia," he wrote, "but I am so impatient that I have the *Blues* all the time." At last, on July 11, 1848, he received a sixty-day leave. In August he entered the doors of White Haven once again. It had been more than three years since Julia had seen her husband-to-be.[16]

Julia saw at once that her lieutenant had changed. Ulysses had left a handsome if untested soldier; he returned a veteran of war. The glamour of soldiering had faded for him, as it had for many of the young men who returned to their homes that year. More than twelve thousand Americans had died during the deadly conflict, brought down by fever, dysentery, and other illnesses as well as wounds suffered on the battlefield. Among those who would not return were several of Julia Dent's former dancing partners during the carefree winter of 1843. The war had also been the first taste of military combat for a group of men who, only a dozen years later, would lead armies of blue and gray: Ulysses S. Grant, George McClellan, Stonewall Jackson, James Longstreet, George Meade, and Robert E. Lee. It had made a hero of Jefferson Davis, who helped turn defeat into victory at the Battle of Buena Vista, and it had brought honor to the Dent family, for the bravery of Frederick Dent, who had been wounded twice, in the battles of Churubusco and Molino del Rey. Ulysses S. Grant would later call the Mexican War "wicked" and unjustified, but in August 1848, his thoughts were not on the morality of the conflict but on marriage.[17]

Julia's thoughts, too, were on marriage. In truth, the war itself had intruded little on her consciousness, except that it had caused a long separation from her lieutenant—now her captain—and occasionally disrupted the steady flow of his love letters to her. She had little to say on the causes of the war or its morality, but she had dreamed of its consequences: her Ulysses would return a hero. In her dream, she had arrived in New Orleans with him "amidst hurrahs, salutes of cannon, a great display of flags and flowers, and . . . bright carpets spread for me to walk upon." Such a hero's greeting from the people of New Orleans did not occur until 1880, when Ulysses Grant was once again a civilian, but for Julia Dent, the dream's prophecy had no expiration date.[18]

Julia and Ulysses set August 22 as the date for their wedding, allowing him time to visit his own family in Ohio. Julia was confident all the arrangements could be quickly made. She had, she observed, had four years to prepare. She chose a bridal gown of India mull muslin, similar to the gown her mother had worn some thirty years before. But Caroline O'Fallon, who had introduced Julia to St. Louis society in 1844, had a grander vision for the young bride. She arrived at the Dents' town house with an elegant dress of watered silk and a veil of white tulle that, Julia reported, "floated around my head and enveloped me in its fleecy folds." Another family friend provided fresh flowers—white cape jessamines—to attach to the veil, and with this, Julia considered her costume complete.[19]

The wedding was simple, the gathering small. The Dent home in St. Louis would not accommodate a large crowd and the August heat would have discouraged attendance. Julia chose three bridesmaids, including her younger sister Nellie; Ulysses's fellow soldiers Cadmus Wilcox and James Longstreet, both destined to surrender to General Grant at Appomattox, along with Bernard Pratte III, were groomsmen. After the ceremony, the guests were treated to ices, fruits, and a wedding cake that Julia judged "a marvel of beauty."[20]

Thirty-two

"HIS LOVING LITTLE WIFE"

Creating a Home and Starting a Family

JULIA DENT WAS NOW JULIA DENT GRANT—and it was time to meet her husband's family. The day after the wedding, the couple boarded a riverboat, headed up the Mississippi to Ohio. Julia's excitement was obvious: it was her first boat trip, her first trip away from St. Louis, and her first act as a married woman. In her old age, Julia remembered the trip as an experience "like a dream to me and always pleasant." The Grants proved an equally novel experience. "This truly interesting family," as she called them, included Ulysses's grandmother Simpson, "tall and robust" and, in Julia's eyes, the "ideal of a Revolutionary mother." Although the formidable Jesse Root Grant was on his best behavior, greeting Julia cordially, he strongly disapproved of his son marrying into a slave-owning family. Hannah Grant, white-haired and bespectacled, remained true to her nature and said little to her son or his wife. In her memoirs, Julia carefully painted a softer picture of Hannah, praising her as "the most self-sacrificing, the sweetest, kindest woman I ever met except my own dear mother." But Hannah, too, disapproved of any connection to slaveholders and their life of ease and luxury. Ulysses's two brothers and three sisters proved more likable and friendlier. Although his sister Clara had inherited her father's sour personality, all the girls adored their brother Ulysses and thus were willing to like his wife.[1]

At last, in October Julia and Ulysses returned to White Haven, to say their goodbyes to the Dents. Ulysses had received orders to report to the military installation at Detroit, Michigan, and, as his wife, Julia would go with him. For Julia, the experience of a separation from her own family was traumatic. The realization that she was leaving her "dear home" in order to make a new life among strangers was wrenching. Gone was the ever-present smile, the ready laugh, the cheerfulness that had long defined her; in their place were the anxiety and uncertainty of a young woman shifting

her identity from daughter to wife. "I could not, could not, think of it without bursting into a flood of tears and weeping and sobbing as if my heart
would break." If Julia's reaction was more dramatic than most, if her
attachment to her father and to her family was more intense than most,
still the transition she faced would be familiar to nineteenth-century
middle-class American women everywhere.[2]

Julia's intense distress both surprised and troubled her husband. He was
at a loss as to how to deal with her tears or her fears. For four years he had
dreamed of this marriage—and it seemed in crisis before it had even
begun. Colonel Dent, however, did know what to do, though his solution
would seem to the young bride and groom worse than the crisis itself.
"Grant," Julia recalled her father saying, "I can arrange it all for you. You
join your regiment and leave Julia with us. You can get a leave of absence
once or twice a year and run on here and spend a week or two with us." He
added, not without a note of triumph, "I always knew she could not live in
the army."[3]

Whatever Ulysses might have thought or wished to say to the Colonel,
he restrained himself. It was Julia's decision, but the choice was not between going to Detroit and remaining at White Haven; the choice, as she
knew, was to begin her life as a married woman or continue her life as a
child. He whispered in her ear: "Would you like this, Julia? Would you like
to remain with your father and let me go alone?" Her answer was no.
"Then," Ulysses instructed, "dry your tears and do not weep again. It makes
me unhappy." In that moment, a husband's prerogative was established:
Julia Dent was, and would remain, Mrs. Ulysses Grant.[4]

Julia had cast her lot with her husband, but her attachment to her father
and family never faded. White Haven, she admitted decades later, would
always feel like home to her. Yet late November 1846 found the Grants
headed to Detroit, stopping in Bethel to visit friends and family along the
way. Julia recalled the trip brightly, she and her new husband, whom she
called "Ulys," riding by moonlight, she singing while the whole world slept.
From there, they boarded a train to Detroit—another exciting first experience for Julia, who later in life would become a world traveler. But bad
news awaited the Grants on their arrival: when Ulysses reported for duty
he discovered that he had been transferred to the more remote outpost at
Sackets Harbor, New York.[5]

Although he protested, they had little choice but to proceed immediately to "this far-off and out-of-the-way place." No sooner had they arrived
at Sackets Harbor than new orders came through: return to Detroit. This

proved impossible since navigation ceased as winter set in. Until the spring thaw, Sackets Harbor's Madison Barracks would be their home.

Julia now demonstrated a surprising adaptability, not only to new surroundings and the relatively Spartan military life but also to her new role as homemaker and wife. She met her first challenge to her authority over the domestic domain quickly. On their arrival, Ulysses invited several officers for dinner without consulting her. Julia insisted he tell them not to come. Her cook, she explained, was untested and she refused to play hostess until she was confident that the meal that was served met her standards. Ulysses was sheepish, but he understood that he had overstepped his boundaries. His friends, invited for the following evening, teased Julia good-naturedly, pretending to be afraid to enter the Grant household without her permission. The evening was a success, and Julia settled comfortably into her role as hostess.[6]

But there was more to domestic duties than making guests feel at ease. Running the household meant a bewildering number of tasks and skills for which life at White Haven had poorly prepared her. In Ellen Dent's household, servants had kept things running so smoothly, cooking, cleaning, and preserving and pickling the fruits of the orchard and the vegetables from the garden, that Julia was "under the impression that the house kept itself." But here in northern New York, there were no battalions of slaves to tend to household chores. Although she had a cook and would always have a maid, Julia knew she would have to take the reins of running the household.[7]

The results were mixed. When she tried to reproduce the meals she enjoyed as a child, she realized she had a faulty memory and little culinary flair. She could not recall—if she had ever actually known—all the ingredients that went into the foods she had relished as a child. She soon turned over the menu and its preparation to her cook. Thus her repertoire, confined to one cake and some "nice currant and quince jelly," did not grow. Years later, while she was in the White House, she was embarrassed to admit she had not a single original recipe to contribute to a cookbook friends were creating.

Julia was equally poor at managing her household budget. From the beginning, she asked Ulysses to provide her with a regular, set allowance. Her reasoning was sound. She knew that bills for household supplies usually came every three to six months, and thus both were large and reflected long-past domestic pleasures and necessities. She had seen other wives criticized by husbands for the extravagance these large bills mistakenly suggested, and she did not want to suffer their fate. But Julia's bookkeeping skills were as limited as her culinary skills. Although she attempted to keep her accounts carefully in the small blank book she'd purchased for that purpose, the sums never added up correctly. "I never was very good at arithmetic," she admitted, "and there was *such* a variety of little items." Sometimes she went over her budget, sometimes she had money to spare, but how and why remained a mystery to her. Ulysses was untroubled by her inability to manage her accounts; indeed, he found this, like many of Julia's failures, endearing. He refused to help her balance her little book, but he always willingly made up any deficit. Like the tolerant schoolmaster she had known as a child, Ulysses neither punished nor demanded mastery. In this, as in so many things, Julia was never challenged; her failures became foibles, and she could remain content with herself.[8]

The winter passed happily for the Grants at Madison Barracks. When spring came, they returned to Detroit, where Ulysses rented a house and equipped it with a maid and his own valet. Soon Julia was pregnant and on her way to St. Louis to give birth to her first son. Frederick Dent Grant, named for her father, was born on May 30, 1850.[9]

Julia and little Fred headed to Detroit for the winter. Her husband, who had fallen back into his bachelor routine of excessive smoking and card playing during her absence, welcomed a return to pleasant suppers on the back porch and relished the new sound of his wife singing lullabies to his son. When spring came, Ulysses was sent to Sackets Harbor once again and Julia and Frederick traveled south to spend the summer at White Haven. By September, Ulysses's loneliness had grown intense, and he ordered her back to Madison Barracks. Julia's shuttling between Missouri, Michigan, and New York ended abruptly when Ulysses's entire regiment received orders to ship out to California.[10]

As Julia was pregnant once again, Ulysses refused to allow her to make the long ocean and land journey to the West Coast. An indignant Julia protested this decision. As she recalled, she threw a temper tantrum. "I said I would go, I would, I would; for him to hush; that I should not listen to him; that he knew nothing whatever about the matter; and that I would go, etc. etc. And of course," she added, "I shed tears." Although Ulysses always grew upset at the sight of his wife in tears, he remained adamant. The trip was both onerous and dangerous; his salary was not enough to provide her and the children with even the bare necessities of life out there; and she had, after all, a comfortable home that would welcome her. The matter was thus settled: White Haven's favorite daughter went home again.[11]

Ulysses understood the sacrifice he was making. Julia's buoyant personality, her ability to make guests feel welcome and valued, and her continuing open affection for her husband had made it possible for Ulysses to enjoy a social life that went beyond cigar smoking and card playing with army cronies. She remained, as she had been from their first meeting, the woman he could talk to, confide in, and cherish. Now, as he headed off to California, all that had to be left behind.

Ulysses sailed from New York City on July 5, 1851; his second son was born seventeen days later, while Julia was visiting his family in Ohio. Had the baby been a girl, Ulysses had given his wife freedom to name her as she wished, but if it was a boy, he gave instructions to name the child Ulysses. "I know you will do this Julia of your own choise but then I want you to know it will please me too." Without complaint, Julia complied. In the end, everyone called the boy "Buck," a nickname that honored his birthplace, the Buckeye State. Buck, like his older brother and the boy and girl who followed, survived all the dangers of infancy and childhood. There would be no small gravestones for the Grants like those that scarred the memories of Varina and Jefferson Davis.[12]

While Julia proudly displayed her children to doting grandparents and joined in the celebrations surrounding her brother Fred's wedding, Ulysses struggled with the long separation from wife and children. Every letter struck the same note of loneliness. "You do not know how forsaken I feel here!" he wrote in February 1854 from his new post at Fort Humboldt, deep in the sequoia country of California, some 250 miles north of San Francisco. Without Julia to create the cheerful environment that ensured a steady round of dinner guests and social calls, Ulysses reverted quickly to his old solitary ways. "I do nothing here but set in my room and read and occationally [*sic*] take a short ride on one of the public horses." No one reading his letters could doubt the depression enveloping him. By March 1854, he was ready to resign from the military rather than endure a longer separation. "I sometimes get so anxious to see you, and our little boys," he told Julia, "that I am almost tempted to resign and trust to Providence, and my own exertions, for a living where I can have you and them with me."[13]

Unfortunately, Ulysses's "own exertions" held out little promise of prosperity. Eager to provide for his growing family from afar, Captain Grant had engaged on arrival in California on one of the many unsuccessful business ventures that would first raise his hopes of prosperity and then dash them. He had clearly inherited none of his father's business acumen. He was too trusting, too hopeful, and too willing to bear the brunt of failures suffered by himself and his partners. In his letters home to wife, father, sisters, and brothers he detailed the ups and downs of his ventures, reporting each of them first with optimism and later with regret. Natural disasters, unscrupulous partners, and bad luck plagued him. Small wonder that his March letter also contained the admission that "whenever I get to thinking upon the subject however *poverty, poverty* begins to stare me in the face."[14]

Julia's letters, few though they might have been, have not survived. But it is likely that they contained, or Ulysses read into them, evidence of a contentment that stood in stark contrast to his own increasing despair. "How do I know," he wrote on March 25, "that you are thinking as much of me as I of you? I do not get letters to tell me so." Only a few weeks later, he tendered his resignation and made plans to head home to his wife and family.[15]

In her memoirs, Julia diminished the toll taken by this extended separation. She dismissed all claims that Captain Grant "was dejected, low-spirited, badly dressed, and even slovenly while in California." She ignored any suggestion that his sudden resignation from the military in the spring of 1854 had been prompted by drinking. Years later, Ulysses himself would concede that "the vice of intemperance had not a little to do with my decision to resign," but Julia never conceded that loneliness and boredom could drive her husband to drink. Of the men who characterized him either as depressed or intemperate, she would only comment: "Well, I am quite sure they did not know *my* Captain Grant, for he was always perfection, both in manner and person, a cheerful, self-reliant, earnest gentleman." Ulysses's own letters shout out a far different tale, but Julia viewed the world through her own bright lens, which added color where there was only gray and shone a corrective light on dark corners. If nothing else, she refused to let a momentary lapse tarnish the image she maintained of her Ulys; he was and would remain "the nicest and handsomest man I ever saw."[16]

In the same fashion, Julia painted a positive picture of the difficult and discouraging years that followed her husband's return to civilian life. Although every venture undertaken turned to dust, despite the help that was provided by Colonel Dent, the Colonel's sons, and even the irascible Jesse Root Grant, Julia recalled these years as happy ones. But if they were happy, they were also filled with failure.

Thirty-three

"CHEER UP, MAKE THE BEST OF THIS"

The Return to Civilian Life

FOR TWO YEARS, ULYSSES TRIED his hand at farming. Colonel Dent willingly provided farmland to his son-in-law, and Julia's brother Louis offered them a house he had built nearby. Here, in the house they called Wish-ton-wish—an Indian name for whippoorwill—Julia's first daughter, Ellen, was born. The White Haven slaves came to see the baby, and the older women among them declared with satisfaction that Ellen (often known as Nellie), unlike Nellie's mother, was "going to look like old Mistress." The younger slave women, showing more tact, told Julia that they had called upon the good fairies to give the child "everything good—beauty, health, and wealth,—and . . . we ask she may be gentle and kind and beautiful like Mistress, her grandma." Like Varina Howell Davis, Julia did not pause to wonder if these slave women knew such wishes were hopeless for their own children.[1]

In Julia's version of their years at Wish-ton-wish, Ulys was a fine farmer and she a "splendid farmer's wife." To her fell the task of raising the chickens, each of which she provided with absurdly fanciful names. Together, Fred, Buck, and Julia tossed handfuls of grain to poultry bearing names such as Celeste and the Great Mogul. And though many a farm wife held that chickens were stupid creatures, Julia insisted that her hens and roosters were remarkably intelligent. For, though their breeds came from foreign lands such as distant China and exotic India, she found they could understand the English language. She discerned this, she explained, because they responded to her call to come and eat and even appeared to pass the word along to other members in the chicken coop. Her proof seems to reveal an almost comic ignorance. But Julia was, after all, a parochial young matron who had never left the country and had no reason to assume that poultry any more than people were the same in Shanghai as in Missouri. She was surprised, in fact, to observe "those foreign birds," her roosters, employing the same "little tricks of gallantry" toward the hens as American roosters were known to employ. Most important to Julia, both domestic and foreign hens seemed as contented as their owner and thus they produced a wealth of chicks and eggs.[2]

Julia managed to bring the same cheery optimism to her home that she brought to her henhouse. She had a moment of despair when Ulys decided to construct a crude cabin for his family despite the superior comforts of Louis Dent's Wish-ton-wish. She recalled this unusual emotion, and the cloud it seemed to cast on the future. "Is this my destiny? Is this my destiny?" she asked herself as she watched the cabin take its ugly shape. "These crude, not to say rough surroundings; to eat, to sleep, to wake again and again to the same—oh, sad is me!" But her confidence returned quickly. She heard what she was certain were the voices of fairies reassuring her: "No, no, *this* is not your destiny. Cheer up, be happy now, make the best of this." And make the best of it she did. She "got out all my pretty covers, baskets, books, etc and tried to make it look home-like and comfortable." Despite her efforts, the cabin remained unattractive; there was nothing to do, Julia concluded cheerfully, but name the ugly place Hardscrabble.[3]

The Grants remained in Hardscrabble until Julia's mother died in 1857. Alone and lonely in his empty mansion, the Colonel persuaded the Grants to move into White Haven with him. Ulysses now took on the task of farming his father-in-law's land as well as his own. The results were discouraging. Profits did not materialize and Ulysses's health suffered. After a year and a half of struggle, Ulysses conceded defeat and put his own farm, the horses, all the equipment, and the crops up for sale. All that remained were Julia's four slaves. Then Ulysses headed to St. Louis, where he entered into a partnership with a cousin of Julia's who bought and sold real estate and negotiated loans. Julia and the children soon followed. But if once Julia had enjoyed the city's fashionable shops and elegant parties, she was now settled in a shabby part of the city far from the St. Louis she had known.

Julia held out little hope that her husband's new business venture would succeed. "I cannot imagine how my dear husband ever thought of going into such a business," she observed in her memoir, "as he could never collect a penny that was owed to him." Julia was correct. This business, too, failed, and reluctantly, Ulysses turned to his own father for help. It was a measure of their desperation that the hopes of Ulys and Julia rested with Jesse Root Grant.[4]

It was not the first time since he had left the military that Ulysses had asked for assistance from his father. An early appeal for a loan had been met with silence, although Jesse certainly had the means to help his son. And when Ulysses, who hated the tanning business, had swallowed both his pride and his distaste and asked for a role in the family operations in Galena, Illinois, Jesse had set unreasonable terms. He would allow Ulysses to join his brothers in the tannery business in Galena, Jesse had said, only if Julia and her children came to live with her in-laws in Bethel, Kentucky, where Jesse and Hannah now resided. Perhaps Jesse's sullen refusal to come to his son's aid at the time arose from open, and vocal, disappointment that Ulysses had resigned his commission in the military. Jesse had tried unsuccessfully to have the army set aside that resignation, much to Ulysses's embarrassment. But one thing is certain: the terms he set for bringing his oldest son into the family business reflected his disapproval of Julia. To Jesse, Julia was spoiled, extravagant, and materialistic; if she set up house-keeping with Ulysses, she would drain his income with demands for servants and fancy household trappings. Under Hannah's watchful eye, Julia could be kept in check and Ulysses would be free to slowly build his fortune.[5]

Julia had cringed at the thought of life in the Spartan Grant household. But she was never in danger, for Ulysses considered another separation of husband and wife unthinkable. Jesse's offer had been turned down, just as Colonel Dent's offer had been rejected when Julia and Ulysses were newlyweds. Now, however, a desperate Ulysses renewed his request for a share in the Galena leather operations. Julia had given birth to their fourth child in February 1858, and at thirty-seven, Ulysses had no other prospects in sight.

He would accept any position and any salary, but his family must move to Illinois with him. This time, Jesse agreed. The Grants packed their belongings and headed north, leaving the four slaves Julia called "these dear family servants of mine" behind. Julia regretted leaving Missouri, but she was greatly relieved that she was not headed for Bethel. Later she would sum up the incompatibility with her in-laws with a brevity and sharpness that spoke volumes: "We were brought up in different schools," she observed. "They considered me unpardonably extravagant, and I considered them inexcusably the other way." Extravagance and parsimony were not the only hallmarks of those "different schools," of course. Jesse Grant continued to be a fierce opponent of slavery throughout his life, and Julia remained a willing owner of slaves until the Emancipation Proclamation began to dismantle the "peculiar institution."[6]

The Grants arrived in Galena in the spring of 1860. Although the town had once been the pride of Illinois, an urban gathering place for miners, traders, explorers, and gamblers when Chicago was just a tiny village, Galena was now on the decline. The city of some fourteen thousand still had gristmills and iron foundries, tanneries and breweries, but its population was no longer growing. Julia and Ulysses found a seven-room brick house, set high on a hill on the more genteel west side of town, roomy enough for them, their four children, and Ulysses's ailing brother Simpson, who would share household expenses. The view was lovely and the neighbors friendly, but soon after arriving, Julia was stricken with homesickness for White Haven and her father. As she was unpacking their possessions, she found that one of her mother's old mirrors had broken into pieces, and she burst into tears, filled with longing for Missouri and fear that it was an omen of bad luck to follow.[7]

Soon enough, however, Julia set aside her worries and her optimism returned. She had much to enjoy: her house was neat and roomy, the view was lovely, and her new servant was both industrious and a good cook. Leaving her maid to handle the housekeeping chores much as her mother before her had done with her slaves, Julia settled into a pleasant routine of reading, sewing, and visiting. In the evening, with Ulys and her three sons and her daughter gathered at the table, Julia was content. Neither Ulysses's humble position as a billing clerk in the family business nor his modest salary could dampen the spirits in the Grant household. Only the nation's growing political instability and the talk of secession threatened to disrupt the domestic tranquillity of Mr. and Mrs. Grant.

Thirty-four

"AS I WAS A DEMOCRAT AT THAT TIME"

The Opportunities of War

GALENA, ILLINOIS, LIKE THE REST OF THE NATION, had been shocked by news of John Brown's raid on Harpers Ferry in 1859. Here, as everywhere, the men and women who had followed the slow but steady unraveling of compromise between slave and free societies now held their breath, frightened by the promise of more bloodshed to come. By mid-1860, rumors of secession moved closer to reality, and Americans such as Jefferson and Varina Davis, Ulysses Grant, and Theodore and Angelina Grimké Weld prepared to confront what contemporaries and later generations would call "the impending crisis." Looking back, the trajectory to war now seemed clear: from the Missouri Compromise to the rise of the Anti-Slavery Societies, the Compromise of 1850, Bleeding Kansas, *Uncle Tom's Cabin,* the Dred Scott decision, John Brown's raid at Harpers Ferry, the ascendancy of a regional Republican political party, and finally the secession of six Southern states from the Union. Suddenly a sense of inevitability settled over the nation.

But for Julia Dent Grant, 1860 brought a jolting introduction to national politics. Unlike Varina or Angelina, Julia came to the news of secession and civil war unprepared by decades of involvement in the larger world outside her home and family. If she was surprised to find herself caught up in the excitement of crisis politics, she was even more surprised to discover that society's concerns could penetrate her own private universe.

Julia's political affiliation, like her acceptance of slavery, had been a birthright rather than a conscious decision. "I was a Democrat," she wrote, "because my father was." No soul-searching had led her, as it did Angelina, to renounce the values and beliefs of her parents; no conscious shift of loyalties from family to husband had taken place as it did for Varina. For Julia, political affiliation did not define her in any significant way and slavery was too much a part of the natural order of things to be questioned. But by

1860, the people she had come to know in Galena as friends and neighbors had begun to openly challenge both of these givens in her life. Their rejection of "the beloved party of my father, of Jefferson, of General Jackson, of Douglas, and of Thomas Benton" in favor of the party of Lincoln and Sumner left Julia "very much disturbed in my political sentiments."[1]

Politics had entered the Grant household. Throughout 1860, Julia listened intently as her Ulys read aloud the speeches and debates that filled the newspapers. But clarity did not come to her. Julia wrestled with these issues in her own way, absorbing the abstract and intellectual arguments by analogy to conflicts in her own life. Secession, she reasoned, was as much the right of a state as choosing not to study subjects that were boring or too overwhelming was the right of a young schoolgirl. Yet efforts to prevent secession were as much the duty of the national government as it was the duty of the long-suffering Misses Mauro to enforce the curriculum of their school. Julia was therefore of two minds on the grave issue of secession. Her dilemma was not based on the ambiguities of the Constitution on critical issues such as state sovereignty, the legality of slavery, or the indivisibility of the Union. In later life she confessed that throughout the years of secession and war, she did not even know what the Constitution was. She recorded a conversation during the war with Confederate women who argued that the actions of Lincoln's government were unconstitutional. After listening to them offer their constitutional arguments, she exclaimed: "Well, I did not know a thing about this dreadful Constitution and told them so. They seemed much astonished and asked, 'Why, surely you have studied it?' 'No, I have not,' " she had replied; " 'I would not know where to look for it even if I wished to read.' "[2]

Ulysses provided little assistance or guidance to his wife as she struggled to parse out the ethics of the impending crisis. He did not challenge her to educate herself on the matter, nor did he demand that she adopt his views. Instead, he found her sudden attention to public affairs amusing and her confusion endearing. When pressed, he said only that she was correct about the Union's obligations, but a bit muddled on the issue of states' rights.[3]

Julia found the internal pressure to create a coherent political critique painfully unsettling. In the end, she made the large, public, and impersonal events swirling around her more manageable, more understandable, by reducing them to their impact on her own narrower, but to her more real, domestic world. Cataclysmic change could be comprehended by subjecting it to one touchstone: how did it affect those she loved? For the wife of

Ulysses S. Grant, the erupting civil war would be a blessing cloaked in a tragedy, for it would bring the acclaim and honor she had dreamed of for her husband.

Unlike Julia, Ulysses faced no moral or intellectual dilemma as the nation moved toward war. He had never given credence to the states' rights argument, and though he had voted for a Democratic presidential candidate in 1856 and supported the Democrat Stephen A. Douglas in 1860, his first loyalty was to the Union. On April 16, the day after Fort Sumter surrendered, he wrote to Colonel Frederick Dent, urging him to set aside his loyalty to the Democratic Party and support President Lincoln. "The times," he wrote, "are indee[d] startling but now is the time, particularly in the border Slave states, for men to prove their love of country. I know it is hard for men to apparently work with the Republican party, but now all party distinctions should be lost sight of and evry true patriot be for maintaining the integrity of the glorious old *Stars & Stripes,* the Constitution and the Union." For Ulysses, the abolition of slavery was not the Union's cause; its cause was preserving the nation. Yet "in all this," he added, "I can but see the doom of Slavery." By the time this letter was written, Ulysses had abandoned his clerk's apron for sword and bayonet.[4]

Julia was sanguine about the prospect of her husband's reentry into the military. Any danger she might have envisioned was offset by her certainty that the war would bring great opportunities for her Ulys to shine. Galena showed its confidence in him, relying on him to recruit and drill local volunteers. She was also contented with the resolution to her own problem of political loyalties. Having domesticated the crisis that was developing around her, Julia abandoned all efforts to resolve the tensions between the right to secede and the need to preserve the Union. It was harder, but no less necessary, to abandon efforts to reconcile filial and marital devotion. Her father was a staunch and vocal supporter of the emerging Confederacy, her husband a firm believer in the Union. For Julia, the choice was bittersweet but clear: her first loyalty must be to her husband and thus to his chosen cause. As for any acts of patriotism on her own, these could be indirect, confined as she felt they should be to *his* household. "As my husband had already offered his sword and his services to his country," she reasoned, her own duty should be "to give all my care to his little ones." And this, she declared with pride in her memoir, "I faithfully did."[5]

The prophecies of her husband's greatness, so vivid in Julia's dreams, now seemed to her to be materializing. Ulysses, however, was less optimistic. He was convinced that the war would be short-lived and thus the chance for glory on the battlefield would have to come more quickly than his circumstances seemed to allow. In April he was appointed as assistant adjutant general of the State, but this was a position far too similar to the bookkeeping and paper pushing he had endured in his family's leather shop. His restlessness and dissatisfaction were obvious: "At present I am on duty with the Governer," he wrote to Julia, describing his duties as "principally smoking and occationally giving advice as to how an order should be communicated."[6]

Ulysses craved a field command, but he believed that these appointments were based as much on patronage and politics as on military experience. In early May, he wrote to his father that he "might have got the Colonelcy of a Regiment possibly, but I was perfectly sickened at the political wire pulling" such an appointment required. Yet soon after writing this gloomy evaluation, Ulysses was made commandant of Illinois's Camp Yates.[7]

Learning of Ulysses's appointment, Julia immediately urged her husband to bring their eleven-year-old son, Fred, along with him to the army camp. Since Ulys's regiment was expected to be on active duty for only three months, Julia thought the time together for father and son would be "a pleasant summer outing for them both." When her husband announced he was sending Fred home because there was likely to be fighting, Julia argued that the boy should remain. Drawing on her knowledge of history, garnered in the happy days at the Mauro family's academy, she reminded Ulysses that the great Macedonian general Alexander had been just as young as Fred when he accompanied his father, Philip, into glory. How could Julia so blithely put her son in harm's way? Unlike Varina Davis, Julia never seemed to doubt that heaven—and the fairies she believed watched over her as well—would keep all those she loved safe, even as bullets rained down on them. In the early weeks of his military service, Ulysses was not persuaded by her historical argument and sent Fred on his way. But as the months of separation from his family began to stretch before him, he changed his mind: throughout the war, he would welcome Fred, Buck, and even little Jesse into military camp. Soon enough, Julia and Nellie would join him, too.[8]

Governor Richard Yates now showed his confidence in the military veteran by appointing Ulysses colonel of the most undisciplined and rebellious of his state regiments: the Twenty-first Illinois Infantry. That regiment's first military assignment set into stark relief Julia's necessary choice between her childhood past and her adult future as wife and mother, for

Ulysses was being sent to her home state, Missouri, to help secure it against the ravages of its own internal civil war. Reports from St. Louis were indeed grim. Although the city's residents had voted to remain in the Union, guerrilla bands of Confederate insurgents roamed the state, and rebels almost succeeded in seizing the United States arsenal in St. Louis. The local federal commander refused any effort to deescalate the conflict: when the State's southern leaders proposed that Missouri adopt a position of neutrality in the war, he declared, "Rather than concede to the State of Missouri the right to dictate to my Government, I would see . . . every man, woman, and child in the State dead and buried." Small wonder that Ulysses wrote to Julia on May 1 that "the state of affairs there is terrible, and no doubt a terrible calamity awaits them. Stationing Ill. troops within striking distance of St. Louis may possibly save the city." Already, Ulysses added, an exodus of Union supporters from the violence-ridden state had begun: "Great numbers of people are leaving Missouri now in evry direction, except South. In some of the Northern towns the state merchants and business men are leaving with all their personal property." Then, drawing back from the dismal picture he was painting for his wife, Ulysses added his reassurance that one day Missouri would be a "great state," despite the destruction the Confederacy would wreak upon it in the coming months.[9]

By May 10, Ulysses was at their old home, Wish-ton-wish, not as a farmer but as a military officer. He reported, with clear regret, that Julia's brother John was readying to join the Confederate army and thus her father would have no one to protect him or his property. The Colonel would soon be "left to the mercy of Mary and the rest of the darkeys," who apparently were now less contented than Julia had believed them to be in her childhood. Ulysses would not hide the old man's personal plight from his wife: "As I told you," he wrote to Julia, "your father . . . says he is ruined and I fear it is too true."[10]

Although the Colonel declared himself a Union supporter, Ulysses labeled him a secessionist. "Your father," he told Julia, "says he is for the Union but is opposed to having army to sustain it. He would have a secession force march where they please uninterrupted." In Missouri, Confederates and Confederate sympathizers seemed to be doing just that. Ulysses found their behavior disgraceful. "The Secessionists," he wrote, "commit evry outrage upon the Unionists. They seize property, drive them out of the state &c. and destroy the railroad track wherever they find it without guard." He suspected that even Colonel Dent, despite his attachment to the South, would soon be a refugee.[11]

Despite the violence in Missouri, Ulysses did not initially believe the war would be long or costly in human life. There would be, he predicted, "much less bloodshed than is generally anticipated." The greatest danger, he told Julia, would come not from the clash of Confederate soldier and Union soldier on the battlefield but from "negro revolts" in the plantation South. If the slaves did rise, he believed white men would stand together: "I have no doubt but a Northern army would hasten South to suppress anything of the kind." He would soon discover how wrong he had been.[12]

Thirty-five

"THE HORRID OLD CONSTITUTION"

Julia's Personal War

WITH ULYSSES GONE, JULIA FACED A NUMBER of unfamiliar challenges. She was on her own, caring for four young children and managing a household without the steady hand of a husband or father, and without the comforting support of her slaves. She could not rely on Simpson, Ulysses's ailing younger brother who shared that household, for the illness that would soon take his life made him one more responsibility she had to shoulder. Although she seemed not to worry excessively about her husband's safety, she could not have been cheered by the news he sent from her home state. Writing from St. Louis once again that August, Ulysses reported that Julia's cousin and his own former business partner, Harry Boggs, had greeted him with open hostility. "He cursed," Ulysses reported, "and went on like a Madman. Told me that I would never be welcome in his house; that the people of Illinois were a poor miserable set of Black Republicans, Abolition paupers that had to invade their state to get something to eat." Ulysses met Boggs's anger with calm and sympathy: "Harry is such a pitiful insignificant fellow that I could not get mad at him and told him so." This response revealed far more than a generous understanding on the part of an officer of an occupying army; the officer's uniform, and the authority it bestowed, had begun to restore Ulysses's confidence in himself.[1]

Jesse Root Grant, who had not concealed his disappointment and lack of respect for his son in the difficult years after Fort Humboldt, was now voicing his pride in Ulysses's rising star. Always tactless, Jesse launched a public tirade of criticism against other military officers, comparing their talents unfavorably to those of his son. Indeed, Jesse's ambition for Ulysses seemed to exceed Ulysses's own. By July 1861, Jesse was already pressuring his son to seek a promotion and a command in the regular army rather than the state volunteer regiments. Ulysses cringed at his father's interference, but he could not deny the satisfaction he took from the steady approval and praise he was now receiving from friends and superiors. "The fact is," he confessed to Julia, "my whole career since the beginning of the present unhappy difficulties has been complimented in a very flattering manner. All my old friends in the Army and out seem to heartily congratulate me." After years of humiliating failures in the civilian world, Ulysses felt he was coming into his own.[2]

Julia had once dreamed of her husband being hailed as a hero. But Ulysses felt he needed her support to make the dream a reality. "You should be cheerful and try to encourage me," he instructed her that August, perhaps in response to her distress at managing affairs at home on her own. And by September, he seemed to need her physical presence as well. Writing from Cairo, Illinois, he declared, "If I am to remain any length of time I want you to come here. Get the children clothed so as to be in readiness to start when I write to you." Whatever added difficulties such preparations might entail, and despite how frightened of entering a war zone Julia confessed she was, she was ready to comply. But the month passed without the hoped-for reunion. "Things begin to look so much like a fight," Ulysses reported on September 12, "that I hardly think it would be prudent."[3]

The timing was bad for Julia as well. Simpson Grant died that month, and Julia and Ulysses debated whether she should move to Covington, Kentucky, where Jesse, Hannah, and Ulysses's sister Clara could help her with her rambunctious sons and her daughter. In the end, Ulysses agreed this was a poor solution to Julia's problems. Clara's "rigid economy"— especially harsh when applied to others—irked even Ulysses; for Julia it would be unbearable. For the moment at least, she would stay put in Galena.[4]

At last, in the fall of 1861, Julia and the children paid a brief visit to Ulysses at Cairo. But as fighting intensified in Kentucky and Tennessee, she made her way to St. Louis, which was now securely in Union hands. Her homecoming was bittersweet. Most of her childhood friends, including Pete Longstreet, had taken up the rebel cause, and she felt out of place as the wife of a Union officer. Although she was happy to see her father, she was relieved to be back in Cairo by mid-December of 1861.

Ulysses was mobilizing his troops for the attack on Fort Donalson and Fort Henry. At the end of January, he sent Julia and the children away, this time to the safety of Covington—and the less than welcoming arms of Jesse, Hannah, and Clara. Small wonder that on board the boat carrying her northward, the usually optimistic and cheerful Julia broke down in tears. "I was very lonely," she recalled, "and, after retiring for the night, I wept like a deserted child; so overcome was I with my desolation that my sobs brought a kind lady passenger to my side." The woman's concern and kindness embarrassed Julia; she was, after all, a grown woman with children, not a child herself. "I could hardly say to her that I was only homesick," Julia wrote—and yet she could not deny it to herself. She would feel the same desolation only once more in her lifetime, she said: when she left the White House in 1877.[5]

Living with the Grants proved as dreadful as Julia knew it would be. Her in-laws disapproved of her liberal child-rearing philosophy and considered the boys shockingly undisciplined and their characters fatally flawed. The rollicking antics that Ulysses and Julia applauded in young Jesse and that the Colonel would have warmly indulged were met with frowns from his paternal grandparents. Although her older children were put in school in Covington, Julia and little Jesse remained ready to flee to Ulysses's side at a moment's notice.[6]

While life in Covington was both tense and dreary for Julia, her spirits were buoyed by the news of Ulys's role in the taking of Fort Henry and Fort Donalson that February. Although she had been anxious about the outcome of the campaign, Julia, as usual, had remained sanguine about her husband's personal safety. "I never once expected to hear bad news from my General. I do not know why, I knew—I felt—he would be victorious and—did not the little ballad I used to sing to him declare 'the faithful soldier to Be God's special care,' and how true it was."[7]

Julia's pride in her husband's success was obvious. It comes through clearly in the *Memoirs*, even though decades had passed by the time she wrote: "The country simply went wild over the success of the General, and he became the recipient of many enthusiastic attentions." Even the tight-lipped Hannah felt compelled to comment on her son's sudden celebrity. Much like Julia, Jesse Grant observed, she seemed "to feel . . . that he had been raised up for the particular purpose of that war, and that the same power that had raised him up, would protect him." Ulysses, however, preferred to give himself credit for his success. He could not resist a small jab at his father. Writing to Julia on February 22, 1862, he inquired if Jesse was still afraid "that I will not be able to sustain myself."[8]

But celebrity carried its own risks. In early April 1862, Union and Confederate armies met in what was then the greatest battle ever fought on the North American continent, the Battle of Shiloh. From the beginning, old friends who had become new enemies led the series of clashes and attacks that resulted in a costly Union victory. The sheer cost in human life of the Shiloh battles was shocking. Grant and Buell lost more than thirteen thousand men; Beauregard lost more than ten thousand. But for some, Ulysses S. Grant's role in the confrontation was far from heroic. Grant, now a major general in the Union army, had not pursued a fleeing Southern army—and almost immediately, criticism rained down on Ulysses. Even before Shiloh, newspaper reporters had considered him fair game, insinuating that the higher command had lost confidence in him. Now papers were filled with commentary on his failings as a military leader. He was attacked for underestimating the enemy's will to fight. Worse, the papers printed rumors that Ulysses had been drunk, on a binge perhaps, causing him to ignore defensive precautions. Rumors that Ulysses had a drinking problem were not new; they had circulated since the Fort Humboldt days. But now the clear message was that alcoholism made him unfit for command and he would soon be relieved of duty.

Ulysses tried to reassure Julia that these rumors were nothing but that: rumors. "What the papers say about relieving me is all a falsehood . . . I am so conscious of having done all things right myself that I borrow no trouble from the lies published." For her part, Julia rejected the accusations of alcoholism as unfounded. Indeed, nothing the reporters printed could shake her confidence in her husband, although their criticisms angered her greatly. She was especially infuriated by a story in a Cincinnati paper that her husband was enjoying himself at a dance hall while the Confederates planned their attack. More than anyone, she knew that her socially awkward husband was unlikely to be waltzing young women around a dance floor, whether in peacetime or during a war. It no doubt stung her that many reporters credited Don Carlos Buell rather than Ulysses with taking control of the Union forces and securing the victory, or that others lauded General William Tecumseh Sherman as the hero of the day. In the end, the most damning criticism of all remained the fact that Grant had failed to pursue the fleeing Confederates; the opportunity to crush the rebellion, it was claimed, had slipped through the fingers of an incompetent military leader.[9]

Ulysses was, in fact, demoted to second in command in the western theater of war under General Henry Halleck. But Julia remained confident that his star would rise once more. In her memoirs, she recalled challenging a news report that Richmond had fallen shortly after the Shiloh battles. The report was clearly false, she declared, for "Richmond will fall only before *Grant* and *his* army."[10]

The fall of Richmond did indeed lie in the future. But the problem of Julia's living arrangements was very much in the present. Criticism had rained down on her as well as on Ulysses—not from the press but from his family. They had complained frequently about the expense of feeding and housing the Grant children, insisting that Julia and her husband were not contributing enough to cover the costs and the inconvenience. Julia's letters on the matter apparently convinced Ulysses that a more protracted stay in Covington would be unbearable for his wife. He conceded as much on March 23: "I see plainly from your letter that it will be impossible for you to stay in Covington. Such unmittigated [*sic*] meanness as is shown by the girls makes me ashamed of them." He gave Julia permission to go to Columbus and rent quarters, or, if she preferred, she could go back to Galena and keep house. The important thing was to put the children in school as soon as possible. The following day, he took a different tack, suggesting she take the children and visit relatives in Louisville. Instead, the end of June found Julia on her way to Memphis to visit Ulysses, leaving her three oldest children behind and traveling only with young Jesse.[11]

If Julia expected her time away to allow a cooling-off period between her and her in-laws, she was to be disappointed. When she returned to Covington in September, the tension had, if anything, increased. Jesse Root Grant and Ulysses were now locked in a battle of words over the older Grant's continuing public outcries against the recent criticism of his son. Ulysses's frustration was obvious: "I have not an enemy in the world who has done me as much injury as you in your efforts in my defence. I require no defenders and for my sake let me alone." As bluntly as he could, Ulysses instructed his father to "keep quiet on this subject."[12]

For the rest of 1862, Julia lived a nomadic existence, spending time at her husband's headquarters or in nearby towns or cities, visiting relatives in Louisville or old schoolmates of her husband in Ohio. Julia clearly felt the impact of the war on her domestic life. The months seemed to pass in flurries of packing and unpacking, traveling by boat and rail, adjusting to life in commandeered quarters or in the homes of friends and relatives, and steeling herself against the criticism of her in-laws. She seemed to be perpetually saying goodbyes and hellos to those she loved—her children, her husband, her father, her friends. Without a home of her own, Julia had become a homemaker in exile. Yet the larger meaning of this civil war between Americans continued to elude her. She lacked—or did not deploy—those antennae that helped an individual perceive the social context of her personal life. Unmindful of this broader context, she was equally unaware of the impact her own actions might have on those more keenly aware of the political and social upheavals in their lives.

Her solipsism could be read in actions both large and small. Almost everywhere she now went, including her husband's military camp, she was accompanied by her "colored nurse Julia," the slave who helped raise Frederick, Buck, Nellie, and Jesse until she ran away to her own freedom. Julia was frankly blind to the incongruity of arriving with a slave in the Union encampment. For her the matter was a simple one: she needed assistance with young Jesse and, where the law did not forbid it, her slave Julia was available to help.[13]

She seemed equally blind to the symbolism of smaller, personal choices. On her way to visit relatives, for example, she stopped in Cincinnati to shop. Here she purchased a bonnet that bore the colors of the Confederacy. When a cousin questioned the tact of the wife of a Union general strolling about town in a hat that proclaimed support for the enemy, Julia was genuinely surprised. She had no idea, she confessed, that gray signified anything at all. And if it did, how should it matter to someone who had simply purchased a bonnet she liked?[14]

As she journeyed to small towns in Tennessee and Mississippi to see her husband in 1862, she could not avoid exposure to the sights and sounds of war and suffering. Although she was by no means callous, she seemed most powerfully affected by those things that resonated with her personal experiences or private memories. Visiting Ulysses in La Grange, Tennessee, for example, evoked in Julia a deep nostalgia for a way of life she had known in her childhood. "In passing through La Grange everything was so familiar—the old Negro quarters, the colored people warming themselves in the sun, the broken windows filled with old clothes—all seemed so familiar that, as I had never been there before, I must have seen them in my dreams."[15]

Even in the midst of civil war, Julia continued to believe that personal loyalties ought to trump the demands imposed by external rules, regulations, or public responsibilities. Moved by the plight of an ailing Confederate prisoner who had broken parole and was returned to military jail, she pleaded the man's cause to her husband. For her, it was a simple matter of a husband granting a wife's request, but for Ulysses she had created a conflict between his obligation to follow established procedures and his desire to please his wife. He told her that she had "no right to ask a personal favor in this matter," but Julia could not acknowledge the boundaries that divided public and private affairs. When he chose to act as a military officer rather than a husband, Julia cried "tears of bitterness." In a rare moment of marital discord, she refused to talk to him, refused even to look at him. She sat, as she put it, "apart from him," using physical space to represent emotional distance. In the end, Ulysses relented and the prisoner was set free.[16]

Throughout the war, Julia's initial responses to hospitality and warmth, as much as to hostility and criticism, were rarely filtered through a consideration of situation or context. The results were sometimes amusing but often wholly inappropriate. When she visited her husband in 1862 in Holly Springs, Mississippi, she found herself sharing a commandeered residence with the wife of a Confederate officer. This woman and her friends received Julia cordially, and Julia responded with her natural openness. In her memoir, she concedes that the women were so charming that she "did not realize for a moment that I was actually in the enemy's camp." The result was what many would consider a disconcerting tableau: there in the parlor, the wife of the Union commander sat cheerily listening to the wives of Confederate officers as they sang "rebel war songs." It was not until the second evening, when the women invited her once again to listen to "their national songs," that Julia at last realized her mistake. "No, never again," she declared, observing what to others might have been immediately obvious: "I would be a traitor to listen again to such songs."[17]

Julia's inability or disinclination to read a political situation correctly was a form of social myopia, but her identification as a Westerner further blurred her vision. While visiting a dressmaker in Holly Springs, she began a conversation with the local customers. When one of the women identified Julia as a Southerner, she promptly denied it. "No," she recalled responding, "I am from the West. Missouri is my native state." When the women insisted that Missouri was, in fact, a Southern state, Julia once again disagreed. "No, indeed," she said, hoping to put an end to the conversation by declaring herself "the most loyal of the loyal." What this meant to her, however, was unclear, for what followed was that remarkable conversation about the Constitution and the constitutionality of secession—the conversation in which she airily admitted she had no idea what the Constitution was.[18]

Ulysses knew his wife well and accepted Julia's lack of interest in matters beyond the intimate world of family and friends. Unlike Theodore Weld, he had not married an active participant in his chosen cause; unlike Jefferson Davis, he would never come to rely on his wife to work as his assistant, confidante, or political adviser. For Ulysses, it was enough that Julia brought warmth and affection to a husband reared to stoicism and now burdened with great public responsibility. Thus his letters to her devoted little space to military strategy, national political trends, or even the inevitable internecine struggles among Union officers. Indeed, Julia often learned of battles her husband had waged after the fact, from the newspapers. Instead, he filled the pages of his letters with news of his health, instructions on budgets and monetary matters, and queries about the children and advice on their schooling. He tried to spare her any anguish, reporting to her that he was safe and urging her to ignore the criticism aimed at him by what he termed "the Abolition press." He mirrored back to her the image of a confident, triumphant Ulysses, a modern hero to a modern Penelope. It was to his favorite sister, Mary Grant, that he confessed his weariness at the burdens of command. In December 1862, he wrote to Mary from Oxford, Mississippi: "For a conciencious person, I confess to be one, this is a most slavish life. I may be envied by ambitious persons but I in turn envy the person who can transact his daily business and retire to a quiet home without a feeling of responsibility for the morrow."[19]

By early 1863, General Halleck had been assigned to the eastern front, and Ulysses Grant had taken command of the long Vicksburg campaign that would, in the end, ensure control of the Mississippi River to the Union. After a brief family reunion in Memphis, Julia and her Ulys thus said their goodbyes. Ulysses traveled down the Mississippi aboard the *Magnolia,* the very steamer that had—in happier days—carried Varina Howell Davis to meet her new husband's family. Julia and her children headed west, to Wishton-wish, for an extended stay with her own father. If the new arrangement was better than life among the Grants, it was far from a happy experience. "My summer was not a happy one," Julia recalled. "Our neighbors were all Southern in sentiment and could not believe that I was not."[20]

These Missourians recognized in her a sensibility shaped by Southern mores and morals, and thus no matter how earnestly she denied a sympathy for the Confederate cause, they did not believe her. They argued, perhaps more astutely than they realized, that her Union loyalty was nothing more than a wife's loyalty to her husband. "It is right for you to say you are Union," they assured her, "but we know better, my child; it is not in human nature for you to be anything but Southern. . . . We know how you have been brought up and an oath would not be more binding than the sanctity of your roof."[21]

Far worse than the efforts of friends to call her back to her roots were her father's efforts to impress upon her the rightness of the Southern cause. He assaulted her with arguments about the constitutionality of secession, just as the Holly Springs women had turned to the Constitution to bolster the South's abandonment of the Union some months before. His harangues were more than Julia could bear. "I was dreadfully puzzled about the horrid old Constitution anyway," she admitted, "and once, when quite worn out with listening, said: 'Papa, why don't they make a new Constitution since this is such an enigma—one to suit the times, you know.'"[22]

For Julia, a frame of government written in the midst of the eighteenth century seemed troublesomely outmoded, since life in mid-nineteenth-century America was so different than it had been for revolutionary Americans. "We have steamers, railroads, telegraphs, etc.," she reminded the Colonel, as if a failure to keep abreast of technological change lay at the heart of the current conflict. Whatever the problem, however, Julia remained supremely confident that Ulysses could supply the proper solution. Government and war were, after all, men's domains.[23]

Thirty-six

"IF YOUR MIND IS MADE UP"

Marital Relations in Wartime

A WAR OF BULLETS AND CANNON might be a man's affair, but a wife and mother's domestic life sometimes generated its own battlefields and required its own strategies for survival. For Julia, this meant not simply the problems of her nomadic life but also the addition of new and challenging duties. Of necessity, Ulysses relied on Julia to manage the family's financial affairs while he waged war. Her trip to St. Louis in 1863 reflected the new burdens she had to shoulder, for she traveled with complex instructions from her husband. She was to go to St. Louis to settle some complicated business affairs, including securing the deed to a hundred acres of land from her brothers John and Lewis, leasing out Hardscrabble to a tenant, and appointing a trustworthy local friend to collect the rent. If Julia's brother John wished to travel to California, she was to offer to buy forty additional acres from him, and if he accepted the offer, she was then to travel to Galena to get the money. As long as she was in Galena, she should also inquire what, if anything, had come to Ulysses from his brother Simpson's estate and collect a number of outstanding debts owed to her husband.[1]

Julia Dent Grant was not the first or only woman who found herself shouldering traditionally male duties during wartime. In fact, for almost two centuries, colonial wives had acted as "surrogate husbands" when men went to war or when death or illness made it necessary. If legal and political rights were a masculine prerogative in both colonial and nineteenth-century society, other arenas could be surprisingly fluid when necessary. A war such as the Civil War made that fluidity a social necessity rather than an individual one. Thus, as men went off to war in the 1860s, thousands of Julia's contemporaries, Union and Confederate alike, shouldered new responsibilities. For many, if not most, not only the tasks themselves but the decision making they entailed proved burdensome.[2]

Julia's challenge was not making decisions but following her husband's explicit and detailed instructions. For Julia, who could not balance her own household account book, the tasks Ulysses now required of her proved especially taxing. Throughout April 1863, Ulysses continued to send her orders, pressing her to act as an astute businesswoman, an attentive mother, and a diplomat in dealing with the Galena branch of the Grant family. "Be sure and attend to the business you went on as I directed," he wrote as the month ended, sounding more like a father instructing his child than a protective and indulgent husband. Only after she had completed her assignments was she free to visit any of her friends or her sister, or take temporary residence once again in Galena. But she must be prepared, he added, to come at once to him when Vicksburg was in his hands. Like the conductor of an orchestra, Ulysses set the tempo of Julia's life, sometimes andante, sometimes allegro, but whatever the tempo, Julia usually danced to its tune.[3]

If Julia felt burdened by assignments that carried her from city to city and into uncharted territory such as rents, land deeds, and debt collection, Ulysses too felt under unusual pressure. The press was once again turning against him, after the Union army's repeated failures to take Vicksburg early that year. Writing to his father, Ulysses admitted, "Was it not for the very natural desire of proving myself equal to anything expected of me, and the evidence my removal would afford that I was not thought equal to it, I would gladly accept a less responsible position." The admission embarrassed him, and he added, "I beg that you will destroy this letter."[4]

No one who knew Ulysses Grant would have believed his wish for a "less responsible position." He was, if nothing else, a dogged and stubborn commander. At last, on April 29 and 30, he managed to cross the Mississippi with his army and confront the Confederates. He fought five battles in the first seventeen days of May and won them all. Still, the real prize—Vicksburg—was not immediately his. Although he assured Julia on May 9 that "the fight which will settle the fate of Vicksburg" was likely to come in two more days, what actually came was a siege of the city that lasted almost two months. At last, on July 4—one day after the Confederate defeat at Gettysburg—the city was his, and with it control of the Mississippi River. The victory was hard won but stunning: an entire Confederate army had surrendered to the husband of Julia Grant. As Ulysses rode into Vicksburg, he received a hero's welcome from his soldiers, and the crowd called out both his name and that of his wife. Small wonder that he could write that August to his brother-in-law in the Union army, Major Frederick Dent, that he "felt younger than he did six years ago."[5]

Vicksburg was a great victory for the Union and a tragedy for its foe.

Even as Julia celebrated her husband's triumph, Varina Davis mourned with her husband their cause's great defeat. Still, the war was far from over for either couple. For the rest of the year, both Julia and Ulysses seemed to lead peripatetic lives. She was off to St. Louis in August to place her three oldest children in school; he was in Chattanooga by October. That same month, Julia headed to Ohio, stopping on the way to see Jesse and Hannah. November found Julia hoping to relocate, if only temporarily, to Nashville, close enough for her husband to visit from Chattanooga. But Ulysses firmly vetoed the idea. "You still ask to come to Nashville!" he wrote on the second of the month. "I do not know what in the world you will do there. There is not a respectable hotel and I leave no one of my Staff there. You would be entirely among strangers and at an expensive and disagreeable place to live." Yet in February 1864, Ulysses himself was in Nashville—and now instructed her to join him as soon as possible. It was clear that his desire to be with Julia had not faded, although the exigencies and un-certainties of war caused his endearing chivalry to give way to brusque command.[6]

On her journey to Nashville, Julia discovered that being the wife of a famous general brought concrete rewards. Local military officers in Louis-ville arranged a private ambulance, or wagon, to take her and Jesse to the train depot, where they were boarded in a car reserved for the highest brass and their guests. Julia greeted this special treatment with her usual mod-est and friendly demeanor. The orderly on board the rail car apparently assumed that Mrs. Grant would be a more imposing and imperious figure. Seeing a short, cheerful, and plain woman, he steered her away from the best seats in the car, explaining that they were reserved "for the General's lady." Julia, being Julia, quietly took her seat on the sunny side of the train.[7]

As they approached Nashville, a fellow traveler, General William Farrar Smith, offered to take Julia to her husband's headquarters in his private ambulance. Julia thanked him but declared, "General Grant will meet us, General." Smith corrected her. "Ah, that is not likely," he said. "General Grant has too weighty matters on his mind to think of these little things. You must not expect him." But Julia remained confident. "He will not fail to meet me," she replied. To Smith's surprise and chagrin, Ulysses was there, waiting to escort his wife and son in a private ambulance of his own.[8]

In Nashville, Julia discovered that gossip and rumor were one price of celebrity. When her husband had to make unscheduled trips to Knoxville and then to Lexington, the story spread that Ulysses had been so annoyed at his wife's arrival that he uprooted his staff and moved his headquarters out of Nashville. Julia's rebuttal to the tale was straightforward: her husband had invited her. But Ulysses, clearly annoyed, regretted that she had not said more. As Julia recalled, he told her: "You might have added that I moved my headquarters to Nashville for the sole reason that I might have you near me." But Julia understood that denials would not put an end to rumors such as this any more than they would squelch the rumors that she was needed in camp to prevent her husband from drinking. She seemed to feel it was best to say little.[9]

Julia *was* needed in her husband's camp, however. She remained, as she had been from their first meeting, the only person Ulysses could relax with, talk freely with, show emotion with. It was Julia alone whom he would allow to minister to him when he was struck by one of the fierce migraines that troubled him throughout the war. It was Julia who pressed hot poultices on his neck and head and gave him a mustard footbath to ease the pain. Varina Davis had ministered in the same way to her husband, but there the similarities ended. For if Varina could restore Jeff Davis to health, she could not delight him by simply being herself, as Julia could her Ulys. Julia's foibles and failings amused her husband, her anecdotes of family and friends delighted him, her cheerful disposition calmed him. He did his best to shelter her from the horrors of the war by forbidding her visits to the hospitals that housed the wounded and dying. He did not want her to share the burdens of war; he wanted her to provide relief from them. "I want and need a little rest and sunshine," he told her—and she was the only one who could brighten his day.[10]

But Ulysses was not the only one who needed Julia. Back in St. Louis, illness had struck. Julia's oldest son, Fred, was seriously ill with dysentery and typhoid fever, and Julia was advised to go to him at once. She headed northwest, escorted by one of Ulysses's officers, with Jesse and his nursemaid in tow. Along the route home, Jesse's nurse, "Black Julia," ran away. "I suppose," Julia mused, "she feared losing her freedom if she returned to Missouri." Now burdened with the care of a young and often rambunctious boy, Julia also faced the task of nursing her older son back to health. For some time, the situation was dire: Fred was not responding to any medication, he had grown skeletal, and he could not keep food down. The memory of William and Ellen Sherman's son, who died of similar symptoms, haunted Julia, and she wrote to Ulysses, asking him to come at once to his oldest child's bedside. At last, a doctor prescribed a new drug, and to Julia's great relief "this medicine acted like a charm and cured him."[11]

By March 1864, Julia, along with Fred, was in Nashville once again. She was now thirty-eight years old, the mother of four, and the wife of a military hero. She was well liked by most who met her, just as she had been well liked as a girl at White Haven. Horace Porter, a member of Ulysses's staff, described her as "a woman of much general intelligence, cheerful and cordial." *New York Tribune* correspondent Albert Richardson was more than a bit chivalrous when he ascribed to her "a sprightly mind" and a "comely" appearance, yet most who knew her would agree with him that she had "a most sterling, lovable character . . . amiable in disposition." Unlike Varina Howell Davis, Julia provoked little jealousy among members of her own sex, for, unlike Varina, she was neither pretty enough nor witty enough to spark rivalry. If anything, many of the sophisticated wives of government officials and society figures she would later encounter in the nation's capital initially underestimated her charm. It was true that she lacked a quick wit, but she could tell an amusing anecdote; she often appeared shy, but she was resolutely self-assured; she sometimes seemed awkward, but it was her poor eyesight, not her lack of manners, that made her so. And, as she was soon to prove, she was keenly aware of how to ingratiate herself with a public who shared her traditional values.

No one would ever mistake Julia Dent Grant for a woman who harbored radical views, like Angelina Grimké; no one would declare her haughty and condemn her for a "masculine intelligence," like Varina Davis. But everyone who knew her believed she was loved by her husband. Indeed, in 1863, after almost sixteen years of marriage, it was clear to all that the affection between Ulysses and Julia had not faded. "They would seek a quiet corner of his quarters of an evening," recalled one of Ulysses's staff officers, "and sit with her hand in his, manifesting the most ardent devotion; and if a staff-officer came accidently upon them, they would look as bashful as two young lovers spied upon in the scenes of courtship."[12]

The Julia Dent that Ulysses S. Grant had fallen in love with in the 1840s had been both naive and provincial, but the war years had greatly broadened Julia's horizons. She had traveled to see her husband, sometimes riding in boxcars, sometimes bounced about in ambulances and other wagons. She had mastered the discipline of an army camp, rising early and eating in mess halls. She had negotiated land sales, honed her diplomatic skills with difficult in-laws, and caught glimpses of the cost of war in human life and human suffering. Despite this, her understanding of the issues that propelled the nation to civil war remained both vague and idiosyncratic. In 1864, as in 1860, she saw the crisis that had enveloped them not as a coherent political event but as a collection of intimate encounters and exchanges with friends and foes, relatives and strangers.

Julia's response to an old friend in St. Louis was typical of this highly personal vision. The woman was now a grieving widow, for her husband had died defending Vicksburg against Ulysses S. Grant. Now alone, the woman was hoping to acquire a pass from the local Union commander so she could join friends in Georgia. Julia responded to the woman's plight with immediate sympathy, helping her get the travel permit and pressing into her hand a large roll of Confederate dollars that had been captured at Vicksburg and given to her as a souvenir. It was not until after the woman left St. Louis that Julia considered the implications of her actions. In helping a friend, she wondered, had she helped the cause of secession as well? Ulysses assured her she had not. Indeed, he told her lightheartedly that putting more of the devalued currency into circulation helped the Union cause. That Julia readily accepted this argument suggests how little an act of near treason mattered to her when weighed against an act of generosity to a friend.[13]

By April 1864, Ulysses was in Virginia, in command of the eastern armies, and Julia took advantage of the move eastward to visit Washington and New York. For his part, Ulysses appeared to have little desire to make an appearance in the capital city unless it was absolutely necessary. Although he had been received with cheers and showered with attention by the city's residents on his last visit there, he did not like "being seen so much about Washington." For this son of Hannah Grant, adulation was embarrassing and suspect; although Ulysses was proud of his accomplishments, he was more comfortable casting them as the result of diligence and attention to duty. Indeed, as his popularity grew, his apparent discomfort grew as well. That winter he would complain to his wife: "Have you read how I was mobbed in Phila? It is a terrible bore to me that I cannot travel like a quiet citizen." Julia, on the other hand, positively reveled in the attention given her husband. Her zest for life and her unshakable sense of entitlement, the legacy of her childhood at White Haven, ensured that she would welcome the celebrity she shared with her husband.[14]

Yet for the first time Julia seemed self-conscious about her own physical appearance. She saw herself suddenly as others who did not love her might see her: short and plump, her face marred by an errant eye, her features frankly plain. She could do little to make herself beautiful, but she might, she hoped, do something to correct the distracting deformity of her eye. If the surgery was successful, she would make a more favorable impression as she stood at her husband's side. But it was not to be. Julia had waited too long, her doctor told her, and the operation could not be performed. If Julia was disappointed, her husband was not. Julia recalled their conversation, she voicing regret but he voicing amazement. "What in the world put such a thought in your head, Julia?" he asked. "Why, you are getting to be such a great man," she explained, "and I am such a plain little wife. I thought if my eyes were as others are I might not be so very, very plain." To this, Ulysses replied: "Did I not see you and fall in love with you with these same eyes? I like them just as they are, and now, remember, you are not to interfere with them. They are mine, and let me tell you, Mrs. Grant, you had better not make any experiments, as I might not like you half so well with any other eyes." His reassurances perfectly combined his affection and his loving paternalism; small wonder that, to Julia's ears, he spoke as "my knight, my Lancelot!" She would never again record any concern about her appearance.[15]

Julia's devotion to the advancement of her husband's reputation and career was as constant as Ulysses's devotion to her. While in New York, Julia attended a Sanitary Fair, one of many fund-raising events staged by the U.S. Sanitary Commission for the relief of Union soldiers. Here, one of the attractions was the offer of a decorative sword to the general who received the most votes from the crowd at the fair. Every vote cost one dollar. Julia paid her dollar—and cast her vote for General McClellan. If Julia was dense about politics writ large, this action showed that she could be shrewd about the small politics of personal gestures. "It would not be in good taste for me to vote for my husband, would it?" she asked her escort. "You see this is a very nice question. I never voted, save at school for our May Queen, and I am sure the etiquette on such occasions should be that the rival queens vote for each other. Any other course there would have been looked on as selfish and dishonorable, and, Colonel, I voted upon that precedent." The explanation, like the gesture, was beautifully conceived and served multiple purposes. By feminizing her voting experience, she assured the public she was no advocate of woman suffrage; by emphasizing her own attention to courtesy and etiquette, she implied that General Grant shared her good manners and thus was, after all, the superior rival for the prize. The newspapers applauded her tact and diplomacy, and in the end, Ulys won the sword.[16]

From New York, Julia headed back to St. Louis, where her three younger children had remained. As always, she welcomed the chance to return to her childhood home, despite the disturbing evidence that the life she had once known was gone and would not return. There were no longer any slaves at White Haven or Wish-ton-wish, where her aging father now resided; the men and women who had made life so pleasant for the Dents in her childhood had been replaced by German and French servants. Although Julia conceded that the new staff "were most excellent substitutes," she missed the personal relationships she had experienced with "our colored people." Perhaps Julia failed to perceive the irony in her own husband's mission: the defeat of the Confederacy that upheld the enslavement of its "colored people."[17]

For his part, Ulysses had long ago realized that secession would spell the doom of slavery. Now, in the spring of 1864, he was preparing his assault on the Confederacy's capital at Richmond and a final victory over its champion, Robert E. Lee. The fighting was fierce and bloody as Confederate and Union forces met at the Battle of the Wilderness, Spotsylvania, North Anna, and then Cold Harbor, where some six thousand Union soldiers died in one hour. Friends turned enemies were wounded in this spring campaign, among them Pete Longstreet at the Battle of the Wilderness. By the end of June, even a battle-hardened soldier such as General Sherman could write to his wife, "It is enough to make the whole world start at the awful amount of death and destruction that now stalks abroad."[18]

Early in July, as Union forces laid siege to Petersburg, Julia returned east with her children. Ulysses sent Julia's brother, Frederick Dent, to meet her at City Point, on the James River, ten miles from the besieged city. That same month, Jubal Early humiliated General Grant by staging a raid on Washington, D.C. Yet Julia's confidence in her husband remained as strong as always. When asked if General Grant would capture Richmond, she replied, "Mr. Grant started out to capture Richmond, and he is a very obstinate man when he undertakes anything."[19]

Thirty-seven

"THERE WILL BE
AN OUTBREAK TONIGHT"
Victory and Assassination

JULIA'S PREDICTION PROVED CORRECT. On April 1, 1865, the war-weary General Lee abandoned the Petersburg defenses and in so doing sealed the doom of Richmond. Varina Howell Davis and her children had already fled the capital, and now the Confederate government itself was frantically planning its escape. On April 2, Ulysses could write to his wife that he was "far inside of what was the rebel fortifications . . . but what are ours now," and, in triumph, President Lincoln began his tour of the fallen city. Fires set by fleeing Confederates burned in Richmond and looters roamed the city, taking what little was left in the abandoned homes and shops. On April 7, General Grant called on General Lee to surrender, and on April 9, at Appomattox Court House, the two men negotiated the terms of that surrender. The victor showed his respect for his enemy by allowing Lee's men to depart with their horses and Lee's officers to retain their sidearms. Within a month, one president, Jeff Davis, would be captured and imprisoned and another, Abraham Lincoln, would be dead.[1]

Julia, along with other officers' wives, was only an observer of the great siege and the final fall of the Confederate capital. Yet for a fleeting moment earlier in the year, she had thought she might play a central role in ending the war. A suggestion had come into the Union camp that a social meeting between Mrs. Grant and Mrs. Longstreet, along with the wives of other high-ranking officers, might be arranged at which the possibility of peace terms could be discussed. Julia was excited by the prospect. "Oh! How enchanting, how thrilling!" she recalled saying to her husband. "Oh, Ulys, I may go, may I not?" But her hopes were dashed, for the general thought the idea itself was absurd and his wife wholly unequipped to act the diplomat. "The men have fought this war," he declared, "and the men will finish it."[2]

When the men did indeed finish it, Ulysses refused to tour the captured capital of the Confederacy. Neither his wife nor his officers could persuade him to change his mind. "I would not distress these people," he told Julia. "They are feeling their defeat bitterly, and you would not add to it by witnessing their despair, would you?" Julia conceded that such sensitivity was appropriate for the leader of the conquering army, but she was certain it did not apply to the conqueror's wife. Thus, in the days that followed the capture of Richmond and the surrender of General Lee, she toured the city.[3]

Julia's curiosity led her to the Confederate White House, where she moved through the rooms in which the Davises had once slept, eaten, and celebrated the holidays with modest, handmade gifts. She saw the porch where Varina's Joe had played—and from which he had fallen to his death. What she saw in Richmond moved her deeply: "I only saw that the city was deserted; not a single inhabitant visible. . . . I remember that all the streets near the public buildings were covered with papers—public documents and letters, I suppose. . . . It was all so sad that I wished to return to the boat." The war had made her husband a hero, yet she felt its tragic personal dimensions. "I fell to thinking of all the sad tragedies of the past four years," she wrote. "How many homes made desolate! How many hearts broken! How much youth sacrificed! How much treasure lost!"[4]

She felt an overwhelming sadness as she traveled through the streets of Richmond, though she could not explain why tears fell from her eyes. "Could it be," she asked decades later as she recalled the scene, "that my visit reminded me of my dear old home in Missouri?" The war had left White Haven, no less than Richmond, in shambles, and it would never be restored to the glories of her childhood past. Her father's health was broken and his fortune gone, her brothers were scattered and divided in their political loyalties, and the slaves she recalled as happy in their bondage had chosen freedom over devotion to the Dents. The world she knew and loved had vanished.[5]

But the present exercised a greater pull on Julia than the past. Amid cries of "The Union forever, hurrah, boys! Hurrah!" the Grants were soon making their way in triumph into Washington, D.C. On the evening of their arrival the whole city was illuminated, with displays of lights in government buildings, embassies, and the homes of prominent citizens. Julia and Ulysses rode out to see the lights with the secretary of war, Edwin Stanton, and his wife, but afterward Ulysses was obligated to join Mrs. Lincoln in her carriage for a similar tour of the city. If Julia felt Mary Todd Lincoln had snubbed her by inviting only Ulysses, she was careful not to suggest this in her memoirs. But, like many other officers' wives, Julia had found the first lady less than cordial. The following day, April 14, 1865, an invitation arrived for both Mr. and Mrs. Grant to join the Lincolns at Ford's Theatre that evening. Perhaps Julia took some pleasure in sending her regrets. But surely it was providential.[6]

Looking back, Julia believed she had somehow sensed the danger she and Ulysses would so narrowly escape. Something had been odd about the man who delivered the invitation, she recalled; he was shabbily dressed and seemed nervous as he announced, "Mrs. Lincoln sends me, Madam, with her compliments, to say she will call for you at exactly eight o'clock to go to the theater." Julia was taken aback both by the man's appearance and by the message he delivered, which sounded, she noted, more like a command than an invitation. She seemed to decide on the spot that the family would depart that day for their new home in Burlington, New Jersey, and she quickly issued her regrets. To her surprise, the man pressed her: "Madam, the papers announce that General Grant will be with the President tonight at the theater." Julia's response was curt: "You deliver my message to Mrs. Lincoln as I have given it to you. You may go now." Thus the Grants were not in the president's box when John Wilkes Booth assassinated Abraham Lincoln.[7]

Abraham Lincoln was the target of the actor's bullet, but Julia firmly believed that her husband's life had been in danger that fateful day. Looking back, she concluded that the shabbily dressed and insistent messenger had himself been one of the conspirators linked to the assassination and had not been sent by Mrs. Lincoln at all. "I am perfectly sure," she wrote with the certainty of hindsight, "that he, with three others, one of them Booth himself, sat opposite me and my party at luncheon that day." Among this suspicious group was a "dark, pale man" who played with his soup spoon, "sometimes filling it and holding it half-lifted to his mouth, but never tasting it." This mysterious man seemed intent on listening to what the women and children at Julia's table were saying. Julia's first thought was that he was crazy, but then it came to her: she was certain he and his companions were members of Confederate Colonel John S. Mosby's guerrilla band, who had come close to capturing Ulysses in Virginia only a year before. Suddenly, a premonition came to her that something terrible would happen that evening. "I believe there will be an outbreak tonight or soon," she told the friend sitting beside her; "I just feel it, and am glad I am going away tonight."[8]

That afternoon, as her family rode to the train depot, Julia was just as certain that the same "crazy" man was the rider who passed them "at a sweeping gallop on a dark horse." The man turned his mount back, rode closely beside the carriage carrying the Grants—and then disappeared. When the Grants reached Philadelphia, Ulysses was handed a telegram and then, in quick succession, two more. Julia, seeing her husband's face turn a deadly pale, knew the telegrams contained terrible news. She asked Ulysses to tell her what had transpired. "Do not exclaim," he told her. "Be quiet and I will tell you. The President has been assassinated at the theater, and I must go back at once." It was agreed that he would continue on to Burlington to see his wife safely home; then he would order a special train to take him back to the nation's capital.[9]

The ride to Burlington was a somber one. Julia watched Ulysses as he sat silent and deep in thought. When she asked him who he thought the assassin was, he said he did not know. Now it was Ulysses's turn to feel a dread come over him: Andrew Johnson would succeed Lincoln as president, and his policies were not likely to be as "kind and magnanimous" as his predecessor's.[10]

That evening, Ulysses returned to Washington. The next morning a letter addressed to him arrived at their home in Burlington, and Julia opened it. The contents were chilling. "General Grant, thank God, as I do, that you still live. It was your life that fell to my lot, and I followed you on the cars. Your car door was locked, and thus you escaped me, thank God."[11]

Thirty-eight

"WHAT SHOUTS WENT UP!"

A Hero and His Wife

JULIA HAD, OF COURSE, always been given to premonitions, and she had great faith in dreams and omens. But on the day the Grants left Washington, her sixth sense had proven accurate. Ulysses, not given to heeding signs and portents, soon confirmed that multiple assassinations had been planned by Booth and his coconspirators. From the capital, he wrote to his wife that he had met with the new president and "there is but little doubt but that the plot contemplated the distruction of more than the President and Sec. of State." Although there was now nothing to fear, he told Julia, one thing was clear: difficult days lay ahead for the nation.[1]

Ulysses had hoped for some relief from the pressures of command, but the government clearly still needed him. The Confederate general Joe Johnston had surrendered to General William T. Sherman, and now the work of restoring order—and winning the loyalty of former rebels—must begin in earnest. As Ulysses made his way to join Sherman in Raleigh, he felt the burden keenly: "I find my duties, anxieties, and the necessity for having all my wits about me, increasing instead of diminishing," he told his wife. "I have a Herculean task to perform and shall endeavor to do it, not to please any one, but for the interests of our great country." Ulysses saw the United States growing in reputation among the world's nations, and with this growing prestige could come great power to do good. America, he predicted, "will have a strength which will enable it to dictate to all others, *conform to justice and right.*"[2]

Ulysses had been a strong supporter of Abraham Lincoln's policy of "malice toward none." For him, this meant a decent regard for all, even the leaders of the Confederacy. He had seen firsthand the impact of the long and bitterly fought war on the South, its people, and its resources, and he did not believe harsh punishment and further deprivation were warranted. "The suffering that must exist in the South the next year, even with the war ending now, will be beyond conception," he told Julia. Only those who could not conceive the impact the war had had, or those who were "heartless and unfeeling," would wish further punishment to be inflicted. Privately, Ulysses believed President Johnson was among the misguided.[3]

Julia's thoughts, as usual, were on more personal and domestic matters. To show their gratitude to the nation's leading general, the people of Philadelphia had presented the Grants with a beautiful home, fully stocked with fine linens and beautiful glassware. The new residence promised them comfort and the company of interesting admirers. But, to Julia's consternation, Ulys was rarely there to enjoy it. His duties carried him to Washington or Raleigh, and at last into Richmond. The truth was, Julia was lonely; her older children were away at school, and only Jesse and Nellie remained with her. She realized that she missed the excitement of her wartime adventures: her husband's bustling headquarters, the debates over strategies and tactics among the officers she listened to, the marshaling of the troops for battle, and the "magnificent reviews" that kept alive a romantic image of war. Here in Philadelphia, in the lovely but too empty house, she felt cut off, isolated. She was thrilled when Ulysses's staff officers wrote suggesting that the general move his household to the capital. Petitioners and admirers filled the corridors of the hotel where Ulysses lived when he was in Washington, and the staff felt their commanding officer needed the comfort and the privacy only a home and caring wife could provide.[4]

Julia wholeheartedly agreed with these sentiments. And so, happily, did her husband. "It does seem that life is too short for us to live apart so," he conceded to Julia. But what would they do with the elegant Philadelphia home? Give it back, Julia said at once. And he did. Julia, Nellie, and Jesse packed their bags, and within a few days, the Grants had moved into a rented house on Georgetown Heights.[5]

Now that she was in the capital city, Julia could fully relish the sights and sounds of Union victory. The armies paraded up Pennsylvania Avenue, reviewed by the president, members of Congress, foreign ministers, and many of the commanding officers. Seated on the platform with these dignitaries was Julia Dent Grant. "As each division marched past with their faded and tattered flags borne proudly aloft, ho, what shouts went up!" she recalled, adding in her memoir that "they thrill me yet." Already, amidst the celebrations of victory, the horrors of war seemed to fade in her memory; what remained vivid for the rest of her life was the glory that war had brought to her husband.[6]

When the parades and celebrations ended, Julia turned her attention to finding a more suitable home for her family—and adjusting to the new, more sophisticated world of Washington political society. It was clear that, lionized though they were, the Grants were out of their depth in the fashionable circles of the capital city. As Ulysses's confidant and military aide Adam Badeau observed, the St. Louis society that Julia came from was "narrow and provincial" in both its outlook and its education. It was, he declared, more like England's eighteenth-century squirearchy than the sophisticated circle that dominated Washington's social and political life. Yet Julia did not enter this new world unarmed: she had the unshakable confidence that defined such a squirearchy; she was astute in decoding personal exchanges; and, despite the deference and compliance she had shown her husband in most matters, she had four years of experience as the acting head of her family. Julia may have been no better informed about formal politics, but she was well prepared to negotiate this new world of personal politics. Indeed, at forty, and at the peak of her husband's fame and popularity, Julia Dent Grant was coming into her own.[7]

Julia Grant's first project was a new home. The Georgetown Heights house did not really suit her or Ulysses, and the rent was high. Although Ulysses toyed with the idea of a farm or a Maryland plantation, Julia preferred to remain in the city. Thus, while Ulysses busied himself writing his report on the army, which he delivered in July 1865, Julia went house hunting on her own. Ulysses's brother-in-law suggested that the Grants buy a home rather than rent, and he made a generous offer to sell them a house on I Street on very liberal terms. Julia was thrilled. Although she was, by her own admission, a terrible mathematician, she laboriously worked out the cost per year and decided that, with a $10,000 down payment, she and Ulysses could afford it.

Julia presented her case to her husband with a surprising confidence, since her management of household finances was sometimes erratic and real estate purchases were, after all, a man's prerogative and a husband's duty. Yet the root of her confidence is not hard to discover: although she had followed her husband's instructions, she had negotiated purchases and sales of land and homes during the war years.

Ulysses did not immediately dismiss his wife's proposal. He examined Julia's arithmetic and then gently reminded her that she had failed to consider the interest on the mortgage. But Julia was undeterred. The initial $10,000 would cover the interest, she replied, and after that the yearly payments would be no more than they were paying for rent. If Ulysses was dubious about her math, he was charmed by her enthusiasm. "Why, you are a financier," he said—and together they went to look at the house. It was a large, four-story house with nice grounds, and it could be theirs for $30,000 with ten years to complete payment. By the middle of January 1866, the Grants had moved into their new home, and within a month, prominent New York financiers showed their appreciation for the man who defeated the Confederacy by paying the full cost of the house.[8]

The generosity of the New York financiers went far beyond the purchase of the I Street home. Included in the gift were over $54,000 in bonds and almost $20,000 in cash. The Grants' Philadelphia benefactors added their support by refusing to take back the home they had provided in their city. Further, they insisted that Julia bring all the furnishings it contained with her to the new Washington home. Clearly Julia's old dreams of cheering crowds hailing her husband as a hero had not been extravagant enough; they had never include this outpouring of material support by the nation's most prosperous citizens.

While Angelina Grimké Weld struggled to make ends meet at a Lexington, Massachusetts, boarding school and Varina Howell Davis viewed both the ruins of her plantation at Brierfield and the poverty brought to friends and neighbors by the South's defeat, Julia Dent Grant basked in the admiration of the wealthy and the gratitude of the ordinary citizens of Washington. The world seemed in love with Ulysses Grant and his wife, and the I Street home became the scene of large receptions and pleasant dinner parties. As Julia recalled with obvious relish, "We only *heard* pleasant words and *saw* smiling faces."[9]

Outside the capital, the reception the Grants received was equally gratifying. Over the next few summers, Julia reported with pride that wherever they went they were greeted by thousands of cheering citizens and admiring veterans of the war. From Baltimore to Boston, Cleveland to New York, in Cincinnati, Louisville, St. Louis, and Galena, bands played, banners waved, and men and women shouted their names. In Detroit, where, Julia recalled, "I had lived so happily when I was first married to Lieutenant Grant," their arrival was greeted by booming cannons and the roar of a thousand huzzas. Women waved from windows, flags and bunting lined the avenues, and veterans filled the streets to catch a glimpse of General Ulysses S. Grant. Years later Julia's intense delight leaps off the pages, but her husband's restrained emotions are equally evident. When the Detroit crowd cried out for a speech from Ulysses, he would not comply. Instead, Detroit citizens were treated to young Jesse Grant's spontaneous recitation of a poem. The boy's affectionate and indulgent upbringing had given him the confidence and exuberance his father lacked.[10]

But away from the cheering crowds and the pleasant company at his dinner table, Ulysses saw a side of Washington Julia rarely glimpsed. President Andrew Johnson was already locked in a struggle with the radicals of Congress; disgruntled military officers chafed at civilian decisions; cabinet members quarreled. Ulysses tried to pursue a neutral path, even agreeing to go on a Western tour with the president in 1866. But there was a psychic cost: every three or four weeks he was struck by the same painful, debilitating migraine headaches that had troubled him during the war. Returning home from his office, he would greet Julia with a warning: "Oh, do not ask me to speak. I have a dreadful headache." She ministered to him as she had done in Memphis or Holly Springs or Nashville, seating him in an armchair, darkening the room, washing his feet with a mustard footbath, and giving him one of her own "little pills" to help him sleep. If Ulysses appreciated her attention, he stubbornly refused to credit her with his recovery when it came. His cavalier response to her care troubled her enough for her to mention it in her memoirs. In a recollection filled with praise for her husband and with repeated evidences of their happy marriage, reports of disagreements and criticism of Ulysses were rare. Yet in this instance, Julia made a point of pressing her claim, appealing to her readers as judges. "But—will you believe it?" she asked those who might read the memoir, "when I would naturally feel that I ought to be commended for curing him and would ask him if I had not made him well nicely and quickly, he was ungracious enough to laugh and say: 'You did not cure me. Why, I got well myself, did I not?' " If Julia's stubborn insistence on recognition was out of character, Ulysses's insistence that he had conquered his pain by himself was not. For the son of Hannah and Jesse Grant, sickness was weakness and pain must be endured or defeated. Years later, when he was dying of cancer, his stoicism and his pride would lead him to hide the extent of his suffering from his wife.[11]

Washington politics were likely to give any reasonable man headaches. By the summer of 1867, President Johnson's struggle with Congress had intensified, and he was now engaged in a conflict with his secretary of war, Edwin Stanton, as well. Ulysses tried to mediate between the president and his cabinet officer, with the result that Johnson decided to replace Stanton with General Grant. Ulysses told the president that he believed Secretary Stanton was protected by the 1867 Tenure of Office Act, passed by a Congress dominated by Radical Republicans, for it denied the chief executive the power to remove any appointee without Senate approval. Nevertheless, he agreed to the portfolio. He explained his decision to Julia, saying, "I think it most important that someone should be there who cannot be used."[12]

Ulysses went to Stanton's home and broke the news to the secretary on August 11. The appointment did little to cement an alliance between the general and the president, however; in fact, their differing understandings of the arrangement drove a wedge between them. Ulysses believed he had made clear he would serve only until the Congress upheld the Tenure of Office Act and reinstated Stanton; Johnson operated on the assumption that Ulysses would remain in the War Department until he chose to resign, regardless of the congressional ruling. On January 13, 1868, Congress acted as expected and reinstated Stanton. Grant's cabinet career was over; Johnson's political troubles had just begun in earnest. And talk of Ulysses S. Grant as the next president grew louder.[13]

Thirty-nine

"ULYS, DO YOU WISH TO BE PRESIDENT?"

The Early White House Years

JULIA HAD HEARD TALK OF her husband as the next president ever since the siege of Richmond. But by the winter of 1867–68, Ulysses was being pressed from many sides to accept a nomination from the Republican Party. Julia was not immediately enthusiastic. It had been her girlhood dream to marry a soldier, and now that her husband was the leading general in the nation, she was contented. As Republicans prepared for the nominating convention in Chicago, Julia asked Ulysses bluntly: "Ulys, do you wish to be President?" His reply probably came as no surprise: "No, but I do not see that I have anything to say about it. The convention is about to assemble and, from all I hear, they will nominate me; and I suppose if I am nominated, I will be elected."[1]

Julia's concern was obvious, and though she was trespassing on masculine terrain, she pressed him. The people had so many differing interests, she said, and the sections of the country had such different priorities. "Think of President Johnson," she said. "What a time he has had." But Ulysses dismissed the comparison to the hapless Tennessean. He believed that he could satisfy all the competing interests more fully than any other possible candidate. Even the South would support him, for Southerners knew that he bore them no malice.[2]

Despite her misgivings, once her husband received the nomination, Julia threw herself into the campaign. "I became an enthusiastic politician," she recalled, willing to meet with and entertain delegations from across the country. But for all her newfound political enthusiasm, she viewed the campaign—as she had viewed the war—largely in personal terms. What was said about her Ulys was more important to her than party platforms, campaign promises, or the jockeying for place and power within the Grant camp. She was outraged by the Democratic campaign propaganda, especially the newspaper articles that attacked her husband's military record, denigrated his skill, and attributed his victories to luck. They called him a drunkard and a dishonest one at that, claiming he did not pay for his drinks. She was amazed at the wild rumors and false reports that masqueraded as news in the papers. On one occasion, while the Grants were in Galena, she read the shocking report that "General Grant is now lying confined in his residence at Galena in a state of frenzy and is tearing up his mattress, swearing it is made of snakes." In fact, Ulysses was sitting beside her, dressed in a linen suit, calmly smoking and reading his own paper. Julia was furious, but Ulysses was amused. He had warned her that she must be prepared to have her husband's character "thoroughly sifted."[3]

The nation's voters clearly approved of her husband's character. Ulysses Grant was carried into office with more than 52 percent of the popular vote and 214 of the 294 electoral votes. Ulysses, who had been so ready to forgive his military enemies, did not show the same charity to his political nemesis, Andrew Johnson. On inauguration day, the new president refused to ride in the same carriage with his predecessor. In front of the Capitol, Samuel Chase, a man who longed to be president, administered the oath to a man reluctant to hold the office. In typical fashion, Ulysses delivered "a plain, practical, common-sense" address, holding his daughter Nellie's hand through the ordeal of public speaking.[4]

Unfortunately, Ulysses's mistakes began at once. He did not consult with anyone about appointments to his cabinet or to key diplomatic posts. Instead, much like future president Warren G. Harding, President Grant surrounded himself—and filled his government—with old friends he trusted. Although he chose wisely in appointing his old military comrade William Sherman to replace him as general in chief of the armies, contemporary commentators believed that most of his appointments were unwise. These early mistakes reflected the fact that Ulysses S. Grant was "without experience, qualifications, or capacity as a civil ruler." Perhaps no one knew this better than the president himself.[5]

Ulysses's finest statesmanship came in his efforts to heal the wounds of war that remained. He appointed his old friend and wedding groomsman, James Longstreet, as surveyor of the port of New Orleans to signal that "reconstructed Confederates" deserved to be welcomed back into public service. He hoped that the appointment would encourage other former Confederates to renew their loyalty to the United States. In this manner, one contemporary declared, "the great conquerer became the great benefactor of those whom he had conquered."[6]

Those who knew Ulysses were not surprised by his generosity of spirit.

And those, including Varina Howell Davis, who had appealed to him for aid could testify to his decency. In December 1865, while her husband languished in the very fort where Julia had been comfortably quartered during the siege of Richmond, Varina had written to General Grant asking his help in improving Jeff's prison conditions. In May 1866, she went to see Ulysses in Washington and, unlike some Union leaders, he met with her and agreed to assist her. The Davises never forgot his kindness. Varina sent him her thanks, declaring, "All know you ever as good as well as great, merciful as well as brave," and in Ulysses's last painful months, Jefferson Davis sent him his good wishes for recovery.[7]

Julia had little if anything to say about her husband's mistakes in creating his administration, but she had a good deal to say about a mistake that threatened to affect her life. Soon after the election, Ulysses announced to Julia that he had sold their Washington home without telling her. Julia was stunned. On one of the rare instances that she challenged him, she pronounced the decision foolish. Where, she asked, would they live after he left office? Ulysses stood firm, confident of his rights as the head of the family. "I have already sold it, I told you, and the matter is settled." But it was not. Julia pressed him once again. "Then have *I* nothing to say in this matter?" she demanded. Her anxiety was understandable; she had spent four years of her life without a home of her own and could not bear to repeat the experience. But Julia's defiant stance signaled her first recognition of another legacy of her wartime experience. In her memoirs, she declared: "I had enjoyed my independence too long to submit quietly to this."[8]

This time, Julia did not plead or cajole. She did not pout. Instead she mounted an aggressive legal argument. She remembered that whenever her father had bought a piece of land, he was obliged to give his wife a "handsome present" to persuade her to sign the deed or else the purchase would not be fully legal. In this, Julia was almost correct. From colonial times until her own day, a husband could not *sell* a piece of property without his wife's consent, as it constituted part of her dower rights in widowhood. This rule was often ignored, but it was a legal restriction nonetheless. Armed with her memory of her parents' practice, she delivered her blow to her husband: "But . . . if I decline to sign the deed, what will the consequences be?" Although this was surely a Julia Dent Grant her husband had rarely seen, Ulysses held his ground. His response was certain to inflame her more. "The General," she recalled, "looked up with an incredulous laugh and said, 'Oh, nothing. It would make no difference except it would be a little embarrassing to me; that is all.' " Now it was Julia who held her ground. "I will not sign it," she said. "Very well," he answered; "I will send word to Mr. Bowen that my *wife* will not *let me* sell the house." And with that, Julia stormed out of the room. But what argument and a woman's rights could not do, a husband's affection could: Ulysses withdrew his promise to sell the house. Better, he apparently reasoned, for the prospective owner to be enraged—as he was—than for his wife to harbor resentment. Apparently he had decided that a good husband could concede to the wishes of his wife without fully conceding his authority.[9]

The Grants moved into the White House in early March 1869. Julia had much to do: new servants had to be hired, new rugs and drapes needed to be installed, and new rules for the existing White House staff had to be established. Although some commentators insisted that Julia could not discipline her servants or her children, she was more than capable of laying down the law to the members of the staff who dealt with the public. First, she took away the room where these men ate their lunches and smoked their pipes. They must take their meals at home and refrain from smoking while on duty. Then she set a dress code: dress suits and white gloves. "Any infringement of the above orders," she warned, "would meet with instant dismissal." Although the press criticized her for this, Julia was unmoved. "The men were well paid and there was no reason why they should not look as neat and respectable as those serving in the houses of private gentlemen."[10]

Clearly, Julia was adjusting quickly to Washington social manners and mores. And so too was her husband. Although his favorite meal remained rare roast beef, boiled hominy, and wheat bread, he presided over better fare when dinner guests were present. Together the Grants took great pains over seating arrangements at dinners that included an array of military men, diplomats, and congressmen and their wives. Adam Badeau believed that Ulysses came to enjoy these social events, for the president "liked to look at pretty girls and listen to the talk of clever women." But Ulysses remained, as he had been in his youth, a man with little skill at small talk.[11]

Soon enough the Grants found their secure footing in the social life of the capital and took the lead rather than remaining as followers. Ulysses set a new standard for the resident of the White House by visiting friends in their homes and attending private parties. Julia established new precedents as well. When guests arrived at her weekly receptions, they found a group of fashionably dressed and well-mannered matrons and young women there to greet them, for rather than stand alone, Julia invited the wives and daughters of senators and cabinet officers as well as personal friends to join her in the receiving line. The new custom was hailed as a success. And with each such success, Julia's confidence grew. Although she continued to welcome suggestions by Washington's leading social lights, such as Mrs. Hamilton Fish, she no longer felt obliged to accept them. Whatever etiquette or custom that was established, Adam Badeau noted, "it either had the sanction of the President or of Mrs. Grant, or it was not introduced at all."[12]

Entertaining as the more formal dinners were, both Julia and Ulysses relished their more private gatherings at home. Seated around the table were good friends, Jesse and Nellie, and the now elderly Colonel Dent, who had come to live with his daughter and son-in-law after the war. "Papa" remained, Julia said, "an uncompromising old-time Democrat," and she skillfully distracted him if someone began an anecdote or story that ridiculed his political party.[13]

The Grant White House was, above all else, a family home. Julia insisted that the gardens be closed to the public so that her children and their friends could have their own place to play. The basement was turned over to Buck, Jesse, and their friends, while Nellie and her friends were given the upper floor. Mary Logan, the wife of one of Ulysses's military friends, observed that "scarcely a Saturday passed without a large theatre-party of children from the White House and the homes of the cabinet officers." Julia's memory of the parties and luncheons and outings for her children were vivid: "dimples and smiles, gleaming white shoulders . . . lace and flowers and tender glances."[14]

Just as her husband had won the hearts of the voting citizens, Julia won the hearts of Washington society. Friends and acquaintances sang her praises, lauding her as the very model of American domesticity. "Mrs. Grant was so gentle, so kind, and so gracious to everyone. . . . She was the same thoughtful, generous, devoted wife and mother, whose gentleness and loyalty to her family and friends made her equally beloved with her husband by the whole nation," wrote Mary Logan. And, like all exemplars of true womanhood, Julia showed herself a benefactor to the poor. "Every Christmas," Logan recalled, "the asylums, hospitals, and charitable institutions in Washington received donations from Mrs. Grant. . . . She was the veritable 'Lady Bountiful' in more than one household." Indeed, if Julia had any fault at all in the eyes of Washington's female observers, it was her indulgent attitude toward her children.[15]

Thus in the early weeks and months of her husband's presidency, Julia could bask not only in the reflected glow of her husband's popularity and fame but also in the widespread approval of her behavior by her peers. The sunny days in the White House seemed as bright as those she remembered at White Haven. No dreams, no visions, no omens appeared to warn her that darker days lay ahead. In this, her second sight failed her.

Forty

"NICE PEOPLE, QUESTIONABLE PEOPLE, AND PEOPLE WHO WERE NOT NICE AT ALL"

Weddings and Scandals in the White House

THE TROUBLE BEGAN IN THE fall of 1869. Jay Gould, whose financial genius was unregulated by either integrity or morality, hatched a scheme to corner the gold market. Among his coconspirators in the plan were the Vermont-born stockbroker "Diamond Jim" Fisk and President Grant's own brother-in-law, Abel Corbin. The plan was simple enough: the men would buy up as much gold as they could, and when the price soared, they would sell for a windfall profit. For the plan to succeed, however, they needed to persuade the president not to infuse more gold into the market by using the United States subtreasury specie to redeem the government's paper dollars, or "greenbacks." They used Corbin, who was married to Ulysses's sister Virginia, to help them establish a social relationship with the president. This allowed them to discuss the pros and cons of government money policies with Ulysses, always urging him not to allow the sale of gold. In case the president did not follow their advice, Gould and Fisk needed a man on the inside, one who could warn them if government gold was about to be released. To this end, Abel Corbin persuaded his brother-in-law to appoint General Daniel Butterfield as assistant treasurer of the United States. Always eager to help friends and family, Ulysses agreed. In exchange for a share in the profits, Butterfield promised to warn the conspirators should a gold release be in the offing.

By mid-September the price of gold had risen sharply. But the plan had already begun to unravel. Ulysses became suspicious of Corbin's sudden, intense interest in the gold market. His suspicion deepened when Julia received a letter from his sister Virginia discussing the issue—a highly unlikely topic for female correspondence. He immediately instructed Julia to send a message to Abel Corbin through Virginia: he must stop at once whatever scheme he was involved in. But it was too late for Corbin to undo what had been done. On September 24, 1869, a date known to history as

"Black Friday," gold reached its peak of $163 an ounce—more than $30 above its value when President Grant took office. The president, however, had already taken steps to quell the financial crisis: he had ordered the sale of $4 million in government gold.

Within minutes, the price of gold tumbled, and legitimate investors who had bought gold as its price climbed now scrambled to sell. Those who had borrowed money to make these purchases—and there were many—found themselves ruined. Among the biggest losers were Abel and Virginia Corbin. Gould, however, escaped the disaster that befell his hapless colleagues, for he had sold his gold before the market collapsed.[1]

Julia's role in the scandal had been small, and it had been played at Ulysses's bidding. But in the troubling days that followed the collapse of the gold market, both the men who hoped to see a bill passed for the relief of the investors and the men who hoped the administration would not intervene pressed their case with the president's wife. Julia found herself in a quandary: she did not understand the issue clearly enough to predict her husband's policy, but she recognized the urgency felt by those who asked her opinion. Reading letters addressed to her on the issue of a pending finance bill to aid the investors, she admitted she was "rather confounded, for they seemed to refer to the same bill, only looked at from a different standpoint." She coped by translating the policy issue into a character issue, for she was more comfortable in the moral realm of right behavior and wrong behavior than in the political realm of fiscal policy and legislation. To those on both sides she replied that whatever the honorable thing was to do, she was certain her Ulys would do it.[2]

Yet Julia realized that as first lady, she could not remain mystified. She found it embarrassing that her ignorance forced her to give equivocal answers. She told Ulysses her dilemma, and, as she recalled, she "reproached him for not informing me sometimes of state affairs." For perhaps the first time, Julia recognized the need to see issues in their broader context, even if it was only to ensure she could better assist her husband. Ulysses's response, however, was disappointing. Now, as so many times in the past, he made light of her dilemma. If her husband's mix of humor, kindness, and comfort usually restored her sunny equilibrium, this time it did not. When he saw that she was hurt rather than comforted by his paternalism, Ulysses quickly made amends. Together, they sat down in the library, where he "kindly and clearly told me the whole story." But Ulys tailored his account to his wife's usual focus on personal character and personal consequences: while it was painful to see the investors and their families lose their fortunes, he said, the government must do nothing that might jeopardize its pledge to redeem with gold the paper money that had helped the Union finance the war. Thus Ulys's explanation did little to stretch Julia's capacity for objectivity. It was easy for her to see the issue once more as a matter of personal honor. "Why, Ulys," she exclaimed, "it is your bounden duty to veto this bill. You will be burned in effigy if you sign it or veto it and I would rather be burned for doing right than wrong."[3]

A second scandal broke, close on the heels of the gold conspiracy. Rumors of corruption surrounding a company known as Crédit Mobilier of America had begun to spread even before the scandal became public in 1872. Beginning in 1864, Crédit Mobilier—whose stockholders were identical to those of the Union Pacific Railroad, which it had acquired—reaped the benefits of generous subsidies, loans, and land grants from the federal government to cover the costs of completing the transcontinental railroad. Not content with the legitimate profits to be made, the directors of the company padded costs, adding almost $20 million to the cost of the rail line. To prevent careful oversight of these expenses, in 1867 the company gave stock to more than thirty Republican and Democratic members of Congress. Almost $33 million found its way into the pockets of congressmen. By the time the extent of the corruption became public in 1872, the liberal members of the Republican Party had begun their revolt against the unethical practices that would earn the postwar era its nickname, the "Gilded Age." Ulysses had little if anything to do with this scandal, but as the party's standard-bearer and candidate for reelection, he became a target of their criticism. Thus by the end of Ulysses's first term in office, a striking dichotomy had emerged: the Grants were moral leaders of the nation in their private life—a loving husband and father and a devoted wife and mother—but they were a couple surrounded by "questionable people, and people who were not nice at all" in their public life.[4]

Despite the cloud hanging over his administration, Ulysses was nominated for a second term. Although this campaign brought out a more aggressive "sifting" of her husband's character than the first, this time Julia was able to find some humor in the situation. The Democratic candidate, reformer and newspaper editor Horace Greeley, had visited the Grants at the White House in 1871. Julia had found him "rather old-fashioned looking" but had liked him at once, for "his face was kind and, when lighted up by a smile, was beautiful." Remembering the evening, she believed she understood Greeley's true motive for seeking the presidency. It was not economic policy or corruption in high places that had prompted this bid for high office; it was simply that Greeley had enjoyed that evening in the White House so much that he wanted a term there himself.[5]

Whatever Greeley's motivation, he did not win a term in the White House. In fact, he died before the election. Ulysses Grant was swept back into office, with over 55 percent of the popular vote and 286 electoral votes. For Julia, two events overshadowed all else in this second administration: her father's death and her daughter Nellie's wedding. In their own ways, both brought sadness. Colonel Dent had been crotchety and often embarrassingly outspoken during his years as part of the Grant household in Washington, yet he had been a central figure in shaping Julia's personality and character. He was the doting father who convinced his homely daughter that she was a princess, worthy of the admiration of all who encountered her.

A wedding in the White House, on the other hand, should have been a cause for celebration and delight. Yet neither Ulysses nor Julia thought Ellen Grant had made a wise choice in a husband. Those who knew her well may not have been surprised at Nellie's decision. She was a beautiful and willful young woman, and she was accustomed—as her mother had been—to being her father's darling girl. Like her mother, she had shown little interest in formal education, and by the age of fifteen she had abandoned school in favor of cotillions and parties. She quickly became a fixture on the Washington social scene. Critics felt she had more social life than was proper for a genteel young woman, but Julia and Ulysses were always ready to indulge their children's wishes.

Nellie had met Algernon Charles Frederic Sartoris aboard ship, coming home from the tour of Europe's major cities that was considered essential for well-bred young women. She was nineteen; he was twenty-three. Although a procession of suitors had appeared at the White House door, it was the handsome, wealthy Algy Sartoris who swept Nellie off her feet. Algy came with a noteworthy pedigree that combined celebrity and wealth: his great-aunt was the famous actress Sarah Siddons; his mother, Adelaide Kemble Sartoris, was an opera singer; his aunt was the actress and antislavery activist Fanny Kemble, who had married an American and divorced him when he inherited a plantation and slaves. Algy's father, the Italian Edward John Sartoris, had added the wealth essential to what might otherwise have been merely an eccentric family. To an American girl, even the daughter of the president, Algernon Sartoris was surely a romantic figure: he was rich and sophisticated, and had grown up in a household whose guests included renowned artists such as Frédéric Chopin and Felix Mendelssohn. What Nellie overlooked during the whirlwind courtship was the fact that the often charming Algy could be, and frequently was, arrogant, boastful, and crude—and that he was already an alcoholic.[6]

During the winter of 1872 and the spring of 1873, Algy and Nellie kept their romance alive through the exchange of passionate letters. When Ulysses realized the relationship was serious, he wrote to Edward Sartoris, expressing a reluctance to part with his daughter that echoed the emotions of Colonel Frederick Dent three decades before. "Much to my astonishment," he said, "an attachment seems to have sprung up between the two young people; to my astonishment because I had only looked upon my daughter as a child with a good home which I did not think of her wishing to quit for years yet." Yet, if marriage was likely, Ulysses was filled with blunt questions for the elder Sartoris. What were his son's "habits, character, and prospects"? What was the likelihood that Algy might become a citizen of the United States and settle here?

The questions came too late. Algy had proposed and Nellie had accepted. When Algy came to ask the president for his daughter's hand, Ulys reluctantly conceded that the young man was sincere. He could do nothing but give the marriage his blessing. Julia, on the other hand, was not so easily pacified. She took the matter directly to her daughter. Did she really want to leave the comforts of home and take up a life with what amounted to a total stranger? she asked Nellie. Nellie's reply ended the discussion: "Why, yes, Mamma. I am sure that is just what you did when you married papa and left grandpa."[7]

The wedding date was set: May 21, 1874. All of Washington society was abuzz with excitement, for this was the first White House wedding in thirty years. But Washington was also buzzing with gossip about the Grants' lack of enthusiasm for the groom-to-be and, far worse, it was buzzing about Algy's frequent public displays of boorish behavior and belittling remarks about his fiancée. The young Sartoris won few supporters with his disparaging remarks about Nellie's intelligence and lack of refinement or with his open penchant for sport rather than hard work or attention to duty. Popular opinion around town—and in newspapers around the nation—was that the marriage was doomed to failure. Sadly, they would prove right.

But whether the young couple's future would be happy or tragic, all of Washington society hoped to attend the wedding. To everyone's surprise and considerable outrage, the wedding was not the extravaganza the city expected. The guest list was shockingly small: only 250 invitations went out, largely to Grant family relatives, close personal friends, and top government officials. Many ambassadors, diplomats, and society matrons were insulted by their exclusion. The press was equally angered when it was announced that all reporters would be banned from the ceremony. None of the Sartoris family attended, for Algy's older brother, Greville, had been killed in a riding accident seven months earlier and Adelaide and Edward were in mourning for the loss of their favorite son. Fanny Kemble, who lived nearby in Philadelphia, refused to attend as well, for she disapproved of President Grant's generosity toward the former slaveholders of the South and his lack of assistance to the freedmen and -women she championed.

Although the wedding was small, it was costly. Ulysses and Julia spared no expense: there was a private railroad car to take Nellie and Julia to New York to consult with dressmakers; thousands were spent on the bridal gown, the bridesmaid's dresses, and accessories; the East Room was filled with flowers and tropical plants, and white roses covered a large wedding bell suspended above the altar. In the absence of any of his own relatives, Algy agreed to have Nellie's oldest brother, Fred, serve as his best man. Eight of Nellie's friends attended her as bridesmaids. The Marine Band played the "Wedding March" as Nellie and her father made their way down the aisle. As bride and groom took their vows, Jesse Grant watched his father standing "silent, tense, with tears upon his cheeks that he made no movement to brush away." For Ulysses S. Grant, son of Hannah and Jesse, it was no small thing to give way to emotions.

After a lavish wedding breakfast, Algy and Nellie headed to New York and from there to London. Surely Julia and Ulysses shared the same thought: a stranger was taking their only daughter to a foreign country. The crowds of Washingtonians who cheered as the newlyweds rode by probably did not grasp the sadness left in their wake. As church bells rang out "Hail Columbia" and, in Algy's honor, "God Save the Queen," Jesse Grant remembered how strangely empty the White House felt.

Nellie's story did not have a happy ending. Algy's alcoholism worsened and his contempt for his wife grew. By 1877, rumors began to spread that the marriage was failing, and even Julia's public assurances that Nellie was neither homesick nor unhappy could squelch them. By 1880 Algy was spending much of his time away from his wife and two children, and in 1883 he was seen in public with another woman. When Nellie returned to America to see her father on his deathbed, Algy would not allow her children to travel with her. She returned to England, but not to her husband, for he had left their home. In 1893, at the age of forty-two, Algernon Sartoris died of pneumonia on the Isle of Capri. He had not lived with his wife for almost eight years. The following year, Nellie Grant Sartoris came home to stay at last.

All of Nellie's sadness lay in the future in that summer of 1874. And soon enough, the emptiness that young Jesse had felt in the White House was filled. That October, Julia and Ulysses's oldest child, Fred, brought home his new bride. She was immediately welcomed into the family, for both Julia and Ulysses wholeheartedly approved of Ida Honoré Grant. Two years later, a second Julia Grant was born to Fred and Ida, and her happy grandmother called on "the fairies of my childhood" to return and bestow their magical favors on her namesake. Looking back, Julia was convinced that the fairies had answered her request. But the delight at becoming a "grandmamma" could not shield Julia from the disappointments that lay ahead for her.[8]

Forty-one

"A WAIF ON THE WORLD'S WIDE COMMON"

Julia Becomes a World Traveler

JULIA HAD HOPED THAT HER HUSBAND would stand for a third term in the White House, for she had come to think of Washington, and the executive mansion, as her home. But Ulys, who had been haunted by scandal and embarrassed by criticism from within his own party, was eager to leave the presidency. If Julia sensed this, she nevertheless hoped she could persuade him to stay.

Ulysses understood his wife's desires well. He knew that she would oppose any concrete steps he took to prevent his renomination. Thus, without telling her, he called his cabinet together, informed them of his decision, and sent off a letter to his party, telling them that he would not run for a third term. Julia was deeply hurt by the deception. "Oh, Ulys! Was that kind to me? Was it just to me?" Though he conceded it was neither, Ulysses clearly believed the deception was necessary. He did not want to be President Grant for four more years. "I do not think I could stand it," he said—and there the matter ended.[1]

Leaving the White House was painful for Julia. She had spent eight happy years there, despite the scandals and the anxiety over Nellie's choice in husbands. After years of a nomadic life, moving from town to town as the wife of a young army officer, then a struggling civilian, and finally a battlefield general, Julia had at last come to rest in the most prestigious home in the nation. Her exit was that mixture of petulance and graciousness to be expected from a well-mannered but spoiled woman accustomed to getting her way. She refused to go to the inauguration of her husband's successor, nor would she vacate the White House so that President and Mrs. Hayes could immediately occupy it after the ceremonies. Instead, she lingered for one moment more in the role of White House hostess, giving a luncheon there for the new residents.

Adam Badeau preserved that moment in his own memoirs, showing tact and sympathy for Julia in his account. Despite the dark cloud of scandal that still hung over the departing president, "Mrs. Grant dispensed her parting hospitalities . . . with dignity." The event served both as a farewell and a welcome, for cabinet members and their families and personal friends were invited as well as guests whom Julia thought the new occupants of the White House might wish to meet. As they entered the dining room, Julia took the arm of President Hayes, "and considering herself still the hostess, as she actually was, she sat at the head of the table." At last, when the meal had ended and the entertainment was over, Ulysses and Julia said goodbye to the house where they had spent so many proud and happy hours. Mrs. Grant, Badeau observed with pride, "kept up her spirit."[2]

The break with Washington and politics seemed complete. In a symbolic gesture of separation, Julia had spent hours burning old letters that she and Ulysses had accumulated over his eight years in office. But what were they to do now? Neither Julia nor Ulysses seemed to know. They were headed for a month's stay with Hamilton and Julia Kean Fish, but after that their future was uncharted. On the train out of Washington, Julia broke down in tears. "Oh, Ulys!" she sobbed. "I feel like a waif, like a waif on the world's wide common." Ulysses was relieved to hear that the source of her tears was emotional rather than physical. "Oh . . . is that all?" he asked. "I thought something had happened." But, after almost twenty-eight years of marriage, Ulysses S. Grant knew how to comfort his wife: "You must not forget that I, too, am a waif. So you are not alone," he said.[3]

By the spring of 1877, the Grants had settled on their destination. On May 17, 1877, Julia, Ulysses, and their youngest child, Jesse, boarded the American steamship *Indiana* for the beginning of a world tour that would eventually take them from Europe to the Middle East, the Far East, and home again at last in the fall of 1879. Friends such as Adolph Borie joined the Grants as they toured India, Egypt, and China, and the European correspondent for the *New York Herald,* John Russell Young, accompanied them, recording every detail of their grand tour. Everywhere the ex-president and his entourage went, they were greeted with enthusiasm and lavish celebration. From Belgium to Tokyo, Ulysses S. Grant was hailed as the victorious general and noble guardian of American liberty, and newspapers back home delighted in carrying accounts of a hero's reception in the courts of Europe and the palaces of the Middle East.[4]

The man at the center of all this attention and adulation, fifty-five-year-old Ulysses Grant, was no longer the trim soldier who had courted Julia Dent. He was fifty pounds heavier than he had been during the Civil War, and his close-cropped beard showed signs of gray. His perennial cigar was always ready at hand. Julia Grant was fifty-one years old, stout and matronly, and still homely in the eyes of all but her husband. Without cares or duties, however, Julia and Ulysses appeared to observers as far younger than their years. They held hands like young lovers, joked with each other, laughed together. The aides and friends and reporters who accompanied the former president and his wife all agreed: after decades together, Julia and Ulysses Grant were still in love.

Despite their age, Julia and Ulysses proved admirably adventurous, as ready to mount a camel or donkey or clamber among ancient ruins as to enjoy a lavish dinner with European and Asian royalty. As they crisscrossed Europe and the Middle East or made their way to India, Japan, and China, they discovered a world opening up to them that was both exotic and filled with splendors. Julia knew that no White House dinner she had ever hosted could compare with dinners in the palaces of the kings of Belgium or Spain, or later at Egypt's Kasr-el-Noussa. Despite this, she, like her husband, retained a firm conviction that her own society was superior to all others in its morals, its customs, and its political system, and that the entire world would be better off if it emulated America.[5]

This pride of place could be seen in Julia's attitude toward everything from cuisine to religion to educational opportunities—and marriage. She boasted readily of the American cornucopia, with its salmon and trout from the Pacific Northwest, beef and mutton and game from the prairies, and fruits and vegetables from the nation's gardens. She declared with conviction that her nation's poor enjoyed the same chance for education as its rich, and even the humblest man could acquire a fortune. And, contrary to the customs in many countries, Americans tolerated no arranged marriages; instead men sought wives who were beautiful and intelligent as well as "amiable and chaste."

Julia was equally confident of Christianity's superiority to other religious beliefs. Throughout her life, she had been a staunch Methodist and a regular churchgoer. If she was far more conscientious in this area than her husband, this was considered fitting: in nineteenth-century America, "true women" were thought to be naturally more spiritual and devout than men. Yet Ulysses, too, believed that Protestant Christianity was the only path to salvation and that those who followed other faiths were in error.

Small wonder that when Julia was asked, "Now that you have seen nearly all the countries of the Continent, how does America compare with them?" she could reply without hesitation. Gazing up at an elaborate chandelier that hung above her head, Julia said: "How does America compare with other countries? As that chandelier is to this room, so is America to other countries."[6]

Clearly not everyone Julia encountered agreed. The queen of England, for example, was not dazzled by the beacon light of America; in fact, though she was a gracious hostess to the Grants, she refused to accord Ulysses the honors due to a former sovereign. The Grants took this slight to their country calmly, but Julia could not resist a reminder to Victoria of the dignity and power of her husband's former office. When the queen lamented her difficult life, filled with labor and duties, Julia sweetly but firmly retorted, "Yes, I can imagine them: I too have been the wife of a great ruler."[7]

If Julia did not charm the queen, she did charm most of the Grant entourage. John Russell Young told his readers back home, "I wish I could lift the veil far enough to show you how much the kind, considerate, ever-womanly and ever-cheerful nature of Mrs. Grant has won upon us all." Only a desire to protect "the privacy of the domestic circle" restrained him from saying more. This cheerfulness and enthusiasm come across vividly in her memoirs as well. Here, in page after page, Julia recalled the sights, sounds, and tastes of the journey in remarkable detail. She wrote of gathering souvenirs from fashionable European shops and exotic Middle Eastern bazaars; of wandering through museums, castles, and gardens; and of dining with emperors and princes. But it was the tours of ancient ruins and the travel to historic sites that most delighted her. Many years before these travels, when she was a girl at the Mauros family's school for young ladies, histories and mythologies had been among the only books to hold Julia's attention. Now, she found herself at the very sites where the first Ulysses was said to have escaped from Calypso or sailed his course between Charybdis and Scylla. Her own Ulysses was less enthralled; even in full flight, his own imagination was limited, and, as Adam Badeau astutely noted, "the practical General was more curious about geography than mythology."[8]

Although paintings in galleries and Greek and Roman ruins did not move Ulysses in the same way they excited his wife, the ex-president was as reluctant as Julia to see his trip end. Even when a wave of homesickness swept over him, he did not give in to it; he was, he told a friend, determined to "see every country in Europe at least." Twenty-six months later, he and Julia at long last decided it was time to return to America. Saying their farewells to their hosts in Japan, they sailed for San Francisco. On September 20, 1879, the Grants were once again on native soil. Julia was happy and relieved to find that their countrymen and -women had not forgotten them. Her tone was triumphant as she recalled the "vast throngs of people who greeted the General with enthusiastic cheers again and again" as they arrived in California.[9]

Forty-two

"DO YOU NOT DESIRE SUCCESS?"

From Politics to Poverty

JULIA AND ULYSSES WERE HOME—but their wanderlust had not been fully quenched. As they slowly wended their way to Galena, they took in the sights of the American West. Here, as in Europe and Asia, the Grants often seemed more like young lovers than a middle-aged married couple: he, reacting to her with what his generation considered manly amusement, exasperation, and indulgence; she, teasing and triumphant, coquettish, stubborn, and charmingly demanding. Both knew their roles; both seemed to delight in them. No better illustration of this could be found than in the episode at Yosemite Valley.

On their trip back from Yosemite Valley, Julia persuaded her husband to let her ride up front with the stagecoach driver. But as the driver sped along the rim of the valley, the coach careening from side to side, Julia grew convinced their lives were in danger. As soon as the coach stopped, Julia leaped to the ground, and refused to join the other passengers when it was time to continue the trip. No amount of coaxing could persuade her to change her mind. The stalemate was resolved when two men with a small carriage and two fine horses volunteered to take seats on the stagecoach and turn their buggy over to the Grants. In her memoirs, Julia conceded that she had been unreasonable. "I behaved so badly," she wrote, although her admission conveyed more humor than self-criticism. And although Ulysses scolded her, declaring "he feared people would think he did not have me under proper discipline," her satisfaction at getting her way was not diminished. Julia's response—hearty laughter—reflected her unshakable confidence that she was adored, a confidence instilled by a doting father and deepened by a long marriage to an indulgent husband. Now in her fifties, Julia remained as certain of Ulysses's forbearance of her whims, her faults, and her self-indulgence as she had been during their courtship so many years before.[1]

The Grants' route took them to Sacramento, Lake Tahoe, Virginia City, Carson City, and on to Omaha, where they reunited with many army friends. At last, they reached Galena and realized they were "home again in reality." But within a week, they were headed for Chicago, then on to Indianapolis, Louisville, Cincinnati, and Harrisburg, and finally to Philadelphia, where, Julia noted, at last "our journey around the globe was completed." Still, Ulysses's wanderlust did not abate. They went on to visit the Southern states, Cuba, and Mexico, where Ulysses had served as a young lieutenant. When at last they returned to Galena, the question that may well have fueled Ulysses's restlessness reemerged: would he seek the presidency once again?[2]

The Republican convention was scheduled to meet in Chicago on June 2, 1880. Julia was convinced that the American people still loved her husband and wanted him to return to the White House. But she feared the leaders of the party did not. She was noticeably anxious and confessed to Adam Badeau that she could barely stand the suspense. Ulysses, on the other hand, remained relatively calm. He followed the selection of delegates carefully and, as Badeau reported, he "considered how every movement would affect the result, and was pleased or indignant at the conversion of enemies or the defection of friends, just as any other human being would have been."

While the delegates wrangled over rules and platform planks, Ulysses prepared to travel to Chicago. He intended to make a brief appearance at the convention on a Monday evening and then immediately depart for Milwaukee, where he would attend the annual reunion of the Grand Army of the Republic. But Julia begged him to go to Chicago on Sunday night so that he could appear on the floor of the convention when it reconvened Monday morning. Ulysses adamantly refused. "Do you not desire success?" Julia recalled asking him. "Well, yes, of course," came the reply. Since his name had been put forward, Ulysses conceded that he would prefer to win the nomination than lose it. But he would do nothing to aid his own cause. When she heard this, Julia's patience evaporated. "Oh, Ulys," she said, "how unwise, what mistaken chivalry. For heaven's sake, go—and go tonight. I know they are already making their cabals against you. Go, go tonight, I beseech you." Whether Julia's urgency sprang from her own ambition to return to the White House or from a desire to see her husband triumph over his enemies is unclear; it is likely it was spurred by both. But Ulysses was unmoved. "Julia," he said, "I am amazed at you"—and with that, Julia ruefully recalled, the matter ended.[3]

Thus Ulysses S. Grant bade farewell to politics. Yet it was not entirely clear what he would now do to earn his living. Although he was not yet sixty years old, he could not reasonably return to a military career, and all his past ventures into business or farming had ended disastrously. Despite their financial uncertainty, the Grants decided to move to New York City, where Ulysses's modest income from savings of $6,000 a year was wholly inadequate. As Julia bluntly put it, "General Grant was poor."[4]

For a brief time, Ulysses served as president of a new railroad venture, the Mexican Southern Railroad, but the enterprise was not likely to make his fortune. Fortunately—or so it seemed at the time—Ulysses's son and namesake came to the rescue. Along with Ferdinand Ward and James D. Fish, the younger Ulysses had formed a New York banking firm. Buck offered his father one-half of his own interest in the business, but Ulysses managed to put in the capital needed to make himself a full partner. Thus in 1880, as the Republican candidate James Garfield vied with his Democratic rival Winfield S. Hancock and the Greenback-Labor Party's James B. Weaver for the presidency, Ulysses S. Grant began his career as a partner in the firm of Grant and Ward.[5]

More good fortune followed. A group of wealthy and influential men presented Julia with a fund that would allow her to purchase a home. By the end of 1881, Julia and Ulysses were settled in a large house on Manhattan's East 66th Street. Julia conceded that she had been a bit extravagant, for the home cost more than they had intended to spend. But, she wrote, "it was so new and sweet and large that this quite outweighed our more prudential scruples." Later she would regret her lack of prudence, as a mortgage of almost $60,000 hung over her head when her husband died. But for now, she was caught up in the happy tasks of ordering furniture and paintings, opening boxes as they arrived, and placing all the souvenirs of their world travels in their new surroundings. By Christmas 1881, with both Fred's and Nellie's families joining them for the holidays and Buck and Jesse happily married and living nearby in the city, Julia had every reason to believe the future was bright. "I think my happiness was quite complete," she wrote, as she settled into a busy social life with family and friends. Sadly, that happiness would not last.[6]

On Christmas Eve, 1883, Ulysses S. Grant made his way home by cab from a business meeting. As he handed the driver the fare, he slipped on the icy ground and fell. Julia was distraught, but Ulysses dismissed the accident as trifling. It was not. The following day, the doctor declared that Mr. Grant needed surgery for a dislocated hip. Soon after the fall, Ulysses suffered an attack of pleurisy. Recuperation was slow; he was bedridden for several weeks, and when he began to walk once again he needed crutches. The busy social season Julia had planned for the family was canceled, and in March, Julia and her husband made their way south, "in search of sunshine." By summer, Ulysses had recovered some of his old energy, although he walked with a slight limp from then on.[7]

Far worse lay ahead for the Grants. The decline of their fortunes—and their fortune—came suddenly in 1884. On Tuesday morning, May 6, Ulysses left his house secure in the knowledge that he was a millionaire. When he reached his office, he discovered he was a pauper. The firm of Grant and Ward had failed; not even a loan from the railroad tycoon William Vanderbilt could save it.[8]

The failure came, "like a thunderclap," without warning. If Ferdinand Ward knew their investments were insecure, he had not shared the knowledge with his partners. Only a few days before, in fact, Ulysses had assured Julia that they had no need to put away money for their children. He was, he said, giving serious thought to increasing his support for the many friends in need that he and his wife already assisted. "Ward," he told her, "is making us all rich—them as well as ourselves—and I have been thinking how pleasant it would be for us to make our impecunious friends ... independent, get them comfortable little homes, and make them allowances." Now it was the Grants who would be numbered among the "impecunious" in need of assistance.[9]

Despite all the scandals that had swirled around him as president, nothing disturbed and humiliated Ulysses more than the collapse of this business enterprise. It was bad enough that he had lost everything, even the trust fund given him by admirers when he left office. His ruin seemed total, for he could not even meet the mortgage payments on their home. But what troubled him most was not his sudden fall from grace, but the fact that the people he loved suffered as well. Buck was ruined; Jesse, too, had invested his entire fortune in the company; Nellie and his sister had invested as well.[10]

Ulysses did what he could to make amends. He made over all his personal property to Vanderbilt, for he felt honor-bound to repay the $150,000 loan that had failed to stem the disaster. Julia waived her dower rights to this property, leaving her with no claim should her husband die. Although Vanderbilt would later restore the property to the Grants, for the moment Ulysses and Julia were without any resources and in no position to help their children. It was painful for Julia to see her sons returning their summer supply of groceries, wines, and cigars, for they could not pay for their orders any more than they could pay for their carfare in the city. To survive, Julia, Ulysses, and their children's families fled New York City and settled at their summer home at Long Branch, New Jersey.[11]

In their prosperity, the Grants had been generous to friends and charitable to strangers; now, both friends and strangers returned the favor. Julia recalled that a gentleman from upstate New York sent Ulysses $500, saying only that he owed it to the General "for Appomattox." A check for $1,000 soon followed from the same man. A foreign minister brought Ulysses a loan of $1,000 as well. Then *Century* magazine asked Ulysses to write an article about the war. This first article, written at a white kitchen table set up in a makeshift office at the house in Long Branch, appeared in February 1885, opening up a new career for the former general and president. By October, Adam Badeau had arrived at the Grants' home to assist Ulysses in writing his memoirs. Ulysses's spirits had risen, and fortune seemed to be smiling on the family once again.[12]

Forty-three

"WARMED IN THE SUNLIGHT
OF HIS LOYAL LOVE AND GREAT FAME"

Julia Becomes a Widow

ALL WAS NOT WELL FOR THE GRANTS, HOWEVER. Bringing back still-painful memories, Julia set down in her memoirs the agonizing battle with cancer that her Ulys would face. It began on a clear summer day in 1884, she wrote. Ulysses had taken a bite of a peach, and as he swallowed, he felt a searing pain in his throat. Julia recalled his exclaiming, "Oh my, I think something has stung me from the peach." Though he rinsed his throat several times, the sharp pain persisted. The water, he said, felt like liquid fire. Julia pleaded with him to see a doctor, but the stoic Ulysses refused, insisting he would be fine "directly." He was not. A few weeks passed, and at last in August, when a doctor came to check on other members of the family, Julia prevailed upon him to look at the General's throat.[1]

The problem, the doctor confirmed, was a serious one, and he recommended Ulysses see a specialist at once. But Ulysses dragged his feet. He was too busy writing to waste time consulting more doctors. It was not until late October that he was examined by Dr. Fordyce Barker. He did not share the doctor's diagnosis with his wife. Julia had to go to Barker herself to discover the "dreadful truth": Ulysses had throat cancer. Sobered by this diagnosis, Ulysses continued to see Barker that November, but his condition did not improve. By December, the pain was unbearable and he could swallow nothing but liquids. By January, he was confined to his room.[2]

Despite the constant pain, Ulysses doggedly worked on his memoirs, stopping only when his grandchildren came to visit him each afternoon. He was determined to complete the project, for the money it would bring was his only hope to provide for his family. Every evening the entire family gathered to read the day's pages aloud and to do their best to lift their father and grandfather's spirits.

Julia was just as dogged in her insistence that her husband would recover. She would not, could not believe that the illness could be fatal. Again and again she asked the doctors: Had anyone been cured? Had anyone survived this illness? "And down in my heart," she wrote, "I could not believe that God in his wisdom and mercy would take this great, wise, good man from us, to whom he was so necessary and so beloved."[3]

As winter dragged on, friends began to visit the Grants. Each day, the Episcopal bishop John Newman and his wife came to comfort their ailing friend. Ulysses, Julia recalled, sat in a large chair, his head resting on a cushion, his eyes closed and his hands clasped before him, as he listened to the clergyman pray. Matías Romero, who had loaned the Grants money in the frightening days following the collapse of Ward and Grant, came up from Washington to sit silently beside his old friend. Those who could not travel to Long Branch sent letters, bouquets, and gifts. Among them was Jefferson Davis, whose respect for the man who defeated his country was conveyed by letter, along with hopes for his speedy recovery. Jeff Davis was not the only Southerner to send his regards; the sons of Robert E. Lee and Albert Sidney Johnston wrote as well. Schoolchildren across the country offered their prayers for the former president's recovery.

But concerns about money weighed heavily on Ulysses and made the completion of his memoirs a near obsession. Once again, friends and admirers came to his aid. William Vanderbilt quietly signed over to Julia all the property Ulysses had surrendered to him in the wake of the failure of Ward and Grant. His only stipulation was that the many gifts the Grants had received over their years in the White House be given to the government when she died. A number of army officers joined with General Sherman to raise a fund for the family, but Ulysses was too proud to welcome this support. He wanted instead, Julia recalled, to be restored to his military rank and thus to receive military pay. After several attempts to win congressional approval for adding Grant to the list of retired military, the bill finally passed both the House and the Senate in March 1885. In the meantime, payment for additional magazine articles helped meet the Grant family's bills.[4]

By January 1885 Ulysses was too ill to visit his doctors. Instead they came to him. The experts took care to shield Julia from the truth that her husband would not recover. Though they shielded Ulysses as well, he slowly realized that the cancer was killing him. Death, however, took its time. Each time he believed the end had come, his body rallied. Each time he rallied, he turned back to the completion of his memoirs. His hopes rested on the book, for he expected half a million dollars in sales. He was racing with death, determined to win. Julia remembered his urgency: "And so he wrote on and on. General Grant, the savior of our Union, General Grant, commander-in-chief of 1,000,000 men, General Grant, eight years President of the United States, was writing, writing of his own grand deeds, recording them that he might leave a home and independence to his family."[5]

In the summer of 1885, the Grants moved to Joseph Drexel's cottage on New York's Mount McGregor. The weather was cooler here, and at the end of each day, Julia and her Ulys sat on the piazza and watched the crowds of well-wishers who passed by, hoping to gain a glimpse of General Grant. Friends such as Generals Simon Bolivar Buckner, William Tecumseh Sherman, and Philip Sheridan traveled here as well, sensing that this was their last opportunity to say goodbye.

On July 19, Ulysses finished his book. Four days later, on the morning of July 23, he passed away, surrounded by his wife and family. Until that moment, Julia had refused to believe her husband would die. Adam Badeau recalled her stubborn denial: "A woman with many of those singular presentiments that amount almost to superstition, but which yet affect some of the strongest minds, and from which General Grant himself was certainly not entirely free, she declared always, even at the moment which everyone else thought would prove the last, that she could not realize the imminence of the end. Her behavior was a mystery and a wonder to those who knew the depth of the tenderness and the abundance of the affection she lavished on her great husband. Her calmness and self-control almost seemed coldness, only we knew that this was impossible . . . once or twice she told me she could not despair . . . she was putting up prayers that were full of confidence."[6]

The despair Julia had refused to feel swept over her with Ulysses's death. She was inconsolable, crying for weeks after he passed away. She sat surrounded by her family in the parlor of the Mount McGregor cottage as the Grants' old friend, Episcopal bishop John Newman, delivered a funeral sermon to the crowd gathered on the front lawn. Like so many others, Newman praised the long and happy marriage of Ulysses and Julia, attributing their happiness to their embrace of appropriate and complementary roles. "Husband and wife, the happy supplement of each other," he declared. "He the Doric column to sustain; she the Corinthian column to beautify. He the oak to support; she ivy to entwine."[7]

Both Julia and Ulysses had always found comfort and satisfaction in the conventional social views of nineteenth-century genteel society. He never doubted that a woman's destiny was to devote her life to her husband and family; she never had reason to challenge this view. Without him, she had no strong and sheltering oak tree around which to entwine. When Julia recorded her husband's death, she could only write: "[h]e, my beloved, my all, passed away, and I was alone, alone."[8]

Forty-four

"LIVING AGAIN, WITH THE AID OF MY FANCY AND MY PEN"

Julia Dent Grant Writes Her Memoirs

SOON AFTER BISHOP NEWMAN DELIVERED his eulogy, the coffin of Ulysses S. Grant was taken to New York City for a more elaborate funeral. In a gesture that surely would have pleased Ulysses, his coffin was escorted by an equal number of Union and Confederate generals serving as honorary pallbearers. Julia, too, would have been touched by this sign of a healing nation, but she was not yet able to face the public. She remained at Mount McGregor until the end of August 1885. At last, with summer over, she returned to the city where she had been both so rich and so poor. There in New York, she made a temporary home with the family of her oldest son, Frederick. He alone had followed in his father's footsteps and risen to the rank of general.

In 1889, Frederick Dent Grant was appointed minister to Austria-Hungary. Julia, still struggling to make a life for herself, agreed to go with Fred's family when they left for Vienna. But if once she had delighted in traveling, this return to the Europe she and Ulysses had toured together only saddened her. By the end of the summer, Julia was back in the United States. And she was alone.

It was four years later that Julia encountered another famous widow, Varina Davis, who was also struggling to define herself now that her husband was gone. They met by chance on a June day, at a West Point resort. Julia had probably gone to escape the humidity and heat of the city; Varina was there to view a parade at West Point. When Julia learned that the widow of the president of the Confederacy was only a few steps away, she knocked on Varina's door to welcome her. Their first exchange was brief and to the point. "I am Mrs. Grant," Julia remembered announcing. "I am very glad to meet you," Varina replied—and a friendship began.[1]

Curious hotel guests might have gawked that evening as the two women sat on the piazza, talking. But Julia and Varina recognized in each other a kindred spirit. Both had been the wives of powerful and important men; both were relics of a slave-owning culture now dismantled; both were mothers and grandmothers; and both had seen the drama, tragedy, and triumphs of the Civil War from a vantage point shared by few. It did not seem to matter that one had known victory and the other humiliating defeat.

There is no record of what they discussed that June day. But they met several times afterward and from time to time wrote to each other. It was Varina who accompanied Julia to the grand tomb built to house her husband's remains on the West Side of Manhattan. And it was Varina who consoled Julia when criticism of Ulysses appeared in print. "I am sorry to know the criticisms . . . have made you unhappy," Varina wrote on April 29, 1901. "There are more hyenas than lions born among beasts. The foul creatures who prey on and tear the dead heroes who have gone to their rest after having done what they could unselfishly to serve their own people cannot do them much harm." She urged her friend to ignore the ingratitude of detractors—as she had, of necessity, learned to do. "If I had not steeled my mind against the attacks of such creatures against my good and great husband I should never have known one hour of peace or comfort." Posterity would be the judge, Varina declared; "in another half century when you and I are where we shall 'see clearly' and are having our merited rest, the world will judge fairly, and commend justly. The picture," she reminded Julia, "is not yet drawn, but perception and memory will paint its fair outlines as time rolls on."[2]

Jefferson Davis and Ulysses S. Grant had treated each other with respect, and now their widows regarded each other with affection. For both Julia and Varina, the character of the men they had married was now more important than the cause that had set them against each other. The following April, Varina—who was far more articulate than her friend—published an article in the New York Sunday World entitled "The Humanity of Grant." "Even in the stress and heat of hostilities, military and political, the humanity of the man shone through the soldier's coat of mail," she wrote. She had experienced that humanity personally, for it was Ulysses Grant, after all, who had responded to her pleas when Jeff was imprisoned at Fortress Monroe. Julia, who had always seen the world through the lens of personal experience, surely understood Varina's gratitude.[3]

The two widows had one more thing in common: the desire to set down on paper their memories. In this they were not alone. For a variety of motives, many of the men responsible for the Civil War, its statesmen and generals, had rushed to publish accounts of their roles in the conflict. Some had put their experiences on paper to vindicate themselves; others, including Ulysses, to provide for their families. Still others had perhaps hoped to exorcise the demon memories of brutality, violence, and death that they carried with them after the war. But it was not only the generals and politicians who took up their pens to shape the history of the conflict. Their wives and widows also chose to write, or authorize the writing of, *their* stories: tales of heroes and villains, of intimacy and devotion. Some sought to be truthful; others spun romantic fantasies, designed to present both wife and husband as exemplars of the nineteenth century's marital ideals. In becoming historians, women such as Mary Anna Jackson, LaSalle Corbell Pickett, Elizabeth Baker Custer, and Jessie Benton Frémont brought purpose to their lives and established a new identity as keepers of the flame and conservators of the nineteenth-century beau ideal. Both the widow of the general who defeated the Confederacy and the widow of that Confederacy's president were among these memoirists.[4]

Soon after Ulysses's death, Julia began to share with her son Fred anecdotes and stories of her world tour with her husband. Soon she was sharing bits of history from Ulysses's childhood and youth as well. Here were stories and revelations that had not even been hinted at in his father's memoirs. Ulysses had committed his military experiences to paper; if he revealed anything of his personal emotions or private life, it was surely accidental. Adam Badeau had once commented that General Grant never engaged in self-reflection, and so it was no surprise that, in his memoirs, Ulysses did not probe the interior of his mind. Julia was no more introspective than her husband, but she had personalized every experience, great or small, and so her memories were rich with emotion and sentiment, even if raw and lacking analysis.[5]

Fred recalled that "every day I devote an hour or more to taking down my mother's reminiscences of him." Together, mother and son filled hundreds of pages with her personal recollections. The fate of these pages was uncertain; like Stonewall Jackson's widow, Julia claimed her account was her legacy to her grandchildren. Yet, like LaSalle Corbell Pickett, Julia hoped to see them reach a far larger, public audience. There were complications, however. The family had agreed with the publishers of the *Personal Memoirs of U. S. Grant* that they would publish no competing accounts for three years. Despite this promise, both Julia and Fred seemed ready to meet what they believed was the public's continuing interest in Ulysses. First, Fred proposed a book about his father's life after the Civil War. Then Julia declared herself eager to publish not only her memoirs but also the many letters written to her by her husband. All the while, she labored over the memoirs, asking friends like Mexican diplomat Matías Romero to send accounts of trips or events that had grown dim in her mind. Both mother and son opened talks with their family friend, the publisher and novelist Mark Twain, but nothing came of it.[6]

Julia pursued publication of her memoirs for some time, diminishing her chances of success by asking for a large advance on royalties. Publishers seemed to feel that her husband's memoirs had sated the public's interest and curiosity. Although Ulysses had revealed no more of his personal life than those who knew him would expect, his stirring accounts of the war's battles and campaigns appeared to satisfy readers both in the North and in the South. Julia could offer the public little that they did not know, in broad outlines, about her husband's character or about their happy marriage. Despite some barbed comments about Ulysses's critics, the tone of Julia's memoir was too gentle, too reminiscent; it lacked shocking revelation or compelling romantic idealization. In the end, the general contentment of their lives together defeated her literary ambitions, and the story she told glided gently on the surface rather than probing the depths of her own or her husband's personality.

Julia reconciled herself to the notion that her memories would be shared only with her family. Still, those memories continued to pour onto the page. She recognized them as the antidote to mourning. Some fifteen years after her Ulys's death, she told an interviewer: "With the general's death . . . I thought my life had been lived, for we had been inseparable. I saw nothing that could brighten or make interesting the remaining years. For two years it was very dreary. Then I began the memoirs." Soon, she confessed, she became "an inveterate scribbler." In recollecting her life, she found a joy she never expected to feel again. "I was living again, with the aid of my fancy and my pen, the life that had been so sweet to me."[7]

If life without her husband was no longer sweet for Julia, neither was it bleak. Ulysses had provided for her material needs before he died. His memoirs generated almost half a million dollars in royalties, and this money, along with a $5,000-a-year pension from the federal government, allowed Julia to live out the remaining years of her life in comfort. She moved to Washington, D.C., settling down among old friends and family. If her world had contracted, it was once again safe and comforting.

Julia, like Varina Davis, lived to see a new century begin. But her health was rapidly failing. In December 1902, she developed bronchitis. This, along with a long-standing heart condition, proved too much for her body to bear. With a doctor, two nurses, and her daughter, Nellie, by her bedside, Julia Dent Grant died as midnight approached on December 14. Major newspapers including the *New York Times* and the *New York Herald* carried news of her death and of her funeral services. She was buried in the riverside tomb created for her husband, in a sarcophagus of red granite identical to the one that held Ulysses. Her funeral was far simpler than his had been. Instead of a million spectators and a long procession of dignitaries, Julia was laid to rest by her family and two hundred friends, including aging veterans who had served under General Grant during the Civil War. Fred, Buck, Jesse, and Nellie were there; Julia's younger sister Emma and two of Ulysses's sisters were beside them.

When these private ceremonies were ended, the tomb was opened once again to the public. The *New York Herald* reported that "fully a thousand men and women, many of whom had stood for hours in the drenching rain, went in to view the flower covered sarcophagus." If Julia was less famous than her husband, she was not entirely forgotten. Her memoirs remained the private treasure of her family until, more than seventy years later, the work of her "fancy and pen" was published in 1975. In it, Julia emerged clearly: confident, optimistic, superstitious, loyal, and loving, too busy living a conventional and generally fortunate life to examine its meaning closely or to marvel at its contradictions and ambiguities.[8]

Epilogue

THE LIVES OF Angelina Grimké Weld, Varina Howell Davis, and Julia Dent Grant spanned a century of rapid changes and major crises as our nation moved into modernity. Their stories cannot encompass everything we seek to know and understand about that century, of course. Angelina Grimké Weld's story is not the whole story of the antislavery or feminist movement. The Confederacy's rise and fall are not perfectly encapsulated in the life of Varina Howell Davis. And the military history of the Civil War and the failures and successes of the postwar years are not exhausted in a biography of Julia Dent Grant. Yet their stories can serve as threads that connect us to our national past and as windows onto a social and political landscape that is both strangely familiar and shockingly foreign to our own.

Angelina Grimké Weld turned her back on a life of luxury as a planter's daughter to become one of the most effective antislavery speakers of the 1830s and one of the first Americans to demand equality for women. Devoting her life to the abolition of an institution whose horrors she had witnessed firsthand, Angelina, with her sister Sarah, traveled the length and breadth of New England, New York, and Pennsylvania, lecturing to supporters, opponents, and those who were simply curious to see the spinster sisters from South Carolina who dared to discuss forbidden topics in front of mixed, or "promiscuous," audiences. Angelina Grimké became the center of controversy, a magnet for criticism from those who felt their comfortable lives threatened by antislavery agitation and from those who felt their moral leadership within the community diminished by the abolitionist crusade. And because she was a woman, each time she stepped upon a stage she was forced to defend not only her views on slavery but also her right to speak them in public. When Angelina married her mentor, Theodore Weld—perhaps the only antislavery orator whose powers matched hers—she abandoned her career as a public advocate of abolition. For almost forty years, as a wife and mother, she struggled to make her life proof that a woman could take up domestic duties without giving up her intellectual and moral equality with her husband. Angelina's successes— and failures—tell us much about the early challenges to hallowed notions of women's sphere. But they also tell us much about the principles and values of an antislavery movement that spurred a woman to defy established rules of behavior and, in the process, create an independent self. That the movement rejected the right of women to see themselves as individuals, not as dependents, perhaps tells us more.

Varina Howell Davis, like Angelina Grimké Weld, was born into the planter class. Beautiful, witty, and vivacious, she ought—in less troubled times—to have lived out her life as the wife of a prosperous and prestigious Southern planter, military hero, and political leader. She did, in fact, become a nineteenth-century matron, but she became more as well. As the wife of Jefferson Davis, Varina was drawn to the very center of American political life, first in Washington, D.C., and later in Montgomery and Richmond, the capitals of the Confederacy. Varina was ill-prepared and ill-suited for the role she was to play as the first lady of the Confederacy who became, at war's end, the supporter of a disgraced cause and the wife of its imprisoned leader. Yet she proved to be more than a tragic survivor. She became an expert political lobbyist for her husband's release, calling in favors from former Senate friends and acquaintances, hiring lawyers, and generating sympathy for her husband in the press. Her campaign to free Jeff Davis brought down upon her a rain of criticism for defying middle-class notions of femininity. Yet there were compensations: her actions allowed her, at long last, to deploy the talents and abilities that Jeff had for so many years labored to suppress in his wife. After his death, she combined two seemingly disparate roles: keeper of her husband's legacy and career woman.

Julia Dent Grant, too, came of age in the conservative and comfortable world of slave society. She recalled her childhood as "one long summer of sunshine, flowers and smiles." But in marrying, she took a risk few of her peers would take: she married a man of uncertain promise and no wealth. Throughout her married life, the presence of sunshine, flowers, and smiles depended entirely on her husband's successes and failures, both of which were spectacular. Unlike Angelina, who struggled to make history, or Varina, who never stopped analyzing the history being made, Julia Grant was able to reduce the epic to the domestic, turning military victories and presidential races into personal moments for her and her beloved Ulys. Not until she was widowed did Julia search for her own voice and her own purpose. She took upon herself the task of memorializing her husband—and, in the process, wrote herself into history at last.

These three lives put a human face on what are otherwise impersonal events. But they do more. Simply put, Angelina, Varina, and Julia were women, and thus their lives allow us to glimpse aspects of the nineteenth century that might otherwise be lost in the roar of cannon and heated political debate. Angelina's life allows us to see the complex connection between a spiritual awakening, a struggle for the liberation of others, and a growing need to assert and articulate the equality of women and men as rational and moral individuals. Varina's life illuminates the ways in which a woman's intellect and her assertiveness could be suppressed and held suspect under some circumstances and released and encouraged under others. Her experience during the years of her husband's imprisonment demonstrates the ways in which women's ingenuity, determination, and talents were, and often continue to be, viewed as latent resources, to be restrained in times of stability and called upon in times of crisis and exigency. And Julia's life offers us an insight into the ways that public events can be experienced in purely personal terms, distorting them yet making them more manageable and comprehensible for those whose primary focus is narrow and whose grasp is not deep. Ironically, Julia empowered herself by reducing war and the great changes it brought from epic to intimate, for she could make an important difference in the life of the man who held victory or defeat in his hands during the Civil War.

The differences in the arcs of these three lives are made more striking by their commonalities. All three were born into slaveholding families but ended their lives in the free society of the Northeast. All married men who were or became major figures in the history of the era. All counted among their friends—and among their enemies—some of the most controversial figures of their day and many of the most brilliant and charismatic leaders of their times. Yet Angelina became a member of a marginalized counterculture, Varina became a symbol of a lost cause, and Julia enjoyed the laurels of victory.

Perhaps the most important commonality among these women of strikingly different temperaments and talents was the ideology that defined middle-class women in the nineteenth century. The conviction that men and women naturally occupied separate spheres, and the idealization of "true womanhood" that this notion fostered, thus emerges as an important leitmotif of this book. Although it was rarely fully realized in any woman's life and was often honored in the breach, this nineteenth-century under-standing of women's place in marriage and society set the terms against which Angelina, Varina, and Julia struggled or to which they succumbed. True womanhood was an ideal, of course, and the demands it made upon women were matched by the demands of true manhood on men. Many historians today argue that the notion of separate spheres and distinc-tive male and female characters and roles blurs as much as it illuminates about the actual lives of nineteenth-century men and women. Yet separate spheres remained the way many of both sexes defined their roles, and true womanhood was the ideal that the century's feminists hoped to dethrone. We can hear this ideology of separate and complementary domains in the eulogy for Ulysses S. Grant that speaks of a good marriage as "husband and wife, the happy supplement of each other . . . He the Doric column to sus-tain; she the Corinthian column to beautify." And we can hear it in the rep-rimands and demands made by Jefferson Davis as he sought to mold his young wife into the "true woman" he so desired. We can hear it as well in the warnings given to Theodore Weld that his activist wife was unfit for marriage and motherhood. The power of this ideology in all three lives can be measured by the fact that on her deathbed, Varina warned her daughter not to show grief by wearing black, for this might disturb her husband's peace of mind.

If all around them radical thinkers and activists were chipping away at the pedestal upon which the true woman was thought to stand, the ideal of true womanhood deeply shaped these three women's inner worlds of thought and desire. In this they were far from alone. Even Charlotte Perkins Gilman, who helped create the feminist theory that challenged sep-arate spheres, could not easily escape the perceptions of marriage and women's destinies ingrained during her childhood. When she married the first time, she knelt together with her husband, wreaths of roses on her head and his, and vowed her loyalty and devotion to him. But Charlotte Perkins Gilman scandalized family and friends by divorcing her husband and leaving her child in his care. Her unceasing efforts over the rest of her lifetime to reform marriage, parenting, and the home itself are more impressive because of her struggle to shed ideas she once accepted as nat-ural and to avoid a destiny she had been taught was ordained.

In their old age, Angelina, Varina, and Julia had their own moments of self-assertion. Widowhood opened up the floodgates for Varina as she moved to New York City, became a newspaper writer, and created a salon where artists, playwrights, actors, and poets gathered. Even Julia tried on the mantle of independence once her husband died, pressing publishers to accept her memoirs and pay her handsomely for them. And in the radical act of acknowledging her brother's mulatto sons, the aging Angelina reasserted her unique vision of racial equality. These may seem small gestures compared to the feminist demands for full equality that began before the Civil War and were rejuvenated after it, but they are gestures worth remembering. They show us how steep the path to equality truly was.

In the end, these three women were captives of one of their era's most demanding ideologies even as it began to lose its potency. Varina Howell Davis lived to see modern America take shape, but her soul—like the souls of Angelina Grimké Weld and Julia Dent Grant—lingered in an earlier century. Perhaps we cannot understand our own modern sensibilities until we understand theirs.

Acknowledgments

AS MOST AUTHORS WILL TELL YOU, we look forward to writing the acknowledgments to our books. This is our chance to thank all those librarians and archivists who helped us find the materials we needed; all those friends who read the manuscript through its many drafts and provided suggestions for improvement with tact and wisdom; our editors, who endured all our excuses for late manuscripts and last-minute changes; and all the members of our family who suffered through bad moods and triumphant whoops of delight from the crazy author hunched over the computer until all hours of the night. Without the assistance of these people, bookshelves would be empty and authors scarce as hen's teeth.

I owe thanks to the scholars who paved the way for this project by editing and annotating many of the papers of Angelina Grimké Weld, Varina Howell Davis, and Julia Dent Grant. To Gilbert H. Barnes and Dwight L. Dumond and to Larry Ceplair, my thanks for bringing Angelina's diary, several of the Grimké and Weld speeches, and much of their correspondence into print. Similarly, Hudson Strode's publication of Varina Howell Davis and Jefferson Davis's personal correspondence started me on the process of understanding this extraordinary woman and her husband. John Y. Simon's edition of the papers of Ulysses S. Grant introduced me to the General and Julia Dent Grant. In addition, the archivists at the Museum of the Confederacy in Richmond provided Varina Davis materials held by its library; Eric Robertson of the New-York Historical Society located microfilms of nineteenth-century newspapers I needed; Kathryn Boone of the Missouri Historical Society found and sent additional Julia Grant materials to me; the University of Alabama archivists shared their rich collection of Davis family records; and Karen Needles patiently reproduced the Julia Dent Grant materials I requested at the Library of Congress. My student David Golland did the initial spade work on a bibliography and, from my home state of Alabama, Scott Kirkland served as researcher at the University in Tuscaloosa. I am equally indebted to Varina and Julia, who chose to write their own memoirs, and to John Y. Simon for publishing Julia's so many years after she penned them. And I owe a deep debt of gratitude to historians including Gerda Lerner, Joan Cashin, Katherine Du Pre Lumpkin, Carol Bleser, Ishbel Ross, and Catherine Birney, all of whom labored before me to reconstruct the lives of Angelina, Varina, and Julia. I only regret that Joan Cashin's splendid scholarly biography of Varina Davis appeared too late for me to draw upon it.

Throughout the three years I have worked on this book, I have been blessed with remarkably generous friends and colleagues. As always, my thanks to the fine group of scholars who gather each month around my dining room table to continue a custom begun when they were my students in the CUNY graduate program. Here, over brunch, we critique one another's works in progress, providing constructive criticism, praise, and moments of welcome humor. These "diss salon" members—Angelo Angelis, Philip Papas, Cindy Lobel, Laura Chmielewski, Mark Sgambettera, Kate Halgren, and Iris Towers—are responsible for much that is good in this book and none that is bad.

My colleague in the Baruch History Department, Julie Des Jardins, took precious time away from her own manuscript on women scientists and from her two young children to help me frame the story of Julia Dent Grant; as a reward, I got to read her brilliant accounts of Madame Curie and Dian Fossey. Roberta McCutcheon listened to me rethink—endlessly, it must have seemed—many of the arguments that appear here in print. Landa Freeman, Julie Des Jardins, and my best critic, Dan Green, read the chapters as they tumbled from my computer. At critical moments, Mary Beth Norton, Mary-Jo Kline, Bert Hansen, Cindy Lobel, and Christopher Miller provided information on much-needed secondary source materials. I owe a debt of gratitude to President Kathleen Waldron of Baruch College and my former dean, Myrna Chase, who supported this project enthusiastically.

When I was all done, Cecelia Hartsell came to my rescue and, using a computer literacy I will never acquire, magically transformed footnotes into endnotes and alphabetized the bibliography. More important, Cecelia's calm and optimistic manner kept me sane during that last great push toward the completion of the project.

I greatly appreciate the privilege of working with Jane Garrett, my editor at Knopf. Her talents are matched only by her patience with authors like myself. I also thank Leslie Levine and my copy editor, Sue Warga.

While it is most unorthodox, I would also like to thank several talented people whom I have never met and who I am certain do not know of me: Jackson Browne, Gregg Allman, Mark Knopfler, Lyle Lovett, Dwight Yoakam, Tom Petty, Bonnie Raitt, and J. D. Souther, storytellers in their own right. My thanks for your music. It restored me to my own moment in time in the hours when I was lost in the nineteenth century.

Last but never least, I thank Hannah and Matthew, who came for dinner and called their mom regularly like the excellent children they are and who declared themselves ready to open a bottle of champagne with me when the book was done.

CAROL BERKIN
New York City, 2008

Notes

Two "I THINK MUCH SUFFERING AWAITS ME":
Angelina Grimké's Journey to Reform

1. Three older biographies of Angelina Grimké exist: Gerda Lerner, *The Grimké Sisters from South Carolina: Pioneers for Women's Rights and Abolition* (New York and Oxford: Oxford University Press, 1998); Katherine Du Pre Lumpkin, *The Emancipation of Angelina Grimké* (Chapel Hill: University of North Carolina Press, 1974); and Catherine H. Birney, *The Grimké Sisters: Sarah and Angelina Grimké, The First American Women Advocates of Abolition and Woman's Rights* (New York: Haskell House, 1885).
2. Lumpkin, *Emancipation*, p. 8; Lerner, *Grimké Sisters from South Carolina*, p. 20.
3. Angelina Grimké, *Walking by Faith: The Diary of Angelina Grimké, 1828–1835*, ed. Charles Wilbanks (Columbia: University of South Carolina Press, 2003).
4. Ibid., pp. 8–9.
5. Ibid., pp. 2–3, 14–15.
6. Ibid., pp. 37–38, 43, 47–48.
7. Ibid., pp. 51–53.
8. Ibid., pp. 48–50, 56.
9. Ibid., pp. 51–53.
10. Ibid., pp. 64, 69.
11. Ibid., pp. 83, 86–89.
12. Ibid., pp. 111, 121.
13. Ibid., pp. 133–35.

Three "MAKE ME INSTRUMENTAL IN THE GREAT WORK OF
EMANCIPATION": *Angelina Grimké's Letter to* The Liberator

1. Julie Roy Jeffrey, *The Great Silent Army of Abolitionism: Ordinary Women in the Antislavery Movement* (Chapel Hill and London: University of North Carolina Press, 1998), p. 43. For the history of Quakers in America, see Thomas D. Hamm, *The Quakers in America* (New York: Columbia University Press, 2003).
2. For Israel Morris's courtship of Sarah Grimké, see Lerner, *Grimké Sisters from South Carolina*, chapter 5.
3. Entries on Edward Beetle's courtship of Angelina Grimké, Grimké, *Walking by Faith*,

pp. 181–201; see also Lerner, *Grimké Sisters from South Carolina*, pp. 73–75; Lumpkin, *Emancipation*, pp. 63–69.

4. Grimké, *Walking by Faith*, p. 183.
5. Ibid., pp. 183–84.
6. Ibid., pp. 188, 196–97.
7. Ibid., p. 201.
8. Ibid., pp. 203–4, 205–7.
9. Ibid., pp. 191–92.
10. "To the Public," January 1, 1831, *The Liberator*, in William Lloyd Garrison and William E. Cain, *William Lloyd Garrison and the Fight Against Slavery: Selections from* The Liberator (New York: Bedford/St. Martin's, 1994), pp. 70–72; see also Henry Mayer, *All on Fire: William Lloyd Garrison and the Abolition of Slavery* (New York: W. W. Norton, 2008), and James Brewer Stewart, *Holy Warriors: The Abolitionists and American Slavery* (New York: Hill and Wang, 1997); Jeffrey, *Silent Army*, pp. 14–52.
11. Lumpkin, *Emancipation*, p. 72; Lerner, *Grimké Sisters from South Carolina*, pp. 92, 96–98; see also Philip S. Foner and Josephine F. Pacheco, *Three Who Dared: Prudence Crandall, Margaret Douglass, and Mytilla Minor* (New York: Greenwood Press, 1984).
12. See Angelina's defense and praise of Thompson in her "Appeal to the Christian Women of the South," in *The Public Years of Sarah and Angelina Grimké: Selected Writings, 1835–1839*, ed. Larry Ceplair (New York: Columbia University Press, 1989), pp. 76–77.
13. Garrison and Cain, *The Liberator*, p. 150; Ceplair, *The Public Years*, pp. 25–27.
14. William Lloyd Garrison's introduction can be found in Ceplair, *The Public Years*, pp. 24–25.

Four "THIS IS ALL LIKE A DREAM NOW; BUT I CAN'T UNDREAM IT": *Angelina Becomes an Abolitionist*

1. Grimké, *Walking by Faith*, pp. 27–28.
2. Ceplair, *The Public Years*, pp. 28–29; Grimké, *Walking by Faith*, pp. 211–13.
3. Grimké, *Walking by Faith*, pp. 211–13.
4. Jeffrey, *Silent Army*, pp. 50–51; Lerner, *Grimké Sisters from South Carolina*, pp. 97–98.
5. Lerner, *Grimké Sisters from South Carolina*, p. 101.
6. Ceplair, *The Public Years*, pp. 33–34.
7. Ibid.
8. Ibid., pp. 36–82.
9. Ceplair, *The Public Years*, pp. 81–82; Sarah Grimké to Theodore Weld, March 10, 1837, in *Letters of Theodore Dwight Weld, Angelina Grimké Weld, and Sarah Grimké, 1822–1844*, ed. Gilbert H. Barnes and Dwight L. Dumond, vol. 1 (New York: Da Capo Press, 1970), p. 373.
10. On the New York women's antislavery societies, see Amy Swerdlow, "Abolition's Conservative Sisters: The Ladies' New York City Anti-Slavery Societies, 1834–1840," in Jean Fagan Yellin and John C. Van Horne, eds., *The Abolitionist Sisterhood: Women's Political Culture in Antebellum America* (Ithaca and New York: Cornell University Press, 1994); Lerner, *Grimké Sisters from South Carolina*, p. 109.

Five "I LAID MY DIFFICULTY AT THE FEET OF JESUS":
The Burden of Being a Woman

1. Yellin and Van Horne, *The Abolitionist Sisterhood*, pp. 1–19; Jeffrey, *Silent Army*, pp. 43–44, 53–54.
2. Lerner, *Grimké Sisters from South Carolina*, pp. 72–73; Phillip Lapsansky, "Graphic Discord: Abolitionists and Anti-Abolitionist Images," in Yellin and Van Horne, *The Abolitionist Sisterhood*, pp. 201–30; for a biography of Fanny Wright, see Cecelia Morris, *Fanny Wright: Rebel in America* (Urbana and Chicago: University of Illinois Press, 1992).
3. For a brief biography of Theodore Weld, see Barnes and Dumond's introduction to Weld's *Letters*, vol. 1.
4. Ceplair, *The Public Years*, pp. 83–84.
5. Ibid., pp. 115–16, 87–90.
6. Ibid., pp. 87–90.
7. Ibid., pp. 116–17.
8. Ibid., pp. 115–16.
9. Ibid., pp. 126–27.
10. Ibid., pp. 119–25.
11. Barnes and Dumond, *Letters*, vol. 1, pp. 364–65.
12. Ceplair, *The Public Years*, pp. 133–34; Barnes and Dumond, *Letters*, vol. 1, p. 388.
13. Ceplair, *The Public Years*, pp. 85–87; *An Appeal to the Women of the Nominally Free States Issued by an Anti-Slavery Convention of American Women* (Boston: Isaac Knapp, 1838), pp. 58–64; "Proceedings of the Anti-Slavery Convention of American Women Held in the City of New York, May 9th, 10th, 11th and 12th" (New York: William S. Dorr, 1837); Dorothy Sterling, *Turning the World Upside Down: The Anti-Slavery Convention of American Women Held in NYC, May 9–12, 1837* (New York: Feminist Press, 1993).
14. Grimké, *Appeal*, p. 58–63.
15. Barnes and Dumond, *Letters*, vol. 1, pp. 270–74.
16. Ibid., pp. 391–92.
17. Ibid., pp. 395–97.
18. Ceplair, *The Public Years*, pp. 141–43.
19. Ceplair, *The Public Years*, pp. 144–46; Barnes and Dumond, *Letters*, vol. 1, pp. 407–10.
20. Barnes and Dumond, *Letters*, vol. 1, pp. 407–10; Ceplair, *The Public Years*, pp. 144–46.
21. Catherine Beecher, *An Essay on Slavery and Abolition with Deference to the Duty of American Females* (Philadelphia: Henry Perkins, 1837).
22. Ceplair, *The Public Years*, pp. 144–46, 146–204. (The original version, published in *The Liberator* and *The Emancipator*, was revised by Grimké, with Weld's help, for publication in book form.)

Six "YOU HAVE HAD MY WHOLE HEART":
A Season of Surprises

1. Lumpkin, *Emancipation*, pp. 111–12.
2. Pastoral Letter of the General Association of Massachusetts, June 28, 1837, Section III,

in Ronald F. Reid, *American Rhetorical Discourse* (Prospect Heights, Ill.: Waveland Press, 1995), pp. 363–67.

3. Chapman's poem can be found in Winston E. Langley and Vivian C. Fox, eds., *Women's Rights in the United States: A Documentary History* (Westport, Conn.: Praeger, 1994), pp. 70–71; see also John Greenleaf Whittier's poem "The Pastoral Letter," in *The Complete Poetical Works of John Greenleaf Whittier*, ed. J. G. Whittier (Whitefish, Mont.: Kessinger Publishing, 2003), p. 46; Ceplair, *The Public Years*, p. 272; Barnes and Dumond, *Letters*, vol. 1, pp. 467–71; Ceplair, *The Public Years*, p. 272.

4. Ceplair, *The Public Years*, p. 272.

5. *The Liberator*, July 21, 1837; Barnes and Dumond, *Letters*, vol. 1, pp. 419–23.

6. Ceplair, *The Public Years*, pp. 273–75, 275–76.

7. Barnes and Dumond, *Letters*, vol. 1, pp. 423–24.

8. Ibid., pp. 411–14.

9. Ibid., pp. 414–19.

10. Ibid., pp. 425–27.

11. Ibid., pp. 427–32.

12. Ibid., pp. 432–36.

13. Ibid., p. 441, 436–41.

14. Ibid., pp. 441–42, 442–45.

15. Ceplair, *The Public Years*, p. 289; Barnes and Dumond, *Letters*, vol. 1, pp. 446–52.

16. Barnes and Dumond, *Letters*, vol. 1, pp. 452–59.

17. Ibid., pp. 459–67.

18. Ibid., pp. 473–75.

19. Ibid., pp. 480–85, 475–78.

20. Ibid., pp. 478–80, 484–88.

21. Ibid., pp. 497–500, 504–10, 520–25.

22. Gilbert H. Barnes and Dwight L. Dumond, eds., *Letters of Theodore Dwight Weld, Angelina Grimké Weld, and Sarah Grimké*, vol. 2 (New York: Da Capo Press, 1970), pp. 520–25.

23. Ibid., pp. 531–36.

24. Ibid., pp. 536–539.

25. Ibid., pp. 553–54, 554–58, 559–63, 575–85, 585–88, 592–603.

26. Ibid., pp. 553–54; for an excellent discussion of abolitionist marriages, see Chris Dixon, *Perfecting the Family: Antislavery Marriages in Nineteenth-Century America* (Amherst: University of Massachusetts Press, 1997), and Robert K. Nelson, "The Forgetfulness of Sex: Devotion and Desire in the Courtship Letters of Angelina Grimké and Theodore Dwight Weld," *Journal of Social History* 37, no. 3 (2004): 663–79.

27. Barnes and Dumond, *Letters*, vol. 2, pp. 585–88.

28. Ibid., pp. 559–63.

29. Ibid., pp. 592–603.

Seven "WE ABOLITION WOMEN ARE TURNING THE WORLD UPSIDE DOWN": *Triumphs and Retirement*

1. Lori D. Ginzberg, *Women and the Work of Benevolence: Morality, Politics, and Class in the Nineteenth-Century United States* (New Haven and London: Yale University Press, 1990), pp. 93, 81; Barnes and Dumond, *Letters*, vol. 2, pp. 536–39.

2. Barnes and Dumond, *Letters*, vol. 2, pp. 553–54.

3. Lumpkin, *Emancipation,* p. 137.
4. Barnes and Dumond, *Letters,* vol. 2, pp. 564–67; Angelina E. Grimké, "Speech to a Committee of the Massachusetts House of Representatives, February 21, 1838," in *The Liberator,* March 2, 1838, p. 35, reprinted in Ceplair, *The Public Years,* pp. 310–12.
5. Barnes and Dumond, *Letters,* vol. 2, pp. 567–70; Jeffrey, *Silent Army,* p. 49.
6. Barnes and Dumond, *Letters,* vol. 2, pp. 567–70.
7. Ibid., pp. 572–75.
8. Lumpkin, *Emancipation,* pp. 139, 137.
9. Barnes and Dumond, *Letters,* vol. 2, pp. 590–92.
10. Ibid., pp. 592–603.
11. Lumpkin, *Emancipation,* p. 140; Lerner, *Grimké Sisters from South Carolina,* pp. 178, 180.
12. Barnes and Dumond, *Letters,* vol. 2, pp. 603–6.
13. Ibid., p. 539.
14. Lumpkin, *Emancipation,* p. 145.
15. Barnes and Dumond, *Letters,* vol. 2, pp. 633–42, 646–51.
16. Ibid., pp. 652–54, 654–56.
17. Ibid., pp. 633–42.
18. Ibid., pp. 678–79; Lerner, *Grimké Sisters from South Carolina,* pp. 178, 180.
19. Lumpkin, *Emancipation,* pp. 147–49; Barnes and Dumond, *Letters,* vol. 2, pp. 678–79.
20. Barnes and Dumond, *Letters,* vol. 2, pp. 617–18.
21. Ceplair, *The Public Years,* p. 318.
22. For accounts of the evening's riot, see Margaret Hope Bacon, "By Moral Force Alone: The Antislavery Women and Nonresistance," in Yellin and Horne, eds., *The Abolitionist Sisterhood,* pp. 275–97; Birney, *The Grimké Sisters,* pp. 237–41; Lerner, *Grimké Sisters from South Carolina,* pp. 183–87.

Eight "I CANNOT TELL THEE HOW I LOVE THIS PRIVATE LIFE":
Angelina and Domesticity

1. Barnes and Dumond, *Letters,* vol. 2, pp. 646–51.
2. Ibid., pp. 607–12.
3. Ibid., pp. 628–32, 633–42, 646–52, 652–54, 662–66, 669–73.
4. Ibid., pp. 628–32.
5. Ibid., pp. 663–66.
6. William Andrus Alcott, *The Young Housekeeper; or Thoughts on Food and Cookery* (1838).
7. See, for example, Charlotte Perkins Gilman, *The Home, Its Work and Influences* (Walnut Creek, Calif.: AltaMira Press, 2002). See also Carol Ruth Berkin, "Private Woman, Public Woman: The Contradictions of Charlotte Perkins Gilman," in Carol Berkin and Mary Beth Norton, eds., *Women of America: A History* (Boston: Houghton Mifflin, 1979), 151–73.
8. Lumpkin, *Emancipation,* p. 168.
9. Barnes and Dumond, *Letters,* vol. 2, pp. 736–37, 724–25, 744–48.
10. Ibid., pp. 753–55.
11. *American Slavery as It Is: Testimony of a Thousand Witnesses* (New York: American Anti-Slavery Society, 1839); Birney, *The Grimké Sisters,* p. 258.
12. Birney, *The Grimké Sisters,* pp. 207–9; Barnes and Dumond, *Letters,* vol. 2, pp. 840–41,

841n; Lerner, *Grimké Sisters from South Carolina,* pp. 190–91; Birney, *The Grimké Sisters,* pp. 260–61. On Graham and the Graham diet, see Stephen Nissenbaum, *Sex, Diet, and Debility in Jacksonian America: Sylvester Graham and Health Reform* (Westport, Conn.: Greenwood Press, 1980), and Cindy R. Lobel, "Consuming Classes: Changing Food Consumption Patterns in New York City, 1790–1860," Ph.D. diss., CUNY Graduate Center, 2003, chapter 5.

13. Birney, *The Grimké Sisters,* p. 246.
14. Lerner, *Grimké Sisters from South Carolina,* pp. 210–11.
15. Lumpkin, *Emancipation,* pp. 167–68; Lerner, *Grimké Sisters from South Carolina,* p. 211.
16. Barnes and Dumond, *Letters,* vol. 2, pp. 807–12.
17. On the schism in the antislavery movement, see Mayer, *All on Fire;* Jeffrey, *Silent Army,* pp. 96–101; Bertram Wyatt-Brown, "William Lloyd Garrison and Antislavery Unity: A Reappraisal," in John McKivigan, ed., *Abolitionism and American Reform* (New York and London: Garland, 1999), pp. 381–400; James B. Stewart, "The Aims and Impact of Garrisonian Abolition, 1840–1860," in McKivigan, ed., *Abolitionism,* pp. 323–36.
18. Barnes and Dumond, *Letters,* vol. 2, pp. 857–60, 836.
19. Ibid., pp. 845–49.
20. Lerner, *Grimké Sisters from South Carolina,* p. 216.
21. Theodore Dwight Weld, *In Memory: Angelina Grimké Weld* (Boston: G. H. Ellis, 1880); Birney, *The Grimké Sisters,* pp. 241, 261; Lerner, *Grimké Sisters from South Carolina,* pp. 216–17.
22. Barnes and Dumond, *Letters,* vol. 2, pp. 865–66, 868–69, 832–33, 834–35, 876–77.
23. Lumpkin, *Emancipation,* p. 182.

Nine "INNUMERABLE, HORRIBLE, UNSPEAKABLE, EARTHY, SENSUAL AND DEVILISH DISTORTIONS OF MARRIED LIFE": *The Crisis Years at Home*

1. See, for example, Barnes and Dumond, *Letters,* vol. 2, pp. 882–84, 884–87, 888–91, 891–94.
2. Ibid., pp. 884–87, 882–84.
3. William Lloyd Garrison also defended Miller, in *The Liberator.* See "The Second Advent, No. 1," *The Liberator,* February 10, 1843; for a history of Miller and his millennial movement, see Francis D. Nichol, *Midnight Cry: A Defense of the Character and Conduct of William Miller and the Millerites, Who Mistakenly Believed that the Second Coming of Christ Would Take Place* (Brushton, N.Y.: TEACH Services, 1994).
4. Barnes and Dumond, *Letters,* vol. 2, pp. 888–90, 891–94.
5. Ibid., pp. 955–57.
6. Ibid., pp. 995–97, 961–63.
7. Ibid., pp. 939–41.
8. Ibid., pp. 993–95, 973–75; Lumpkin, *Emancipation,* pp. 200–1.
9. Birney, *The Grimké Sisters,* p. 265; Lerner, *Grimké Sisters from South Carolina,* pp. 232, 234–35, 236.
10. Lumpkin, *Emancipation,* p. 211.
11. Birney, *The Grimké Sisters,* pp. 272–73, 274; Lerner, *Grimké Sisters from South Carolina,* pp. 236–38, 244.
12. For an excellent discussion of events leading to this crisis and its psychological impact, see Lumpkin, *Emancipation,* pp. 155–203.

13. Lerner, *Grimké Sisters from South Carolina*, p. 239; Lumpkin, *Emancipation*, p. 202.
14. Barnes and Dumond, *Letters*, vol. 2, pp. 939–40; Lerner, *Grimké Sisters from South Carolina*, p. 240.

Ten "THIS IS NOT AN *IN MEMORIAM,* IT IS A WAR-CRY":
The Last Years of Angelina Grimké

1. Lerner, *Grimké Sisters from South Carolina*, p. 247.
2. David Walker's *Appeal, in Four Articles Together with a Preamble to the Coloured Citizens of the World, but in Particular, and Very Expressly, to Those of the United States of America* (New York: Hill and Wang, 1995); Henry Highland Garnet's "Call to Rebellion" (1843), in Deidre Mullane, ed., *Crossing the Danger Water: Three Hundred Years of African-American Writing* (New York: Doubleday, 1993). For the best recent biography of John Brown, see David Reynolds, *John Brown, Abolitionist: The Man Who Killed Slavery, Sparked the Civil War, and Seeded Civil Rights* (New York: Vintage, 2006).
3. See Paul Finkelman, *Dred Scott v. Sandford: A Brief History with Documents* (New York: Bedford/St. Martin's, 1997).
4. John Brown, "Address to the Virginia Court at Charles Town, Virginia," November 2, 1859, in Birney, *The Grimké Sisters.*
5. Lerner, *Grimké Sisters from South Carolina*, p. 257; Birney, *The Grimké Sisters*, pp. 286–87.
6. Lerner, *Grimké Sisters from South Carolina*, pp. 261–62.
7. Angelina Grimké Weld, "Address at the Women's National Loyal League," May 14, 1863, in Elizabeth C. Stanton, Susan B. Anthony, and Matilda J. Gage, *History of Woman Suffrage*, vol. 2 (New York: Fowler & Wells, 1881–1922), pp. 60–61; for a discussion of the League, see Wendy Hamand Venet, *Neither Ballots nor Bullets: Women Abolitionists and the Civil War* (Charlottesville and London: University Press of Virginia, 1991), pp. 110–22.
8. Lerner, *Grimké Sisters from South Carolina*, pp. 258–61.
9. Stanton et al., *History of Woman Suffrage*, vol. 2, p. 406; Lerner, *Grimké Sisters from South Carolina*, p. 266.
10. For full accounts of the relationship between Angelina Grimké Weld and her brother's sons, see Birney, *The Grimké Sisters*, pp. 289–94; Lerner, *Grimké Sisters from South Carolina*, pp. 267–69; Lumpkin, *Emancipation*, pp. 220–27.
11. Birney, *The Grimké Sisters*, pp. 295–97.
12. Birney, *The Grimké Sisters*, p. 308; Stephen Howard Browne, *Angelina Grimké: Rhetoric, Identity and the Radical Imagination* (East Lansing: Michigan State University Press, 1999), p. 167; Birney, *The Grimké Sisters*, pp. 310–11.
13. Birney, *The Grimké Sisters*, pp. 316–18; Browne, *Angelina Grimké*, p. 170.
14. Birney, *The Grimké Sisters*, p. 319.

Eleven "THE HAPPY FIRESIDE": *The Deep South Before the Civil War*

1. Lieut. Col. John J. Craven, M.D., *The Prison Life of Jefferson Davis* as published in 1866 (Scituate, Mass.: DSI Digital Reproductions, 2001), 270.

Twelve FROM THE BRIARS TO THE HURRICANE:
Varina Banks Howell and Jefferson Davis

1. Ishbel Ross, *First Lady of the South: The Life of Mrs. Jefferson Davis* (New York: Harper and Brothers, 1958), pp. 13–17; Varina Davis, *Jefferson Davis: A Memoir by His Wife,* vol. 1 (Baltimore: Nautical and Aviation Publishing Company of America, 1990), pp. 51, 187–88.
2. Gerry Van Der Heuvel, *Crown of Thorns and Glory: Mary Todd Lincoln and Varina Howell Davis: The Two First Ladies of the Civil War* (New York: E. P. Dutton, 1988), p. 51; Bell Irvin Wiley, *Confederate Women* (New York: Barnes and Noble Press, 1994), pp. 83–84.
3. See Elizabeth Fox-Genovese, *Within the Plantation Household: Black and White Women of the Old South* (Chapel Hill: University of North Carolina Press, 1988).
4. Davis, *Davis,* vol. 1, p. 51.
5. Jefferson Davis to Sarah Knox Taylor, December 16, 1834, in *Jefferson Davis: Private Letters, 1823–1889,* ed. Hudson Strode (New York: Da Capo Press, 1995), pp. 10–12; Davis, *Davis,* vol. 1, pp. 95–96, 166–67; Wiley, *Confederate Women,* p. 84; Joan Cashin, "Varina Howell Davis," in G. J. Barker-Benfield and Catherine Clinton, eds., *Portraits of American Women from Settlement to the Present* (New York and Oxford: Oxford University Press, 1998), pp. 259–77.
6. Davis, *Davis,* vol. 1, p. 164.

Thirteen "THE DESIRE I HAVE TO BE WITH YOU EVERY DAY
AND ALL DAY": *The Courtship of Jefferson Davis and Varina Howell*

1. Davis, *Davis,* vol. 1, p. 193; Hudson Strode, *Jefferson Davis, American Patriot, 1808–1861* (New York: Harcourt, Brace and Company, 1955), pp. 125–29; Wiley, *Confederate Women,* pp. 85–86; Van Der Heuvel, *Crown,* p. 51.
2. Ross, *First Lady,* p. 8.
3. Van Der Heuvel, *Crown,* p. 52.
4. Jefferson Davis to Varina Howell, March 8, 1844, in Strode, *Private Letters,* pp. 18–20; Jefferson Davis to Varina Howell, March 15, 1844, in Strode, *Private Letters,* pp. 20–22.
5. Ross, *First Lady,* p. 20.
6. Jefferson Davis to Varina Howell, March 15, 1844, in Strode, *Private Letters,* pp. 20–22.
7. Jefferson Davis to Varina Howell, September 6, 1844, in Strode, *Private Letters,* pp. 23–24; Jefferson Davis to Varina Howell, June 22, 1844, in Strode, *Private Letters,* p. 22; Strode, *Jefferson Davis,* pp. 134–35.
8. Jefferson Davis to Varina Howell, November 22, 1844, in Strode, *Private Letters,* pp. 24–25.
9. Jefferson Davis to Varina Howell, December 11, 1844, in Strode, *Private Letters,* pp. 25–26; Van Der Heuvel, *Crown,* p. 53; Strode, *Jefferson Davis,* pp. 136–38.
10. Van Der Heuvel, *Crown,* p. 54; Strode, *Jefferson Davis,* pp. 137–38.

Fourteen "CALMER, DISCREETER, LOVELIER": *The Months at Brierfield*

1. Strode, *Jefferson Davis*, p. 138; Davis, *Davis*, vol. 1, pp. 200–2.
2. Jefferson Davis to Margaret Howell, April 25, 1845, in Strode, *Private Letters*, pp. 29–30.
3. Paul Starr, *The Social Transformation of American Medicine* (New York: Basic Books, 1984); John Duffy, *From Humors to Medical Science* (Urbana: University of Illinois Press, 1993).
4. Varina Howell Davis to Margaret Howell, n.d., 1845, Varina Howell Davis to William Howell, April 11, 1845, Jefferson Davis Papers, University of Alabama Library, Tuscaloosa.
5. James H. Cassedy, *Medicine in America: A Short History* (Baltimore: Johns Hopkins University Press, 1991); Charles E. Rosenberg, "Belief and Ritual in Antebellum Medical Therapeutics," in John Harley Warner and Janet A. Tighe, eds., *Major Problems in the History of American Medicine and Public Health* (Boston: Houghton Mifflin, 2001), pp. 108–13.
6. Varina Howell Davis to Margaret Howell, n.d., 1845, Jefferson Davis Papers, University of Alabama Library, Tuscaloosa.
7. Davis, *Davis*, vol. 1, p. 206.
8. Joseph David Howell to Margaret Howell, November 21, 1845, in Strode, *Private Letters*, pp. 33–34.
9. Davis, *Davis*, vol. 1, p. 209.

Fifteen "HOW GRAND AND *BLASÉ* THE PEOPLE ALL LOOKED":
The First Washington Experience

1. Davis, *Davis*, vol. 1, pp. 209, 216–19.
2. Ibid., vol. 1, p. 220; Strode, *Jefferson Davis*, pp. 145–46.
3. Davis, *Davis*, vol. 1, p. 235; Varina Davis to Margaret Howell, January 30, 1846, in Strode, *Private Letters*, pp. 35–36.
4. Varina Davis to Margaret Howell, January 30, 1846, in Strode, *Private Letters*, pp. 35–36.
5. Varina Davis to Margaret Howell, April 3, 1846, in Strode, *Private Letters*, pp. 37–38; Davis, *Davis*, vol. 1, pp. 265, 159, 257.
6. Davis, *Davis*, vol. 1, pp. 268–83.
7. Varina Davis to Margaret Howell, January 30, 1846, in Strode, *Private Letters*, pp. 35–36.
8. Davis, *Davis*, vol. 1, p. 235; Strode, *Jefferson Davis*, pp. 149–50.
9. Davis, *Davis*, vol. 1, p. 243; Van Der Heuvel, *Crown*, p. 61; Strode, *Jefferson Davis*, pp. 156–57.
10. Varina Davis to Margaret Howell, June 6, 1846, in Strode, *Private Letters*, pp. 38–39.

Sixteen "THE HEART AT LAST, IF IT IS WELL GOVERNED,
MAKES THE HEAVEN": *War, Injury, and Domestic Discord*

1. Jefferson Davis to Lucinda Davis Stamps, July 8, 1846, in Strode, *Private Letters*, p. 40; Varina Davis to Margaret Howell, June 6, 1846, in ibid., pp. 38–39.
2. Varina Davis to Margaret Howell, June 6, 1846, in Strode, *Private Letters*, pp. 38–39; Strode, *Jefferson Davis*, p. 132; Van Der Heuvel, *Crown*, pp. 60–61.

3. Varina Davis to Margaret Howell, June 6, 1846, in Strode, *Private Letters,* pp. 38–39; Jefferson Davis to Lucinda Davis Stamps, in ibid., p. 40.
4. Jefferson Davis to Varina Davis, July 29, 1846, in *The Papers of Jefferson Davis,* eds. James T. McIntosh, Lynda L. Crist, and Mary S. Dix, vol. 3 (Baton Rouge: Louisiana State University Press, 1981), pp. 13–14; Strode, *Jefferson Davis,* p. 132.
5. Davis, *Davis,* vol. 1, pp. 356–357; Strode, *Jefferson Davis,* pp. 172–74; Van Der Heuvel, *Crown,* pp. 61–62.
6. Jefferson Davis to Varina Davis, December 10, 1846, in *Papers of Jefferson Davis,* vol. 3, pp. 93–95.
7. Varina Davis to Margaret Howell, January 2–5, 1847, Jefferson Davis Papers, University of Alabama Library, Tuscaloosa.
8. Ibid.
9. Jefferson Davis to Varina Davis, May 27, 1847, in *Papers of Jefferson Davis,* vol. 3, p. 178; Strode, *Private Letters,* p. 47.
10. Davis, *Davis,* vol. 1, pp. 356–57; Varina Davis to Margaret Howell, summer 1847, in Strode, *Private Letters,* pp. 48–49; Ross, *First Lady,* pp. 46–47; Jefferson Davis to Varina Davis, January 3, 1848, quoted in William J. Cooper Jr., *Jefferson Davis, American* (New York: Vintage Books, 2001), pp. 171–72; Carol K. Bleser, "The Marriage of Varina Howell and Jefferson Davis: 'I Gave the Best and All My Life to a Girdled Tree,' " *Journal of Southern History,* 65, 1 (February 1999): 2–40.
11. Varina Davis to Margaret Howell, summer 1847, in Strode, *Private Letters,* pp. 48–49.

Seventeen "THE SOUTHERN RIGHTS CAUSE IS THE LOSING ONE NOW": *The Return to Washington, D.C.*

1. Varina Davis to Margaret Howell, [November] 17, 1847, Jefferson Davis Papers, University of Alabama, Tuscaloosa.
2. Varina Davis to Margaret Howell, November 12, 1847, Jefferson Davis Papers, University of Alabama, Tuscaloosa.
3. Jefferson Davis to Varina Davis, April 18, 1848, in *The Papers of Jefferson Davis,* vol. 3, pp. 301–3; Jefferson Davis to Varina Davis, January 3–4, 1848, quoted in Cooper, *Jefferson Davis, American,* 173–74.
4. Varina Davis to Jefferson Davis, January 24, 1849, in *The Papers of Jefferson Davis,* ed. Lynda L. Crist, Mary S. Dix, and Richard E. Beringer, vol. 4 (Baton Rouge: Louisiana State University Press, 1983), pp. 7–8.
5. Varina Davis to Jefferson Davis, January 25, 1849, in Strode, *Private Letters,* p. 58.
6. Ibid., p. 58.
7. See, for example, Varina Davis to Margaret Howell, April 3, 1846, in *The Papers of Jefferson Davis,* ed. James T. McIntosh, vol. 2 (Baton Rouge: Louisiana State University Press, 1974), pp. 533–35.
8. Varina Davis to Margaret Howell, December 27, 1849, Jefferson Davis Papers, University of Alabama Library, Tuscaloosa.
9. Varina Davis to Margaret Howell, December 13, 1847, Jefferson Davis Papers, University of Alabama Library, Tuscaloosa; Varina Davis to Margaret Howell, December 27, 1849–January 6, 1850, Jefferson Davis Papers, University of Alabama Library, Tuscaloosa.
10. Varina Davis to Margaret Howell, May 18–20, in Strode, *Private Letters,* pp. 61–62.

11. Davis, *Davis,* vol. 1, p. 314; Strode, *Jefferson Davis,* pp. 195–96, 230; Wiley, *Confederate Women,* 90.
12. Davis, *Davis,* vol. 1, pp. 419–20.
13. Ibid., pp. 479–80.
14. Strode, *Jefferson Davis,* p. 230.
15. See Eric Foner, *Free Soil, Free Labor, Free Men: The Ideology of the Republican Party Before the Civil War* (New York: Oxford University Press, 1995), and Jonathan H. Earle, *Jacksonian Antislavery and the Politics of Free Soil, 1824–1854* (Chapel Hill: University of North Carolina Press, 2004).
16. Davis, *Davis,* vol. 1, pp. 424–26.
17. For a full discussion of Henry Clay and the Compromise of 1850, see Robert V. Remini, *Henry Clay: Statesman for the Union* (New York: W. W. Norton, 1993).
18. Davis, *Davis,* vol. 1, pp. 459–62; Ross, *First Lady,* p. 61.
19. Ross, *First Lady,* p. 62; Varina Davis to Margaret Howell, April 1850, in Strode, *Private Letters,* p. 60.
20. Varina Davis to parents, July 10, 1850, in Strode, *Private Letters,* pp. 62–63.
21. Strode, *Jefferson Davis,* p. 235; Cooper, *Jefferson Davis, American,* p. 214; Varina Davis to parents, October 28, 1851, in Strode, *Private Letters,* pp. 63–64.
22. Strode, *Jefferson Davis,* pp. 235–36; Ross, *First Lady,* pp. 63–64.
23. Varina Davis to parents, October 28, 1851, in Strode, *Private Letters,* pp. 63–64.
24. Strode, *Jefferson Davis,* p. 238.
25. Varina Davis to Jefferson Davis, July 25 [1852], in Strode, *Private Letters,* pp. 291–92.
26. Cooper, *Jefferson Davis, American,* p. 242.

Eighteen "WE FELT BLOOD IN THE AIR":
Personal and Public Tragedies

1. Strode, *Jefferson Davis,* pp. 245–51, 255; Davis, *Davis,* vol. 1, pp. 477–78.
2. Strode, *Jefferson Davis,* p. 258; Ross, *First Lady,* p. 71.
3. Davis, *Davis,* vol. 1, pp. 555–56, 560.
4. Jefferson Davis Howell to Varina Davis, November 14, 1853, Jefferson Davis Papers, University of Alabama Library, Tuscaloosa.
5. For a vivid account of "Bleeding Kansas," see Thomas Goodrich, *War to the Knife: Bleeding Kansas, 1854–1861* (Mechanicsburg, Penn.: Stackpole Books, 1998). See also David M. Potter, *The Impending Crisis, 1848–1861* (New York: Harper and Row, 1976).
6. Varina Davis to Margaret Howell, June 29, 1854, Jefferson Davis Papers, University of Alabama Library, Tuscaloosa; Varina Davis to parents, July 1854, in Strode, *Private Letters,* pp. 78–79; Davis, *Davis,* vol. 1, p. 535.
7. Dr. Robert C. Wood to Mrs. William [Margaret] Howell, January 24, 1857, in Strode, *Private Letters,* p. 81; Varina Davis to Margaret Howell, January 31, 1857, in ibid., p.82; Davis, *Davis,* vol. 1, p. 571.
8. Varina Davis to Margaret Howell, February 10, 1857, Jefferson Davis Papers, University of Alabama Library, Tuscaloosa; Varina Davis to Margaret Howell, summer 1857, Jefferson Davis Papers, University of Alabama Library, Tuscaloosa.
9. Varina Davis to Margaret Howell, summer 1857, Jefferson Davis Papers, University of Alabama Library, Tuscaloosa.
10. Davis, *Davis,* vol. 1, p. 540.

11. Jefferson Davis to Varina Davis, July 20, 1857, in Strode, *Private Letters,* pp. 129–30.

12. Jefferson Davis provided financial support to the Howell family. See, for example, Varina Davis to Margaret Howell, October 1857, in Strode, *Private Letters,* p. 96; Davis, *Davis,* vol. 1, p. 223.

13. Varina Davis to parents, September 15, 1856, in Strode, *Private Letters,* pp. 80–81.

14. Davis, *Davis,* vol. 1, pp. 575–78.

15. Virginia Clay-Clopton, *A Belle of the Fifties: Memoirs of Mrs. Clay of Alabama,* ed. Leah Rawls Atkins, Joseph H. Harrison Jr., and Sara A. Hudson (Tuscaloosa and London: University of Alabama Press, 1999), pp. 114–28.

16. Davis, *Davis,* vol. 1, p. 587.

17. Varina Davis to Margaret Howell, September 15, 1858, in Strode, *Private Letters,* p. 90.

18. Cooper, *Jefferson Davis, American,* pp. 310–12.

19. Varina Davis to William Howell, November 14, 1858, Jefferson Davis Papers, University of Alabama Library, Tuscaloosa; Varina Davis to Margaret Howell, November 21, 1858, in Strode, *Private Letters,* pp. 100–101.

20. Cooper, *Jefferson Davis, American,* pp. 315–16.

Nineteen "everybody is scared": *John Brown,*
the Fire Eaters, Lincoln, and Secession

1. Varina Davis to Margaret Howell, March 1, 1859, in Strode, *Private Letters,* p. 102; Varina Davis to Jefferson Davis, April 17, 1859, in *The Papers of Jefferson Davis,* ed. Lynda L. Crist and Mary S. Dix, vol. 6 (Baton Rouge: Louisiana State University Press, 1989), pp. 243–45.

2. Varina Davis to Margaret Howell, April 25, 1859, in Strode, *Private Letters,* pp. 108–9.

3. Varina Davis to Jefferson Davis, July 2, 1859, in Strode, *Private Letters,* p. 111.

4. Davis, *Davis,* vol. 1, p. 645; David S. Reynolds, *John Brown, Abolitionist.*

5. Davis, *Davis,* vol. 1, p. 650.

6. Franklin Pierce to Jefferson Davis, January 6, 1860, in Strode, *Private Letters,* pp. 113–14.

7. Strode, *Jefferson Davis,* pp. 331, 356–58; Strode, *Private Letters,* pp. 116–19.

8. Varina Davis to Jefferson Davis, November 15, 1860, in Strode, *Private Letters,* pp. 114–15.

9. Strode, *Private Letters,* p. 120.

10. Davis, *Davis,* vol. 1, pp. 696–97.

11. Ibid., pp. 696–97.

12. Davis, *Davis,* vol. 2, p. 5.

Twenty "civil war has only horror for me":
Varina Becomes the First Lady of the Confederacy

1. Strode, *Private Letters,* p. 120; Davis, *Davis,* vol. 2, p. 12.

2. Strode, *Private Letters,* p. 119; Jefferson Davis to Varina Davis, February 20, 1862, in ibid., p. 123; Strode, *Jefferson Davis,* p. 408.

3. Van Der Heuvel, *Crown,* p. 151.

4. See James M. McPherson, *Battle Cry of Freedom: The Civil War Era* (New York: Oxford University Press, 2003), and David H. Donald and Richard Nelson Current, *Why the North Won the Civil War* (Baton Rouge: Louisiana State University Press, 1960).

5. Strode, *Private Letters,* p. 121.

6. Davis, *Davis,* vol. 2, pp. 35–36.

7. Abraham Lincoln, *Selected Speeches and Writings* (New York: Vintage, 1992), pp. 284–92.

8. Davis, *Davis,* vol. 2, pp. 161–63; Varina Davis to Margaret Howell, June 1861, in Strode, *Private Letters,* pp. 123–24.

9. Davis, *Davis,* vol. 2, pp. 848–81.

10. Van Der Heuvel, *Crown,* p. 153; Ross, *First Lady,* 142; Davis, *Davis,* vol. 2, pp 161–63.

11. Wiley, *Confederate Women,* p. 97.

12. Mary Boykin Miller Chesnut, *Mary Chesnut's Civil War,* ed. C. Vann Woodward (New Haven and London: Yale University Press, 1981), p. 746.

13. Davis, *Davis,* vol. 2, pp. 202–3.

14. Chesnut, *Chesnut's Civil War,* pp. 482–83; Davis, *Davis,* vol. 2, pp. 848–81.

15. Varina Davis to Margaret Howell, June 1861, in Strode, *Private Letters,* pp. 123–24.

Twenty-one "THE PEOPLE OF OUR COUNTRY ROSE IN THEIR MIGHT": *From First Lady to Refugee*

1. Davis, *Davis,* vol. 2, p. 183.

2. Andrew DeVilbiss to Mary DeVilbiss, 1862, in Andrew Carroll, *Behind the Lines: Powerful and Revealing American and Foreign War Letters—and One Man's Search to Find Them* (New York: Scribner's, 2005), p. 123. On Shiloh, see Larry J. Daniel, *Shiloh: The Battle That Changed the Civil War* (New York: Simon and Schuster, 1998), and James L. McDonough, *Shiloh: In Hell Before Night* (Knoxville: University of Tennessee Press, 1977).

3. See Kevin Dougherty and J. Michael Moore, *The Peninsular Campaign of 1862: A Military Analysis* (Jackson: University Press of Mississippi, 2005).

4. Davis, *Davis,* vol. 2, pp. 268–69.

5. Ibid., p. 267; Van Der Heuvel, *Crown,* p. 155.

6. Van Der Heuvel, *Crown,* pp. 154–55; Davis, *Davis,* vol. 2, pp. 311–12; Cooper, *Jefferson Davis, American,* pp. 389–90.

7. Davis, *Davis,* vol. 2, pp. 321–22; Van Der Heuvel, *Crown,* p. 156.

8. Davis, *Davis,* vol. 2, pp. 208, 210, 323–25.

9. Ibid., pp. 209–10.

10. Davis, *Davis,* vol. 2, pp. 218–19; Chesnut, *Chesnut's Civil War,* p. 568; Van Der Heuvel, *Crown,* p. 167.

11. Van Der Heuvel, *Crown,* p. 159.

12. Chesnut, *Chesnut's Civil War,* p. 434.

13. Davis, *Davis,* vol. 2, pp. 298–99.

14. Ibid., pp. 495–96.

15. Ibid., p. 375.

16. *New York Herald,* April 2, 1863; *Richmond Examiner,* April 7–11, 1863.

17. Jefferson Davis to Margaret Howell, March 19, 1863, Jefferson Davis Papers, University of Alabama Library, Tuscaloosa; Van Der Heuvel, *Crown,* p. 166.

18. Varina Davis to Jefferson Davis Howell, March 4, 1864, in Strode, *Private Letters,* pp. 135–37.

19. Davis, *Davis,* vol. 2, pp. 496–97; Chesnut, *Chesnut's Civil War,* pp. 601–2.

20. Varina Davis to Mrs. Richard Griffith, May 8, 1864, in Strode, *Private Letters,* pp. 137–38; Ross, *First Lady,* 199–200.

21. Davis, *Davis*, vol. 2, pp. 529–36, 571, 575–76.
22. Ross, *First Lady*, pp. 189–90.
23. Davis, *Davis*, vol. 2, p. 575.
24. Ibid., p. 577; Jefferson Davis to General Gorgas, March 29, 1865, in Strode, *Private Letters*, p. 143.
25. Varina Davis to Jefferson Davis, April 7, 1865, in Strode, *Private Letters*, pp. 150–51.
26. Varina Davis to Jefferson Davis, April 13, 1865, in Strode, *Private Letters*, p. 152; Davis, *Davis*, vol. 2, pp. 578, 610–12.
27. Varina Davis to Jefferson Davis, April 19, 1865, in Strode, *Private Letters*, p. 153.
28. Davis, *Davis*, vol. 2, pp. 614–15.
29. Jefferson Davis to Varina Davis, April 23, 1865, in Strode, *Private Letters*, pp. 155–57; Varina Davis to Jefferson Davis, April 28, 1865, in ibid., pp. 158–59.
30. For Jeff Davis's route after leaving Richmond, see Cooper, *Jefferson Davis, American*, pp. 562–75; Strode, *Private Letters*, pp. 165–66; Davis, *Davis*, vol. 2, pp. 620–46. On the controversy of Jefferson Davis's clothing when captured, see Davis, *Davis*, vol. 2, pp. 640–41; Ross, *First Lady*, p. 414; Varina Davis to Francis P. Blair, June 6, 1865, Jefferson Davis Collection, Eleanor S. Brockenbrough Library, Museum of the Confederacy, Richmond, Virginia.
31. Cooper, *Jefferson Davis, American*, p. 577.
32. Davis, *Davis*, vol. 2, p. 648.
33. Ibid., p. 649; Clay-Clopton, *A Belle of the Fifties*, p. 266.

Twenty-two "I NEVER REPORT UNFIT FOR DUTY":
Varina Begins Her Campaigns for Freedom

1. Davis, *Davis*, vol. 2, pp. 696–98; Cooper, *Jefferson Davis, American*, pp. 576–84.
2. Cooper, *Jefferson Davis, American*, pp. 584–85; Van Der Heuvel, *Crown*, pp. 224, 226.
3. Varina Davis to Mary Boykin Chesnut, September 20, 1865, in Ross, *First Lady*, p. 270.
4. Ross, *First Lady*, pp. 261–66; Van Der Heuvel, *Crown*, pp. 226–29.
5. Ross, *First Lady*, pp. 262–63.
6. Varina Davis to the Secretary of State, Mr. Seward, July 10, 1865, Brockenbrough Library; Ross, *First Lady*, p. 264.
7. Mrs. Jefferson Davis to Mrs. Howell Cobb, September 9, 1865, in *The Correspondence of Robert Toombs, Alexander H. Stephens and Howell Cobb*, ed. U. B. Phillips (New York: Da Capo Press, 1970), pp. 667–68; Ross, *First Lady*, p. 268.
8. Varina Davis to J. J. Craven, June 1, 1865, in Craven, *Prison Life*, pp. 88–89.
9. Varina Davis to J. J. Craven, July 2, 1865, in ibid., pp. 169–71.
10. Varina Davis to J. J. Craven, October 10, 1865, in ibid., pp. 331–48.
11. Varina Davis to Jefferson Davis, September 14, 1865, in Strode, *Private Letters*, pp. 173–75.
12. Jefferson Davis to Varina Davis, November 21, 1865, in Strode, *Private Letters*, pp. 206–7; Jefferson Davis to Varina Davis, September 26, 1865, in ibid., pp. 177–79; Strode, *Jefferson Davis*, p. 588.
13. Varina Davis to Jefferson Davis, November 13, 1865, in Strode, *Private Letters*, pp. 200–2.
14. Varina Davis to Jefferson Davis, December 14, 1865, in Strode, *Private Letters*, pp. 215–16; Varina Davis to Armistead Burt, October 20, 1865, Rare Books and Special Collections Library, Duke University, Durham; Varina Davis to Jefferson Davis, December 25, 1865, in Strode, *Private Letters*, pp. 217–19.

15. Varina Davis to Jefferson Davis, February 2, 1866, in Strode, *Private Letters,* pp. 227–29; Varina Davis to Jefferson Davis, March 18, 1866, in ibid., pp. 240–41; Varina Davis to Jefferson Davis, n.d., 1866, Jefferson Davis Papers, University of Alabama Library, Tuscaloosa; Van Der Heuvel, *Crown,* pp. 232–33.

16. Van Der Heuvel, *Crown,* pp. 232–33.

Twenty-three "I SAW MR. DAVIS'S SHRUNKEN FORM AND
GLASSY EYES": *The Reunion at Fortress Monroe*

1. Davis, *Davis,* vol. 2, pp. 758–59.
2. Ibid., p. 762.
3. Ibid., p. 765.
4. Ibid., p. 768.
5. Ibid., pp. 768–69.
6. Ibid., pp. 769–71.
7. Varina Davis to Horace Greeley, September 2, 1866, in Strode, *Private Letters,* pp. 251–52.
8. Varina Davis to Margaret Howell, October 18, 1866, in ibid., p. 252.
9. Davis, *Davis,* vol. 2, p. 775.
10. Varina Davis to William Preston Johnston, September 27, 1866, in Marvin Shaw, "Mrs. Jefferson Davis at Fortress Monroe, Virginia," *Notes and Documents, Journal of Southern History* 16, no. 1 (February 1950): 73–76.

Twenty-four "THE BUSINESS IS FINISHED:" *Jefferson Davis Goes Free*

1. For Varina Davis's account of the entire proceedings leading to Jefferson Davis's parole, see Davis, *Davis,* vol. 2, pp. 775–802. See also Cooper, *Jefferson Davis, American,* pp. 605–10.
2. Varina Davis to Horace Greeley, November 21, 1866, in Strode, *Private Letters,* pp. 253–54.
3. Varina Davis to Jefferson Davis, December 8, 1866, in ibid., pp. 254–55.
4. Varina Davis to Jefferson Davis, March 15, 1867, in ibid., pp. 263–64.
5. Varina Davis to Jefferson Davis, March 18, 1867, in ibid., p. 265; Varina Davis to Jefferson Davis, March 20, 1865, Jefferson Davis Papers, University of Alabama Library, Tuscaloosa; Varina Davis to Jefferson Davis, April 9, 1867, in Strode, *Private Letters,* pp. 266–67; Varina Davis to Jefferson Davis, [April] 1867, Jefferson Davis Papers, University of Alabama Library, Tuscaloosa.
6. Varina Davis to Jefferson Davis, April 25, 1877, in Strode, *Private Letters,* pp. 267–68.
7. Davis, *Davis,* vol. 2, pp. 794–95; Burton Harrison to Constance Cary, May 13, 1867, in Strode, *Private Letters,* pp. 269–70.
8. On February 26, 1869, the U.S. attorney general wrote to Jeff Davis's attorneys that he had given instructions to *nolle prosequi* all indictments for treason allegedly committed during the late war. His office, he added, had "no information of any such prosecutions" pending anywhere against Jefferson Davis. Roy Franklin Nichols, "United States vs. Jefferson Davis, 1865–1869," *American Historical Review* 31, no. 2 (January 1926): 266–84. Joseph E. Davis to Jefferson Davis, May 14, 1867, in Strode, *Private Letters,* p. 270; James Murray Mason to Jefferson Davis, May 14, 1867, in Strode, *Private*

Letters, pp. 272–73; John H. Reagan to Jefferson Davis, May 21, 1867, in Strode, *Private Letters,* pp. 273–74; Robert E. Lee to Jefferson Davis, June 1, 1867, in Strode, *Private Letters,* pp. 274–75; George Parsons Lathrop, "The Bailing of Jefferson Davis," *Century Illustrated Magazine* 33, no. 4 (February 1887).

Twenty-five "OUR ONCE HAPPY HOMES": *Varina's Postwar Odyssey*

1. James Murray Mason to Jefferson Davis, May 14, 1867, in Strode, *Private Letters,* pp. 272–73.
2. Davis, *Davis,* vol. 2, pp. 796–99.
3. Strode, *Private Letters,* p. 289; Davis, *Davis,* vol. 2, p. 797.
4. Jefferson Davis to Howell Cobb, July 6, 1868, in Strode, *Private Letters,* p. 290; Jefferson Davis to Varina Davis, November 22, 1868, in ibid., pp. 294–95; Mrs. Jefferson Davis to Mrs. Howell Cobb, July 6, 1868, in Phillips, *Correspondence of Robert Toombs,* pp. 699–700.
5. Mrs. Jefferson Davis to Mrs. Howell Cobb, October 22, 1868, in Phillips, *Correspondence of Robert Toombs,* pp. 704–6.
6. Jefferson Davis to Varina Davis, February 7, 1869, in Strode, *Private Letters,* pp. 297–98.
7. Jefferson Davis to Varina Davis, October 11, 1869, in Strode, *Private Letters,* pp. 318–19; Jefferson Davis to Varina Davis, October 15, 1869, in ibid., p. 319; Varina Davis to Jefferson Davis, October 16, 1869, in ibid., pp. 319–20; Jefferson Davis to Varina Davis, November 9, 1869, in ibid., pp. 320–21.
8. Varina Davis to Jefferson Davis, December 3, 1869, in ibid., pp. 325–27; Mrs. Howell Cobb to Varina Davis, February 26, 1870, in ibid., p. 337.
9. Bleser, *Marriage,* pp. 3–40.
10. Ibid., p. 26.
11. Varina Davis to Jefferson Davis, March 4, 1870, in Strode, *Private Letters,* pp. 338–39.
12. Jefferson Davis to Lucinda Stamps, January 4, 1873, in ibid., p. 361; Jefferson Davis to Varina Davis, August 24, 1873, in ibid., pp. 365–66; Jefferson Davis to Varina Davis, August 26, 1873, in ibid., p. 367.
13. Jefferson Davis to Varina Davis, September 1, 1873, in ibid., p. 369; Jefferson Davis to Varina Davis, January 8, 1874, in ibid., pp. 377–78.
14. Jefferson Davis to Varina Davis, February 15, 1874, in ibid., pp. 384–85.
15. Jefferson Davis to Varina Davis, February 26, 1874, in ibid., pp. 388–89.
16. Davis, *Davis,* vol. 2, pp. 819–22; Jefferson Davis to Varina Davis, January 11, 1876, in Strode, *Private Letters,* pp. 422–23.
17. Jefferson Davis to Varina Davis, March 22, 1876, in Strode, *Private Letters,* pp. 426–27.
18. Varina Davis to Jefferson Davis, March 25, 1876, in ibid., pp. 427–28.
19. Varina Davis to Jefferson Davis, March 8, 1874, in ibid., pp. 389–91.

Twenty-six "IN THE COURSE OF HUMAN EVENTS I SHALL PROBABLY GO DOWN TO MR. DAVIS'S EARTHLY PARADISE": *Separation and Reconciliation*

1. Jefferson Davis to Varina Davis, November 18, 1875, in Strode, *Private Letters,* pp. 421–22; Davis, *Davis,* vol. 2, p. 824.

2. John Q. Anderson, "Sarah Anne Ellis Dorsey," in Edward T. James, ed., *Notable American Women: A Biographical Dictionary,* vol. 1 (Cambridge, Mass.: Belknap Press of Harvard University Press, 1975), pp. 505–6; Davis, *Davis,* vol. 2, pp. 825–26.
3. Jefferson Davis to Maggie Hayes, February 1, 1877, in Strode, *Private Letters,* p. 447.
4. Winnie and Varina Davis to Jefferson Davis, February 18, 1877, in ibid., pp. 448–49; Maggie Hayes to Varina Davis, June 11, 1877, Jefferson Davis Papers, University of Alabama Library, Tuscaloosa.
5. Varina Davis to Jefferson Davis, August 2, 1877, in Strode, *Private Letters,* pp. 460–61.
6. Varina Davis to Jefferson Davis, September 9, 1877, in ibid., pp. 462–63.
7. Varina Davis to Constance Harrison, November 7, 1877, in ibid., p. 467.
8. Maggie Hayes to Varina Davis, June 9, [1877], Jefferson Davis Papers, University of Alabama Library, Tuscaloosa.
9. Varina Davis to Jefferson Davis, February 4, 1878, in Strode, *Private Letters,* pp. 468–71.
10. Jefferson Davis to Varina Davis, February 16, 1878, in ibid., pp. 471–72.
11. Varina Davis to Jefferson Davis, April 7, 1778, Jefferson Davis Papers, University of Alabama Library, Tuscaloosa.
12. Jefferson Davis to Varina Davis, April 10, 1878, in Strode, *Private Letters,* pp. 477–78.
13. Jefferson Davis to Addison Hayes, October 18, 1878, in ibid., p. 490; Jefferson Davis to Maggie Hayes, November 8, 1878, in ibid., p. 491.
14. Jefferson Davis to Varina Davis, July 2–4, 1879, quoted in Bleser, *Marriage,* p. 33; Cooper, *Jefferson Davis, American,* pp. 677–78; Strode, *Private Letters,* p. 495.

Twenty-seven "OTHER REFUGE HAVE WE NONE": *Life and Death at Beauvoir*

1. Varina Davis to Winnie Davis, April 25, 1880, in Strode, *Private Letters,* p. 500.
2. Judah P. Benjamin to Varina Davis, April 25, 1781, in Strode, *Private Letters,* pp. 505–6, 508–9.
3. Cooper, *Jefferson Davis, American,* pp. 681–82, 695–98; Ross, *First Lady,* 335–41, 349; Strode, *Private Letters,* pp. 551–52.
4. Jefferson Davis to Varina Davis, November 12, 1889, in Strode, *Private Letters,* p. 561.

Twenty-eight "HER CONVERSATION IS SUPERLATIVELY INTERESTING": *Varina's Years of Independence*

1. For a discussion of Varina's life after 1889, see Suzanne T. Dolensky, "Varina Howell Davis, 1889 to 1906: The Years Alone," *Journal of Mississippi History* 47 (May 1985): 90–109.
2. Dolensky, "Varina Howell Davis," p. 92.
3. Varina Davis to General and Mrs. Lee, April 20, 1890, Brokenbrough Library; Varina Davis to Major William H. Morgan, October 5, 1890 (copy), Brokenbrough Library; Van Der Heuvel, *Crown,* p. 253; Wiley, *Confederate Women,* p. 133.
4. Varina Davis, "To the Veterans and People of the Southern States," July 11, 1891, Jefferson Davis Papers, University of Alabama Library, Tuscaloosa; Dolensky, "Varina Howell Davis," pp. 101–3.
5. Van Der Heuvel, *Crown,* p. 253; Dolensky, "Varina Howell Davis," pp. 103–5.
6. Varina Davis to Mrs. Dial, November 21, 1897, Brokenbrough Library.

7. Dolensky, "Varina Howell Davis," p. 96.
8. Varina Davis to Addison Hayes, n.d., Jefferson Davis Papers, University of Alabama Library, Tuscaloosa; Van Der Heuvel, *Crown,* p. 256.
9. Van Der Heuvel, *Crown,* p. 257.
10. Dolensky, "Varina Howell Davis," pp. 101, 105–8; Van Der Heuvel, *Crown,* p. 254.
11. Van Der Heuvel, *Crown,* pp. 255, 258.
12. Ibid., pp. 259–60.
13. Varina Davis to Maggie Davis Hayes, n.d., Jefferson Davis Papers, University of Alabama, Tuscaloosa; Van Der Heuvel, *Crown,* p. 261.

Thirty "ONE LONG SUMMER OF SUNSHINE": *Growing Up in Missouri*

1. Julia Dent Grant, *The Personal Memoirs of Julia Dent Grant,* ed. John Y. Simon (New York: G. P. Putnam's Sons, 1975), pp. 42–43; Emma Dent Casey, "When Grant Went A-Courtin': The Personal Recollections of His Courtship and Private Life by His Wife's Sister, Emma Dent Casey," in *Voices: Online Magazine of the Missouri Historical Society,* spring 2008, pp. 1–2.
2. Casey, "When Grant Went A-Courtin'," p. 2; J. Grant, *Memoirs,* p. 46.
3. J. Grant, *Memoirs,* p. 33.
4. Ibid., pp. 33, 34, 42.
5. Ibid., p. 38.
6. Ibid.
7. Ibid., p. 40.
8. Ibid., pp. 39, 49.

Thirty-one "BUT ONE SWEETHEART IN HIS LIFE":
The Courtship of Julia Dent Grant

1. Casey, "When Grant Went A-Courtin'," pp. 2–9.
2. Jean Edward Smith, *Grant* (New York: Simon and Schuster, 2001), p. 26.
3. Smith, *Grant,* pp. 21–22; Ulysses S. Grant, *Personal Memoirs of U. S. Grant,* ed. E. B. Long (New York: Grosset and Dunlap, 1962), pp. 3–10; Ishbel Ross, *The General's Wife: The Life of Mrs. Ulysses S. Grant* (New York: Dodd, Mead, 1959), pp. 49–51.
4. Ross, *General's Wife,* p. 5.
5. J. Grant, *Memoirs,* p. 49.
6. Ibid., pp. 49–50.
7. Ibid., p. 50.
8. For Grant's letters to Julia, see *The Papers of Ulysses S. Grant,* vol. 1: 1837–1861, ed. John Y. Simon (Carbondale: Southern Illinois University Press, 1967).
9. Ulysses S. Grant to Julia Dent, July 28, 1844, Simon, *Papers,* vol. 1, pp. 30–32; Ulysses S. Grant to Julia Dent, August 31, 1844, in ibid., pp. 33–36.
10. Ulysses S. Grant to Julia Dent, September 7, 1844, in ibid., pp. 37–39.
11. J. Grant, *Memoirs,* p. 51.
12. Ibid., pp. 52–53.
13. Ulysses S. Grant to Julia Dent, September 14, 1845, in Simon, *Papers,* vol. 1, pp. 53–54.
14. Ulysses S. Grant to Julia Dent, November 11, 1845, in ibid., pp. 61–63.

15.   Casey, "When Grant Went A-Courtin,'" p. 7.
16.   Ulysses S. Grant to Julia Dent, June 4, 1848, in Simon, *Papers,* vol. 1, pp. 160–61.
17.   Smith, *Grant,* pp. 34–69; U. S. Grant, *Personal Memoirs,* pp. 22–95; Ross, *General's Wife,* pp. 35–43.
18.   J. Grant, *Memoirs,* p. 54.
19.   Ibid., p. 55.
20.   Ibid.

Thirty-two "HIS LOVING LITTLE WIFE": *Creating a Home and Starting a Family*

1.   J. Grant, *Memoirs,* p. 57.
2.   Ibid., p. 58.
3.   Ibid.
4.   Ibid.
5.   Ibid., pp. 58–59.
6.   Ibid., pp. 59–60.
7.   Ibid., p. 60.
8.   Ibid., pp. 60–61; Smith, *Grant,* pp. 74–76.
9.   J. Grant, *Memoirs,* pp. 65–71.
10.   Ross, *General's Wife,* pp. 64–68.
11.   J. Grant, *Memoirs,* p. 71.
12.   Ulysses S. Grant to Julia Grant, July 15, 1852, in Simon, *Papers,* vol. 1, pp. 247–49.
13.   Ulysses S. Grant to Julia Grant, February 2, 1854, in ibid., p. 319; Ulysses S. Grant to Julia Grant, March 6, 1854, in ibid., pp. 322–24.
14.   Ulysses S. Grant to Julia Grant, March 6, 1854, in ibid., pp. 322–24.
15.   Ulysses S. Grant to Julia Grant, March 25, 1854, in ibid., pp. 326–28.
16.   Smith, *Grant,* pp. 86–88; J. Grant, *Memoirs,* p. 75.

Thirty-three "CHEER UP, MAKE THE BEST OF THIS": *The Return to Civilian Life*

1.   J. Grant, *Memoirs,* p. 76.
2.   Ibid., p. 77.
3.   Ibid., pp. 78–79.
4.   Ibid., p. 80.
5.   Ibid.
6.   Smith, *Grant,* p. 95; J. Grant, *Memoirs,* p. 83.
7.   Ross, *First Lady,* pp. 100–2; J. Grant, *Memoirs,* p. 84.

Thirty-four "AS I WAS A DEMOCRAT AT THAT TIME": *The Opportunities of War*

1.   J. Grant, *Memoirs,* p. 86.
2.   Ibid., p. 106.

3. Ibid., p. 87.
4. Ulysses S. Grant to Frederick Dent, April 19, 1861, in Simon, *Papers*, vol. 2, pp. 3–4.
5. J. Grant, *Memoirs*, p. 89.
6. Ulysses S. Grant to Julia Grant, May 1, 1861, in Simon, *Papers*, vol. 2, pp. 15–16.
7. Ulysses S. Grant to Jesse Root Grant, May 6, 1861, in ibid., pp. 20–23; Smith, *Grant*, pp. 103–8.
8. J. Grant, *Memoirs*, p. 92; Ulysses S. Grant to Julia Grant, October 1, 1861, in Simon, *Papers*, vol. 3, pp. 10–11.
9. Smith, *Grant*, p. 114; Ulysses S. Grant to Julia Grant, May 1, 1861, in Simon, *Papers*, vol. 2, pp. 15–16.
10. Ulysses S. Grant to Julia Grant, May 15, 1861, in Simon, *Papers*, vol. 2, pp. 30–32; Ulysses S. Grant to Julia Grant, May 10, 1861, in ibid., pp. 26–29.
11. Ulysses S. Grant to Julia Grant, May 10, 1861, in ibid., pp. 26–29; Ulysses S. Grant to Julia Grant, July 19, 1861, in ibid., pp. 72–73.
12. Ulysses S. Grant to Julia Grant, May 6, 1861, in ibid., pp. 23–24.

Thirty-five "THE HORRID OLD CONSTITUTION": *Julia's Personal War*

1. Ulysses S. Grant to Julia Grant, August 10, 1861, in Simon, *Papers*, vol. 2, pp. 96–97.
2. Ulysses S. Grant to Julia Grant, August 26, 1861, in ibid., pp. 140–41.
3. Ulysses S. Grant to Julia Grant, August 29, 1861, in ibid., pp. 148–49; Ulysses S. Grant to Julia Grant, September 3, 1861, in ibid., pp. 180–81; Ulysses S. Grant to Julia Grant, September 12, 1861, in ibid., pp. 246–47.
4. Ulysses S. Grant to Julia Grant, September 29, 1861, in ibid., p. 327.
5. J. Grant, *Memoirs*, p. 98.
6. Ross, *General's Wife*, p. 121.
7. J. Grant, *Memoirs*, p. 97.
8. Ibid.; Ross, *General's Wife*, p. 121; Ulysses S. Grant to Julia Grant, February 23, 1862, in Simon, *Papers*, vol. 4, p. 271.
9. Ulysses S. Grant to Julia Grant, March 24, 1862, in Simon, *Papers*, vol. 4, pp. 418–19; J. Grant, *Memoirs*, p. 99.
10. J. Grant, *Memoirs*, p. 99.
11. Ulysses S. Grant to Julia Grant, March 23, 1862, in Simon, *Papers*, vol. 4, pp. 412–13; Ulysses S. Grant to Julia Grant, March 24, 1862, in ibid., pp. 418–19.
12. Ulysses S. Grant to Jesse Grant, September 17, 1862, Simon, *Papers*, vol. 6, pp. 61–62.
13. J. Grant, *Memoirs*, p. 83.
14. Ibid., p. 102.
15. Ibid., p. 105.
16. Ibid., pp. 110–11.
17. Ibid., p. 106.
18. Ibid.
19. Ulysses S. Grant to Julia Grant, December 15, 1862, in Simon, *Papers*, vol. 7, pp. 43–45.
20. J. Grant, *Memoirs*, p. 113.
21. Ibid.
22. Ibid.
23. Ibid.

Thirty-six "IF YOUR MIND IS MADE UP": *Marital Relations in Wartime*

1. Ulysses S. Grant to Julia Grant, April 20, 1863, in Simon, *Papers,* vol. 8, pp. 100–1.
2. See Carol Berkin, *Revolutionary Mothers: Women in the Struggle for America's Independence* (New York: Vintage, 2006). See also Drew Gilpin Faust, *Mothers of Invention: Women of the Slaveholding South in the American Civil War* (Chapel Hill: University of North Carolina Press, 1996), and Nina Silber, *Daughters of the Union: Northern Women Fight the Civil War* (Cambridge, Mass.: Harvard University Press, 2005).
3. Ulysses S. Grant to Julia Grant, April 28, 1863, in Simon, *Papers,* vol. 8, pp. 132–33.
4. Ulysses S. Grant to Jesse Root Grant, April 21, 1863, in ibid., pp. 109–10.
5. Ulysses S. Grant to Julia Grant, May 9, 1863, in ibid., p. 189; Ulysses S. Grant to Major Frederick Dent, August 23, 1863, in Simon, *Papers,* vol. 9, pp. 200–1; for a full discussion of Grant's role in the Vicksburg campaign, see Smith, *Grant,* chapter 7, pp. 206–57.
6. Ulysses S. Grant to Julia Grant, November 2, 1863, in Simon, *Papers,* vol. 9, pp. 352–53; J. Grant, *Memoirs,* p. 124.
7. J. Grant, *Memoirs,* p. 124.
8. Ibid., pp. 124–25.
9. Ibid., p. 125.
10. Ibid.
11. Ibid., p. 126.
12. Ross, *General's Wife,* p. 140.
13. Ross, *General's Wife,* p. 157; J. Grant, *Memoirs,* p. 126.
14. Ulysses S. Grant to Julia Grant, April 17, 1864, in Simon, *Papers,* vol. 10, pp. 315–16; Ulysses S. Grant to Julia Grant, November 25, 1864, in Simon. *Papers,* vol. 13, pp. 26–27.
15. J. Grant, *Memoirs,* pp. 126–27.
16. Ibid., pp. 130–31.
17. Ibid., p. 131.
18. Ross, *General's Wife,* p. 169. For a full discussion of the battles involved in the Richmond campaign, see Smith, *Grant,* pp. 284–407.
19. *Colonel Alexander K. McClure's Recollections of Half a Century* (Salem: Salem Press Company, 1902); Ross, *General's Wife,* p. 167.

Thirty-seven "THERE WILL BE AN OUTBREAK TONIGHT":
Victory and Assassination

1. Ulysses S. Grant to Julia Grant, April 2, 1865, in Simon, *Papers,* vol. 14, p. 330.
2. J. Grant, *Memoirs,* p. 141.
3. Ibid., p. 153.
4. Ibid., pp. 151–52; Ross, *General's Wife,* p. 188.
5. J. Grant, *Memoirs,* p. 151.
6. Ibid., p. 154. For several instances of Mary Todd Lincoln's hostile behavior toward Julia Grant and the wives of Ulysses S. Grant's officers, see ibid., chapter 5.
7. Ibid., p. 155.

8. Ibid., pp. 155–56.
9. Ibid., p. 156.
10. Ibid.
11. Ibid., pp. 156–57.

Thirty-eight "WHAT SHOUTS WENT UP!": *A Hero and His Wife*

1. Ulysses S. Grant to Julia Grant, April 16, 1865, in Simon, *Papers*, vol. 14, pp. 396–97.
2. Ulysses S. Grant to Julia Grant, April 21, 1865, in ibid., pp. 428–29.
3. Ulysses S. Grant to Julia Grant, April 25, 1865, in ibid., p. 433.
4. J. Grant, *Memoirs*, pp. 157–58.
5. Ibid., p. 158.
6. Ibid., pp. 158–59.
7. Adam Badeau, *Grant in Peace from Appomattox to Mount McGregor, a Personal Memoir* (Freeport, N.Y.: Books for Libraries Press, 1971), p. 170.
8. J. Grant, *Memoirs*, pp. 160–61, 167n.
9. Ibid., p. 161.
10. Ibid., p. 164.
11. Ibid., p. 162.
12. Ibid., p. 165; Smith, *Grant,* pp. 438–53.
13. J. Grant, *Memoirs,* p. 166.

Thirty-nine "ULYS, DO YOU WISH TO BE PRESIDENT?": *The Early White House Years*

1. J. Grant, *Memoirs,* p. 170.
2. Ibid., p. 171; Smith, *Grant,* pp. 454–57.
3. J. Grant, *Memoirs,* p. 172.
4. Badeau, *Grant in Peace,* p. 113; J. Grant, *Memoirs,* p. 172; Benjamin Perley Poore, *Perley's Reminiscences of Sixty Years in the National Metropolis,* vol. 2 (Philadelphia: Hubbard Brothers, 1886), pp. 251–52.
5. Badeau, *Grant in Peace,* p. 157; Poore, *Perley's Reminiscences,* p. 237; Smith, *Grant,* pp. 464–66.
6. Mary Logan, *Reminiscences of the Civil War and Reconstruction* (Carbondale and Edwardville: Southern Illinois University Press, 1970), p. 184.
7. Badeau, *Grant in Peace,* p. 29.
8. J. Grant, *Memoirs,* p. 173.
9. Ibid.
10. Ibid., p. 174.
11. Badeau, *Grant in Peace,* p. 174.
12. Ibid., p. 242; J. Grant, *Memoirs,* pp. 175–76.
13. J. Grant, *Memoirs,* p. 177.
14. Logan, *Reminiscences,* pp. 186–87; J. Grant, *Memoirs,* p. 177.
15. Logan, *Reminiscences,* pp. 186–187; Laura C. Holloway, *The Ladies of the White House; or, In the Home of the Presidents* (Philadelphia: Bradley and Company, 1881), pp. 603–4.

Forty "NICE PEOPLE, QUESTIONABLE PEOPLE, AND PEOPLE WHO
WERE NOT NICE AT ALL": *Weddings and Scandals in the White House*

1. For detailed accounts of this scandal, see Kenneth D. Ackerman, *The Gold Ring: Jim Fisk, Jay Gould and Black Friday, 1869* (New York: Da Capo Press, 2005), and Edward J. Renehan Jr., *Dark Genius of Wall Street: The Misunderstood Life of Jay Gould, King of the Robber Barons* (New York: Basic Books, 2006).
2. J. Grant, *Memoirs*, p. 183.
3. Ibid., p. 184.
4. Poore, *Perley's Reminiscences*, p. 290; Smith, *Grant*, pp. 552–53.
5. J. Grant, *Memoirs*, p. 180.
6. For a full account of the courtship, wedding, and marriage of Algernon Sartoris and Ellen Grant from which this is taken, see Christopher Gordon, "A White House Wedding," *Missouri History Organization*, Summer 2005, pp. 9–19.
7. J. Grant, *Memoirs*, p. 181.
8. Ibid.

Forty-one "A WAIF ON THE WORLD'S WIDE COMMON":
Julia Becomes a World Traveler

1. J. Grant, *Memoirs*, p. 186.
2. Badeau, *Grant in Peace*, pp. 259–60.
3. J. Grant, *Memoirs*, pp. 196–97.
4. See John Russell Young, *Around the World With General Grant*, ed. Michael Fellman (Baltimore: Johns Hopkins University Press, 2002).
5. For Julia Grant's account of their trip, see J. Grant, *Memoirs*, Chapters 7–11, pp. 201–320.
6. J. Grant, *Memoirs*, p. 237–38.
7. Badeau, *Grant in Peace*, p. 288.
8. Young, *Around the World*, p. 83; Badeau, *Grant in Peace*, p. 307.
9. Young, *Around the World*, p. 435; J. Grant, *Memoirs*, p. 307.

Forty-two "DO YOU NOT DESIRE SUCCESS?": *From Politics to Poverty*

1. J. Grant, *Memoirs*, pp. 309–10.
2. Ibid., p. 312.
3. Smith, *Grant*, pp. 614–17; J. Grant, *Memoirs*, p. 322.
4. J. Grant, *Memoirs*, p. 322.
5. Smith, *Grant*, pp. 618–20; J. Grant, *Memoirs*, pp. 322–23.
6. J. Grant, *Memoirs*, pp. 323–24.
7. Ibid., p. 326–27.
8. Smith, *Grant*, pp. 620–22; Ross, *General's Wife*, p. 284.
9. J. Grant, *Memoirs*, p. 327.
10. Ibid., p. 328.

11. Ibid.; Smith, *Grant*, p. 622; Ross, *General's Wife*, pp. 284–85.
12. J. Grant, *Memoirs*, p. 328; Ross, *General's Wife*, pp. 287–89; Badeau, *Grant in Peace*, pp. 421–24.

Forty-three "WARMED IN THE SUNLIGHT OF HIS LOYAL LOVE AND
GREAT FAME": *Julia Becomes a Widow*

1. J. Grant, *Memoirs*, pp. 328–29. Julia Grant's full account of her husband's illness can be found in chapter 12, pp. 321–33.
2. Ibid., p. 329.
3. Ibid.
4. Smith, *Grant*, pp. 624–25.
5. J. Grant, *Memoirs*, p. 331.
6. Badeau, *Grant in Peace*, pp. 451–52.
7. J. Grant, *Memoirs*, Introduction, p. 17.
8. Ibid., p. 331.

Forty-four "LIVING AGAIN, WITH THE AID OF MY FANCY
AND MY PEN": *Julia Dent Grant Writes Her Memoirs*

1. Ross, *General's Wife*, pp. 388–89.
2. V. Jefferson Davis to Julia Grant, April 29, 1902, Ulysses S. Grant Papers, Library of Congress, Manuscripts Division, Washington, D.C.
3. Ross, *General's Wife*, pp. 389–90.
4. Sarah E. Gardner, " 'A Sweet Solace to My Lonely Heart': Stonewall and Mary Anna Jackson and the Civil War," in Carol Bleser and Lesley J. Gordon, eds., *Intimate Strategies of the Civil War: Military Commanders and Their Wives* (New York: Oxford University Press, 2001), pp. 49–68; Lesley J. Gordon, " 'Cupid Does Not Readily Give Way to Mars': The Marriage of LaSalle Corbell and George E. Pickett," in ibid., pp. 69–86; Shirley A. Leckie, "The Civil War Partnership of Elizabeth and George A. Custer," in ibid., pp. 178–98; Pamela Herr, "Permutations of a Marriage: John Charles and Jessie Benton Fremont's Civil War Alliance," in ibid., pp. 199–224.
5. Badeau, *Grant in Peace*, p. 119.
6. John Y. Simon, Foreword, in J. Grant, *Memoirs*, pp. 17–26; Matías Romero to Julia Grant, August 6, 1898, Ulysses S. Grant Papers, Library of Congress, Manuscripts Division, Washington, D.C.
7. Quoted in Simon, Foreword, in J. Grant, *Memoirs*, p. 20.
8. *New York Times*, December 14, 1902; *New York Herald*, December 15, 1902.

Bibliography

ARCHIVES

Jefferson Davis Collection, Eleanor S. Brockenbrough Library, Museum of the Confederacy, Richmond, Virginia.

Jefferson Davis Papers, William Stanley Hoole Special Collections Library, University of Alabama Library, Tuscaloosa.

Ulysses S. Grant Collection, Missouri History Museum, Archives, St. Louis.

Ulysses S. Grant Papers, Family Correspondence, Library of Congress, Manuscripts Division, Washington, D.C.

New-York Historical Society, Newspaper Collection, Library, New York.

John O'Fallon Collection, Missouri History Museum, Archives, St. Louis.

Isaac H. Sturgeon Papers, Missouri History Museum, Archives, St. Louis.

PUBLISHED DOCUMENT COLLECTIONS

Barnes, Gilbert H., and Dwight L. Dumond, eds. *Letters of Theodore Dwight Weld, Angelina Grimké Weld, and Sarah Grimké, 1822–1844.* 2 vols. New York: Da Capo Press, 1970.

Ceplair, Larry, ed. *The Public Years of Sarah and Angelina Grimké: Selected Writings 1836–1839.* New York: Columbia University Press, 1989.

Cramer, Jesse Grant. *Letters of Ulysses S. Grant to His Father and His Youngest Sister, 1857–1878.* New York and London: G. P. Putnam's Sons, 1912.

Crist, Linda Laswell, ed. *The Papers of Jefferson Davis.* 12 vols. Baton Rouge: Louisiana State University Press, 1971–2008.

Phillips, U. B., ed. *The Correspondence of Robert Toombs, Alexander H. Stephens, and Howell Cobb.* New York: Da Capo Press, 1970.

Simon, John Y., ed. *The Papers of Ulysses S. Grant.* 30 vols. Carbondale: Southern Illinois University Press, 1967–2008.

BOOKS, ARTICLES

Ackerman, Kenneth D. *The Gold Ring: Jim Fish, Jay Gould and Black Friday, 1869.* New York: Da Capo Press, 2005.

Alcott, William Andrus. *The Young Housekeeper: Or Thoughts on Food and Cookery.* Whitefish, Mont.: Kessinger Publishing, 2007.

Ames, Mary Clemmer. *Ten Years in Washington.* Hartford: A. D. Worthington and Company, 1873.

Badeau, Adam. *Grant in Peace from Appomattox to Mount McGregor, A Personal Memoir.* Freeport, N.Y.: Books for Libraries Press, 1971.

Beecher, Catherine E. *An Essay on Slavery and Abolition with Reference to the Duty of American Females.* Philadelphia: Henry Perkins, 1837.

Berkin, Carol. "Private Woman, Public Woman: The Contradictions of Charlotte Perkins Gilman." In Carol Berkin and Mary Beth Norton, eds. *Women of America: A History.* Boston: Houghton Mifflin, 1979, pp. 150–76.

———. *Revolutionary Mothers: Women in the Struggle for America's Independence.* New York: Vintage, 2006.

Birney, Catherine H. *The Grimké Sisters: Sarah and Angelina Grimké: The First American Women Advocates of Abolition and Women's Rights.* New York: Haskell House Publishers, 1970.

Bleser, Carol, and Lesley J. Gordon, eds. *Intimate Strategies of the Civil War: Military Commanders and Their Wives.* New York: Oxford University Press, 2001.

Bleser, Carol K. "The Marriage of Varina Howell and Jefferson Davis: 'I Gave the Best and All My Life to a Girdled Tree.' " *Journal of Southern History* 65, no. 1 (February 1999): 2–40.

Boritt, Gabor, ed. *Why the Civil War Came.* New York: Oxford University Press, 1996.

Boydston, Jeanne, Mary Kelley, and Anne Margolis, eds. *The Limits of Sisterhood: The Beecher Sisters on Women's Rights and Woman's Sphere.* Chapel Hill: University of North Carolina Press, 1988.

Briggs, Emily Edson. *The Olivia Letters.* Washington, D.C.: Neale Publishing Company, 1906.

Browne, Stephen Howard. *Angelina Grimké: Rhetoric, Identity, and the Radical Imagination.* East Lansing: Michigan State University Press, 1999.

Cadwallader, Sylvanus. *Three Years with Grant.* New York: Knopf, 1955.

Carroll, Andrew. *Behind the Lines: Powerful and Revealing American and Foreign War Letters—and One Man's Search to Find Them.* New York: Scribner's, 2005.

Casey, Emma Dent. "When Grant Went A-Courtin': The Personal Recollections of His Courtship and Private Life by His Wife's Sister, Emma Dent Casey." *Voices: Online Magazine of the Missouri Historical Society* (spring 2008): 1–9.

Cashin, Joan. "Varina Howell Davis." In G. J. Barker-Benfield and Catherine Clinton, eds., *Portraits of American Women from Settlement to the Present.* New York and Oxford: Oxford University Press, 1998.

Cassedy, James H. *Medicine in America: A Short History.* Baltimore: Johns Hopkins University Press, 1991.

Chesnut, Mary Boykin Miller. *Mary Chesnut's Civil War.* Ed. C. Vann Woodward. New Haven and London: Yale University Press, 1981.

Clay-Clopton, Virginia. *A Belle of the Fifties: Memoirs of Mrs. Clay of Alabama.* Ed. Leah Rawls Atkins, Joseph H. Harrison, and Sara A. Hudson. Tuscaloosa: University of Alabama Press, 1999.

Clinton, Catherine. *The Plantation Mistress.* New York: Pantheon, 1984.

Colman, Edna. *White House Gossip.* Garden City, N.Y.: Doubleday, 1927.

Cooper, William J. *Jefferson Davis, American.* New York: Vintage Books, 2001.

Craven, Lieut. Col. John J. *The Prison Life of Jefferson Davis as Published in 1866.* Scituate, Mass.: DSI Digital Reproductions, 2001.

Daniel, Larry J. *Shiloh: The Battle That Changed the Civil War.* New York: Simon and Schuster, 1998.

Davis, Jefferson. *Jefferson Davis: Private Letters, 1823–1889.* Ed. Hudson Strode. New York: Da Capo Press, 1995.

Davis, Varina. *Jefferson Davis: A Memoir by His Wife.* 2 vols. Baltimore: Nautical and Aviation Publishing Company of America, 1990.

Dixon, Chris. *Perfecting the Family: Antislavery Marriages in Nineteenth-Century America.* Amherst: University of Massachusetts Press, 1997.

Dolensky, Suzanne T. "Varina Howell Davis, 1889 to 1906: The Years Alone." *Journal of Mississippi History* 47 (May 1985): 90–109.

Donald, David H., and Richard Nelson Current. *Why the North Won the Civil War.* Baton Rouge: Louisiana State University Press, 1960.

Dougherty, Kevin, and J. Michael Moore. *The Peninsular Campaign of 1862: A Military Analysis.* Jackson: University Press of Mississippi, 2005.

DuBois, Ellen. "Struggling into Existence: The Feminism of Sarah and Angelina Grimké." *Women: A Journal of Liberation* 1 (spring 1970): 4–11.

Duffy, John. *From Humors to Medical Science.* Urbana: University of Illinois Press, 1993.

Earle, Jonathan H. *Jacksonian Antislavery and the Politics of Free Soil, 1824–1854.* Chapel Hill: University of North Carolina Press, 2004.

Faust, Drew Gilpin. *Mothers of Invention: Women of the Slaveholding South in the American Civil War.* Chapel Hill: University of North Carolina Press, 1996.

Foner, Eric. *Free Soil, Free Labor, Free Men: The Ideology of the Republican Party Before the Civil War.* New York: Oxford University Press, 1995.

Foner, Philip S., and Josephine F. Pacheco. *Three Who Dared: Prudence Crandall, Margaret Douglass, and Mytilla Minor.* Westport, Conn.: Greenwood Press, 1984.

Fox-Genovese, Elizabeth. *Within the Plantation Household: Black and White Women of the Old South.* Chapel Hill: University of North Carolina Press, 1988.

Garrison, William Lloyd, and William E. Cain. *William Lloyd Garrison and the Fight Against Slavery: Selections from* The Liberator. New York: Bedford/St. Martin's, 1994.

Giesberg, Judith Ann. *Civil War Sisterhood: The U.S. Sanitary Commission and Women's Politics in Transition.* Boston: Northeastern University Press, 2000.

Gilman, Charlotte Perkins. *The Home: Its Work and Influence.* Walnut Creek, Calif.: AltaMira Press, 2002.

Ginzberg, Lori. *Women and the Work of Benevolence: Morality, Politics, and Class in the Nineteenth-Century United States.* New Haven and London: Yale University Press, 1990.

Goodrich, Thomas. *War to the Knife: Bleeding Kansas, 1854–1861.* Mechanicsburg, Penn.: Stackpole Books, 1998.

Gordon, Christopher. "A White House Wedding." *Missouri History Organization* (summer 2005): 9–19.

Grant, Julia Dent. "The Married Life of General Grant." *The Home-Maker* (October 1890), Old Dominion University Libraries, Norfolk.

Grant, Julia Dent. *The Personal Memoirs of Julia Dent Grant.* Ed. John Y. Simon. New York: G. P. Putnam's Sons, 1975.

Grant, Ulysses S. *Personal Memoirs of U. S. Grant.* Ed. E. B. Long. New York: Grosset and Dunlap, 1962.

Hamm, Thomas D. *The Quakers in America.* New York: Columbia University Press, 2003.

Hardesty, Nancy A. *Women Called to Witness: Evangelical Feminism in the Nineteenth Century.* Knoxville: University of Tennessee Press, 1999.

Hoganson, Kristin. "Garrisonian Abolitionists and the Rhetoric of Gender, 1850–1860." *American Quarterly* 45, no. 4 (December 1993): 558–95.

Holloway, Laura C. *The Ladies of the White House or, In the Home of the Presidents*. Philadelphia: Bradley and Company, 1881.

Jeffrey, Julie Roy. *The Great Silent Army of Abolition: Ordinary Women in the Antislavery Movement*. Chapel Hill: University of North Carolina Press, 1998.

Keckley, Elizabeth. *Behind the Scenes: Thirty Years a Slave and Four Years in the White House*. New York: Arno Press and the New York Times, 1968.

Langley, Winston E., and Vivian C. Fox, eds. *Women's Rights in the United States: A Documentary History*. Westport, Conn.: Praeger, 1994.

Lathrop, George Parsons. "The Bailing of Jefferson Davis," *Century Illustrated Magazine* 33, no. 4 (February 1877).

Lee, Olive. "The Women of the Grant Family." *New England Magazine* 29, no. 4 (December 1903): 435–42.

Lerner, Gerda. *The Grimké Sisters from South Carolina: Pioneers for Women's Rights and Abolition*. Boston: Houghton Mifflin Company, 1967.

Lincoln, Abraham. *Selected Speeches and Writings*. New York: Vintage, 1992.

Lobel, Cindy R. "Consuming Classes: Changing Food Consumption Patterns in New York City, 1790–1860." Ph.D. diss., CUNY Graduate Center, 2003.

Logan, Mary. *Reminiscences of the Civil War and Reconstruction*. Carbondale and Edwardville: Southern Illinois University Press, 1970.

Lumpkin, Katharine Du Pre. *The Emancipation of Angelina Grimké*. Chapel Hill and London: University of North Carolina Press, 1974.

Mayer, Henry. *All on Fire: William Lloyd Garrison and the Abolition of Slavery*. New York: W. W. Norton, 2008.

McClure, Alexander K. *Colonel Alexander K. McClure's Recollections of Half a Century*. Salem, Mass.: Salem Press Company, 1902.

McDonough, James L. *Shiloh—In Hell Before Night*. Knoxville: University of Tennessee Press, 1977.

McKivigan, John, ed. *Abolitionism and American Reform*. New York and London: Garland, 1999.

McPherson, James M. *Battle Cry of Freedom: The Civil War Era*. New York: Oxford University Press, 2003.

Melder, Keith E. "Forerunners of Freedom: The Grimké Sisters in Massachusetts, 1837–1838." *Essex Institute Historical Collections* 103 (July 1976): 223–49.

Morris, Cecelia. *Fanny Wright: Rebel in America*. Urbana and Chicago: University of Illinois Press, 1992.

Nelson, Robert K. " 'The Forgetfulness of Sex': Devotion and Desire in the Courtship of Angelina Grimké and Theodore Weld." *Journal of Social History* 37, no. 3 (2004): 663–79.

Nichol, Francis D. *Midnight Cry: A Defense of the Character and Conduct of William Miller and the Millerites, Who Mistakenly Believed That the Second Coming of Christ Would Take Place*. Brushton, N.Y.: TEACH Services, 1994.

Nissenbaum, Stephen. *Sex, Diet, and Debility in Jacksonian America: Sylvester Graham and Health Reform*. Westport, Conn.: Greenwood Press, 1980.

"Pastoral Letter of the Massachusetts Congregationalist Clergy." In Aileen S. Kraditor, ed., *Up from the Pedestal: Selected Writings in the History of Feminism* (Chicago: Quadrangle Books, 1968): 50–52.

Pendel, Thomas F. *Thirty-Six Years in the White House*. Washington, D.C.: Neale Publishing Company, 1902.

Pickett, LaSalle (Corbell). *Across My Path: Memories of People I Have Known*. Freeport, N.Y.: Books for Libraries Press, 1970.

Poore, Benjamin Perley. *Perley's Reminiscences of Sixty Years in the National Metropolis.* 2 vols. Philadelphia: Hubbard Brothers, 1886.

Potter, David M. *The Impending Crisis, 1848–1861.* New York: Harper and Row, 1976.

Reid, Ronald F. *American Rhetorical Discourse.* Prospect Heights, Ill.: Waveland Press, 1995.

Remini, Robert V. *Henry Clay: Statesman for the Union.* New York: W. W. Norton and Company, 1993.

Renehan, Edward J., Jr. *Dark Genius of Wall Street: The Misunderstood Life of Jay Gould, King of the Robber Barons.* New York: Basic Books, 2006.

Reynolds, David S. *John Brown, Abolitionist: The Man Who Killed Slavery, Sparked the Civil War, and Seeded Civil Rights.* New York: Vintage, 2006.

Rosenberg, Charles E. "Belief and Ritual in Antebellum Medical Therapeutics." In John Harley Warner and Janet A. Tighe, eds., *Major Problems in the History of American Medicine and Public Health.* Boston: Houghton Mifflin, 2001.

Ross, Ishbel. *First Lady of the South: The Life of Mrs. Jefferson Davis.* New York: Harper and Brothers, 1958.

———. *The General's Wife: The Life of Mrs. Ulysses S. Grant.* New York: Dodd, Mead, and Company, 1959.

Shaw, Marvin. "Mrs. Jefferson Davis at Fortress Monroe, Virginia." *Notes and Documents, Journal of Southern History* 16, no. 1 (February 1950): 73–76.

Silber, Nina. *Daughters of the Union: Northern Women Fight the Civil War.* Cambridge, Mass.: Harvard University Press, 2005.

Smith, Jean Edward. *Grant.* New York: Simon and Schuster, 2001.

Starr, Paul. *The Social Transformation of American Medicine.* New York: Basic Books, 1984.

Sterling, Dorothy. *Turning the World Upside Down: The Anti-Slavery Convention of American Women Held in New York City, May 9–12, 1837.* New York: Feminist Press, 1993.

Stevenson, Janet. "A Family Divided." *American Heritage* (April 1967): 6–91.

Steward, James Brewer. *Holy Warriors: The Abolitionists and American Slavery.* New York: Hill and Wang, 1997.

Strode, Hudson. *Jefferson Davis, American Patriot, 1808–1861.* New York: Harcourt, Brace and Company, 1955.

Van Der Heuvel, Gerry. *Crown of Thorns and Glory: Mary Todd Lincoln and Varina Howell Davis: The Two First Ladies of the Civil War.* New York: E. P. Dutton, 1988.

Venet, Wendy Hamand. *Neither Ballots nor Bullets: Women Abolitionists and the Civil War.* Charlottesville and London: University Press of Virginia, 1991.

Walters, Ronald G. *American Reformers, 1815–1860.* New York: Hill and Wang, 1978.

Weld, Angelina Grimké. *Walking by Faith: The Diary of Angelina Grimké, 1828–1835.* Charles Wilbanks, ed. Columbia: University of South Carolina Press, 2003.

Weld, Theodore Dwight. *In Memory. Angelina Grimké Weld.* Boston: G. H. Ellis, 1880.

Whittier, J. G. *The Complete Poetical Works of John Greenleaf Whittier.* Whitefish, Mont.: Kessinger Publishing, 2003.

Wiley, Bell Irvin. *Confederate Women.* New York: Barnes and Noble Books, 1975.

Yellin, Jean Fagan, and John C. Van Horne, eds. *The Abolitionist Sisterhood: Women's Political Culture in Antebellum America.* Ithaca: Cornell University Press, 2007.

Young, John Russell. *Around the World with General Grant.* Ed. Michael Fellman. Baltimore: Johns Hopkins University Press, 2002.

Index

Page numbers in *italics* refer to illustrations. The initials AGW, JDG, and VHD refer to Angelina Grimké Weld, Julia Dent Grant, and Varina Howell Davis.

ILLUSTRATION CREDITS

The Jefferson Davis portrait (c. 1845) is in the National Portrait Gallery. Smithsonian Institution Art Resource, NY.

The Varina Howell Davis portrait (c. 1849) is in the Picture Collection, Louisiana and Lower Mississippi Valley Collection, LSU Libraries, Louisiana State University, Baton Rouge.

The Julia Grant portrait is in the Library of Congress, Brady-Handy Collection, reproduction #LC-USZ62-25791 DLC.

The Ulysses Grant portrait is in the Library of Congress, Brady-Handy Collection, reproduction #LC-BH82601-3703 DLC.

The Angelina Grimké portrait is in the Library of Congress, negative #LC-USZ61-1609.

The Theodore Weld portrait is courtesy of the Ohio Historical Society, Collection #SC3053, Image #AL00618.

A NOTE ON THE TYPE

This book was set in Minion, a typeface produced by the Adobe Corporation specifically for the Macintosh personal computer, and released in 1990. Designed by Robert Slimbach, Minion combines the classic characteristics of old-style faces with the full complement of weights required for modern typesetting.

Composed by North Market Street Graphics
Lancaster, Pennsylvania

Printed and bound by Berryville Graphics,
Berryville, Virginia

Designed by M. Kristen Bearse